# BUILDING SOCIALISM



By placing the party grassroots at the centre of its focus, *Building Socialism* presents an original account of the formative first two decades of the Soviet system. Assembled in a large network of primary party organisations (PPO), the Bolshevik rank-and-file was an army of activists made up of ordinary people. While far removed from the levers of power, they were nevertheless charged with promoting the Party's programme of revolutionary social transformation in their workplaces, neighbourhoods and households. Their regular meetings, conferences and campaigns have generated a voluminous source base. This rich material provides a unique view of the practical manifestation of the Party's revolutionary mission and forms the basis of this insightful new narrative of how the Soviet republic functioned in the period from the end of the Russian Civil War in 1921 to its invasion by Nazi Germany in 1941.

Yiannis Kokosalakis is a Research Fellow in the Faculty of History, Philosophy and Theology at Bielefeld University. His research focuses on the history of the socialist states of the twentieth century and the experience of revolutionary movements in government and has published a number of articles on Soviet labour relations, ideological instruction and political reform. He has held a European Marie Sklodowska Curie Fellowship and received a National University of Ireland Early Career Award for his work.

# NEW STUDIES IN EUROPEAN HISTORY

*Edited by*



The aim of this series in early modern and modern European history is to publish outstanding works of research, addressed to important themes across a wide geographical range, from southern and central Europe to Scandinavia and Russia, from the time of the Renaissance to the present. As it develops, the series will comprise focused works of wide contextual range and intellectual ambition.

*A full list of titles published in the series can be found at:*

www.cambridge.org/newstudiesineuropeanhistory

# BUILDING SOCIALISM

*The Communist Party and the Making of the Soviet System, 1921–1941*

YIANNIS KOKOSALAKIS

*Bielefeld University*

CAMBRIDGE
UNIVERSITY PRESS

CAMBRIDGE UNIVERSITY PRESS

Shaftesbury Road, Cambridge CB2 8EA, United Kingdom

One Liberty Plaza, 20th Floor, New York, NY 10006, USA

477 Williamstown Road, Port Melbourne, VIC 3207, Australia

314–321, 3rd Floor, Plot 3, Splendor Forum, Jasola District Centre, New Delhi – 110025, India

103 Penang Road, #05–06/07, Visioncrest Commercial, Singapore 238467

Cambridge University Press is part of Cambridge University Press & Assessment, a department of the University of Cambridge.

We share the University's mission to contribute to society through the pursuit of education, learning and research at the highest international levels of excellence.

www.cambridge.org
Information on this title: www.cambridge.org/9781009218849

DOI: 10.1017/9781009218870



First published 2023
First paperback edition 2025

*A catalogue record for this publication is available from the British Library*

*Library of Congress Cataloging-in-Publication data*
NAMES: Kokosalakis, Yiannis, 1987- author.
TITLE: Building socialism : the communist party and the making of the soviet system, 1921-1941 / Yiannis Kokosalakis.
DESCRIPTION: 1 Edition. | New York, NY : Cambridge University Press, 2023. |
SERIES: Nseh new studies in European history | Includes bibliographical references and index.
IDENTIFIERS: LCCN 2022053366 (print) | LCCN 2022053367 (ebook) | ISBN 9781009218863 (hardback) | ISBN 9781009218849 (paperback) | ISBN 9781009218870 (epub)
SUBJECTS: LCSH: Soviet Union–Economic policy–1928-1932. | Soviet Union–Economic policy–1938-1942. | Industrial organization–Soviet Union–History. | Industrial policy–Soviet Union–History. | Kommunisticheskaia͡ partii͡a Sovetskogo Soi͡uza–History.
CLASSIFICATION: LCC HC335.2 .K595 2023 (print) | LCC HC335.2 (ebook) | DDC 338.947–dc23/eng/20221103
LC record available at https://lccn.loc.gov/2022053366
LC ebook record available at https://lccn.loc.gov/2022053367

ISBN 978-1-009-21886-3 Hardback
ISBN 978-1-009-21884-9 Paperback

Дорожка скатертью!
Мы и кухарку
каждую
выучим
управлять государством!

Vladimir Maiakovskii, *Vladimir Il'ich Lenin*, 1924

# *Contents*

Acknowledgements

Like many first monographs, this book began its journey as a doctoral project. In the several years that have passed since I started my graduate research at the University of Edinburgh, I have accumulated a significant number of intellectual and personal debts to people and institutions. This short note can only hope to address some of those. My doctoral supervisors Iain Lauchlan and Julius Ruiz provided helpful comments and corrections to my work. The School of History, Classics and Archaeology of the University of Edinburgh and the Scottish Consortium of Russian Central and East-European Studies provided financial support for travel and training. Without the friendly introduction to the Russian archives provided by Polly Jones and Alexander Titov through the Russian Archives Training Scheme, the primary research that made this book possible would have been a much less pleasant experience.

Many of the following chapters were written during a research fellowship I held at the School of History of University College Dublin (UCD). This was funded by a European Marie Sklodowska Curie Fellowship for which I am very grateful. This book incorporates adapted material dispersed in various chapters from my articles 'Bolshevik Bargaining in Soviet Industry' and '"Merciless War" against Trifles', which were originally published in *The Journal of Modern History* (vol. 93, no. 2) and *Revolutionary Russia* (vol. 28, no. 1), respectively. Many thanks to Chicago University Press and Taylor & Francis for allowing republication.

I am highly indebted to Robert Gerwarth for being the source of invariably excellent advice on all kinds of academic matters, but especially on how to turn a thesis into a book. Emma Lyons, Kate O'Hanlon, Sarah Feehan and Suzanne Darcy offered invaluable administrative support throughout my time at UCD. Lior Tibet, Elisabeth Piller, Ronan Macnamara, Peter Hession and Mark Jones provided a fruitful combination of entertaining conversation, intellectual stimulation and occasional comments on my written work. James Harris has offered much advice and challenging feedback from the late stages of my doctoral studies to the present day. Roland Boer has kindly shared his encyclopaedic knowledge of the theoretical underpinnings of socialist state-building. Bob Chase has generously read and commented on draft chapters of this book.

Personal friendships have been as important as collegial relationships in making this book possible. Many thanks to Veronica Lykou, Richard Yuel and Jaume Miro for putting up with me during my early doctoral years in Edinburgh. Dina Veriutina, Liana Mukhamedzyanova and Sasha Skorobogatova provided not only accommodation, but also the company necessary to prevent me from losing all touch with the twenty-first century during the most immersive phase of my archival work in Saint-Petersburg. Michał Palacz, Chelsea Sambells and Victor Cazares Lira went through the trials of doctoral training at the same time as I did and provided collegial and friendly support without which it would have been much harder to complete the doctoral phase of this project. The ideas underlying my work have been formed over many years in friendly conversations with Andrew Weir, Phil McGuinness, Euan Oliphant, Keir Lawson, Jon Black and Neil Bennet. It is a privilege to have friends that do not regard my interest in the Soviet Union as a curious obsession. On a similar note, there are few people I share more views with than Alexis Synodinos. Our conversations are a great source of pleasure every day.

I have left the best for last. My parents have been a source of infinite support throughout my life in more ways than can be enumerated in this note. Neither this book nor many other things would have been possible without their love and trust. Finally, no contribution to the completion of this work deserves to be acknowledged more than that of Alkistis Elliott-Graves. Her support, patience and constant encouragement have been my greatest source of strength throughout these years.

# *Abbreviations and Russian Terms*

| | |
|---|---|
| *agitprop* | agitation and propaganda |
| *aktiv* | activist group |
| *artel'* | traditional Russian work-crew |
| CC | Central Committee of the Communist Party |
| *edinonachalie* | one-person management principle |
| *gorkom* | city committee of the Communist Party |
| *gubkom* | province (guberniia) committee of the Communist Party, *obkom* from 1929 |
| KP | *Krasnyi Putilovets*, Red Putilovite works in Leningrad |
| *kul'tprop* | culture and propaganda, department and head of |
| *obkom* | province (oblast') committee of the Communist Party |
| *partkom* | party committee |
| *partorg* | party organiser |
| *partorg TsK* | party organiser assigned directly by the CC |
| *partsec* | party secretary |
| PPO | Primary Party Organisation |
| *rabkor* | workers' correspondent |
| *raikom* | district committee of the Communist Party |
| RGASPI | Russian State Archive of Social and Political History |
| RGAVMF | Russian State Archive of the Navy |
| *spetseedstvo* | specialist-baiting |
| TsGAIPD | Central State Archive of Historical-Political Documents, Saint-Petersburg |
| VKP (b) | All-Union Communist Party (bolsheviks), the Communist Party |
| *zapiska* | note to speaker, often question |
| *zavkom* | factory committee |

# *Introduction*
## *The Communist Party in Leninist Theory, Soviet Practice and Historical Scholarship*

The Soviet Union claimed to be a state founded on a class alliance of workers and peasants engaged in the world-historical task of building a communist society.[1] Workers were explicitly recognised as the senior members of this partnership, leading the way in historical progress by means of their political hegemony over the state, exercised through the monopoly in power of the Communist Party. The Party, as the 'highest form of [the proletariat's] class organisation', united in its ranks the most advanced elements of the working class in the struggle for the 'victory of socialism'.[2] It was, in Lenin's expression, the vanguard of the proletariat.[3] Ever prone to literary references, Stalin once likened the Communist Party to Antaeus, the giant of Greek mythology who was invincible as long as he remained in contact with his mother, the earth.[4] By this metaphor, the general secretary suggested that the Soviet Communist Party was not only a leader of the Soviet people, but also born of them and reliant on them for its strength. The premise of this monograph is that such claims reflected strong ideological commitments on the part of the Bolshevik leadership, which ultimately made their way to the institutional architecture of the

[1] The first article of the 1936 Constitution of the USSR stated: 'The Union of Soviet Socialist Republics is a socialist state of workers and peasants.' A similar idea was expressed by the lengthier introduction to the 1924 Constitution, which declared that the formation of the USSR had divided the world into socialist and capitalist camps. Iu. S. Kukushkin and O. I. Chistiakov, *Ocherk istorii Sovetskoi Konstitutsii* (Moscow: Politizdat, 1987), pp. 264, 285.

[2] Thus stated the preamble to the 1934 Party Rules (*Ustav*) of the All-Union Communist Party (bolsheviks). All subsequent references to the *Ustav* shall be given in the form *Ustav* (*date*): (*section*). (*article*). These will refer to the text as it appears in the documentary collection *Kommunisticheskaia Partiia Sovetskogo Soiuza v rezoliutsiakh i resheniakh s'ezdov, konferentsii i plenumov TsK, 1898–1988*, vols. 1–16 (Moscow: Izdatel'stvo Politicheskoi Literaturi, 1983–90). Hereafter, the terms Party, Communist Party and the acronym VKP (b) will be used interchangeably.

[3] V. I. Lenin, 'Tezisy ko II-mu kongressu kommunisticheskogo internatsionala', in V. I. Lenin (ed.), *Polnoe sobranie sochinenii*, 5th ed., vol. 41 (Moscow: Izdatel'stvo Politicheskoi Literatury, 1974): 160–212, p. 166.

[4] *Pravda*, 1 April 1937.

USSR and the way it was governed. The chapters that follow will provide an account of the implications of the institutional reflection of these claims for social and political life in the interwar Soviet Union. It will seek, in short, to answer the question: what did the vanguard party actually do?

This book is the first to place the party grassroots at the centre of its account of the formative first two decades of the Soviet system. Though leading Bolsheviks are the protagonists of most works of political history, this study focuses instead on the activities of the many thousands of ordinary communists who acted as the Party's concrete presence throughout Soviet society. Assembled in a large network of primary party organisations (PPO), the Bolshevik rank-and-file was an army of activists made up of ordinary people. While far-removed from the levers of power, they were nevertheless charged with promoting the Party's programme of revolutionary social transformation in their workplaces, neighbourhoods and households. Their incessant meetings, conferences and campaigns have generated a voluminous source base offering a unique view into the practical manifestation of the Party's vanguard mission. The chapters that follow draw on this rich material to craft a new account of how the Soviet republic functioned in the period from the end of the Russian Civil War in 1921 to its invasion by Nazi Germany in 1941.

One of the most influential social historians of the Soviet Union described party activism as a paradox, pointing out that communist rank-and-filers were representatives of political authority but their activities brought them to conflict with functionaries of the state everywhere.[5] This dual nature of the grassroots party membership as the promoter of state policy and supervisor of its implementation is the main theme of the following pages, where it will be argued that, instead of a paradox, communist activism is best viewed as a central feature of state–society relations in the Soviet Union. Rank-and-file activism was inseparable from the policy implementation process, with the party leadership and government unleashing successive waves of political campaigns to generate support for their policy initiatives.

There is much in this that is similar to what sociological literature terms political mobilisation.[6] What differentiates the Leninist concept of the vanguard from agents of political mobilisation more broadly is that the

[5] Sheila Fitzpatrick, *Everyday Stalinism: Ordinary Life in Extraordinary Times: Soviet Russia in the 1930s* (New York: Oxford University Press, 2000).

[6] An extensive sociological discussion of the concept of mobilisation is Birgitta Nedelmann, 'Individuals and Parties – Changes in Processes of Political Mobilization', *European Sociological Review* 3, no. 3 (1987): 181–202. For examples of the use of the concept in historical research, see

activity of the Party was intended to achieve more than a mere enhancement of the state's instrumental capacity of policy implementation. The vanguard party was conceived of as the means by which the communist content of policy would be safeguarded, ensuring the successful transition of the USSR to communism at some future point. For this, the active involvement of the rank-and-file in the everyday running of industry, agriculture, the military and everything else was as important as the leadership's control of government and the formulation of policy. This was despite the fact that the existence of a purely technical dimension of administration was recognised by Lenin and the acquisition of technical competence by the state apparatus would regularly emerge as a desideratum in policy pronouncements throughout the interwar period.[7] Getting the state to do what it was told to do was not enough for the Bolsheviks. It had to do things the right way and in the right direction. The very process of policy implementation thus acquired an ideological dimension.

This is crucial for the account offered in this book, because the vanguard principle transformed the party rank-and-file into an ineluctable aspect of the system of government in the USSR. For as long as the leadership remained committed to Marxism–Leninism, it was compelled by its worldview to insist that its policies were implemented by means of activism as well as administration. As will be shown in the chapters that follow, this was so even when it became clear that activism was getting in the way of policy implementation. Significantly, because ideology was more ambiguous than policy, the involvement of the party rank-and-file with the implementation process almost invariably took the form of party activists taking advantage of their status to address their myriad concerns as workers and non-elite members of Soviet society more broadly. This should not be viewed as a cynical attempt to manipulate public discourse. Rank-and-file influence over the implementation process was implied in the vanguard party concept. These people were doing what they were expected to do, even if particular outcomes left much to be desired from the perspective of the leadership.

The paradox in this, if any, is that the party grassroots moved politically closer to the leadership the more they disorganised policy implementation

Stefano Bartolini, *The Political Mobilization of the European Left, 1860–1980: The Class Cleavage* (Cambridge: Cambridge University Press, 2007); Gregory M. Luebbert, *Liberalism, Fascism, or Social Democracy: Social Classes and the Political Origins of Regimes in Interwar Europe* (Oxford: Oxford University Press, 1991); Susan Whitney, *Mobilizing Youth: Communists and Catholics in Interwar France* (Chapel Hill: Duke University Press, 2009).

[7] V. I. Lenin, 'Luchshe men'she, da luchshe', *PSS*, vol. 45: 389–406.

by getting involved in it. Reliant as it was on the input of non-professional activists, this mode of governance gave the latter significant opportunities to pursue their own interests, thus also giving them a stake in the system. Before expanding further on the content of this monograph, it is necessary to clarify its motivation; why study the communist rank-and-file?

The central argument of this book is that the Soviet Union remained a revolutionary polity committed to deep social transformation throughout the interwar period. The vanguard party was the main agent of this revolutionary process, not only as the producer of policy that sought social change, but also as the main instrument by which elements of Soviet society were themselves involved in bringing about this change. The PPO was the organisational space where the policies conceived by the Party leadership who held state power were put into practice by those workers, technicians and administrators who held party cards. It thus acted as an institutional interface between the Soviet state and the society it governed. The account that follows is predicated on an understanding of revolution as a rapid transformation of the relationship between society and the state.[8] It shows that the turbulent fluidity of this relationship received institutional form in the way the vanguard party functioned at its grassroots. In that regard, this book contributes to a broader historiographical trend exploring how the class tensions, political strategies and cultural outlooks that animated revolutions were subsequently transcribed onto the practices and institutions they produced.[9]

The nature of Soviet state–society relations has also been the central question of historical scholarship on the USSR. Telling the story of the early years of Soviet power from the perspective of the party rank-and-file makes it possible to rethink this relationship by sidestepping the problem of primacy that fuelled much of the heated debate that dominated the field

[8] This classic definition is in Theda Skocpol, *States and Social Revolutions: A Comparative Analysis of France, Russia and China* (Cambridge: Cambridge University Press, 1979), p. 4.

[9] David Armitage and Sanjay Subrahmanyam (eds.), *The Age of Revolutions in Global Context, c. 1760–1840* (New York: Palgrave, 2009); Gail Bossenga, 'The Nobility's Demise: Institutions, Status, and the Role of the State', *The American Historical Review* 124, no. 3 (2019): 942–49; Stephan Fender, *The Global Perspective of Urban Labor in Mexico City, 1910–1929: El Mundo al Revés* (New York: Routledge, 2020); Robert Gerwarth, *November 1918: The German Revolution* (Oxford: Oxford University Press, 2020); Sebastian Heilmann et al., *Mao's Invisible Hand: The Political Foundations of Adaptive Governance in China* (Cambridge, MA: Harvard University Press, 2011); Ralf Hoffrogge, *Working-Class Politics in the German Revolution: Richard Müller, the Revolutionary Shop Stewards and the Origins of the Council Movement* (Leiden: Brill, 2014); Mark Jones, *Founding Weimar: Violence and the German Revolution of 1918–1919* (Cambridge: Cambridge University Press, 2016); Julia C. Strauss, *State Formation in China and Taiwan: Bureaucracy, Campaign, and Performance* (Cambridge: Cambridge University Press, 2019).

in its pre-archival period and has remained implicit in much of its intellectual output to the present day. Virtually every student of Soviet history learns about the acrimonious controversy between scholars subscribing to the totalitarian model of the Soviet state and the younger generation of revisionist historians that sought to deconstruct it. Totalitarianists argued that the power of the state over society was for analytical purposes boundless and consequently framed their scholarship around the intentions of state actors. By contrast, revisionists sought to demonstrate that social realities constrained the power of the state and even forced policy changes, even if, ultimately, all initiative came from above. The debate was to a large extent one about primacy. The problem with this was pointed out by J. Arch Getty at the height of the controversy. Being the product of a revolution, the Soviet Union had no obvious boundaries between state and society. 'An internally divided, improvised, inexperienced, and constantly renovating officialdom shaded almost imperceptibly into a dynamic, mobile, dramatically changing society.'[10]

As the disintegration of the USSR and the decline of the world communist movement appeared to make Cold War categories redundant, the heat generated by these debates died down. A more synthetic picture emerged, where Party leaders for whom Marxist–Leninist ideas matter can and do employ ruthless state power but are constrained by several factors leaving their own mark on historical development. Combined with the vastly increased availability of archival sources after 1991, the fading of old demarcations has led to a reorientation of scholarly efforts to highly empirical research eschewing attempts at broader interpretative syntheses. Some two decades after the archival revolution, one reviewer of the state of the field suggested that the collapse of old intellectual certainties could produce better history, even though it made for duller headlines.[11] Though there is much to agree with in this assessment, this book begins from the premise that the old bottom-up versus top-down binary remains implicit in much of the contemporary literature.[12]

[10] J. Arch Getty, 'State, Society, and Superstition', *The Russian Review* 46, no. 4 (1987): 391–96, p. 394.

[11] Catriona Kelly, 'What Was Soviet Studies and What Came Next?', *The Journal of Modern History* 85, no. 1 (2013): 109–49, p. 149.

[12] A recent book-length historiographical examination of debates on Stalinism is for the most part structured around the totalitarian–revisionist divide and suggests that pre-archival arguments have remained remarkably resilient in the present era. Mark Edele, *Debates on Stalinism* (Manchester: Manchester University Press, 2020), pp. 4–6. Quaint accusations of Stalinist apologia also still appear in book reviews: Oleg Khlevniuk, 'Top Down vs. Bottom-up: Regarding the Potential of

This becomes apparent if we consider more recent attempts at developing interpretative frameworks for the Soviet interwar period. One fertile departure in the literature has sought to frame the Soviet project of socialist construction within the broader framework of modernisation. tracing the origins of Marxism–Leninism in the intellectual tradition of the Enlightenment as an attempt to use reason and technological progress in order to improve human life, both materially and culturally.[13] The specificity of the Soviet Union lay in the particular historical legacy of the Russian Empire, combined with the explicitly non-capitalist path of development prescribed by Marxism–Leninism. A quest to overcome the backwardness of old Russia by revolutionary means and at any cost was the essential element of what a prominent contributor to the modernisation literature termed 'Stalinism as a civilization'.[14] By contrast, other scholars took issue with the concept of modernity as a descriptor of Soviet realities, arguing that whatever the intellectual lineage of Marxism–Leninism, the Party's transformative project was thwarted by the weight of Russian history. On their views, the persistence or re-emergence of informal power networks, authoritarian rule and ethnic particularism, among other things, betrayed the nature of the USSR as a neo-traditional or neo-patrimonial state.[15]

Contemporary "Revisionism"'. trans. Aaron Hale-Dorrell and Angelina Lucento, *Cahiers du monde russe. Russie – Empire russe – Union soviétique et États indépendants* 56, no. 56/4 (2015): 837–57; Hiroaki Kuromiya, 'Stalin's World: Dictating the Soviet Order', *Revolutionary Russia* 28, no. 2 (2015): 199–201; E. A. Rees, 'On Stalin's Team: The Years of Living Dangerously in Soviet Politics', *Revolutionary Russia* 29, no. 1 (2016): 110–12.

13 Michael David-Fox, *Crossing Borders: Modernity, Ideology, and Culture in Russia and the Soviet Union* (Pittsburgh: University of Pittsburgh Press, 2015); David L. Hoffmann, *Cultivating the Masses: Modern State Practices and Soviet Socialism, 1914–1939* (Ithaca: Cornell University Press, 2011); David L. Hoffmann, *Stalinist Values: The Cultural Norms of Soviet Modernity, 1917–1941* (Ithaca: Cornell University Press, 2003); Peter Holquist, '"Information Is the Alpha and Omega of Our Work": Bolshevik Surveillance in Its Pan-European Context', *The Journal of Modern History* 69, no. 3 (1997): 415–50; Amir Weiner, ed., *Landscaping the Human Garden: Twentieth-Century Population Management in a Comparative Framework* (Palo Alto: Stanford University Press, 2003).

14 Stephen Kotkin, *Magnetic Mountain: Stalinism As a Civilization* (Berkley: University of California Press, 1997).

15 J. Arch Getty, *Practicing Stalinism: Bolsheviks, Boyars, and the Persistence of Tradition* (New Haven: Yale University Press, 2013); Yoram Gorlizki, 'Ordinary Stalinism: The Council of Ministers and the Soviet Neopatrimonial State, 1946–1953', *The Journal of Modern History* 74, no. 4 (2002): 699–736; Terry Martin, *The Affirmative Action Empire: Nations and Nationalism in the Soviet Union, 1923–1939* (Ithaca: Cornell University Press, 2001); Yuri Slezkine, 'The USSR as a Communal Apartment, or How a Socialist State Promoted Ethnic Particularism', *Slavic Review* 53, no. 2 (1994): 414–52.

There has occurred a certain inversion of analytical focus, whereby scholars interested in the ideological motivations of state policy look for its effects on the granular everyday practices of social life, while those interested in the deeper structures of Russian society examine their manifestations in the political behaviour of the Soviet leadership. This tends to reproduce the analytical distinction between state and society and, implicitly, the search for first causes in their relationship. We seem to be left with much the same picture as before the archival revolution, whereby the state tried to shape society according to its revolutionary vision and society responded in ways that yielded unexpected outcomes, modern or neo-traditional. We are still missing a way to put the insight gained by access to the archives into a clearer account of socio-political dynamics than was the case before.

It is not the purpose of this monograph to propose anything as ambitious as a new theory of state–society relations in Soviet history. Instead, it will show that studying a particular feature of the institutional structure of the USSR points the way to a better understanding of the concrete functioning of this relationship in the interwar period. That feature is the rank-and-file of the Communist Party, the mass membership whose party status did not translate into executive positions in the state apparatus. The dual status of party rank-and-filers as *ipso facto* supporters and functionaries of the Soviet system on the one hand and as regular citizens on the other renders the state–society distinction null in their case. The party grassroots were both functionally and by design the locus in the Soviet system (*stroi*) where state and society overlapped. This is because the primacy question emerged as problem of policy for the Bolsheviks well before it became a problem of research for historians. The Leninist concept of the vanguard party was an attempt to provide a solution to the problem of how the state apparatus would remain under the control of a specific part of society – the proletariat – while at the same time pursuing a consistent political project, the historical transition to communism. The chapters that follow will show that the ideological underpinnings of the Soviet system had a concrete institutional reflection in the Communist Party, with profound effects on the way the Soviet state was governed.

This book then speaks to a number of more specialised scholarly debates. First, it contributes to a long tradition of works examining the capacity of the state to implement its policy at different levels of the apparatus. Getty's major contribution to the original revisionist challenge was to show that the Party and state apparatuses had been in such a chaotic state during the interwar period as to make the complex political intrigues posited by totalitarian scholars implausible.[16] Post-archival research added further layers of complexity to the question of administrative weakness, with James Harris demonstrating that regional power holders such as industrial managers and local party bosses had the ability to mislead the centre and avoid implementing directives they found impossible or simply inconvenient.[17] This centre–periphery power contest had important implications for the question of the origins of the mass repression campaigns of the mid–late 1930s. Political violence was a tool used to bring powerful barons to heel, but was also driven by the information provided by the very same local leaders. Threat inflation was a key tactic used by regional leaders to secure extra power and avoid accountability for policy failures.[18]

By focusing on the party rank-and-file, this study enhances our understanding of how the Soviet system functioned, highlighting a level of politics that has received scarce attention. As the following pages will show, PPO activities blurred the lines between the managers and the managed, by delegating aspects of policy implementation to the latter. This meant that the problem of administrative weakness, actual and perceived, was exacerbated the stronger the Party's presence became on the ground. For the leadership, this was both a source of frustration and a resource in its tussles with regional power centres.

The party rank-and-file emerges here as an additional factor that further complicates known power dynamics. With regard to mass repression, the PPO provided a distinct channel through which existing social tensions could become entangled with state security concerns and thus contribute to the proliferation of violence. This book thus contributes to the literature on the social dynamics of Soviet political violence, but its focus remains broader.[19] Through their membership in the PPO, grassroots communists

[16] John Arch Getty, *Origins of the Great Purges: The Soviet Communist Party Reconsidered, 1933–1938* (Cambridge: Cambridge University Press, 1987).

[17] James R. Harris, *The Great Urals: Regionalism and the Evolution of the Soviet System* (Ithaca: Cornell University Press, 1999).

[18] J. Arch Getty, '"Excesses Are Not Permitted": Mass Terror and Stalinist Governance in the Late 1930s', *The Russian Review* 61, no. 1 (2002): 113–38; J. Arch Getty, 'The Rise and Fall of a Party First Secretary: Vainov of Iaroslavl', in James Harris (ed.) *The Anatomy of Terror* (Oxford: Oxford University Press, 2013); James Harris, *The Great Fear: Stalin's Terror of the 1930s* (Oxford: Oxford University Press, 2016).

[19] Archival studies of the social dynamics of repression include Wendy Z. Goldman, *Inventing the Enemy: Denunciation and Terror in Stalin's Russia* (Cambridge: Cambridge University Press, 2011); Wendy Z. Goldman, *Terror and Democracy in the Age of Stalin: The Social Dynamics of Repression* (Cambridge: Cambridge University Press, 2007); Cynthia Hooper, 'Terror from within: Participation and Coercion in Soviet Power, 1924–1964'. Unpublished dissertation, Princeton University, 2003; James Hughes, *Stalinism in a Russian Province: A Study of Collectivization and Dekulakization in Siberia* (London: Palgrave Macmillan, 1996).

became involved in all of the cataclysmic transformations that defined the Soviet interwar period but also every little intermediary policy adjustment. Neither dissidents nor state executives, but both militantly communist and fiercely protective of their workplace interests, these people were the concrete manifestation of the twin ideals of activist governance and participatory citizenship that lay at the heart of Marxist–Leninist ideology.

Questions of citizenship and grassroots politics form a significant part of the research agenda on the evolution of the Soviet system after the Second World War. Soviet elections, party conferences and anticorruption campaigns are often framed as attempts to reinforce the system's legitimacy with the demanding public of citizen-soldiers, or as mechanisms of containing tensions within a much expanded and more assertive administrative apparatus.[20] This study shows that post-war political practices had a long pedigree in the institutional experimentation of the 1920s and 1930s, thus placing them in the long(er) durée of the Soviet state-building project.

Finally, this monograph speaks to the perennial question of the role of ideology in Soviet governance. Marxism–Leninism features prominently in the chapters that follow, both as a causal factor and, more importantly, as the boundary of possibility and desirability with respect to policy for all actors involved. What is more, the main object of this study, the party organisation, was itself a product of Marxist–Leninist ideology rather than a deep structure of Russian history. The account that follows contributes to a tradition of scholarship examining the tension in Soviet governance between the demands of technical competence and ideological purity. In a detailed account, David Priestland traced the origins of this tension to an uneasy balance between scientific and romantic elements that was already present in Marx's thought.[21] Other scholars have approached this problem with reference to competing factions of 'reds' and 'experts' or puritans and pragmatists in the leadership, with policy content reflecting the balance of power between them.[22]

[20] Edward Cohn, *The High Title of a Communist: Postwar Party Discipline and the Values of the Soviet Regime* (DeKalb: Northern Illinois University Press, 2015); Yoram Gorlizki and Oleg V. Khlevniuk, *Substate Dictatorship: Networks, Loyalty, and Institutional Change in the Soviet Union* (New Haven: Yale University Press, 2020); Serhy Yekelchyk, *Stalin's Citizens: Everyday Politics in the Wake of Total War* (New York: Oxford University Press, 2014). See also Alexei B. Kojevnikov, *Stalin's Great Science: The Times and Adventures of Soviet Physicists* (London: Imperial College Press, 2004), chapter 8.

[21] David Priestland, *Stalinism and the Politics of Mobilization* (Oxford: Oxford University Press, 2007), pp. 21–34.

[22] Sheila Fitzpatrick, 'Ordzhonikidze's Takeover of Vesenkha: A Case Study in Soviet Bureaucratic Politics', *Soviet Studies* 37, no. 2 (1985): 153–72; J. Arch Getty, 'Pragmatists and Puritans: The Rise and Fall of the Party Control Commission', *The Carl Beck Papers in Russian and East European*

This study shows that the PPO was an inherently 'red' institution. By its very function, it tended to amplify the radical aspects of party policy and make any technocratic retrenchment hard to implement in practice. At its most direct point of contact with society, the Soviet system was always ideologically charged, in a manner reflecting the views and preferences of grassroots party activists. This argument also has implications for our understanding of how Soviet citizens internalised and interpreted official ideology. A significant body of work has approached this as a process of linguistic adaptation – 'speaking Bolshevik' – reflecting various levels of psychological transformation.[23] In the pages that follow, the PPO emerges as the political space where Soviet citizens could both learn and effectively deploy Bolshevik rhetoric. The ability to act Bolshevik was both an incentive and a prerequisite for mastering this vernacular.

Communist rank-and-filers were as much Marxist–Leninist advocates and executors of government policy as they were workers and functionaries concerned with their immediate environment. Their activity was a fundamental element of the Soviet political system, one that renders the contours of the imperceptible shading of the state into society much more discernible to the historian. For the state, the party rank-and-file was a section of society that could be relied upon to promote its policies. For the large majority of people who had little influence over state power, it was a part of the Soviet system that could make sure these policies were implemented in a way consistent with their needs. This monograph will examine how communist activists mediated state–society relations in the Soviet interwar period. The remainder of this introduction will outline how.

## I.1 Methodological Leninism: Studying the Communist Rank-and-File

Due in large part to the persistence of the state–society binary, the Communist Party as a distinct political institution with specific traits

*Studies*, no. 1208 (1997); Jonathan Harris, *The Split in Stalin's Secretariat, 1939–1948* (Lanham: Lexington Books, 2008); Daniel Stotland, *Purity and Compromise in the Soviet Party-State: The Struggle for the Soul of the Party, 1941–1952* (Lanham: Lexington Books, 2017).

[23] Igal Halfin, *Red Autobiographies: Initiating the Bolshevik Self* (Seattle: University of Washington Press, 2011); Igal Halfin, *Stalinist Confessions: Messianism and Terror at the Leningrad Communist University* (Pittsburgh: University of Pittsburgh Press, 2009); Igal Halfin and Jochen Hellbeck, 'Rethinking the Stalinist Subject: Stephen Kotkin's "Magnetic Mountain" and the State of Soviet Historical Studies', *Jahrbücher Für Geschichte Osteuropas* 44, no. 3 (1996): 456–63; Jochen Hellbeck, *Revolution on My Mind: Writing a Diary under Stalin* (Cambridge, MA: Harvard University Press, 2009); Kotkin, *Magnetic Mountain*, p. 198.

deriving from its vanguard mission has received very little attention in post-1991 scholarship. Because the USSR was a single party state, research on the Soviet political process has tended to treat the Party as a layer of the state apparatus, with one researcher having explicitly argued that it was not a political organisation in any meaningful sense of the term.[24] However, although administrative tasks did make up a significant share of the Party's workload, there are strong reasons to reject the view of the Party as an all-Union staffing agency. Not only has research on ideology demonstrated its close connection to policy formulation, but the only recent budgetary study of VKP (b) has shown that 'the Party's most significant expenditure item was for ideology'.[25] The same study also showed that the Party was financially independent of the state, relying increasingly on membership dues and publishing revenues, and concluded that it was an autonomous actor within the Soviet system.[26] If the Party can be shown to have been both institutionally distinct from the state and primarily concerned about ideology-related activities, it follows that a study of the Party must take into account the tasks it set for itself on the basis of its ideological principles. For the purposes of this investigation, it is therefore necessary to set out the implications of the vanguard concept for the way the Party functioned.

Some cultural histories of the Soviet interwar period have described the vanguard status of the Party as being predicated on a claim of possession of esoteric knowledge in the form of Marxism–Leninism.[27] This is incorrect because, although the precepts of Marxism–Leninism did acquire a dogma-like status of unquestionability, there was nothing esoteric about them. Whatever its epistemic value, Marxism–Leninism had the cultural status of a scientific discipline and was, therefore, in principle accessible to

24 I. V. Pavlova, *Stalinizm: stanovlenie mekhanizma vlasti* (Novosibirsk: Sibirskii Khronograf, 1993), introduction. McAdams's recent transnational account of the Communist Party as a political institution makes a similar point, suggesting that VKP (b) essentially ceased to be a political institution after Stalin's elimination of all opposition. A. McAdams, *Vanguard of the Revolution: The Global Idea of the Communist Party* (Princeton: Princeton University Press, 2017). This understanding of the Party as an essentially administrative organ was strongly related to the view that Stalin's ultimate victory in the power struggles of the NEP-era was founded on his control of staffing appointments. For a recent refutation of this view, see Harris, *Great Fear*, pp. 58–75. Harris argues that Stalin's tactical advantage did not lay in control of appointment, but in gaining the loyalty of regional party secretaries by providing them with security of tenure (p. 59). This argument is convincing, but it still turns on the administrative functions of the party apparatus.

25 Eugenia Belova and Valery Lazarev, *Funding Loyalty: The Economics of the Communist Party* (New Haven: Yale University Press, 2013), pp. 17–18.

26 Ibid., p. 8.

27 Fitzpatrick, *Everyday Stalinism*, p. 16. Kotkin goes further, describing Communist Party rule as akin to a theocracy. Kotkin, *Magnetic Mountain*, pp. 293–95.

any interested and literate person. Members of the non-party public were encouraged to acquaint themselves with Marxism–Leninism, as with science in general, as part of their general education through books, periodicals and activities organised by party members. Acquiring and disseminating knowledge of Marxism–Leninism as the science of revolution was a core aspect of a communist's vanguard mission, but possessing this knowledge was not what vanguard status consisted in.

Being part of the vanguard was instead a matter of commitment. The distinctive feature of Bolshevism lay in the fact that it ascribed crucial ideological importance to certain organisational principles, central amongst which were discipline, centralism and active participation of members in all activities.[28] These were initially conceived as means to defend the Party from repression by the tsarist state while also training and socialising increasing numbers of working-class militants in the ways of revolutionary activity. When after revolution and civil war the Bolsheviks successfully established their authority over what would become the USSR, the Party's main task became the implementation of the dictatorship of the proletariat. This consisted of the twin tasks of preventing capitalist restoration by any means necessary and involving the greatest part possible of the country's working population in the implementation of the Party's programme of socialist transformation and cultural enlightenment.[29] Institutionally, this translated on the one hand into the familiar mirroring of the state by the party apparatus in a supervisory capacity. On the other, it meant that the broad ranks of the membership were expected to actively promote party policy and become involved in the day-to-day running of their workplace, in order to ensure that things were being done in the spirit of policy and ideology.

To better ground the discussion that follows in this book, it is worth devoting some space to examining the Bolsheviks' ideas about the place of their party in a post-revolutionary society in more detail. The nature of the transformation of the Bolshevik party from an instrument of

[28] This is a theme running through all the early works of Lenin on the Party, but expressed most clearly in *What Is to Be Done?* V. I. Lenin, 'Chto Delat'?, *PSS*, vol. 6: 1–192, especially pp. 111–54. The question of active participation was among the core elements of the organisational differences that led to the schism between Mensheviks and Bolsheviks at the Second Congress of the Russian Social-Democratic Labour Party in 1903. In his speech, Lenin argued that it would be extremely dangerous to extend party membership rights to people who were not members of a party organisation. 'Every member of the Party is responsible for the Party and the whole of the Party is responsible for every member . . . It is our duty to protect the solidity, consistency and purity of our Party'. V. Lenin, 'II S"ezd RSDRP', *PSS*, vol. 7: 260–312, p. 290.

[29] Lenin, 'Tezisy', pp. 185–86.

revolution to one of government was to a large extent determined by their understanding of the nature of state power in the transition from capitalism to communism. Before the October revolution, Lenin had followed Marx and Engels in regarding the state as an evil of class society that would gradually become unnecessary as more and more people became involved in public administration to run the common affairs of society. His pamphlet on the *State and Revolution* was Lenin's most extensive statement on the subject, proposing a system of direct, mass participation in state affairs that would largely render organised hierarchies of enforcement superfluous. To be sure, some sort of coercion would have to exist, but its character would be more akin to the intervention of concerned citizens to prevent a crime, rather than an organised apparatus of repression. The state would, thus, 'wither away'.[30]

Within that context, the role of the party was to provide the core of conscious workers who, leading by example, would draw the broader toiling masses into the task of governance. Although this is not explicitly stated in *State and Revolution*, Lenin made the point in a subsequent article responding to critics of Bolshevism who denounced their radicalism as the demagoguery of political dilettantes who had no intention to actually govern. Published weeks before the October uprising, *Will the Bolsheviks hold State Power?* contained a striking passage that is worth quoting at some length.

> We are not utopians. We know that every unskilled labourer, every kitchen-maid cannot right now join in state governance. In this we agree [with other parties]. But we differ ... in that we demand an immediate break with the prejudice that only the rich and bureaucrats from rich families can run the state. ... *Conscious workers must lead*, but they are able to draw into the task of governance the masses of toilers and the oppressed.[31]

Lenin proceeded to note that the Russian proletariat had created a quarter-million strong party to 'to take control and set in motion the state apparatus in a planned manner', thus being able to demonstrate in practice that the working class was up to the task of providing its own 'food, milk, clothing, accommodation'.[32] He, thus, introduced into Bolshevik political thought two ideas that went on to play a significant role in laying the

[30] Lenin, 'Gosudarstvo i Revoliutsiia', in *PSS*, vol. 33, pp. 102. Lenin wrote *State and Revolution* in hiding following the Provisional Government's crackdown on workers' organisations after the failed rising known as the July Days. This suggests that the Bolshevik leader viewed the development of a theoretical framework to guide a post-revolutionary polity as a matter of great urgency.

[31] Lenin, 'Uderzhat li bol'sheviki gosudarstvennuiu vlast'?, in *PSS*, vol. 34, pp. 315–16.

[32] Ibid., pp. 329–33.

intellectual framework for Soviet mass politics. First, he defined political participation in terms of engaging with the process of production and provision for people's everyday needs, thus advocating a type of social citizenship.[33] Second, Lenin concretised the sketch of socialist state–society relations provided in *State and Revolution* while at the same time qualifying it. The mass involvement of the toiling masses in public administration that was to lead to the withering away of the state would have to be pioneered by the most daring and advanced of workers, that is the party. These two concepts are crucial for the argument made in this book.

Within months of October, with the Russian economy collapsing under the strain of the developing Civil War, Lenin was forced to signal a retreat from the principles of the commune-state proclaimed in *State and Revolution*. Shortly after the signing of the controversial Brest–Litovsk treaty with Imperial Germany, which saw revolutionary Russia lose roughly a quarter of its European territory and a similar part of its economic capacity, Lenin issued a forceful call for retrenchment.[34] In *The Immediate Tasks of Soviet Power* he reiterated the two principles of socialist governance sketched out in his September article, but also dispensed with any wishful thinking over the prospect of a decline in state coercion. Lenin argued that, faced with a catastrophic crisis, the first priority of the revolutionary state was the 'organisational task' of preventing socio-economic disintegration by providing elementary public security and economic growth. Leaving little room for doubt on whether this would involve the use of repressive means, Lenin declared that the 'construction of socialism requires orderly organisation' which in turn required

[33] The concept of social citizenship was developed by the British sociologist T. H. Marshall. Marshall argued that welfare rights established in the twentieth century were part of an evolutionary process of citizenship and, thus, a necessary element of the latter in modern societies. T. H. Marshall and Tom Bottomore, *Citizenship and Social Class* (London: Pluto Press, 1992). Lenin's position was of course more radical, in that he argued in favour of the active engagement of worker-citizens in the executive process of welfare provision. Interestingly, the contemporary idea of the Communist Party of China regarding economic welfare as a fundamental human right draws on Lenin but is also rooted in the Three Principles of the People enunciated by the father of Chinese nationalism Dr Sun Yat-Sen. See on this, Liu Hainian, 'The Struggle for Human Rights by the Communist Party of China (1921–1949)', Institute of Law of the Chinese Academy of Social Sciences website, available at: www.iolaw.org.cn/global/en/new.aspx?id=44851, last accessed 9 February 2019. The significant point here is that the notion of economic and social welfare as a fundamental right was not peculiar to Bolshevism in twentieth century political thought. Lenin's view was extraordinary in that it advocated that those concerned (workers) should seize control of the very process of welfare provision (production and distribution).

[34] Borislav Chernev, *Twilight of Empire: The Brest–Litovsk Conference and the Remaking of East-Central Europe, 1917–1918* (Toronto: University of Toronto Press, 2017).

'coercion in the form of dictatorship'.[35] Crucially, Lenin defined dictatorship as 'iron authority' which acted ruthlessly 'against exploiters as well as hooligans' and concluded that it was the party's responsibility to lead the masses down the 'path of labour discipline'.[36]

The *Tasks* represented a significant departure from *State and Revolution* in that they represented an acceptance on Lenin's part of a legitimate coercive role for the state beyond defence against counter-revolutionaries (exploiters) to include the provision of public order (against hooligans) and the maintenance of economic activity (labour discipline). Combined with the principles of mass participation and communist leadership, Lenin's notion of revolutionary proletarian dictatorship proved to be a winning strategy for the Bolsheviks in the Russian Civil War.[37] In the years that followed, Lenin's party proceeded to reconquer most of the former Tsarist empire by destroying their opponents on the battlefield while using a combination of tactics to co-opt or suppress anti-Bolshevik supporters of the Soviet cause.[38] A crucial turning point came in July 1918 when, following a failed coup by their former partners, the Left Socialist Revolutionaries, the Bolsheviks were left in sole charge of the Soviet state apparatus, effectively establishing one-party rule. By the time the Red Army had emerged victorious in the Civil War, some of the Party's prominent members were beginning to wonder about the increasingly authoritarian direction the nascent Soviet state was taking, as well as about the effects this was having on the Party itself and its relationship with the country's working class. These concerns generated the first major oppositionist challenge to the general line launched during the Party's Tenth Congress in 1921. The account offered in this book picks up the thread from there.

Its argument will be illustrated by means of a study of party activism in Leningrad in the period 1921–41. The year of the German invasion of the

[35] Lenin, 'Ocherednye zadachi Sovetskoi vlasti', in *PSS*, vol. 36, pp. 194. [36] Ibid., 196, 203.

[37] For an interesting regional study of how the Bolsheviks generated support among neutral populations by organising participatory structures, see Aaron B. Retish, *Russia's Peasants in Revolution and Civil War: Citizenship, Identity, and the Creation of the Soviet State, 1914–1922* (Cambridge: Cambridge University Press, 2008).

[38] The literature on the Russian Civil War is vast, but see indicatively Jonathan Smele, *The 'Russian' Civil Wars, 1916–1926: Ten Years That Shook the World* (Oxford: Oxford University Press, 2016). For examples of Bolshevik coalitions with other groups, see Lara Douds, *Inside Lenin's Government: Ideology, Power and Practice in the Early Soviet State* (London: Bloomsbury Academic, 2018), chapter 2; Alex Marshall, 'The Terek People's Republic, 1918: Coalition Government in the Russian Revolution', *Revolutionary Russia* 22, no. 2 (2009): 203–21; Donald J. Raleigh, *Experiencing Russia's Civil War: Politics, Society, and Revolutionary Culture in Saratov, 1917–1922* (New Haven: Princeton University Press, 2002), pp. 142–73.

USSR has been selected as the end point of the account offered here, on the assumption that the commencement of the Great Patriotic War transformed the relationship between Party, state and society to a significant extent and that, as a consequence, the study of party activism in war conditions would constitute a different subject of inquiry. Leningrad has been selected as the geographical focus for this study because of its interesting political history, its solid industrial economic base and the quality of its party records. The purpose of this book is not to suggest that Leningrad party life was representative of that of the rest of the country. Instead, the focus on Leningrad is intended to frame this study within the conditions best suited to an examination of the practical implications of the Leninist concept of the vanguard party. These include high party density in a highly urbanised environment and, also, a series of important political convulsions such as the fall of Zinoviev, the assassination of Sergei Kirov and the front-line status of the city in the run up to the Second World War, all of which required and elicited different responses from the 'most advanced elements' of Leningrad's working class.

A combination of sources is deployed to support the argument offered in the following chapters. Published materials, the press and secondary literature are used to demonstrate the political objectives of Party leaders, the conditions in which these were pursued, as well as the role assigned to the rank-and-file in the leadership's vision. The archival records of the Leningrad Region party committee and its bureau are used to demonstrate how all-Union policy was regionally concretised and to shed light on the ways in which the regional leadership sought to mobilise the grassroots. The concrete response of rank-and-file communists to the policy initiatives of the centre is examined by means of a micro-historical case study on the Primary Party Organisation (PPO) of Leningrad's Red Putilovite (*Krasnyi Putilovets*, KP) machine building plant, later renamed Kirov factory.

This is based on the stenographic records of the organisation's general assemblies – later conferences – and the protocols (minutes) of various other activities organised by the factory's communists. The value of this source material lies in that it affords us a unique close-up view into the workings of the party organisation. Stenographic records of conferences preserve a large volume of rich and often entertaining detail, including heckling from the floor and the occasional joke, providing rare texture to the world of factory political activism. The often-handwritten protocols of lower-level gatherings similarly offer rare insight into the way that even the most mundane aspects of the production process could become entangled with ideological affairs in the highly politicised world of Soviet industry.

Equally important is the information that can be gleaned from the more formalised features of these records, like the notes on attendance, participation and of course the meetings' agendas. Thus, the fact that conference attendance rarely fell below the 1,000 mark gives us an indication of both the sheer scale of these events and the size of the audience reached by the discussions held therein. Similarly, that even small groups of communists in the shop cells could and did hold structured meetings on often seemingly obscure party affairs is testament to the influence of Bolshevik political culture down to the very bottom of the apparatus. Furthermore, protocol and stenographic records often include a large volume of question notes (*zapiski*) that reached speakers from the floor. Usually anonymous, *zapiski* contained in their majority topical questions, but could often be simple statements of opinion or (perceived) fact. Their value as sources lies in that their anonymity gave their authors the opportunity to express views that were beyond the boundaries of political acceptability.[39] Deploying them alongside the transcripts of speeches made at party gatherings makes it possible to compare what it was possible to say in the context of a party meeting to what was of actual concern to the rank-and-filers.

The KP/Kirov case study takes its methodological cue from Lenin's insistence on the centrality of the organisational form of the Party for its vanguard mission. As the primary party organisation was the 'foundation of the Party', a study of party activism is best conducted by means of a detailed investigation of such an organisation.[40] A micro-historical study of a specific organisation provides the opportunity to examine the activity of the party rank-and-file in a sustained manner through time, in order to appreciate both the continuities and disruptions in the reception of policy initiatives by the mass membership. Again, the selection criterion has not been typicality. The giant KP/Kirov plant was far from typical, having an illustrious revolutionary history and being at the cutting edge of Soviet industrial technology, pioneering the country's tractor and later tank

39 For a more detailed discussion of *zapiski* as sources, see Gleb J. Albert, '"Comrade Speaker!" Zapiski as Means of Political Communication and Source for Popular Moods in the 1920s', *The NEP Era: Soviet Russia 1921–1928*, 8 (2015): 43–54.

40 *Ustav 1936*, VIII: 48. The *Ustav* of 1926 referred to the same level of organisation as 'cell' (*iacheika*). *Ustav 1926*, X: 57. For the sake of clarity, I have used the term 'primary party organisation' and abbreviation PPO throughout this book. Because of its size, the KP/Kirov PPO included sublevels of organisation known as 'shop-cells' (*tsekhiatseiki*), operating in the enterprise's various workshops and departments. Whenever the term 'cells' appears, it refers to the factory's shops.

production processes. The factory's engineers visited and hosted their American counterparts, while famous foreign communists like Ernst Thälmann and Clara Zetkin addressed the enterprise's workers on several occasions, as did esteemed Soviet dignitaries like Maksim Gorkii.[41] Its immense organisation was one of seventeen out of 1,814 in the city of Leningrad to be made up of over 1,000 members.[42] Party saturation at KP/Kirov was also particularly high, floating around the 14 per cent mark throughout most of the period studied while the city average never exceeded a brief highpoint of 8 per cent in 1933 and was usually just over 5 per cent.[43]

The KP/Kirov Primary Party Organisation was, thus, a special party group in an exceptional enterprise. The purpose of the case study is therefore not to produce a readily generalizable picture of Soviet interwar party activism but, rather, to provide a detailed account of this aspect of the Soviet political system in what were near ideal conditions for its operation. If the party were to lead the working class to the 'victory of socialism', there were few places better to do that than a factory where more than one in ten workers were communists. By contrast, conditions in the countryside were far less hospitable to the Bolshevik political project.[44] Nevertheless, maintaining awareness of the favourable environment in

[41] For a discussion of the fame and special status of KP, see the introduction in Clayton Black, 'Manufacturing Communists: "Krasnyi Putilovets" and the Politics of Soviet Industrialization, 1923–1932'. Dissertation, Indiana University, 1996.

[42] *Leningradskaia Organizatsiia KPSS* v. *Tsifrakh, 1917–1973* (Leningrad: Lenizdat, 1974), p. 135. Roughly two thirds, or 1,254 organisations had between 3 and 49 members. There were also 258 PPOs numbering between 50 and 100 members and 285 between 101 and 1,000.

[43] KP/Kirov party saturation is given on the basis of statistical reports available at TsGAIPD, f. 1012, op. 1, d. 480; op. 2, d. 1012; d. 1478, ll. 7, 14. The city-wide figure has been derived from the total membership numbers given in *Leningradskaia Organizatsia*, pp. 69–70 and the population estimates provided in I. I. Eliseeva and E. I. Gribovaia (eds.), *Sankt-Peterburg, 1703–2003: Iubileiinyi statisticheskii sbornik* (Saint-Petersburg: Sudostroenie, 2003), pp. 16–17.

[44] In 1941, the end-year of this study, there were 5,708 active PPOs in the entire Leningrad region, of which 1,967 operated in industrial, communications, transport and construction enterprises. At the same time, kolkhoz and sovkhoz PPOs amounted to 142 and 123, respectively. *Leningradskaia Organizatsia*, p. 130. The matter is further complicated if we consider the significant variation in social organisation that existed within the distinct parts of the Soviet population grouped together as 'rural'. One should be conscious about transposing the insights gained from the account offered in this book onto social contexts where the class categories of Marxism–Leninism bore little relevance to everyday life. The Bolsheviks themselves also had to confront this problem in designing and implementing policy in rural areas. Their shifting, contradictory policy towards the Cossacks during the Civil War is among the most striking examples. Peter Holquist, *Making War, Forging Revolution: Russia's Continuum of Crisis, 1914–1921* (Cambridge, MA: Harvard University Press, 2002), pp. 166–205. Similarly, attempts to introduce collectivisation to small hunter–gatherer societies were derailed by the irrelevance to local conditions of theoretical categories derived from Russian agriculture. Yuri Slezkine, *Arctic Mirrors: Russia and the Small Peoples of the North* (Ithaca: Cornell University Press, 1996), pp. 187–264.

which the KP/Kirov PPO operated makes it possible to appreciate the ways in which its activities may have been similar or different to that of other organisations in both process and outcomes. In that regard, this book is grounded in a tradition of micro-historical scholarship that views the value of case-studies in their ability to illuminate macro-processes rather than represent social averages. KP/Kirov is an excellent point on which to focus a study of the Soviet endeavour to build a polity based on the industrial working class. Many findings of this book will likely apply to other factories of such scale. Others can and should be challenged and supplemented by studies of socialist construction in, for example, small workshops, rural settlements and white-collar working environments.[45]

The argument is developed in a chronological narrative structure. Chapter 1 examines how the Bolsheviks attempted to rebuild their links with the industrial working class after the Russian Civil War. It considers the generalised sense of crisis within the Party generated by the precipitous fall in the urban population and the increasingly authoritarian direction of the Soviet state. Beginning with a discussion of the issues and outcomes of the Tenth Congress, the chapter moves on to show that the leadership decided to rebuild the Party's links with its proletarian constituency by means of a massive expansion in membership that irrevocably transformed the Bolsheviks. Chapter 2 considers how the factional struggles of the mid-1920s played out at the lower levels of the party apparatus, thus beginning the books engagement with rank-and-file activity. It will show that the programmatic differences between the leadership under Stalin on the one hand and the oppositionist challenges led by Trotsky and Zinoviev on the other were seriously engaged with at the grassroots level, with the rank-and-file ultimately siding with the Central Committee. Chapter 3 examines how the political environment created on the ground during the factional struggle shaped the way the rank-and-file responded to the campaign of rapid industrialisation launched by the leadership in the late 1920s, playing a crucial part in mediating the myriad social tensions that emerged during that critical period. In industry, this resulted in the process of production becoming politicised, with far-reaching consequences for workplace relations.

[45] That the value of micro-historical research is not limited to typical or representative case-studies is a point that has been made by practitioners of micro-history in various areas. See indicatively Richard D. Brown, 'Microhistory and the Post-Modern Challenge', *Journal of the Early Republic* 23, no. 1 (2003): 1–20; Carlo Ginzburg et al., 'Microhistory: Two or Three Things That I Know about It', *Critical Inquiry* 20, no. 1 (1993): 10–35; Marion W. Gray, 'Microhistory As Universal History', *Central European History* 34, no. 3 (2001): 419–31.

In Chapter 4, the book's focus shifts to the cultural and educational aspects of party activism, stressing its significance for acculturating the rank-and-file into Bolshevism. It will show that because of the important material dimensions of cultural activities, these too attracted the interest and efforts of grassroots communists who selectively engaged with this aspect of party policy in a way consistent with their concerns. Chapter 5 follows the party rank-and-file as it engaged with the democratisation campaigns surrounding the introduction of a new constitution in 1936. It shows that activists welcomed these initiatives as a way to strengthen their position relative to the state administrative apparatus, eventually becoming willing agents of the campaigns of repression that swept the country in 1937. Chapter 6 shows that, despite the disruption caused by mass repression, the leadership embarked on a renewed push for institutional renewal within the Party at the same time as it was trying to place the country's economic life on a military footing. The Conclusion offers some comments regarding the implications of the book's arguments for Soviet history beyond 1941 as well as the history of twentieth century communism more broadly.

# CHAPTER 1

# *Building a Workers' Party*

## 1.1 Introduction

When the delegates of the Tenth Congress of the Russian Communist Party (Bolsheviks) gathered in Moscow in early March 1921, the military phase of the Russian revolution was drawing to a close. In his opening speech, Lenin remarked that this was the first time after three and a half years of brutal fighting that a Party Congress was convening in conditions of complete absence of hostile troops on Soviet soil. Having secured the immediate survival of the fledgling workers' state and planted the seeds of proletarian revolution abroad by establishing the Comintern, the victorious Bolsheviks were now faced with the task of peaceful economic reconstruction and political consolidation. Lenin argued that this challenge was no less formidable, as the Civil War had not only decimated the country economically and ruined its infrastructure, but also shredded its social fabric and completely rearranged its class structure. For a Marxist party, correctly diagnosing the new balance of class forces was a necessary precondition for the development of an effective policy framework. The smouldering tensions within the Party, reflected in the 'extraordinary abundance of platforms, tendencies, little tendencies, almost-like-tendencies' circulating amongst the membership, were a sure sign that the Bolsheviks had yet to complete this vital task.[1]

Lenin was typically perceptive. The Tenth Congress has long been recognised as a watershed moment in Soviet history, putting in motion a range of policy initiatives that would have enduring influence on the development of the relationship between Party, state and society in the Soviet system. These included the ban on organised factions, the working out of the place of trade unions in the socialist state and the launching of the New Economic Policy (NEP). None of these policies was without controversy and their adoption by the Party laid the groundwork for an

[1] *Protokoly X S'ezda RKP (b)* (Moscow: Partiinoe Izdatel'stvo, 1933), pp. 3–5.

extended period of internal strife that would consume much of its energies for the remaining decade.

The policy initiatives that established the party rank-and-file and its primary organisations as a distinct element in Soviet politics were launched within the context of these conflicts. An investigation into the role of the communist grassroots in the formation of the Soviet system must, therefore, start here. The following pages will consider the content of the post-Civil War controversies and provide a sketch of the ideological and practical motivations behind the early institutional development of the Soviet polity and the role of the Communist Party therein. The account will proceed in three parts: first, an outline of the policy debates of the Tenth Congress and their context; second, an examination of the concrete implementation by the party leadership of the policy directives issued and, third, an overview of the first major crisis experienced by the emerging political system, namely the launching of Leon Trotsky's Left Opposition.

## 1.2 The Tenth Party Congress: Challenges and Responses

Despite the remarkable improvement in the military fortunes of the Soviet state, the Tenth Party Congress carried out its business in rather inauspicious circumstances. In the last week of February 1921, minor disturbances surrounding an industrial dispute at Petrograd's *Trubochnyi* factory led to limited clashes with a detachment of Red Fleet cadets guarding the enterprise. The offended workers appealed for support to their colleagues at the nearby Baltic shipyards and a combined group subsequently made a failed attempt to seize arms from a local barracks. Although the conflict was quickly contained without violence, rumours of a generalised rebellion triggered a more organised challenge to Bolshevik power. On 28 February, the Battleship *Petropavlosk* mutinied and issued a resolution calling for a 'third revolution' against the Bolshevik 'commissar regime'. The following day, a public meeting held at the Anchor square of the naval fortress-city Kronstadt elected a 'revolutionary committee' and put forward its demands for 'Soviets without communists', an end to civil war measures limiting freedom of speech and assembly but also in favour of 'freedom to trade'. The committee then moved to arrest the leading cadres of the Kronstadt Soviet and some 600 communists, including the commissar of the Baltic Fleet, Nikolai Kuzmin, who had arrived the day before to diffuse the situation.[2]

[2] RGASPI, f. 17, op. 109, d. 27, ll. 17, 21–23; S. Semanov, *Likvidatsiia antisovetskogo Kronshtadtskogo miatezha 1921 goda* (Moscow: Nauka, 1973), pp. 82–87.

The Kronstadt mutiny involved 2 battleships, more than 100 batteries of coastal artillery and some 27,000 sailors and soldiers. The government responded by declaring a state of siege in Petrograd and, following an unsuccessful negotiation attempt on 8 March, put down the rebellion by force ten days later. The troops of the Seventh Army that carried out the assault numbered over 40,000. The scale of this crisis naturally cast a shadow over the proceedings of the Tenth Congress. Indeed, such was the political significance of a former Bolshevik stronghold staging an armed uprising while the supreme party body was in session, that a number of Congress delegates were mobilised to go to Petrograd as part of the negotiation team and subsequently joined the Red Army storming of Kronstadt. One of the mobilised delegates was I. Sladkov, a seaman representing Kerch and the Azov flotilla.

On 7 March, Sladkov penned a situation report to Ephraim Sklianskii that has been preserved in the archives and offers useful insight into the way low-ranking cadres perceived the Kronstadt uprising. Sladkov stated that attempts to negotiate with the mutineers had failed as they had been duped by Left SR activists who had then handed over command to White officers who were committed counter-revolutionaries. There was, therefore, no solution to the crisis but a military one. Significantly, Sladkov opined that the susceptibility of the Kronstadt garrison to counter-revolutionary agitation was the result of the persistence of 'amateur tendencies' in the Navy. He went on to warn that there was no guarantee against future mutinies if the Navy was not thoroughly reconstituted into a disciplined, 'strong-spirited' organisation in the mould of the Red Army.[3]

Sladkov's denunciation of amateurism echoed Lenin's earlier attacks on indiscipline and 'hooliganism' as counter-revolutionary phenomena that undermined Soviet power. Delivering the main report of the Central Committee at the Tenth Congress, Lenin returned to this theme in connection with the events concurrently unfolding in Kronstadt. The Bolshevik leader described the uprising as a 'petty-bourgeois counterrevolution' that was 'without a doubt more dangerous than [White generals] Denikin, Iudenich and Kolchak taken together'. In a country where the proletariat was in a minority and peasant households had been ruined by war, the ongoing military demobilisation provided an endless supply of potential mutineers. Lenin argued that events in Kronstadt demonstrated that, in these conditions, seemingly innocuous demands for trade freedom or political reform put forward by non-aligned people could easily function

[3] RGASPI, f. 17, op. 109, d. 27, ll. 13–15.

as a stepping-stone for a counter-revolutionary uprising directed against Soviet power.[4]

The red thread running through Lenin's Congress speech was the vital need for the Party to work out an accommodation with the highly differentiated petty-bourgeois mass of people that constituted the overwhelming majority of the country's population. One part of this was the vast peasantry. Starved, exhausted and armed after years of war, Russia's primary producers were a necessary but volatile ally for the Bolsheviks who needed to feed the cities but had little to offer in return for grain. Lenin argued that the only way to restore proper economic exchange between town and countryside was to abolish wartime requisitioning in favour of an agricultural tax in kind and allow foreign investment in specific sectors. Having the ability to market its surplus produce, the peasantry could then buy up the output of industry kickstarted by foreign capital. Diligent state management of this exchange would ensure the development of state industry and take the insurrectionary edge off slogans like 'freedom to trade'.[5]

The multitude of peasant households was not the only component of the elemental petty-bourgeois forces (*stikhii*) besieging the revolution. Towards the end of his report, Lenin touched upon the creeping threat of 'bureaucratism' spreading through the state apparatus. Shorthand for negligence and corruption, bureaucratism was a threat of petty-bourgeois degeneration both due to the fact that the state apparatus was staffed with officials who were not necessarily of working-class origin or even communist sympathies and because economic collapse had encouraged the development of a network of graft that necessarily took the form of small private exchange. Out of need or disposition, the functionaries of the proletarian state were turning into small-time crooks and petty traders. They could thus not be relied upon to fulfil the complex task of economic reconstruction. No less alarmingly, they were also alienating the Soviet state from its proletarian constituency.[6]

What was then to be done if the future of the nascent socialist state could not be entrusted to its functionaries? For Lenin, the enormity of the challenge posed to the revolution by the petty-bourgeois hydra could only be met through more effective control of the state apparatus by the Party and closer attention to the needs and moods of Soviet workers. This would require a massive show of 'cohesion, resilience and discipline' on the part

[4] Lenin, 'X S'ezd RKP(b)', in *PSS*, vol. 43, pp. 24–25. [5] Ibid., pp. 28–31.
[6] Ibid., pp. 31, 46–47.

of the Bolsheviks. Unfortunately, the Party was not demonstrating these qualities. The 'luxury' of discussion that had generated the multitude of platforms Lenin ridiculed in his opening speech had allowed the petty-bourgeois mentalities prevalent in Russian society to seep into the Party. As a result, a quasi-anarchist syndicalist tendency had formed within the ranks and been allowed to propagate demands that were incompatible with the proletarian dictatorship and effectively indistinguishable from those of the Kronstadt mutineers. In response to this threat, the CC introduced a resolution 'On Party Unity' forbidding the operation of organised internal party groupings and declaring the struggle against factionalism to be a key political priority.[7]

Along with the abolition of grain requisitions, the ban on factions was the most consequential of the resolutions passed at the Tenth Congress. The combination of a mixed economy with a monolithic single-party state provided the context within which all subsequent developments would unfold. Although Lenin got his way, neither his diagnosis nor his proposed remedies to the maladies of the revolution were without controversy. The chief bearers of the syndicalist 'deviation' condemned by Lenin were a group of mostly Moscow-based leading cadres who had organised themselves into an internal 'Workers' Opposition' to what they saw as the Party's drifting away from proletarian interests. The Workers Opposition had first emerged as a distinct group about a year earlier, when in February 1920 its members took control of the Tula provincial committee (*gubkom*). It rapidly gained considerable popularity with disaffected workers on a platform of democratisation of Soviet institutions and direct workers' management of production. Its leadership included prominent trade-unionists like the metal worker Sergei Medvedev and the former Commissar of Labour Aleksei Shliapnikov. Employing a combination of active campaigning and tactical alliances with smaller groups, the Workers' Opposition made quick gains in Moscow and the surrounding area. Its most significant organisational success was gaining support for its theses by the central committee of the Metalworkers' Union.[8]

On 25 January 1921, *Pravda* published a pamphlet on *The Workers' Opposition* in which the leading Bolshevik Aleksandra Kollontai offered a programmatic explication of the group's differences with the CC majority.

7 Ibid., pp. 89–92.

8 Barbara Allen, 'Alexander Shliapnikov and the Origins of the Workers' Opposition, March 1919–April 1920', *Jahrbücher Für Geschichte Osteuropas* 53, no. 1 (2005): 1–24; Tat'iana A. Sandu, 'Rabochaia Oppozitsiia v RKP(b): 1920–1921 gg.', *Vestnik Tiumenskogo Gosudarstvennogo Universiteta* 3 (2003): 166–72.

The pamphlet, which was subsequently circulated at the Tenth Congress, traced the origins of the brewing party crisis to much the same causes as Lenin's political report. The non-proletarian, petty-bourgeois character of Russian society was preventing the Party from plotting and holding a true socialist course. For Kollontai, however, the chief symptom of this malaise was not syndicalism, but a growing alienation of the committed, true working-class base of rank-and-file party activists, the *nizi* (lows), from an aloof leadership of *verkhi* (highs). Having lost touch with the *nizi*, the *verkhi* presumed to rule in the name of the working class by staffing important posts with toadies who were more interested in pursuing 'Soviet careers' than serving the socialist transformation of society.[9]

To address this crisis of estrangement, the Workers' Opposition proposed a radical shake-up of the relationship between Party, state and society as it had developed during the Civil War. The Party was to return to its role as a collective intellectual leader and educator of the working class by being deprived of its administrative control over the state apparatus. This was to be achieved by abolishing the Party's informal power of executive appointment (*naznachenstvo*), ensuring that all levels of the state apparatus were instead democratically elected. To ensure that working-class interests would prevail in this new constitutional set-up, the Opposition also demanded that industrial management be put under the control of the trade unions, all the way from the administrations of individual enterprises to the agencies and commissariats responsible for national economic planning.[10]

In his concluding remarks on the CC political report, Lenin urged delegates to read Kollontai's pamphlet as 'the best material against the "workers' opposition"'. He ridiculed the notion that operational control of production and national planning could be taken over by assemblies of trade-unionists ('are they joking, can we take these people seriously?') and accused the oppositionists of empty sloganeering. Lenin argued that the whole party agreed that bureaucratism was a major problem but that the remedy proposed by the Opposition was disingenuous because they knew that the reason the Party could not 'implement consistent democratism' was that 'we are too weak'. Weakening party control over state administration would enfeeble the Soviet state and the revolution

[9] Aleksandra Kollontai, 'Rabochaia Oppozitsiia', in *Levye Kommunisty* v *Rossii* (Moscow: Praksis, 2008): 165–206, pp. 167–68, 178, 200.

[10] Ibid., pp. 194, 202.

itself. It was in this sense that the Workers' Opposition represented an intra-party Kronstadt.[11]

The oppositionists protested against Lenin's accusations and defended their record as loyal soldiers of the CC. Rather than undermine the party, the objective of their intervention had been to strengthen it by remedying the growing isolation (*otorvannost'*) of the leadership from the rank-and-file and the broader working class. Indeed, they had never countenanced the founding of a separate organisation. Essentially, the Bolsheviks were experiencing a clash between their early revolutionary vision of bottom-up politics and engaged activism with the deflating compromises necessary in order to maintain power as a governing party. In his own Congress speech, Shliapnikov, a keen memoirist, said that he was partly motivated by a sense that the party had lost the unity of purpose and sense of camaraderie that had been a defining trait of underground Bolshevism.[12]

Although the Workers' Opposition was comprehensively defeated at the Congress, its rapid growth and the solid political and class credentials of its members indicated that their concerns were probably shared by a substantial part of the Bolshevik membership. Warnings of rank-and-file alienation were, thus, not easy to dismiss and Lenin did in fact promise that the CC would take on board anything of value in the oppositionists' platform, even as he refused to countenance the introduction of any of its concrete proposals. Addressing the problems exposed by the twin crises of Kronstadt and the Workers' Opposition would be the chief task of the party in the early years of the NEP period.

## 1.3 Party Building and the Formation of Grassroots Institutions

Lenin's interventions at the Tenth Congress had essentially been a reiteration of the principles of governance formulated in *The Immediate Tasks of Soviet Power* at the outset of the Russian Civil War. Experience and exigency had demonstrated the impracticability of the vision of a commune-state and the necessity of maintaining robust, effective chains of command staffed by professionals. For as long as this remained the case, the attendant danger of bureaucratism could only be combatted by the involvement of the popular masses in state administration through a

11 Lenin, 'X S'ezd', pp. 39, 45.

12 *Protokoly X S'ezda RKP (b)*, p. 77; David Priestland, 'Bolshevik Ideology and the Debate over Party–State Relations, 1918–21', *Revolutionary Russia* 10, no. 2 (1997): 37–61, p. 38.

process of permanent consultation and activism that would not, however, infringe upon the prerogatives of state executives.

Against the protests of Shliapnikov, Kollontai and their comrades, Lenin argued that the conditions which had originally led the Bolsheviks to adopt this course were still in place. He did, nevertheless, admit that the pressing demands of the Civil War had led to the neglect of the second half of the political formula proposed in the *Immediate Tasks*. In order to right this forced deviation of the Party's course, the Congress passed two substantial resolutions: *On the Role and Tasks of Trade-Unions* and *On Questions of Party Building*. Both documents began with a reassertion of the correctness of the political line the Party had adhered to since 1918 and stressed that the military-like organisational principles that had governed party life and trade-union activity since that time had been dictated by military force majeure. The transition to a state of peace thus necessitated a corresponding change in the modus operandi of these pillars of the Soviet republic towards a greater application of 'workers' democracy' (*rabochaia demokratiia*).[13]

A dispute on the role of trade-unions in the Soviet state had been raging in the Party since mid-1920 when, at the initiative of Leon Trotsky, the CC had implemented a merger of the rail and water transport unions into a single apparatus staffed by direct appointees. Trotsky had subsequently argued for an extension of this scheme to all trade unions as part of a broader plan to restore the Russian economy by militarising labour. Although Lenin and the majority of the CC had condemned Trotsky's views, the extreme authoritarianism of this proposal had galvanised the Workers' Opposition and been the chief motive for their presentation of a programme against the CC line.[14]

Significantly, the CC-sponsored resolution on trade-unions was tabled against a minority proposal by Trotsky and his supporters as well as the Opposition platform. The majority line attempted to strike a middle ground between the latter's syndicalist demands for the subordination of industry to the trade-union apparatus and Trotsky's authoritarian project to incorporate unions into the state. The CC resolution stipulated that the

[13] *Protokoly X S'ezda RKP (b)*, pp. 590–91, 605–7.

[14] Barbara C. Allen, *Alexander Shlyapnikov, 1885–1937: Life of an Old Bolshevik* (Leiden: Brill, 2015), pp. 162–69; Simon Pirani, *The Russian Revolution in Retreat, 1920–24: Soviet Workers and the New Communist Elite* (London: Routledge, 2008), pp. 68–69; William G. Rosenberg, 'The Social Background to Tsektran', in *Party, State and Society in the Russian Civil War*, ed. Diane P. Koenker, William G. Rosenberg and Ronald Grigor Suny (Bloomington: Indiana University Press, 1989), 349–73.

purpose of professional associations at the current phase of the revolution was to function as 'schools of communism', that is as organisational spaces where workers would acquire the habits and hone the skills necessary to become masters of their own state. Although there was no question of trade-unions assuming direct operational control of industry, the resolution listed a number of aspects of the organisation of production that could be immediately placed under union control.

These included the determination of skill-brackets and norm-setting for the remuneration of labour, as well as inspection and control functions over the disposal of resources by the industrial apparatus and the distribution of the labour force. In addition, trade-unions were to participate in the formulation of economic plans and the cadre selection process at all levels. They would further promote technical literacy amongst their members and select candidates from the ranks of workers for training and promotion to executive posts. At the same time, however, the unions would have to assume greater responsibility for work discipline, taking a strong line against manifestations of unconscientious attitudes towards labour such as truancy and embezzlement of factory equipment.[15]

Unions were, thus, to perform some of the functions of the apparatus of industrial administration without being subordinate to the latter, while also acting as an institutional counterweight to its power without being superior to it. To maintain this delicate institutional balance, trade-union leadership was to remain in the hands of reliable, experienced communists who could be trusted to defend their organisations from managerial intervention while also preventing their transformation into hotbeds of anarcho-syndicalist activism. In this context, it was vital to ensure that the party apparatus remained grounded in a politically robust rank-and-file membership of solid proletarian character. The Congress resolution on party building had precisely this purpose.

The document preamble asserted that the organisational form of a Marxist party depended upon its concrete revolutionary tasks. Army-like methods of command and control employed during the Civil War had contributed to the alienation of the grassroots *nizi* from the leading *verhki* and led to the fragmentation of the Party into often hostile clans of 'soldiers and civilians, trade-unionists and Soviet officials, old members and new'. The chief task of the Party in the post-war period was to overcome this crisis by reuniting the membership around the common purpose of extending its influence over the non-aligned masses and

[15] *Protokoly X S'ezda RKP (b)*, pp. 599–600.

combatting counter-revolution. 'Workers' democracy' was the basic principle that would have to guide the development of the organisational form appropriate to the new revolutionary tasks.[16]

The resolution stipulated that the main purpose of the new organisational form was to ensure the maximum possible involvement of rank-and-file members in party life and public affairs more broadly. The chief method by which this would be achieved was the broadest possible discussion of all major policy issues, provided that the Party had not yet reached a binding decision on the matter at hand. This transition required a renewed attention to the Party's recruitment practices, the attraction of new members of solid proletarian background into the ranks and the purging of the apparatus from unreliable elements that had colonised it in the chaos of war. Special attention would have to be paid to the political education and ideological acculturation of the new recruits, in order to secure the Party's revolutionary integrity against the prevailing petty-bourgeois mentality of the Russian masses.[17]

In addition to laying out the basic principles for future organisational development, the resolution contained a special section on the work of cells, the primary party organisations in which the vast majority of communists exercised the rights and duties of membership. Strengthening these grassroots institutions was a necessary condition for healing the rift between *nizi* and *verkhi* and to that effect the Congress resolved that factory-based cells should not be confined to the task of political education but be transformed into 'militant organs of the Party's economic work'. This entailed each and every member becoming actively involved in the formation and activities of trade-union committees and the organs of economic control. Party rank-and-filers were expected to lead their non-party colleagues by example. They were to demonstrate initiative in discovering new ways to raise productivity and provide meaningful support to the ideas of other workers. At the same time, communists had to be militant defenders of workers' interests against managerial abuse, taking swift action to ensure grievances were addressed in a way that strengthened the bond between the Party and its proletarian constituency. Thus, the resolution identified party cells as the main institutional framework for interacting with its social support base.[18]

The discussion on party building was the longest at the Tenth Congress, taking up three of its sixteen sessions and involving seventeen speakers. The oppositionists, who had been represented on the resolution's drafting

[16] Ibid., p. 609. [17] Ibid., p. 610. [18] Ibid., pp. 613–14.

committee, admitted that it was in the right direction and did not vote against it. This rare show of unity indicated the extent to which, even at their most fractious, Bolsheviks of all shades were agreed that their party remained the chief representative of working-class interests and the natural leader of the revolution.[19]

The Tenth Congress resolutions on trade-unions and party building would have long-term implications for the relationship between the Party, its working-class base and the state apparatus. Party building as a permanent concern with the recruitment of new members and their political upbringing became a major theme of party activity for the entirety of the period examined in this study. More significantly, the Party-sponsored social partnership between unions and management proposed in the trade-union resolution gave rise to a distinctively Soviet institutional framework that came to be known as the industrial triangle.

The place of factory administrations in this system was simple enough. They had to formulate plans, manage resources and put their staff to work. Trade-union organisations had the slightly more complicated task of defending their members and providing them with important services, while also taking over some aspects of the labour side of industrial management. Party organisations were the lynchpin of the system by ensuring that the other two sides performed their functions without coming to blows and derailing industrial production. It was within the party framework that communist workers and trade-unionists could confront communist factory directors as equals and work out compromises on the common ground of party policy.[20]

The Soviet industrial triangle was, thus, not an aggregate of separate organisations but a form of institutional enmeshment and overlapping boundaries between Party, state and society. A long historiographical tradition has regarded the formation of the triangle as a sign of failure or retreat of the Russian revolution and the socialist project, a collusion

[19] Ibid., pp. 553–54; Pirani, *Russian Revolution*, p. 68. Shliapnikov stated that the opposition would abstain because the draft resolution was still not good enough to vote for.

[20] Nataliia Ofitserova, 'Informatsionnye Dokumenty o Vzaimootnosheniiakh Zavodskogo Soobshchestva i Vlasti v 1920-Kh Godakh: Problemy i Ikh Resheniia', *Nauchno-Tekhnicheskie Vedomosti SPbGPU* 2, no. 111 (2010): 155–60; Nataliia Ofitserova, 'Rol' Profsoiuzov v Bor'be s Rabochim Aktivizmom v Zavodskom Soobshchestve v 1920-e Gody', *Nauchno-Tekhnicheskie Vedomosty SPbGPU. Gumanitarnye i Obshschestvennye Nauki* 3, no. 131 (2011): 165–69; Svetlana Borisovna Ul'ianova, 'Formirovanie "Treugol'nika" Na Sovetskikh Predpriiatiiakh v Pervoi Polovine 1920-Kh Gg.', *Noveishaia Istoriia Rossii*, no. 2 (2013): 169–84; Oksana Zaitseva, 'Metody Predotvrashcheniia Trudovykh Konfliktov Na Predpriiatiiakh Petrograda, Leningrada v Nachale 1920-Kh Gg.: Sistema Opoveshcheniia o Besporiadkakh, Kontrol' Za Povedeniem Mass, *Vestnik Leningradskogo Gosudarstvennogo Universiteta Im. A. C. Pushkina* 4, no. 1 (2012): 114–23.

between the Bolsheviks, unions and industrial authorities leading to the political dispossession of Soviet workers who could no longer rely on any independent institutions.[21] To be sure, trade-unions in the NEP era expended considerable efforts to contain labour militancy and prevent strikes at state-owned enterprises. Their membership declined in the first half of the 1920s, likely reflecting a loss of authority among workers. Nevertheless, it would be facile to dismiss the triangle as a mere con. Although acting as a brake on the more militant forms of industrial activism, trade-unions played an important role in securing mediated resolutions to labour disputes in favour of workers, while also monitoring standards of workplace health and safety and helping the unemployed.[22]

The function of party cells within this institutional framework will be examined at greater length in subsequent chapters. In early 1921, when the Tenth Congress concluded its business, the triangle existed only on paper. After three years of Civil War, the trade-union apparatus had been decimated by staff and membership loss, as millions of workers had abandoned the cities in search of food and shelter in the countryside.[23] The 'declassing' of the proletariat that vexed many a Bolshevik mind was real enough. It was, however, reasonable to expect that this dramatic trend would eventually be reversed by the restoration of economic growth attracting workers back to the factories and their unions. However, in terms of the Party and its upgraded role, the prospects looked less promising. Party building could not be left to the forces of the market or the

[21] Allen, *Shliapnikov*, p. 226; Kevin Murphy, *Revolution and Counterrevolution: Class Struggle in a Moscow Metal Factory* (Chicago: Haymarket Books, 2007), pp. 105–6; Pirani, *Russian Revolution*, pp. 156, 167.

[22] O. A. Chernova, 'Deiatel'nost' Professional'nikh Soiuzov Po Razresheniiu Trudovykh Konfliktov Na Predpriiatiiakh Tsentral'nogo Chernozem'ia v 1920-e Gody (Po Materialam Kurskoi i Voronezhskoi Gubernii)', *Nauchnye Vedomosty. Seriia Istoria, Politologiia, Ekonomika, Informatika* 16, no. 19 (2010): 188–96; Sergei Iarov, 'Predposylki konformizma: prekrashchenie zabastovok v Petrograde v 1917–1925 gg.', *Sotsiologicheskii Zhurnal*, no. 2 (2007): 109–47; Taisiia Iudina, 'Profsoiuzy kak instrument regulirovaniia obshchestvennykh otnoshenii v SSSR v 1920-e gg. (na primere kontsesii "Gruzinskii Marganets")', *Vestnik RUDN, Seriia 'Istoriia Rossii'*, no. 1 (2011): 58–65; Diane P. Koenker, *Republic of Labor: Russian Printers and Soviet Socialism, 1918–1930* (Ithaca: Cornell University Press, 2005), pp. 161–64; Konstantin Kozlov, 'Uchastie ural'skikh profsoiuzov v predotvrashchenii i uregulirovanii zabastovochnogo dvizheniia v gody nepa', *Vestnik Cheliabinskogo Gosudarstvennogo Universiteta*, no. 12 (2013): 36–41; Svetlana Urazova, 'Izmeneniie funktsii profsoiuzov v nachal'nyi period nepa', *Izvestiia Vyshikh Uchebnykh Zavedenii. Povolzhskii Region*, no. 1 (2011): 36–42; Zaitseva, 'Metodi predotvrashcheniia'.

[23] Between 1917 and 1920, the populations of Moscow and Petrograd declined, respectively, from 2 to 1 million and 2.5 million to just over 700,000. Most other large industrial cities experienced similar, though not as acute population loss. Diane Koenker, 'Urbanization and Deurbanization in the Russian Revolution and Civil War', *The Journal of Modern History* 57, no. 3 (1985): 424–50, pp. 424–25.

ingenuity of state planners. The Party would have to build itself through its own efforts and, by the same token, transform itself into the vanguard revolutionary force envisaged by its leaders.

The first step in this process was a thorough survey of Bolshevik forces and a weeding out of politically unreliable elements. In the summer of 1921, the CC passed resolutions mandating a general purge (*chistka*) of the ranks, followed by an all-Russian party census, in order to determine the state of the Party's local organisations, the exact size of its membership and its social composition. The *chistka* aimed to rid the Party of the double-dealing 'also-communists' who had joined it after victory, as well as those erstwhile honest proletarian cadres who had become 'commissarified' and turned into stale bureaucrats. The aim was to protect the ideological integrity of Bolshevism and restore the trust of the rank-and-file but also ensure the smoother functioning of the apparatus by breaking up networks of convenience and corruption. To that end, local organisations were instructed to involve non-party workers in the purge, relying on their assistance to expose the bad apples in their midst.[24]

For the census, the CC statistical department developed a system involving separate forms to register individual party members, cells and party committees. Individual forms consisted of fifty-nine entry fields for information such as personal details and demographic traits like class, age, and nationality, but also for information like a member's pre-1917 political credentials, such as participation in the labour movement and prison sentences for underground revolutionary work. The census thus also acted as a secondary purge, with the cards of those deemed unfit for membership being confiscated.[25]

The results of the two processes were probably less than reassuring for the leadership. At the outset of the purge, the Party had a membership of roughly 710,000. At its conclusion, the number of communists stood at just under 500,000. This figure was further trimmed during the census and subsequent rounds of the purge in remote provinces, so that the first results published in late 1922 indicated a membership of roughly 410,000.

[24] *Pravda*, 30 June 1921; 'Ob ochistke partii', in *Protokoly odinnadtsatogo S'Ezda RKP(b)* (Moscow: Partizdat, 1936), pp. 722–25; A. Miasnikov, 'Partiinaia chistka 1921-go goda v provintsii (po materialam Kaluzhskoi i Tul'skoi gubernii)', *Omskii Nauchnyi Vestnik* 12, no. 6 (2009): 37–41, p. 38.

[25] RGASPI, f. 17, op. 18, 'Predislovie opisi', p. 2; Sergei Vorob'ev, 'Sotsial'nyi portret kommunistov Urala nachala 1920-kh gg. Istochnikovedcheskoe issledovanie materialov vserossiiskoi perepisi chlenov RKP (b)', Unpublished doctoral thesis (avtoreferat). Institut Istorii Ural'skogo Otdeleniia RAN (2003), pp. 19–21.

Over the course of a year, more than a third of party members had been deemed unfit for membership or had chosen to walk out before being shown the door. What is more, the alarmist warnings of the Workers' Opposition about the Party's catastrophic loss of authority amongst the working class now appeared to contain a grain of truth. Party saturation in the two capitals stood at 26.5 per thousand and barely exceeded 5 per thousand in the other industrial provinces of central Russia. Organisations in industrial enterprises that had been stalwarts of Bolshevism in previous years had shrunk to a few hundred members amongst thousands of workers. To make matters worse, although on paper the Party appeared to be remaining healthily working-class, with workers accounting for over half of its membership, more detailed qualitative indicators revealed a worrying trend. A large proportion of communists of proletarian origin were no longer directly involved in production, having taken up professional party posts or managerial positions in their enterprises. Even in the two capitals, only about 15 per cent of members were workers by occupation.[26]

To remedy these alarming trends, the Bolshevik leadership decided to step up the pace of party building. In March 1922, the Eleventh Party Congress passed a resolution *On the strengthening of the Party and its new tasks* which reiterated the previous year's party building directives but introduced a range of new measures. Barriers to entry were set up via a system of differential recruitment prescribing a longer candidacy period for non-workers. To restore the Party's prestige, factory-based organisations were instructed to demonstrate greater initiative in defending workers' interests and maintain a critical distance from management. In order to enhance the capacity of PPOs to intervene in factory life, the secretaries of those operating in enterprises of over 1,000 workers were 'relieved of other work' and became paid cadres. District party committees (*raikomy*) were set up to oversee and coordinate the work of PPOs in large population centres.[27]

By mid-1922 then, the basic contours of the lower end of the party apparatus had taken shape. However, although the purge had cleared out

[26] *Protokoly odinnadtsatogo S'ezda*, p. 396; RGASPI, f. 17, op. 18, dd. 680, 683, etc.; Statisticheskii Otdel TsK RKP, *Vserossiiskaiia perepis' chlenov RKP 1922 goda*, 5 vols. (Moscow: Izd. Otd. TsK RKP, 1922): vol. 3, p. 60; E. G. Gimpel'son, *Sovetskii rabochii klass 1918–1920 gg. Sotsial'no-politicheskie izmeneniia* (Moscow: Nauka, 1974), pp. 199–201; John B. Hatch, 'The "Lenin Levy" and the Social Origins of Stalinism: Workers and the Communist Party in Moscow, 1921–1928', *Slavic Review* 48, no. 4 (1989): 558–77, p. 562.

[27] *Protokoly odinnadtsatogo S'ezda*, pp. 577–79, 589–90.

the ballast accumulated during the Civil War, the census had also made the Party's uncoupling from its working-class base stand out in stark relief. The measures proposed by the Eleventh Congress reoriented the Party's political work towards the grassroots but could not in themselves remedy the fact that there were simply too few communists left amongst workers in Soviet factories. The breakthrough on that front would come towards the end of the following year when the Bolshevik leadership settled upon a dramatic reversal of the priorities of party building from quality to quantity.

In December 1923, a joint session of the Politburo and the presidium of the Central Control Commission (CCC) – the Party's disciplinary organ – resolved to recruit 100,000 workers 'from the bench (*ot stanka*)', or directly employed in production. The recruitment campaign was put into motion following Lenin's death in January 1924 and promoted as the Lenin Levy (*Leninskii Prizyv*) in honour of the deceased leader. In both its symbolic and its organisational aspects, the Lenin Levy was designed to reforge the links between the Party and the working-class. Prospective members announced their intention to join in public factory meetings before funerary portraits of Lenin. The standard recruitment procedure requiring references from existing party members was suspended in favour of a majority vote on candidacies by the workers present. Throwing open of the gates of membership yielded impressive quantitative results. The campaign was repeated the following year, leading to the induction of some 500,000 new members by 1926. A staggering 92 per cent of the *Lenintsy* were workers directly employed in production and 80 per cent were classed as skilled. In 1927, the Party launched the October recruitment campaign to mark the ten-year anniversary of the revolution, attracting another 100,000 candidates.[28]

Over the course of three years, the Party more than doubled its membership by means of these successive recruitment drives. Dissociation from its proletarian constituency was no longer a problem as thousands of workers poured in to populate the grassroots institutions set up by the party building policies of the early 1920s. Only a few hundred strong at the time of the 1922 census, PPOs in major industrial plants now counted thousands in their ranks. Their assemblies were no longer the private affairs of tight-knit groups, but mass events that punctuated time in the factories. The vanguard of the proletariat envisioned by Lenin had thus been assembled. There remained the no less formidable task of integrating

[28] Hatch, 'Lenin Levy', p. 565.

the fresh recruits in the political culture of Bolshevism and deploying them in the struggle to build socialism. Before examining this process in greater detail, we must take a step back to consider the political context in which this rapid expansion of party ranks took place.

## 1.4 Party Democracy and the Left Opposition

The routing of the Workers' Opposition and the attendant ban of factions did not put an end to challenges to the leadership line. In the months that followed the conclusion of the Tenth Congress, Shliapnikov and his followers focused their efforts on extending their influence in the trade-union apparatus, aiming to push it towards a more assertive exercise of its upgraded authority and in this way draw the Party closer to the Opposition's position on direct workers' management. What galvanised the oppositionists into action was the rapid evolution of the Party's economic policy from the modest reconciliation with the peasantry signalled by the tax in kind to the acceptance of market mechanisms and private property rights that became a pillar of the NEP.

Keen to avoid charges of factionalism, Shliapnikov at first chose to voice his concerns about the direction of the Soviet economy directly to the Politburo, warning the Party against relying on foreign capital for the country's economic development and arguing that an industrial policy based on the profit motive would end up severing the last bonds between the Party and the proletariat. After the Supreme Council of the People's Economy (VSNKh) stonewalled his suggestions on the NEP, Shliapnikov and his supporters engaged in more active attempts to influence the trade-union apparatus and the party rank-and-file, addressing factory meetings and campaigning in the unions while seeking to preserve their organisational presence by accepting transfers and demotions when the party disciplinary organs caught up with them. On two occasions, the Workers' Opposition attempted to internationalise their dispute with the Party leadership by bringing their criticism of the NEP and its implementation to the Comintern.[29]

Others took more radical action. Disillusioned with Shliapnikov's timid response to what they regarded as an abject betrayal of communist principles, less prominent oppositionists defied the ban on factions to set up organised groups pushing the workerist line condemned by the Tenth Congress. At the most extreme end, Vasili Paniushkin's Worker–Peasant

[29] Allen, *Shliapnikov*, pp. 193–200, 210–11, 222.

Socialist Party renounced Bolshevism and echoed the Kronstadt rebels' demands in calling for the Soviets to be taken over by workers who had not betrayed their class. The student-based group behind the Workers' Truth platform developed a theory of the Bolshevik Party as the incubator of a new technical-bureaucratic bourgeoisie. Less radical groups like Gavril Miasnikov's Perm'-based Workers' Group refrained from writing off the Party as an agent of counter-revolution, but insisted that, without the lifting of political repression to allow workers' to organise in defence of their system, NEP could well be the antechamber to a new system of exploitation.[30]

Ultra-left opposition to the NEP never posed a serious threat to Bolshevik power. The Cheka made short work of the minor splinter groups. Shliapnikov, the most senior and high-profile of the oppositionists, had his hands tied by the much stricter disciplinary framework adopted at the Tenth Congress. On 9 August 1921, a joint session of the CC and CCC convened to consider whether Shliapnikov had violated the ban on factions, after a rank-and-file worker of the Moscow Hydroelectric Plant denounced him for allegedly stating that the Party had become petty-bourgeois and was 'guilty of driving the workers to thievery' during a meeting called to discuss rumours that the factory was about to be leased to a foreign investor. The plenum resolved to retain him as a CC member but threatened to consider his expulsion if further evidence of factionalism emerged. His room for manoeuvre severely constrained, Shliapnikov proceeded to lose a number of battles in his remaining power bases in the unions and the party apparatus. The following year, the Eleventh Party Congress condemned Shliapnikov and his associates' appeal to the Comintern and threatened them with expulsion from the Party if they continued opposing the CC line.[31]

Miasnikov and Paniushkin were both revolutionary fanatics who had gained a reputation of ruthlessness to the class enemy during the Civil War. They would have probably struggled in any transition to peace and the ensuing politics of compromise. Shliapnikov was a more experienced and pragmatic politician who sought to pursue his objectives through established party channels. That all of them would begin opposing the NEP so soon after its introduction is indicative of how radical a departure

[30] Pirani, *Russian Revolution*, pp. 126–28, 142, 204; Tat'iana A. Sandu, '"Rabochaia Oppozitsiia" v RKP (b)'. Unpublished doctoral thesis (Tiumen', 2006), pp. 192–94.

[31] Robert V. Daniels, *The Conscience of the Revolution: Communist Opposition in Soviet Russia* (Cambridge, MA: Harvard University Press, 1960), pp. 160–65; Allen, *Shliapnikov*, pp. 237, 251.

it was from established Bolshevik economic thought. It was not, however, the content of the NEP that turned opposition to it into a political crisis. As the workerists came to realise, the problem was that the emerging political system gave them no means to oppose the leadership's compromise with capitalism.

Having decisively defeated their opponents on the battlefield, the Bolsheviks monopolised political power in the Soviet republic. Being, in Lenin's words, too weak to allow the proliferation of platforms in their own ranks, they also left no space for dissent within their own party. Following the ban on factions, any form of sustained, organised opposition to party policy would inevitably come up against state repression or the Party's disciplinary organs. Rejection of the NEP was, thus, immediately coupled with criticism of the political regime and demands for more 'workers' democracy'. After the renewed condemnation of this political programme at the Eleventh Congress, it seemed as if there would be no further challenge to the political course set by the leadership. When the latter's own unity started to give way, however, a new, far more extensive crisis began to brew.

The Left Opposition made its first appearance in Bolshevik politics in October 1923, when Leon Trotsky wrote a letter to the CC and CCC condemning its handling of economic matters, followed a week later by a declaration raising similar concerns and signed by forty-six prominent communists, including sitting CC members. The Declaration of the forty-six further criticised the 'inner-party regime' of secretarial appointments for stifling internal democracy in order to support a 'factional dictatorship' of the Politburo. It demanded the convocation of a conference of the CC and 'prominent party workers' whose views opposed the majority line in order to discuss ways out of the current impasse.[32]

Trotsky's emergence as a crusading democrat appears bizarre given his long record of ridiculing constitutional liberties and his then still recent plans for militarising labour.[33] His decision to break ranks with the Politburo rather appears to have been motivated by his growing impatience with the NEP. As head of the Politburo commission on heavy industry, Trotsky had been charged with devising a workable plan for the survival and gradual expansion of large, loss-making enterprises in the new market

[32] E. H. Carr, *The Interregnum, 1923–1924* (Baltimore: Penguin Books, 1969), pp. 375–80.

[33] Ian Thatcher, 'Trotsky and the Questions of Agency, Democracy and Dictatorship in the USSR, 1917–1940', in *The Fate of the Bolshevik Revolution: Illiberal Liberation 1917–1941*, ed. Lara Douds, James Harris and Peter Whitewood (London: Bloomsbury Academic, 2020), pp. 96–98.

environment. In a report he delivered to the Twelfth Party Congress in spring 1923, he warned that the core NEP strategy of funding industrial growth from rural surpluses would soon be derailed due to the persistent divergence of the prices of manufactured and agricultural products. This 'scissors crisis' meant that peasant production would fail to provide the state with sufficient tax income to replenish its coffers, which were constantly being drained by generous subsidies to the sluggish industrial sector.[34]

Against this looming crisis, Trotsky had attempted to convince CC and Politburo meetings held before the Congress that the solution lay in comprehensive economic planning and a reorientation of agricultural policy to prioritise state over private farming. Essentially arguing for abandoning the NEP, Trotsky had been rebuffed at both party organs and his proposals were further defeated in a special commission on industrial financing elected at the Congress to examine his concerns. Trotsky's letter and the Declaration of the forty-six had appeared – and was leaked – in the aftermath of these defeats, indicating that Trotsky had become convinced that his economic policies could not be adopted without a shake-up of the political rules of the game.[35]

In subsequent meetings with the leadership, Trotsky insisted on a complete overhaul of the system of party governance. He demanded that the electoral principle be universally enforced against the common practice of direct appointments to leading posts, and that dissenting members be allowed to voice their views collectively, though he refrained from calling directly for a lifting of the ban on factions. The two sides eventually agreed on a common draft for a resolution unanimously passed at a joint session of the Politburo and Presidium of the CCC on 5 December 1924. The text reiterated the essential nature of 'workers' democracy' for the further progress of party building, including the freedom to discuss and debate vital political issues. Similarly, leading officials were to be elected at all levels of the apparatus. There were, however, caveats. Freedom of discussion would not be allowed to develop into factionalism. Further, although elections remained the preferred means of filling leading posts, higher party bodies were still to verify elected officials and retained the right of direct appointment in special circumstances. Nevertheless, such administrative practices were expected to fall into disuse as the twin processes of

34 Carr, *Interregnum*, pp. 29–30.

35 James R. Harris, 'Discipline versus Democracy: The 1923 Party Controversy', in *The Fate of the Bolshevik Revolution: Illiberal Liberation 1917–1941*, ed. Lara Douds, James Harris and Peter Whitewood (London: Bloomsbury Academic, 2020), pp. 115–17.

party building and socialist development led to the practical overcoming of political tensions. In service of this goal, the same resolution also proposed the mass recruitment of industrial workers that became known as the Lenin Levy.[36]

Aside from the quantitative pivot, there was very little that was not already party policy in this new resolution *On Party Building*. Despite, or perhaps because of this fact, Trotsky chose to declare victory and renew his attacks on the leadership. Within days of the document's publication, he penned a new article denouncing the bureaucratisation of the apparatus, this time in the form of a letter to the entirety of the membership. Published in *Pravda* on 11 December, the *New Course* argued that the recent resolution on party building represented an admission on the part of the leadership that a serious change of political direction was necessary, against the wishes of 'conservatively predisposed comrades, who are inclined to overestimate the importance of the apparatus and underestimate the Party's spontaneous action (*samodeiatel'nost'*)'. The article encouraged the younger generation of members to become more actively involved in political matters in order to remedy the danger of the 'degeneration of the Old Guard' leading the Party.[37]

Trotsky was throwing down the gauntlet to the rest of the party leadership, placing himself at the head of a purported youthful revitalising force against the stale bureaucratism of an aloof ruling clique. The battle lines thus drawn, there followed a series of escalating clashes between the leadership and the newly minted opposition in the press and a series of party meetings held in the run up to the Thirteenth Conference in early 1924.

The story of this political struggle has been told so many times as to make a recounting of its details here redundant. The oppositionist platform was published in the central and regional party press and dissenting communists were given the opportunity to voice their criticisms of the party line at pre-Conference meetings. Archival records indicate that these were heated events with few punches pulled, as the opposition accused the majority and its supporters of using their stranglehold over the apparatus in order to promote a catastrophic economic policy that was carrying the seed of capitalist restoration. Trotsky and his supporters made a good showing in the heavily student-populated Moscow Party Organisation but

[36] *Pravda*, 7 December 1923; Carr, *Interregnum*, pp. 314–15; Daniels, *Conscience of the Revolution*, pp. 220–21.

[37] *Pravda*, 11 December 1923.

also managed to secure the support of more purely proletarian sections of the apparatus like the Cheliabinsk city committee. Such limited gains were not enough to undermine support for the majority line. The opposition was defeated and condemned as a 'petty-bourgeois deviation' first at the Thirteenth Conference and then, more conclusively, at the Thirteenth Congress in May 1924.[38]

For the purposes of this study, the significance of this leadership struggle lies not so much in its outcome, as in the fact that it was carried out in the form of a discussion on the nature of 'worker's democracy', the fundamental principle that was to guide the process of party building. In that regard, the most striking aspect of the conflict is how little the platform of the Left Opposition differed from the CC majority line. At no point did Trotsky present any concrete amendments to the constitutional make-up of the Soviet Union or the Party's governing statutes. The democratisation proposed was to take place within the context of the single-party state and with the ban on factions remaining in place. As a contribution, the *New Course* offered the rather strained argument that democratisation entailed 'the Party subordinating its own apparatus to itself, while not for a single minute ceasing to be a centralised organisation'. There were no institutional guarantees for the survival of the Party's true 'revolutionary spirit', but it certainly required the 'permanent interaction of the old generation with the new'.[39]

It takes a very charitable reading to view the formation of an oppositionist platform on such vague ruminations as anything but an attempt to provide an ideological pole around which to build a political base for the purpose of forcing through Trotsky's far more concrete economic views. This was not lost on the CC majority, whose members and supporters accused Trotsky of inventing major political differences out of thin air in order to pursue his own ends.[40] Regardless, however, of Trotsky's motives, his decision to wield the notion of party democracy as a weapon against the leadership led the latter to adopt a renewed emphasis on party discipline as a major theme in the polemics against its renegade member.

38 Carr, *Interregnum*, pp. 326–28, 346–47; Daniels, *Conscience of the Revolution*, pp. 227–30; Harris, 'Party Controversy', pp. 120–24; Aleksandr Reznik, *Trotskii i tovarishchi: Levaia Oppozitsiia i politicheskaia kul'tura RKP(b), 1923–1924* (Saint-Petersburg: Evropeiskii Universitet v Sankt-Peterburge, 2017), pp. 105, 216–17, etc.

39 *Pravda*, 11 December 1923.

40 *Trinadtsatyi S"ezd RKP(b). Stenograficheskii otchet* (Moscow: Gospolitizdat, 1963), pp. 215, 220, 229, etc.

Everyone agreed in principle that workers' democracy was a fundamental element of Bolshevik politics and there was no better proof of the majority's commitment to involving the youth in party affairs than the Lenin Levy. What marked the opposition, now increasingly labelled 'Trotskyist', as a dangerous 'petty-bourgeois deviation' was its flagrant disregard for monolithic unity as a no less important core trait of true Bolshevism or 'Leninism'. These arguments were made at the Thirteenth Congress but also, more importantly, in several articles appearing on the pages of a constellation of recently founded journals and newspapers aiming to shape the worldview of freshly minted communists.[41]

Stalin enunciated the new political formula in a series of lectures at Sverdlov University subsequently published under the title *On the Foundations of Leninism*. The general secretary described the Party as an 'organised detachment of the working-class' with the mission of imbuing the masses with a work-ethic promoting perseverance and a methodical approach to all aspects of production and political life. To achieve this, the Party itself needed to be 'the personification of organisation and discipline'. Stalin concluded that the essence of Leninism as a theoretical and practical school of revolutionary governance was the combination of 'Russian revolutionary fervour (*revolutsionnii razmakh*)' with 'American professionalism (*delovitost'*)'. Revolutionary fervour was the 'revitalising force that wakens thought, presses ahead [and] smashes the past'. Professionalism was the necessary counterweight anchoring revolutionary fervour to concrete reality and preventing it from turning into empty sloganeering and ultimately undermining revolutionary policy.[42]

Tellingly, Stalin's *Foundations* were dedicated to the Lenin Levy. The fresh recruits joined the party just as a conflict within the leadership gave rise to a perception of Bolshevism privileging unity over open debate. Opposition became increasingly coterminous with deviation; it was at best a useless distraction from practical work, at worst a manifestation of the insidious influence of alien social forces. Discipline would henceforth be the boundary of democracy within the party and 'revolutionary fervour', while an essential quality for communists, would have to be checked by

[41] Roger Pethybridge, 'Concern for Bolshevik Ideological Predominance at the Start of NEP', *Russian Review* 41, no. 4 (1982): 445–53. Indicative titles of articles published in the journal *Bol'shevik* include 'Trotskyism and the Dictatorship of the Proletariat', 'Does Trotskyism exist in organisational questions' (no. 15–16, 1924) and 'An example of petty-bourgeois degeneration' (no. 3–4, 1924).

[42] Iosif Stalin, 'Ob osnovakh Leninizma' in *Sochineniia*, 13 vols. (Moscow: Gospolitizdat, 1946–52), pp. 174–76, 186–88.

professionalism. Maintaining this delicate balance was naturally the responsibility of the Party's leadership. With these fundamental organisational principles established and thousands of workers taking the pledge of membership, the process of party building was now firmly in motion.

## 1.5 Conclusion

In his last major speech at a party Congress, Lenin gave the following assessment of the Bolsheviks' prospects as a party of government:

> We are still a drop in the ocean amongst the popular masses and we can govern only in so far as we express correctly what the people are already conscious of. [Otherwise] the party will not be leading the proletariat, the proletariat will not be leading the masses and the whole [system] will fall apart.[43]

Subsequently quoted with approval by Stalin in his didactic contributions to the elucidation of Leninism, this formulation captured the essence of Lenin's thought on the role of the vanguard party in power. A small minority among the population of the USSR, the Bolsheviks could only survive and grow by patiently gaining the trust of the masses. This they could only do by being aware of people's needs and working out policies that addressed these. Leadership consisted in channelling the energies of the masses into activities that best served their own interests. Several years later this notion would be codified in the constitution of the Soviet Union and other socialist states as the leading role of the communist party in society. In the early years of the Soviet republic, this idea and its institutional implications were only vaguely grasped.

Lenin read the popular discontent that eventually culminated in the Kronstadt uprising as a clear sign that the Party was failing in its role as revolutionary leader. It was necessary to take a step back, let peasants do what they knew best – grow food and trade it – and lay the groundwork for a renewed attempt at socialist development sometime in the future. Nevertheless, the coincidence of external discontent with brewing grievances inside party ranks convinced Lenin that endless discussion was a 'luxury' the Party could no longer afford. If they were to remain in power and carry their revolutionary project through, the Bolsheviks had to act with monolithic unity. Factionalism could no longer be tolerated. Party cadres were to implement leadership directives with professional commitment.

[43] Lenin, 'XI S'ezd RKP(b)', in *PSS* 45, p. 112.

Disciplinary measures were, however, to be completed by a reorganisation of the party apparatus on the principle of 'workers' democracy'. This included the further institutional development of the bottom level of the party apparatus and renewed attention to the recruitment and education of new working-class communists. Rejuvenated with new blood, party organisations were now to demonstrate greater initiative in the everyday life of industrial enterprises, where they were to check that directors managed production competently while at the same time making sure that trade-unions defended their members' interests and made use of their new powers.

The new line was not without its detractors. The Workers' Opposition contended that workers should have more direct control of production and Trotsky's Left Opposition criticised the leadership for not implementing 'workers' democracy' with sufficient conviction. Tellingly, however, neither of the two challengers rejected any of the foundations of the emerging political system. Despite their sharp exchange of invective, oppositionists and majority supporters alike remained committed to a system of benevolent authoritarianism whereby the single ruling party would consult with the governed and rule in their interest but could not be legitimately removed from power. All leading Bolsheviks shared a notion of democracy as mass participation in the practical implementation of policy, initiative for which remained a prerogative of the leadership. Thus, the basic contours of the relationship between Party, state and society in the Soviet Union were set.

CHAPTER 2

# *Which Way to Socialism?* *NEP and the Struggle for Power*

By the time the New Course controversy had come to a close, the basic contours of Soviet politics had been firmly established. Following the defeat of the Left Opposition, the fundamental elements of the relationship between the Communist Party and the Soviet state would never again be seriously challenged. Similarly, unity of will and action around the political line of the leadership would remain the highest of Bolshevik virtues, a defining trait of communist political culture for decades to come. To be sure, these were not particularly radical departures. As we saw earlier, elements of the party-centric conception of politics had already been present in Lenin's revolutionary theory prior to the October revolution and had certainly become common currency by 1921. What is more, all but the most marginal party dissidents had been reluctant to countenance a radical overhaul of the Soviet political system. Clashes of vision would have to give way to debates over policy implementation, or at least be camouflaged in such terms.

As the New Economic Policy provided the overarching framework for all other policy initiatives, the political struggles that followed Lenin's death revolved around the way the leadership managed the NEP and the extent to which this was consistent with the party's broader goal of socialist transformation. The new contours of Bolshevik politics determined the tactics available not only to the Left but to all factions that would emerge to challenge the CC majority after Lenin's passing. Crucially, the decision to open the Party's doors to a new cohort of rank-and-file communists introduced a new variable to internal politics. The Lenin enrolment had transformed primary party organisations from isolated, demoralised groups of communists to mass institutions tightly woven into the fabric of factory life. Both oppositionists and the centre tried to manoeuvre this new dynamic to their advantage. This chapter will examine this process as it unfolded during the bitter factional struggles against the so-called New and United Oppositions, the last major challenges to the NEP consensus.

Before delving into the ways in which the clashing sides attempted to mobilise the rank-and-file for their own ends, it would, however, be helpful to consider in some more detail the effects the first years of the NEP had on Soviet society.

## 2.1 Ambiguous Recovery

At face value, the NEP was a resounding success. It had been introduced in order to remedy the economic collapse of the Civil War years and afford the Soviet government some breathing space while it devised a workable industrial strategy. Sure enough, agricultural production was restored so that the country no longer faced the threat of famine. By one account, workers and peasants were better fed in 1926 than they had been before the revolution. Industry was recovering too, albeit at a slower pace. In the same year, industrial production reached near parity with its pre-war levels from roughly 15 per cent of the same in 1921.[1] These, however, were modest goals. The long-term prospects of socialist development remained under the persistent shadow of the scissors crisis described by Trotsky in 1923. What is more, even the modicum of prosperity achieved by the mid-1920s had not come without its own difficulties. The NEP era was marked by a broad array of social tensions that provided ample reasons for political disgruntlement in party ranks.

We have already encountered the horror with which the Bolshevik left experienced the legalisation of private property over the means of production by the NEP, as well as the attendant re-emergence of a class of capitalists. Quite apart from the leftists' cultural and ideological revulsion to the grotesque spectacle of a conspicuously consumerist bourgeoisie operating under the auspices of a workers' state, the party rank-and-file had to readapt to life in the context of a capitalist economy. Although the Nepmen operated in a labyrinthine regulatory framework of tax brackets and licensing laws designed to limit their expansion and divert as much surplus as possible to state coffers, they remained bosses within their own enterprises. In the early years of the NEP, employers were able to take advantage of underdeveloped labour inspection mechanisms and the low levels of unionisation amongst the workforce in the private sector to impose shockingly exploitative conditions of work. Some 60 per cent of all 1922 court cases relating to breach of labour legislation were brought

[1] E. H. Carr and R. W. Davies, *Foundations of a Planned Economy*, 3 vols. (London: Macmillan, 1969), 1: pp. 271, 625.

against private businessmen. The most common accusations related to violations of limits to the working day and laws against the employment of children.[2] Nepmen were also skilled in the use of piece-rates and bonuses to promote norm-busting. Speaking at a conference of private sector workers in 1925, an employee at a stockings manufacturer described managerial tactics thus:

> With the move to piece-rates, we deliver 150% of our pre-war norm. They drive us, they hover over us . . . and work goes on at such pace that you have no time to drink water. The piece-rate in itself exerts pressure, every worker wants to earn more, and the bosses craftily take advantage of this. Before the signing of a collective agreement they swamp you with work and make it possible to earn three-times the norm. The benefit is clear: the boss achieves a higher norm at the time of the collective agreement [negotiations].[3]

The numerous communists sceptical of the NEP were probably not reassured by the fact that private enterprise soon began to outgrow its prescribed limits. Despite the original NEP legislation limiting the size of private businesses to those employing no more than twenty workers, this stipulation was soon abandoned in practice. Private leasing of state-owned enterprises was a popular means of circumventing the cap on hired labour, so that by the end of 1924 the average private or leased factory employed more than twenty labourers and roughly a hundred of these operated with workforces exceeding 300. To make things worse, about a third of all leased enterprises had returned to the hands of their pre-revolutionary owners.[4]

Workers employed in state industry, a majority overall, should at least in theory have been shielded from the harshest aspects of the new economic environment.[5] Nevertheless, the fiscal frugality necessitated by the dire financial straits of the Soviet state made it impossible to insulate the publicly employed workforce from the general belt-tightening. From 1921, the government began to introduce the principle of economic cost-accounting (*khozraschet*) for state enterprises. A series of decrees enacted greater operational independence for industrial trusts and

[2] G. Belkin, 'Formy chastnoi promishlennosti', in *Chastnyi kapital v narodnom khoziaistve SSSR*, ed. A. M. Ginzburg (Moscow: Promizdat, 1927), pp. 218–19.

[3] Ia. R. Emdin, 'Polozhenie truda v chastnoi promishlennosti', in *Chastnyi kapital v narodnom khoziaistve SSSR*, ed. A. M. Ginzburg (Moscow: Promizdat, 1927), p. 212.

[4] Alan M. Ball, *Russia's Last Capitalists: The Nepmen, 1921–1929* (Berkeley: University of California Press, 1990), p. 133; Lyubov' Suvorova, *Nepovskaia mnogoukladnaia ekonomika: mezhdu gosudarstvom i rynkom* (Moscow: AIRO, 2013), p. 96.

[5] Ball, *Nepmen*, pp. 131–32; Koenker, *Republic of Labor*, 29–30.

individual production units and mandated that the financial viability was the responsibility of their respective administrations. Thus, the 9 August 1921 SNK decree 'On the Implementation of the Principles of the New Economic Policy' stipulated that administrations were responsible for plan fulfilment and quality control, while permitting them to sell a limited amount of their output on the market in order to cover enterprise costs that were not covered by the stage budget.[6]

A subsequent decree published on 27 October relaxed the limitations placed on the disposal of output, allowing enterprises to sell it at market price in order to cover the non-fixed capital costs of production, including wages, fuel and raw materials. The April 1923 'Decree on Trusts' went considerably further in institutionalising market relations in the Soviet economy, defining trusts as 'state industrial enterprises which are independent in their transactions and function according to the principle of commercial accounting (*kommercheskii raschet*) with the aim of extracting profit (*izvlechenie pribyli*). Such liberties with respect to output notwithstanding, trusts and enterprises were nevertheless forbidden to transfer or liquidate their fixed assets such as buildings and machinery, while mergers and closures were only allowed with the express permission of higher state organs, so as to prevent the embezzlement of socialised public property.[7]

Although not quite the same as being exposed to free market pressures, this seemed a fine distinction from the workers' point of view. Faced with constant stoppages caused by aging equipment and irregular supply of raw materials and spare parts, industrial managers were often forced to balance their books by docking or delaying pay. With consumer goods remaining scarce and expensive in the post-war economy, such managerial tactics caused much resentment amongst the Bolsheviks' working-class constituency, especially when they were combined with heavy-handed or insulting behaviour towards workers. As a result, the introduction of NEP was accompanied by several waves of industrial unrest of varying intensity, attracting the watchful eye of the secret police, who dutifully informed the Party leadership.

[6] *Dekrety Sovetskoi vlasti*, 18 vols. (Moscow: Politizdat, 1957–89), 13: pp. 92–96.

[7] This is certainly a very schematic outline of the complex rules underpinning the NEP. Light industry was for example much more self-reliant financially than heavy industry, while the state maintained direct control over enterprises deemed of special importance. The intricacies of the NEP-era legal framework regulating the market are, however, too complex to examine here in detail. The point is that the Soviet leadership made a serious effort to develop a functioning market mechanism in a broader socialist economic framework. For a more detailed discussion, see V. N. Bandera, 'Market Orientation of State Enterprises during NEP', *Soviet Studies* 22, no. 1 (1970): 110–21; Suvorova, *Nepovskaia mnogoukladnaia ekonomika*, etc.

According to a Moscow Soviet report from early 1923, strike action in the capital was almost invariably the result of wage arrears and workers were generally willing to return to work after being paid their dues.[8] Union-wide figures collated by the GPU showed that some 100 enterprises employing roughly 50,000 workers went on strike in July 1923, the figures climbing to 140 and 80,000, respectively, the following month.[9] In September, a four-day strike involving some 7,000 workers at Moscow's *Prokhorovskaia Manufaktura* succeeded in attracting the support of workers at the nearby *Tsindel'* factory, who gave notice of their intention to engage in secondary action.[10] Although this particular spike in industrial action was attributed to the effects of currency reform on the purchasing power of workers, disputes over remuneration and work conditions continued to fuel workplace conflict in the years that followed. Thus, although real wages rose steadily and the wage debt was eliminated by late 1924, strike activity persisted with disputes centred mostly around the terms of labour contracts, such as skill-based pay scales and norms for workers on piece-rates.[11] Despite however, an absolute increase in the number of strikes during the first NEP years, their average duration declined so that already by the end of 1923, it did not exceed 24 hours.[12]

Strained industrial relations were not the only form of capitalist recrudescence to trouble Soviet society and its leaders in the NEP period. After the initial spurt of economic activity delivered by the expansion of private trade, the winding up of the war economy led to the re-emergence of one of the most familiar aspects of free labour markets: unemployment. Joblessness was a persistent element of economic life in the NEP era, maintaining an alarmingly upward trend in both absolute and relative numbers. Already in the first NEP year, the numbers of the unemployed began to swell, with the introduction of *khozrashchet* leading to significant layoffs as enterprise directors attempted to cut their costs. By the start of 1922, the railways alone reportedly reduced their workforce by some 300,000 employees. The following year, the number of registered unemployed climbed steadily in the fifty-two province (*gubernskie*) capitals, averaging 560,000 and peaking at 755,000 in December. Soviet labour

8 Murphy, *Revolution and Counterrevolution*, p. 97.

9 Vladimir Brovkin, *Russia after Lenin*: Politics, Culture, Society (London: Routledge, 1998), p. 174.

10 Andrew Pospielovsky, 'Strikes during the NEP', *Revolutionary Russia* 10, no. 1 (1997): 1–34: p. 25.

11 William Chase, *Workers, Society and the Soviet State: Labor and Life in Moscow, 1918–29* (Champaign: University of Illinois Press, 1987), pp. 228–32; Koenker, *Republic of Labor*, p. 136; *Trud v SSSR: Diagrammy. 1924–1926* (Moscow: Izdatel'stvo VTsSPS, 1926), p. 35.

12 Pospielovsky, 'Strikes', pp. 25–26.

economists were particularly concerned by the fact that although the initial spike had been due to cuts in the size of administrations and the Soviet sector (i.e., the civil service), the upward trend soon spread to industry.[13] Between 1923 and 1925, the overall percentage of unemployed trade-union members jumped from 8 per cent to 13.8 per cent.[14]

The defining feature of NEP unemployment was that, in marked contrast to what has been the case in developed capitalist economies, it was rising at the same time as overall employment was growing. The ranks of industrial workers expanded from 1.2 million in 1922 to some 1.9 million in 1925, which did not however prevent unemployment registering a new peak at 1.1 million in the same year.[15] This quandary was a result of intensifying rural immigration into industrial areas, as the displaced of the Civil War gradually making their way back to the cities were joined by rural youth attracted to the prospect of urban living beyond the patriarchal authority of the peasant household.[16] A corollary of the rural sources of unemployment was that a large number of the jobless were unskilled workers. Thus, at the same time as it called forth a new reserve army of workers, the NEP could not provide industry with sufficient skilled labour to sustain its growth. In 1924, the People's Commissariat of Labour reported labour shortages in multiple urban centres.[17] It is indicative of the contradictions of the NEP that the Soviet economy was simultaneously experiencing industrial growth, unemployment and labour shortages.

The Party's experiment with a market economy was therefore working, but the results were mixed. A catastrophic collapse of agriculture had been averted and heavy industry was on track to matching its pre-war output levels. The Civil War era flight from the cities was being reversed. Nevertheless, these improvements carried the price of ideological compromise and, consequently, the straining of the relationship between the party leadership and the rank-and-file, as well as the Party and its proletarian constituency more broadly. This was particularly vexing to the committed ideologues of the far left of the Party and there is some evidence that

[13] A. Isaev, *Bezrabotitsa v SSSR i bor'ba s neiu (za period 1917–1924 g.g.)* (Moscow: Voprosy Truda, 1924), pp. 33, 40–42.

[14] L. S. Rogachevskaia, *Likvidatsiia bezrabotitsy v SSSR 1917–1930 gg.* (Moscow: Nauka, 1973), p. 81.

[15] E. H. Carr, *Socialism in One Country*, vol. 1 (London: Macmillan, 1958), p. 365. The trend would continue, with unemployment reaching 1.3 million in 1926, despite a further improvement in employment. Rogachevskaia, *Likvidatsiia bezrabotitsy*, p. 142.

[16] Vladimir Andrle, *A Social History of Twentieth-Century Russia* (London: Edward Arnold, 1994), p. 82.

[17] Isaev, *Bezrabotitsa*, pp. 44–45.

activists connected to the Workers' Opposition attempted to revive their activity in the first years of the NEP.[18]

Unemployment and skill depletion were, however, far more worrying to the Party leadership, as it was these phenomena that cast doubt upon the viability of Soviet industrial growth and, by extension, the prospects of socialist development. Having already drawn attention to the scissors crisis during their first clash with the CC majority, the leaders of the Left Opposition highlighted the inability of industry to absorb rural immigration as proof that the Party would have to pursue a more aggressive policy of industrial expansion even at the cost of its hard-won peace with the peasantry. For its part, the leadership was above all concerned by the persistently low productivity of labour, which painted a grim picture of the country's industrialisation prospects.[19]

In any case, the Stalin-led CC majority began to signal a reorientation of economic policy towards an intensification of industrial growth but would not countenance any course of action that might endanger the delicate recovery of the rural economy. Over the course of 1925, however, the CC drew up ambitious plans for the expansion of heavy industry which would go on to form a major part of the agenda of the 14th Party Congress in December of that year. Nevertheless, the economic agenda of the so-called Congress of Industrialisation would be overshadowed by some of the most dramatic political developments of the NEP era. Newly inducted into the Party's ranks and freshly equipped with Bolshevik ideological precepts, the raw recruits of the Lenin enrolment found themselves at the centre of a bitter leadership clash.

## 2.2 The Zinoviev Opposition: A Leningrad Mutiny

Having failed to prevail during the New Course discussion, Trotsky and the Left refrained from launching any major political challenge against the CC in the immediate aftermath of their defeat. Nevertheless, the 1924 hiatus from factional activity turned out to be short-lived. Over the course of

[18] Sandu, '"Rabochaia Oppozitsiia" v RKP (b)', pp. 192–94.

[19] The importance attached to the issue of labour productivity by the Party leadership is reflected in the many speeches of Felix Dzerzhinskii in his capacity as head of the VSNKh. For example, in his conclusive remarks on his report on the state of the metal industry to the XIV Party Conference given on 29 April 1925, Dzerzhinskii stated that output per single worker had to be increased 'whatever it may take' ('*vo chto by to ni stalo*'). Felix Edmundovich Dzerzhinskii, *Izbrannye proizvedeniia v 2-kh tomakh*, vol. 2, 2 vols. (Moscow: Izdatel'stvo Politicheskoi Literatury, 1967), p. 135.

1925, the political alliance that had seen off the Left Opposition began to come apart. In what came to be known as the New Opposition, Grigorii Zinoviev aligned with Lev Kamenev and other leading party figures to present the most serious organisational threat to the CC majority of all the leadership struggles of the 1920s.[20] As head of the Leningrad Party Organisation (LPO), Zinoviev was able to mobilise the party membership and apparatus of the second largest city in the USSR in support of his struggle against the leadership. It was the first and last time in Soviet political history that an opposition had gained significant purchase on the party machine. Precisely for this reason, and significantly for the purposes of this investigation, the New Opposition was also the only one that mobilised large numbers of the Party's recently expanded rank-and-file. The importance of the eventual defeat of the New Opposition in the process of Stalin's ascendance to political supremacy has concentrated scholarly interest onto the implications of the affair for central politics. There are, however, strong reasons to suggest that the origins of this factional fight lay in the tensions generated by the NEP and that the central role Leningrad played in the events was due to more than Zinoviev's control of the northern capital's party organisation.[21]

A closer look at the grassroots dynamics that fuelled Zinoviev's leadership bid indicates that the party rank-and-file had by that time emerged as a crucial factor in Soviet politics. Their interests and immediate concerns dominated political life in the bottom rungs of the party apparatus, that were now almost exclusively populated by the new recruits. As the country's most heavily industrialised region, Leningrad experienced the side-effects of the NEP particularly acutely. Thus, despite being a symbol of proletarian Bolshevism and the flagship of Soviet industry, the factory *Krasnyi Putilovets* (KP) faced closure on two separate occasions in 1923 and 1924, as the enormous enterprise accounted for some 90 per cent of the Leningrad region machine-building trust's debt while operating at less than 5 per cent capacity. It took a direct intervention from members of the CC for the government to intervene and remove KP from the hands of

[20] Other prominent members of the New Opposition were Nadezhda Krupskaia and Grigorii Sokol'nikov, the People's Commissar for Finance. Daniels, *Conscience of the Revolution*, pp. 253–54.

[21] Daniels denied that the crisis had any significance beyond that of a clash between the personalities involved, arguing that '[t]here is no evidence that any bona fide rank and file movement was involved'. Daniels, *Conscience of the Revolution*, p. 271. Schapiro offered a similar interpretation of the events. Leonard Schapiro, *The Communist Party of the Soviet Union*, 2nd rev ed. (New York: Routledge, 1970), p. 320.

the trust and place it under direct central control by the VSNKh. Even so, the loan extended was barely enough to keep the enterprise afloat and was certainly not enough to provide for the expansion of its activities.[22] Lack of credit was a recurring problem for industrial enterprises during the NEP period both because the government was trying to encourage rationalisation and because the Soviet state was just starting to come to grips with the intricacies of public finance.[23]

Working-class communists, however, perceived official thriftiness as indifference to the fate of heavy industry and, in Leningrad's case, as discrimination against their region. At the 20th conference of the LPO in May 1924, S. S. Lobov of the organisation's industrial bureau accused Moscow of withholding credit and subsidies worth millions of roubles. As a result of this, he argued, the regional machine-building trust was unable to pay its workers.[24] Such economic uncertainty inevitably strained the relationship between the Party and its working-class base. Thus, as in other enterprises throughout the country, KP industrial life in the early NEP was marked by a tense relationship between workers and management, with disputes over pay, norm-setting and the provision of safety equipment often leading to strikes or stoppages. To make things worse, communists were often found to be the chief instigators of such disturbances, at the same time as attendance at production conferences was in decline.[25]

Circumstances were driving workers to the tried and tested methods of confrontational industrial action and away from Party-approved forms of labour activism. Left unchecked, this tendency could lead to a breach in the vital relationship between the Party and its proletarian constituency, a prospect made particularly alarming by the fact that a large part of the membership now consisted of freshly recruited workers. Such worries were reflected in a September 1925 report by the party organiser of KP Aleksandr Aleksandrov to the regional secretary and prominent

[22] Clayton Black, 'Party Crisis and the Factory Shop Floor: Krasnyi Putilovets and the Leningrad Opposition, 1925–26', *Europe–Asia Studies* 46, no. 1 (1994): 107–26, p. 109.

[23] In September 1924, for example, the Soviet metal industry received only 70 per cent of the credits planned by Prombank. S. M. Kiselev, 'Kredit v sisteme narodnogo khoziaistva SSSR', *Planovoe khoziaistvo*, 2 (1925): 22–38, pp. 35–37.

[24] Black, 'Party Crisis', pp. 111–12.

[25] Production conferences were enterprise-based gatherings organised by the trade-unions where workers discussed and proposed solutions to problems in the production process. They were thus the approved channel of workers' input into the management of production in the context of the emerging industrial 'triangle' (see Chapter 1). Ibid., p. 112; Chase, *Workers*, pp. 256–57; Svetlana Borisovna Ul'ianova, '"Leningradskii pochin": proizvodstvennye soveshchaniia v sisteme motivatsii i stimulirovaniia truda v 1920-e gg', in *Rynok truda v Sankt-Peterburge: problemy i perspektivy*, ed. B. V. Korneychuk (Saint-Petersburg: Nestor, 2003).

oppositionist Piotr Zalutskii, claiming that the insufficient growth rate of the factory was a 'serious danger' with respect to the political moods of its workforce.[26] There were thus strong reasons for Leningrad's communists to rally behind a political programme attacking the retreat from socialist principles represented by the NEP and in favour of an expansionist economic policy oriented towards the development of heavy industry. Zinoviev, their leader, purported to offer them just such a programme.

Tensions between the centre and the Party in the northern capital started to become explicitly apparent after the April 1925 14th Party Conference which devoted most of its time to agrarian policy debates. Zinoviev did not speak against the Conference resolution proposing tax cuts to stimulate the rural economy and seems to have been content to accept that a strengthening of capitalist elements in the countryside was an acceptable price to pay for economic growth as late as May 1925.[27] This, however, was a substantially less attractive idea to the Leningrad rank-and-file whose expanded ranks now included many thousand workers from the city's troubled factories. From mid-1925 onwards, the combative Leningrad press began to accuse Moscow and parts of the leadership of political deviationism, of essentially aiding and abetting the growth of a strong and vibrant bourgeoisie in town and countryside. The Leningraders were not so much explicitly opposed to the broad aims of the NEP but had grown concerned by what seemed to be a rather cavalier attitude towards its inherent dangers by some prominent Bolshevik leaders. Nikolai Bukharin had become notorious for a speech to Moscow party activists where he called on peasants to enrich themselves, while his close ally Vladimir Bogushevskii had used the pages of no less prestigious a publication than *Bol'shevik* to argue that the kulak threat was fictitious and that the category no longer held meaning.[28]

It was one thing to argue that temporarily tolerating capitalist relations was a necessary retreat in order to create the conditions for socialist development, it was quite another to suggest that socialist development itself entailed the enrichment of kulaks and Nepmen against the backdrop of sluggish industrial growth. The party organisation of the heavily industrial Moskovsko–Narvskii district, home of KP, became a hotbed of such sentiment. Addressing a meeting of more than 1,000 KP communists in

[26] V. Iu. Cherniaev, *Piterskie rabochie i 'Diktatura Proletariata': Oktiabr' 1917–1929* (Saint-Petersburg: Russko-Baltiiskii Informatsionnii Tsentr BLITs, 2003), p. 350.

[27] Carr, *Socialism*, vol. 1, pp. 262–71.

[28] Vladimir Bogushevskii, 'O derevenskom kulake ili o role traditsii v terminologii', *Bol'shevik*, no. 9–10 (1925): 63–64.

June, the *raikom* secretary A. D. Sarkis spoke in favour of maintaining a constructive relationship with the peasantry but stressed that the proletariat should maintain the leading role. He was preaching to the converted. The KP party organiser Aleksandrov, who as we have seen was growing anxious about the possibility of the factory's woes undermining the loyalty of its workforce, made the same point at a subsequent meeting. He also warned that growing stratification in the countryside made the kulak class a clear and present danger that needed to be confronted.[29]

The party grassroots had become an institutional space where widespread resentment with the NEP could be articulated in official language and amplified by engaging with fundamental policy debates taking place at the top. It was this development that created the opportunity for Zinoviev to launch his oppositionist bid and perhaps prompted him to do so. Responding to the combative sentiment among the party base, Zinoviev joined the critics of the deviation with two major publications laying out his differences with those elements in the leadership fudging the party line.[30] In his pamphlet *The Philosophy of the Epoch*, Zinoviev employed a shrewd tactic to signal his concern about the direction of the country, without, however, openly breaking with the CC. Instead of attacking any of the other leaders directly, he used the writings of the Harbin-based émigré professor Nikolai Ustrialov as a foil. An erstwhile opponent of the Bolsheviks with service in the Whites, Ustrialov had emerged as a leading voice in the *smenovekhovtsy* movement since the end of the civil war. Named after the Prague-based journal *Smena Vekh* (Change of Signposts), this group of liberal and nationalist intellectuals argued that opponents of Communism had to accept Bolshevik victory as an irreversible fact and seek common ground with the Soviet state so as to influence the further historical development of Russia. Crucially, this conciliatory line did not signify abject surrender. Ustrialov had argued in a series of articles that the NEP signified a reorientation away from the dead-end of socialism towards a more normal path of bourgeois development.

29 Black, 'Party Crisis', p. 114.

30 Zinoviev emerges as little more than an unprincipled opportunist in most accounts of the factional struggle. More recently, some attempts have been made to paint a more balanced picture of him as a political leader operating in and influenced by his concrete historical context. See indicatively, Lars T. Lih, 'Zinoviev: Populist Leninist', *The NEP Era: Soviet Russia, 1921–1928*, 2 (1928): 1–24; Clayton Black, 'Zinoviev Re-examined: Comments on Lars Lih's "Populist Leninist"'. *The NEP Era: Soviet Russia, 1921–1928*, 2 (1928): 25–38. What is significant for the purposes of this investigation is that, whatever Zinoviev's motives, he sought to appeal to a pro-industry sentiment that was already present amongst the party rank-and-file.

Zinoviev cited some of his more poignant formulations: 'The torch has almost burned out, but the world did not burn'; 'The old bourgeoisie is dead – a new bourgeoisie is being born. . . . The old bureaucracy is dead too, but a new bureaucracy is also inevitably being born.' Even more helpfully to the Leningrad chief's case, Ustrialov had also identified the social forces that would drive Russia's bourgeois regeneration. These included the 'peasant-producer', 'the new generation of managers' and the 'ordinary capitalist bourgeoisie'. There was likely nothing that could stoke rank-and-file hostility to the NEP more than the image of a foreign-based counter-revolutionary publicly placing his hopes on kulaks, bureaucrats and Nepmen. In his conclusion, Zinoviev, pretending still to be arguing against Ustrialov, stressed that the NEP was a tactical evasion rather than a change in course. He then admonished the Party to hold firm in its correct line but warned that the influence of hostile classes might lead to 'vacillations, here and there' even within its own ranks.[31]

These arguments were elaborated further in *Leninism*, a quotation-laden book-length study of the theory and practice of the late leader. Organised as a historical overview of all the political disputes Lenin had taken part in, Zinoviev's book attempted to position Leninism as upholding the true revolutionary line in the labour movement against umpteen 'petty-bourgeois deviations'. In his chapters on the NEP, Zinoviev cited numerous passages from the master's works describing the NEP as a tactical retreat that was fraught with the danger of capitalist restoration.[32] In this way, the NEP was cast as correct but only insofar as it delivered the goods for socialist construction. For it to do so, the Party would have to follow the correct Leninist policies. According to Zinoviev, the Party did naturally have the right policy. It followed, therefore, that if the NEP was not yielding the desired results, it had to be the case that some elements within the Party were not sufficiently committed to implementing it in the appropriate manner. It could scarcely have been hard for Zinoviev's readers to divine the targets of his allegations. Bukharin, Rykov, and other NEP enthusiasts had become notorious as class-collaborationists among Leningrad communists. By attacking their views as deviationist, Zinoviev was effectively presenting *them* as oppositionists subverting the line pursued by the legitimate leadership, of which he was a member. Zinoviev thus attempted to stake out a position that appealed to his heavily

[31] Grigorii Zinoviev, *Filosofiia epokhi* (Leningrad: Priboi, 1925).

[32] Grigorii Zinoviev, *Leninizm: vvedenie v izuchenie Leninizma* (Leningrad: Gosudarstvennoe Izdatel'stvo, 1925), pp. 221–24.

proletarian Leningrad base, without becoming vulnerable to the criticism of anti-NEP adventurism that had been directed to the Left Opposition. It was a delicate balancing act which ultimately failed, but not before leading to a direct clash between the LPO and the CC majority.

After their leader had provided theoretical and political cover for their views, Leningrad communists became increasingly more outspoken in their criticisms of the NEP. During the autumn of 1925 and in anticipation of the upcoming party Congress, the regional press carried combative interventions from local activists which publicised the growing dissatisfaction of the LPO with the direction the Party was taking. In September, O. S. Tarkhanov, the propagandist of the KP party organisation, attacked the leadership of the Komsomol as a key conduit of petty bourgeois influence on the rank-and-file. The estrangement of the northern capital from the mainstream reached crisis levels in October, when regional secretary Zalutskii denounced the line pursued by the leadership as amounting to a Thermidor.[33]

For its part, the leadership attempted to avoid a public confrontation with the Party's most historic organisation by offering some recognition to the concerns of the LPO while also indicating that it would not tolerate further insubordination. On 29 October, the CC published a letter identifying vacillation around the kulak question as a major threat to party work. The text identified two deviations from the Party's rural policy. Many Leningraders may have been relieved to find out that the first of these was the under-estimation of the threat of kulak expansion in the countryside. The anti-NEP hardliners among them, however, were probably less impressed by the fact that the CC letter identified over-estimation of the kulak danger as the second deviation, denouncing it in equal measure.[34]

Whatever the merits of the political diagnosis of the CC, it failed to satisfy the LPO radicals. The twenty-second conference of the LPO convened on 1 December 1925, to review the Party's activity in the region, elect office-bearers for the subsequent period and, more importantly, discuss the Central Committee's theses and report to the Fourteenth Party Congress. Despite the growing tensions of the preceding period, there was little in the conference proceedings that could have foreshadowed the scale of the subsequent conflict. There were, however, clear indications of significant grassroots resentment towards the broader state of

[33] Black, 'Party Crisis', p. 114; Carr, *Socialism*, vol. 1, p. 112.
[34] *Leningradskaia Pravda* (*LP*), 29 October 1925.

affairs in the country, as well as of a feeling of neglect and alienation from the central leadership.

Among the first contributors from the floor, Korolev from the *Proletarskii* factory complained about the Central Committee decision to organise the forthcoming Congress in Moscow, despite a XIII Congress resolution stipulating that it was to take place in Leningrad. His assessment of the decision as demeaning for Leningrad workers was echoed by Bogdanov from the Leonov Tram depot.[35] Far more important politically, however, was the large number of speakers who expressed concern about the rapid growth of social inequality in both city and countryside as a result of the NEP. Although speakers generally refrained from openly attacking the leadership, there were several warnings about the dangers of political deviations developing within the Party that led to complacency about the growth of kulak and Nepman power. The most blistering critique along these lines was delivered by Sarkis. The secretary of KP's home district identified a number of issues over which the Party was 'wavering', chief among which were the class character of the Soviet state, the flourishing of non-Marxist ideas within the Party, and, naturally, the threat of the kulak. He lambasted Bukharin as the chief promoter of such petty-bourgeois views and, in order to alert his audience to the gravity of the situation, alleged that a by then withdrawn decree by the People's Commissariat of Agriculture of the Georgian Republic had ordered the denationalisation of land.[36]

Although Sarkis's alarmist tone reflected the mood of much of the delegate body, there were numerous contributions that did not carry the same sense of urgency. Pichurin, from Volodarskii district, argued that the main weakness of party work was practical rather than ideological, stemming mainly from the inability of rural cadres to promote the party line among the peasantry accurately. He suggested that '[t]he kulak must be controlled like the NEPman', arguing that this was to be achieved by a reinforcement of party presence in the countryside, rather than a political reorientation. Petrova, another delegate, went even further, stating that she could not understand the cause of such worries. Given the circumstances, party work in the countryside was in her opinion quite solid.[37]

The Lenin enrolment had brought swathes of NEP discontents into the Party and provided them with the rhetorical and organisational tools necessary to make their views known. This did not, however, translate into automatic grassroots support for an anti-NEP programme, much less

[35] RGASPI, f. 17, op. 21, d. 2668, ll. 7–8. [36] Ibid., ll. 14–15. [37] Ibid., l. 15.

for a rebellion against the central leadership. Interestingly, notwithstanding the frustration voiced by several delegates on various aspects of party work, Zinoviev and his supporters made no attempt to prepare the organisation for a full confrontation with the Central Committee. This suggests that they were not confident in their ability to carry the conference, or that they had not fully decided on such a course at the time.[38] The mass rank-and-file politics inaugurated by the Lenin Levy was as new to the Old Bolshevik Zinoviev as party membership was to the new recruits. Zinoviev understood that the radical inclinations of the Leningraders gave him some leverage with the rest of the leadership. He nevertheless appears to have been uncertain in terms of the extent to which he could mobilise anti-NEP sentiment and the ultimate purpose of such a move.

The turning point came after the simultaneous Moscow Party Organisation conference published its political resolution, which the Leningrad leadership interpreted as a direct attack on themselves. Although the text did not directly mention Leningrad, there were enough references to the dangers of anti-NEP adventurism to make Zinoviev nervous. In a closed session of the Leningrad conference, he expressed himself thus: 'I affirm that there is here a definite political verdict, and not only on my real or imaginary errors; here are words directly referring to the Leningrad organization, to the Leningrad workers ... You should clearly recognize that the affair is now being conducted under the slogan "Beat the Leningraders".'[39]

Still, Zinoviev stuck to his tactic of casting his opponents as a faction operating in Moscow, thus masking the growing isolation of the LPO from the mainstream. This is reflected in the final conference resolution which warned of the danger of the kulak and stressed the need to keep a close watch on social stratification in the countryside, but still condemned the leftist deviation of over-estimating this danger and declared the LPO to be 'fully and wholly' in agreement with the CC.[40] Even the alarmist Sarkis maintained that there were 'no differences' between Leningrad and Moscow and that the argument over the direction of the country was with 'individual comrades' rather than any organisation. In any case, the LPO would stand firmly by the decisions of the CC. Sarkis was addressing

[38] Zinoviev had attempted to sound out the leanings of the party organisation of the Leningrad-based Communist University. Its activists, who presumably knew something about Marxist theory, seemed unconvinced that there was anything wrong with the Muscovites' view. Igal Halfin, *Intimate Enemies: Demonizing the Bolshevik Opposition, 1918–1928* (Pittsburgh: University of Pittsburgh Press, 2007), pp. 193–94.

[39] Zinoviev, in Carr, *Socialism*, vol. 1, p. 124.

[40] RGASPI, f. 17

a 1,400 strong meeting of KP communists, which then went on to draft a letter to the Fourteenth Congress, calling 'all members of our party to stand as a monolithic wall and pull out by the roots all deviations'.[41] His audience could not have imagined that they were about to become part of the largest internal mutiny in the Party's history.

Notwithstanding his countless pronouncements on the correctness of party policy, Zinoviev took the unprecedented step of delivering a supplementary report (*sodoklad*) to the main political report of the CC to Congress read out by Stalin. The forty-three delegates signing the request to the Congress presidium for *sodoklad* speaking rights to Zinoviev all came for Leningrad.[42] Zinoviev, thus, took the floor as a representative of the LPO rather than a minority viewpoint within the leadership that could at least in principle claim all-Union appeal. What is more, the content of the supplementary report offered little more than Zinoviev's already published concerns about the NEP, while failing to develop them into a coherent programmatic statement that was substantively different from the CC political report.

Speaking in the evening of 19 December 1925, Zinoviev opened by subscribing to the conventional wisdom that the NEP was the correct path to socialism, that in the absence of world revolution socialist construction would have to begin in one country and that the peculiarities of said country necessitated a carefully managed policy towards the peasantry. He warned that the main challenge confronting the Party was drawing 'ever wider layers of the people' closer to the proletarian state, while also remaining true to the revolutionary endgame without sinking into *obydenshchina*, the comforting habit of managing the Soviet system in its current, not quite socialist state.

None of these points were absent from Stalin's CC report. Instead of directly challenging any of the CC theses, Zinoviev opted to criticise Bukharin's views on the question of whether production relations in publicly owned industry in the USSR were socialist or, because of the state sector's interaction with extensive commodity exchange elsewhere in the economy, 'socialist, but not fully'. This arcane debate has some merit for Marxist political economy but carried scarcely any concrete policy implications for the NEP. Zinoviev certainly could not offer any.[43]

41 Black, 'Party Crisis', pp. 115–16.

42 *XIV S"ezd Vsesoiuznoi Kommunisticheskoi Partii (b). Stenograficheskii Otchet* (Moscow: Gosudarstvennoe Izdatel'stvo, 1926), p. 96.

43 Ibid., p. 101.

The lack of specific policy alternatives was easily seized upon by subsequent speakers as evidence of the unprincipled motives of this new faction. The suspicions of most delegates were confirmed when Politburo member Lev Kamenev took the floor to lend his support to the *sodoklad*. Kamenev dropped a bombshell in the conclusion of his speech, when following sustained challenges from the audience to offer specific proposals he stated that he had 'come to the conclusion that comrade Stalin cannot act as the unifier of the Bolshevik [Party]'.[44] Kamenev's words elicited a cascade of indignant heckling from the audience, as furious delegates denounced the hypocrisy of the oppositionists. When less senior oppositionists subsequently spoke in favour of the *sodoklad*, they faced such hostility that they could barely complete their speeches. Thus, when on the following day Sarkis attempted to reiterate his earlier arguments from *Leningradskaia Pravda* about the proletarian composition of the Party, he was interrupted so often that Rykov, no friend of the opposition, had to intervene as Chair to extend his timeslot. Sarkis used his extra time to remind his audience that the LPO delegation represented some of the largest industrial enterprises of the country, including of course KP.[45]

Sarkis's invocation of the romantic image of Leningrad as the cradle of the proletarian movement could hardly counterweigh the comfortable majority of Congress delegates enjoyed by the CC. The isolation of the oppositionists was so evident that, when the time came for Congress to vote on a resolution on the CC report, Kamenev announced that the delegates who had spoken in favour of Zinoviev's *sodoklad* would not be tabling one of their own. He claimed instead that the Moscow-sponsored resolution approving the report had incorporated enough of the arguments of the minority view that it was possible to move forward without the divisive spectacle of Congress voting on competing texts. Kamenev went on to suggest a number of revisions that would reflect minority concerns with greater clarity, but his proposal was rejected by an overwhelming 559 to 65 delegates.[46]

This was not the end of the drama. After Congress delivered its rebuke, leading LPO delegates left Moscow without attending subsequent sessions. Returning to base, the local leaders dug in their heels and resolved to go down fighting. On 28 December, Leningrad's rank-and-file membership was summoned to mass meetings in order to hear reports on the deliberations of the Party's supreme decision-making body. More than 2,000 activists of the Moskovsko–Narvskii district assembled on the grounds of

[44] Ibid., p. 275. [45] Ibid., pp. 349–51. [46] Ibid., p. 524.

the rubber plant *Krasnyi Treugol'nik* to hear Sarkis's account of the events in Moscow. Rallies of similar size were held in other districts and on the following day *Leningradskaia Pravda* carried their near-unanimous resolutions supporting the local leadership against potential recriminations from the CC.[47]

This was unprecedented. Factional scheming was certainly not unheard of in Bolshevik history, but on previous occasions defeat at Congress meant that the minority accepted at least formally the new line and, by implication, its diminished political status. The concentrated organisational power of Zinoviev's supporters, however, made it possible for them to attempt to resist the centre by mobilising the local apparatus to shield themselves from recriminations. District secretaries like Sarkis and loyal rank-and-file organisers like KP's Aleksandrov refused to distribute Congress literature to the grassroots in order to obscure the isolation of the LPO from the party mainstream and maintain the illusion that it was being hounded by a nefarious Moscow-based faction within the leadership.[48] By rallying Leningrad's activist base around them, the Zinovievites were essentially challenging the CC either to launch disciplinary action against the entirety of the LPO, thus paralyzing the apparatus, or leave them at their posts, thus legitimising their factional activity. The Party's freshly established grassroots institutions were being used as a weapon against the CC.

Realising that regaining control of the LPO by administrative means would at best be a pyrrhic victory, the leadership opted for a more complicated course of action. After the conclusion of Congress business on 31 December, the CC dispatched a delegation of its most experienced members to the northern capital to try and win back the LPO to the majority line. Prominent Bolsheviks including Viacheslav Molotov, Mikhail Kalinin, Sergei Kirov and Kliment Voroshilov toured the city addressing party cells in industrial districts in order to expose the duplicitous conduct of the local leadership.

This was far from an easy task, however, and the CC representatives had to employ some shrewd organisational tactics to get their way. Rather than speaking at formally organised meetings which could be controlled by the LPO apparatus, the CC representatives linked up with so-called 'initiative groups' of local communists who were loyal to the centre and showed up unannounced in factories and workers' clubs to speak directly to the rank-and-file. These gatherings were rowdy affairs attracting several hundred

[47] *LP*, 29 December 1925. [48] Black, 'Party Crisis', p. 117.

activists who were keen to defend their local leadership or find out if rumours of their factionalism were true. Two weeks after his arrival in the city, Sergei Kirov penned a letter to Sergo Ordzhonikidze where he described one such meeting as follows:

> Yesterday we were at Treugol'nik, [with a party] collective of 2,200 people. It was an incredible fight. It was a kind of meeting I hadn't seen since the days of October and didn't even imagine possible among party members. At times, in some parts of the meeting people even came to blows. I am not exaggerating.[49]

By 16 January, the CC delegation had succeeded in prying most key Leningrad districts out of opposition control. Nevertheless, several party cells in the heavily industrial Moskovsko–Narvskii district remained stubbornly loyal to the Zinovievites including, above all, KP. At this point, the organisations that had declared against the opposition represented a majority of Leningrad's party membership and it would have thus been possible for the centre to declare victory and oust the oppositionists in a new regional conference where the latter would have been in a minority. Because, however, the opposition had mobilised the rank-and-file against the CC by passing resolutions supporting its conduct through individual PPO meetings, only a complete reversal of this process could signify its total and irreversible defeat. Otherwise, whatever the outcome of a regional conference, the oppositionists would still be able to point at their control of key organisations to present themselves as a legitimate current of thought within the Party. As the most important of opposition strongholds, KP became the site of the last and most intense clash between the CC delegation and the Zinovievites.

The KP initiative group had already become active before the Opposition had shown its hand at Congress. As in other enterprises, this was essentially an attempt to out-factionalise the Zinovievites by bringing together a core group of loyal communists with proletarian background and impeccable revolutionary credentials. Commanding the respect of the workforce, these CC-loyalists could use their influence to undermine support for the local leadership. At KP, this effort was spearheaded by Ivan Gaza, a Putilovite metalworker of pre-revolutionary party standing who had spent the Civil War as political commissar of an armoured train at the Northern Front. After the war, Gaza remained in the Red Army as

[49] Oleg Khlevniuk et al. (eds.), *Bol'shevistkoe Rukovodstvo Perepiska. 1912–1927* (Moscow: ROSSPEN, 1996), p. 318. An older communist, Voroshilov (p. 320) likened his experience in Leningrad to the revolutionary days of 1905 and admitted feeling 'literally rejuvenated' (*bukval'no omolodel*).

commissar and commander of the armoured forces of the Leningrad military region. Nevertheless, he maintained contact with his factory as Leningrad armour was under the patronage (*shefstvo*) of KP.[50]

As the crisis was gaining steam, Gaza liaised with KP workers who had served under him in order to establish a network of agitators to bring the CC position to workers and break the Zinovievites' press monopoly in the factory. On 28 December, having been barred from speaking at the Moskovsko–Narvskii district meeting addressed by Sarkis, Gaza set up an impromptu counter-rally where he denounced the Leningrad delegates' behaviour at Congress. A couple of weeks later, the KP initiative group published an 'Appeal to VKP (b) members of *Krasnyi Putilovets*' imploring them to turn away from factionalism and declaring the fate of the revolution to be 'fully and entirely dependent' on the monolithic unity of the Party.[51] *Leningradskaia Pravda*, by then taken over by CC loyalists, carried the text, thus making it accessible to all interested KP workers.

Still the Zinovievites held fast. On 16 January, a meeting of KP party activists passed a resolution defending the LPO Congress delegation and condemning the initiative groups as a threat to party unity. Two days later, a meeting at the cannon casting shop also expressed support for the Zinovievites, its resolution stating that 'if our delegates are guilty then we are guilty too'. By that time, however, the opposition's hold on the KP organisation had begun to loosen. Meeting a day after the cannon-casters, the communists of the electrical shop condemned the Congress delegates, removed all oppositionists from their cell bureau, and replaced them with CC loyalists headed by Frants Giats, an active member of the KP initiative group.[52]

On 20 January, after almost a month of bitter factional struggle, the CC representatives turned up *en masse* at an expanded plenary session of the KP organisation to confront its leadership. Kirov, Tomsky, Voroshilov, Molotov and Kalinin – himself a former Putilovite – took the floor to denounce Zinovievite demagogy and lay out the Congress-approved policies on the construction of socialism and the expansion of heavy industry. Even then, the oppositionists did not give in easily. The organisation had

[50] *Smena*, November 1940. The practice of *shefstvo* was intended to reinforce the proletarian class character of the Red Army by establishing institutional links between enterprises and military units or formations. For more details, see David R. Stone, 'Shefstvo: Lev Trotsky and the Military Origins of Revolutionary Patronage', *Revolutionary Russia* 19, no. 1 (2006): 21–36.

[51] *LP*, 13 January 1926.

[52] Black, 'Party Crisis', p. 119; Stanislav Kostiuchenko, *Istoriia Kirovskogo Zavoda, 1917–1945* (Moscow: Mysl', 1965), p. 233.

become so divided that the normally straightforward process of electing a presidium for the session took over two hours because the two sides could not agree on its composition. In the end it was agreed that two separate presidiums would conduct the plenum. Still, there was more shouting than reasoned debate during the proceedings, with speakers often interrupted by hecklers, some of the rowdiest of whom had to be ejected from the meeting area. In the end, the presence of the CC heavyweights swayed the plenum, which voted 800 to 400 to 'condemn the behaviour of the bureaus of the [KP] collective, the *raikom* and the *gubkom*'.[53] The last bastion of the Zinovievites had fallen.

The mass involvement of the Leningrad rank-and-file in the New Opposition set it apart from previous political crises and is testament to the extent of the transformation undergone by the party since the Lenin Levy. The various shades of leftism faced down by the CC majority in the preceding years had been manifestations of programmatic differences within the Party over its tasks in government, reflecting the unease of sizeable parts of the membership with the Bolsheviks' transformation from a party of revolution to a party of power. Once these political differences had been aired and debated at the appropriate party organs, it had been relatively easy to end the discussion and move on, as party statutes bound all members to uphold the majority decisions. By contrast, there was no alternative policy platform articulated by Zinoviev, Kamenev, and their allies at the Fourteenth Congress. Instead, the oppositionists mobilised the support of the LPO on the basis of the claim that the party leadership had been taken over by a shadowy faction that was attempting to warp the otherwise correct general line of the Party. This lack of pronounced differences of principle has led most historians of the 1920s to overlook the true historical significance of these events.

This lay not so much in the proceedings of the Fourteenth Congress itself but in what came after. The Leningrad rank-and-file was so committed to supporting the regional leadership that the CC despatched its most prominent members to the city and they in turn had to employ their old revolutionary toolkit in order to win back the LPO factory by factory. Even after having been addressed by the likes of Molotov, Kalinin, and Voroshilov, a full third of KP communists refused to condemn the LPO Congress delegation, with results elsewhere in the city showing similar levels of recalcitrance.[54] A revolt of such scale and depth yet so obviously lacking in clear ideological motivation presented a particularly complex

[53] TsGAIPD, f. 1012, op. 1, d. 266, ll. 2–25. [54] Black, 'Party Crisis', p. 121.

challenge to the Bolshevik leadership. It suggested that the large numbers of workers who had joined the Party since 1924 had brought with them the smouldering proletarian disgruntlement with the NEP. For these politically inexperienced proletarian communists it was likely of less consequence whether state industry was socialist or 'socialist but not fully' than that it remained in operation. The first years of the NEP had not demonstrated that this would necessarily be the case, as demonstrated by the near closure of KP, where 90 per cent of the membership at the time of the Fourteenth Congress had only joined during the previous year.[55]

The Lenin Levy had, thus, succeeded in its primary task of bringing the Party closer to the masses, at the price of bringing the multitude of social contradictions inherent in the NEP into the Party itself. The Leningrad crisis had demonstrated that an alienated rank-and-file could act as a launching board for opposition factions that could seize extensive parts of the apparatus. In this sense, it is of little importance whether Zinoviev was cynically manipulating the LPO membership or genuinely concerned about the prospects of the NEP. What is crucial is that the New Opposition brought home to the leadership that the Party's expanded rank-and-file was a new political force that had to be reckoned with. A corollary of this was that the new regional leadership would have to rebuild the trust of the LPO to the centre, refraining from a punitive treatment of the oppositionists.[56] The key task would be to address the concerns of the Leningraders regarding the prospects of industrial expansion, while also demonstrating to them that the CC majority was in fact on their side.

Convening on 10 February 1926, the extraordinary conference of the LPO attempted to do just that. The party leaders that had toured that city's factories at the height of the crisis appeared again to reiterate the commitment of the CC to industrial growth. They were joined by Felix Dzerzhinskii, the head of the VSNKh whose fame as founder of the secret police was bound to reassure those who were concerned about the CC yielding ground to the class enemy. Nikolai Bukharin, the bogeyman of anti-NEP alarmism, also delivered a lengthy speech to the conference assuring the delegates that, should the need arise, the Party retained the means to 'pacify' (*omirotvorit'*) the kulak as 'in 1918'.[57] Sergei Kirov, who had taken over as secretary of the *gubkom*, delivered the main report in

[55] Kostiuchenko, *Istoriia*, p. 237.

[56] A session of the new *gubkom* under Kirov held on 19 January explicitly forbade any disciplinary measures against rank-and-file oppositionists. RGASPI, f. 17, op. 21, d. 2674, l. 11.

[57] RGASPI, f. 17, op. 21, d. 2669, ll. 2–5, 70–72.

which he stressed unity around the CC as the main principle that would guide the work of the LPO in the future. The resolution adopted by the conference on the basis of Kirov's report provided a succinct statement of the leadership's understanding of the crisis and its intentions in terms of moving past it.

According to the text, the unity of the Party had been undermined by the practice of indiscriminate recruitment of new members that had had the effect of swelling its ranks with untested working-class elements without sufficient experience of organised class struggle. This had resulted in a 'radical alteration of the organisational nature of [the] Party'. The conference resolved that the only guarantee against future manifestations of factionalism was the careful studying of Leninist theory and Congress materials, as well as the strengthening of party democracy to frustrate the plans of future factionalists. It would also be necessary to raise the quality of the Party's intervention among the broader masses, by having communists become more actively involved in the work of trade unions, soviets and cooperatives.[58]

The contributions of the CC representatives to the LPO conference and the resolution of the latter suggest that the leadership traced the origins of the crisis to the following two factors. First, the prioritisation of rural economic growth had put a strain on the relationship of the Party with its working-class base. Second, a large part of that base was absorbed into party ranks without sufficient experience in Bolshevik politics, thus becoming open to manipulation by a demagogic clique. The first problem would be addressed by the gradually improving pace of industrial growth. In terms of the second, the remedies prescribed by the conference resolution rather echoed the principles that had driven party building since the revolution and inspired the Lenin Levy. Education to make the membership more politically astute and activist participation in public affairs to empower rank-and-file communists and strengthen their links with the broader masses of people. Having survived the crisis, the leadership had decided to stay its course. As the most prominent stronghold of the opposition, KP would become a major testing ground for this policy.

## 2.3 Rejuvenating the Party Organisation

Having spearheaded the CC-aligned initiative group, Ivan Gaza was demobilised from the Red Army and became the new party organiser at

[58] Ibid., ll. 57–58.

KP. The first major party meeting held under Gaza's leadership was an expanded joint session of the PPO bureau with its shop-level equivalents, shop-section organisers, communist foremen and trade-union activists that took place on 9 February 1926, one day before the LPO's extraordinary conference. Attended by 306 members, the first meeting of the factory's new leadership had been called to review and discuss ways to remedy the effects of the factional struggle that had shaken the organisation.[59] Gaza spoke first, declaring that the main task before the organisation was rebuilding party discipline, a major casualty of the factional conflict. This was seconded by Anushenko, a communist from the ironworks shop, who argued that shop-level party activity had taken a particularly hard hit during the crisis, as unruly young party members 'had been walking all over their shop cells'.[60]

The political discussion was, however, soon derailed into a comprehensive attack on the factory administration from members of the trade-union factory committee (*zavkom*) and communists from various shops, as well as an exchange of accusations between these two groups over who was to blame the most for not containing the labour unrest caused by bad management. This was not a purely economic concern. Industrial grievances had been a major source of the recent political crisis. They continued to set the agenda for the new PPO leadership. *Zavkom* member Kir'ianov spoke of conflicts in several shops and accused managers of withholding pay for stoppages (*prostoi*). At the same time, he attacked party members for not bringing the problem to the attention of the *zavkom* early enough, which would have prevented things from escalating. Glushkov, a communist from the iron-rolling shop, responded that Kir'ianov had in fact been informed a week in advance but chose to do nothing. Zadvinskii, from the steam-boiler shop, also blamed the factory administration for the problem of truancy, claiming that workers had not been provided with warm clothes and reiterating the problem of unpaid stoppages.

Others expressed more serious concerns about management. Nazimov, from the wagon shop, cautioned against the administration's purported slackness and then went on to argue that factory security had to be tightened as there were people who were trying to take advantage of the situation to cause trouble. This comment was made in relation to fires that had recently broken out on factory grounds, which the director Grachev conceded as reflective of the lack of adequate security measures but not of

59 TsGAIPD, f. 1012, op. 1, d. 268, l. 10.

60 '[S]hagnuli po golovam tsekhiacheek'. Ibid.

integrity on the administration's part. While other speakers went on to criticise the administration on pay and related issues, Gubanov, a communist from the instrument making shop, chose to remain on the security theme. Gubanov stated that former White Army officers and generals had been discovered at *Krasnyi Treugol'nik*, another one of Leningrad's iconic factories. He went on to muse if it would not be a good idea to investigate if the same was true for KP as well, concluding that it was 'necessary to shake-up' all of the factory's staff. Grachev, the factory director, attempted to provide some cover for his white-collar staff, saying that while there certainly were some who were damaging factory work, it was not fair to say that all the administration was 'worthless' (*negodniaia*).[61]

The views expressed at the meeting are indicative of the state of affairs prevalent at the party grassroots after the defeat of the Zinovievites. The rejection of the opposition by the PPO had not resolved the industrial tensions that had fuelled it in the first place. What is more, intervention like Gubanov's indicated that party activists continued to look at factory conditions and draw negative political conclusions about the country's prospects of socialist development. Recast by mass recruitment and tempered in a rough factional struggle, the PPO appears here as a political microcosm, its grassroots leadership viewing the arguments taking place at higher levels of the party apparatus through the lens of factory conditions.

In any case, the meeting seems to have concluded on an uncertain tone, with Gaza reiterating that rebuilding party discipline was a task of paramount importance but without any concrete measures being agreed on. In line with the policy adopted by the new regional leadership, such discipline had less to do with persecuting the remnants of the opposition than with the more mundane task of promoting a modicum of organisational culture amongst the membership, still overwhelmingly composed of recent recruits.[62] Thus, of the eleven disciplinary cases reviewed by the organisation's conflict commission on 17 March, six were about lost party cards.[63] The remainder concerned internal squabbles as well as accusations of 'careerism' and corruption, as in the case of Ivan Balashov, a storekeeper accused by the main factory store bureau of not informing the organisation of his criminal convictions for bribe-taking, blackmail, and theft of

[61] Ibid., l. 11.

[62] At that time, about half of the organisation's members had joined the Party in 1925. TsGAIPD, f. 1012, op. 1, d. 266, l. 60.

[63] TsGAIPD, f. 1012, op. 1, d. 268, l. 103.

evidence.[64] None of the cases reviewed had any connection to the events of the preceding winter, or to any subsequent oppositionist activity.

The promotion of party discipline with respect to organisational matters seems to have remained the primary political concern of the Party at KP for most of the remainder of 1926. Low meeting attendance and high levels of arrears in party dues emerged as major issues in the organisation's general assembly held on 27 May. According to Gaza, the organisation had only collected 60 per cent of subscription dues in March and 56.3 per cent in April. Similarly, the shop bureau re-election campaign that had taken place after the organisation withdrew its support for the opposition had only been attended by 65 per cent of the membership, although this was apparently an improvement on past performance.[65] Similar concerns were expressed by the *raikom* bureau during a review of the performance of some of KP's shop-level party organisers held in August. The district party organ deemed the work of the organiser of the open-hearth furnace shop party group Morozov to be 'very weak', demanding 'decisive measures against disciplinary offences' like unexcused absences and delays in the payment of subscription dues. Ivanov, a party activist from the tractor department was also criticised for failing to keep good attendance records, despite the rest of his work having been 'satisfactory'.[66]

None of these problems related to oppositionist activity. The issues highlighted by the *raikom* review were purely organisational, reflecting a concern with the performance of the budding grassroots apparatus. However, despite the repeated complaints about the state of party work expressed by the leadership at both the enterprise and the district level, things do not actually seem to have been so bad in every shop. The wagon shop organisation, for example, held regular meetings throughout the year, with an average attendance by members and candidates of around 66 per cent, as well as a regular though fluctuating presence by non-members. Although perhaps being an exception in that regard, the wagon shop party group had by May 1926 collected 90 per cent of its members' subscription dues.[67] Its activities included presentations followed by discussion on a variety of topics ranging from the perennial problems of production to more abstract issues like the state of the worker–peasant alliance and the international political situation. Throughout the year, the group seems to have also conducted its organisational affairs in a more or less orderly

[64] Ibid., l. 106. [65] TsGAIPD, f. 1012, op. 1, d. 266, ll. 60–62.
[66] TsGAIPD, f. 1012, op. 1, d. 264, ll. 15–25. [67] TsGAIPD, f. 1012, op. 1, d. 287, l. 20.

manner; managing to hold a smooth re-election of its bureau in January and elect other officer-bearers in subsequent months.[68] These are hardly disappointing results for an organisation composed predominantly of new recruits of overwhelmingly low education levels.[69] That the leading cadres of the organisation found them substandard is more reflective of the importance they attached to the task of party building rather than the performance of the rank-and-filers.

It should not be surprising that the KP organisation focused on party building while devoting little time to the events of the winter crisis. Both the CC and the new regional leadership had resolved that the factional activity of the opposition had become possible because of demagogic exploitation of legitimate grievances amongst the party's rank-and-file by Zinoviev and his allies. Having neutralised the opposition organisationally, it had become possible for CC loyalists to begin to remedy the problems that were the source of its political legitimacy. By making rank-and-file communists more politically astute – or 'conscious' in the parlance of the time – Bolshevik leaders expected to make them less susceptible to similar demagogy in the future. To be sure, there can be little doubt that, from the perspective of the leadership, adherence to the CC-line was the measure of political maturity. Nevertheless, a satisfactory level of political awareness – and therefore loyalty – could in the spirit of Marxism–Leninism only be gained by getting party members fully involved in the everyday life of the organisation, through participating in meetings and actively promoting party policy amongst their fellow workers. In other words, discipline was expected to be the product of political education.

More importantly, this was also a necessary component of the Party's response to the economic problems at the root of the crisis. The Fourteenth Congress had resolved to step up industrial expansion but, in order to do so, the chronic weaknesses of Soviet industry would have to be addressed. In response to these problems, the April 1926 CC plenum of the Party formulated a new economic initiative known as the Regime of Economy.[70] Unlike previous attempts to save resources by putting

[68] The new bureau consisted of eight Party and one Komsomol members, all with over twelve years' experience in production but, with one exception, less than two years of party membership. During the election, the candidate member Georgii Danilov was removed from the list due to his incapacity to work and replaced by Georgii Smirnov, who also became the organiser. Some months later, the bureau also held a three-way contested election on the post of 'plenipotentiary' (*upolnomochennyi*) for newspaper subscriptions. Ibid., ll. 1–4, 7, 33.

[69] Members with only primary education made up 91 per cent of the organisation in 1926. TsGAIPD, f. 1012, op. 1, d. 266, l. 61.

[70] *KPSS* v. *resoliutsiiakh*, vol. 4, pp. 8–17.

pressure on wages, the CC resolution that introduced the Regime of Economy explicitly stated that the current level of workers' earnings was not to be affected.[71] Instead of this, measures were to be taken to improve labour productivity, including strengthening labour discipline and rationalisation of the working day. At the same time, the resolution pointed at other aspects of the production process that could benefit from greater frugality, like administrative expenditures.

Feeding into already tense relations between workers and management, the question of where the most economising was to be made and, consequently, who was to bear most of the burden, quickly became a matter of dispute at party meetings. With the LPO fresh after the opposition crisis, industrial policy was so sensitive an issue that Stalin himself made a rare visit to Leningrad a few days after the April plenum to address the *gubkom* and a gathering of party activists.[72] On 22 April, Sergei Kirov visited KP to personally report on the results of the plenum. Addressing the meeting of about 1,000 members and sympathisers Kirov stressed the importance of the Regime of Economy for the development of Soviet industry, arguing that the lack of hard currency and the inability of the Soviet government to obtain foreign loans meant that the USSR would have to rely primarily on its internal resources for development. Every kopeck had to be seen as 'one's own sweat and blood'. Nevertheless, Kirov's speech was not a one-sided call for belt-tightening. The discipline of the Regime of Economy was not to be imposed on labour alone, but also on the administrative apparatus. 'Every plan – Kirov stated – goes through twenty revisions before being implemented. The state apparatus must be brought to order.'[73]

At the end of Kirov's speech, the floor was opened to contributions from the floor. These are remarkable for the consistency with which they attacked administrative staff as the main culprit of excessive expenses. Pavlov stated that while wage-rates bureaus were necessary, 'proletarians can't afford bureaus of 20–25 members'. Artamonov complained that the main store of the factory employed five inspectors (*kontrolery*) who were

[71] The August 1924 CC plenum had passed a resolution 'On the Policy of Wages' (*O politike zarabotnoi plate*) which sought to address the growing disparity between wages and labour productivity. Ibid., vol. 3, pp. 293–96. Some of the measures proposed were effectively measures of labour intensification, leading to a spike in labour unrest the following year. See on this Svetlana Borisovna Ul'ianova, 'Rabochie v massovykh khoziaistvenno-politicheskikh kampaniiakh 1920-kh gg.', in *Predprinimateli i rabochie Rossii v usloviiakh transformatsii obshchestva i gosudarstva v XX stoletii. Materialy mezhdunarodnoi nauchnoi konferentsii, posviashchennoi pamiati professora Iu. I. Kir'ianova*, ed. A. M. Belov (Kostroma: Kostromskoi Gosudarvstennii Universitet im. N. A. Nekrasova, 2003), pp. 83–93.

[72] Stalin, *Sochineniia*, 8, p. 394.

[73] TsGAIPD, f. 1012, op. 1, d. 266, l. 42.

paid ninety roubles per month to 'do nothing'. Isakov hinted at corruption, alleging that storemen were paid sixty roubles per month, had families of four or five members, but could be seen on a drinking binge ten evenings a month. Only Grachev spoke in defence of the factory's administrative staff and tried to shift the focus of the conversation onto questions of labour discipline. Amongst the last to take the floor, he stated that white-collar employees (*sluzhaschchie*) made up only 12 per cent of factory staff and that any discussion on the regime of economy should start with the problem of truancy (*progulki*) as well as the disorderly state of shop-floors.[74]

A similar mood can be glimpsed from the notes (*zapiski*) passed to Kirov from the floor. Although most notes contained questions about the CC plenum and technical suggestions regarding aspects of the production process, some of them revisited the theme of administrative wastefulness with increased belligerence. In order to give a better picture of the terms in which the issue was framed, it is worth quoting some of them at full length:

> How does the Regime of Economy agree with the administration receiving 200–300 roubles plus bonuses?
>
> There is too much administration in the factory. We should economise a bit.
>
> If we do not put a stop to the squandering and embezzlement of our property, we will never get the masses involved in our community. My suggestion is to expose the squanderers publicly, send them back to the workers where they came from and we will try them in our own way (*svoim sudom*).
>
> Measures must be taken against squandering, up to and including capital punishment.[75]

In his concluding remarks, Kirov attempted to bridge the gap between workers and the administration by suggesting that the Regime of Economy was the concern of both. He argued that the decline of labour productivity was primarily the result of the wearing out of equipment and the inability of administrative staff to effectively deploy the workforce at its disposal but that truancy was also a major contributing factor.[76]

From his perspective as a senior party leader, Kirov's approach made sense. In order to tap into the mobilising potential of communist activists, he needed to offer some recognition to their concerns. Nevertheless, Kirov's balanced address did little to dampen the anti-managerial

[74] Ibid., l. 43. [75] Ibid., ll. 45–47. [76] Ibid., l. 43.

sentiment of the rank-and-file. The implementation of the Regime of Economy reappeared as a major theme in the organisation's general assembly that convened on 27 May 1926. Delivering the main report, Gaza noted that there had been a significant decline in the productivity of labour in the second quarter of 1926 compared to the previous year but attributed the fall primarily to the post-crisis discussion that had taken up much of February. He went on to say that stoppages and truancy were the other main causes of falling labour productivity, stressing that the latter was the fault of workers alone, having reached an alarming rate of 13.55 per cent in April.[77]

The need to address such problems of labour discipline was a major theme of Gaza's report, but some of the comments he made with respect to the attitude of rank-and-file communists towards these issues are of particular interest here. Speaking of a series of slow-downs (*volynki*) that had taken place in the factory in connection with some labour-disputes, Gaza claimed that rank-and-file communists had often been found to be the main leaders, wryly commenting that 'having learned at the party school that communists are the vanguard of the proletariat, it appears that they think that if workers want to kick up a row they have to step in and do it for them'. Gaza urged party members to promote the correct line amongst workers and rounded off his speech with an assessment of the organisation's work as politically correct but often weak in practice.[78]

The discussion after the report followed a pattern similar to that of the previous meeting. The perceived large numbers of highly paid administrative staff were attacked by rank-and-file members like Ukkonen who stated that the only redundancies that had taken place had been of employees in the third and fourth brackets (*razriady*) of the skill-based pay scale. 'Start cutting from the top', he advised, 'and the Party will grow to new heights'.[79] Chervinskii complained that administrative staff had in fact increased in the tractor department where he worked. Chervinskii also

[77] Ibid., l. 58–59. [78] Ibid., ll. 59–63.

[79] Ibid., l. 65. Soviet wage policy went through a large number of reviews and overhauls throughout the interwar period, all of which created new sources of confusion and conflicts. In 1926, there was a seventeen-bracket scale in all-union use, but there were variations according to industry and enterprise with respect to norm-setting and the use of piece-rates. See on this L. I. Borodkin and E. I. Safonova, 'Gosudarstvennoe regulirovanie trudovykh otnoshenii v gody nepa: formirovanie sistemy motivatsii truda v promyshlennosti', *Ekonomicheskaiia Istoriia: Obozrenie* 5 (2000): 23–46; E. I. Safonova, 'Moskovskie tekstil'shchiki v gody nepa: kvalifikatsiia i differentsiatsiia v oplate truda', *Ekonomicheskaiia Istoriia. Ezhegodnik* (2001): 389–419; Lewis H. Siegelbaum, 'Soviet Norm Determination in Theory and Practice, 1917–1941', *Soviet Studies* 36, no. 1 (1984): 45–68, pp. 47–52.

criticised the weak development of shop-floor party organisations, bemoaning the bureau's negligence of this key task.[80] Smirnov, a former oppositionist, attacked the new leadership for making a series of mistakes in matters of party development and economic administration, claiming that the factory was in fact losing more workers than admin staff.[81] Notes to Gaza from the floor reiterated these points but also inquired about the state of production conferences, which the secretary conceded had very low attendance.[82]

It was again left to the director, Grachev, to provide some defence for the factory's white-collar personnel. Grachev argued that management had already made significant staff reductions amongst them, having closed the commercial sub-department whose head had been enjoying a monthly salary of 300 roubles. He added that administrative staff were also labourers and that the factory could not be run without them, warning that their continued marginalisation might lead to their political alienation.[83] Grachev finished his contribution by saying that the Regime of Economy would be successful only if all 2,000 members of the organisation worked to put it into practice.

After a few more short speeches, the floor was taken by Podol'skii, the *raikom* instructor present at the meeting. Podol'skii warned that the inexperienced, newly-expanded activist base of the organisation could fall into the trap of tailing, rather than leading the non-party mass. He then encouraged party activists to tell their fellow workers the truth about the inescapable difficulties of industrial development and admonished the rank-and-file to cease the unacceptable practice of putting forward demands that are impossible to fulfil.[84]

The tensions expressed at the meeting were reflected in the resolution produced at its end. Very much a compromise document, it stipulated that labour productivity was to be raised primarily by rationalising production and renewing equipment. The text also declared the development of shop-floor organisations to be a priority area of work and made regular meetings and reports obligatory for their organisers while the administration was

[80] TsGAIPD, f. 1012, op. 1, d. 266, l. 65.

[81] Ibid. Smirnov claimed that only four admin staff had been laid off at the wagon department, compared to some eighty workers.

[82] The total number of workers participating in conferences was 1,428 – out of who 530 were Party members – from a total workforce of over 10,000. According to Gaza, however, this was just on paper, attendance being even more disappointing in reality. Ibid., l 69.

[83] 'We mustn't treat them as a foreign body. Perhaps this is why only 100 showed up at the May Day celebrations'. Ibid., l. 66.

[84] Ibid., l. 68.

instructed to attach technical staff to production conferences, in order to assist workers in the formulation of workable suggestions. At the same time, the resolution instructed communists to be model workers and declared the promotion of labour discipline to be a priority issue for the organisation.[85]

Thus, in the immediate aftermath of the Fourteenth Congress and for most of 1926 the KP party organisation was kept busy with the task of getting its apparatus in working order and promoting political activism among its members while also trying, without spectacular success, to prevent it from getting in the way of plan fulfilment. A slight shift of the scales can, however, be observed in the general assembly of June 1927.[86] By that time, the Regime of Economy had been succeeded by a new industrial campaign, the Rationalisation of Production. Unlike its predecessor, Rationalisation was meant to be achieved on the basis of technical and organisational measures, such as mechanisation of particular tasks, reorganisation of the workplace, and training of new cadres. Socialist rationalisation, it was argued, could not proceed at the expense of the country's working class as was the case in the capitalist world. It should instead contribute to the improvement of workers' living standards and the expansion of the range of opportunities available to them.[87] This political recalibration at the centre strengthened the hand of party militants on the shop-floor.

Giving his annual report on the work of the organisation's bureau, Gaza presented figures showing that overhead costs had fallen by 2.8 per cent over the preceding year.[88] He then reported approvingly that there had been no labour disturbances during the same period, attributing this achievement to improving relations between workers and the administration.[89] Despite these positive developments, Gaza followed up with what seemed like an unprovoked attack on management, echoing many of the rank-and-file criticisms voiced at previous meetings. The party organiser criticised the factory administration for its behaviour towards workers' correspondents (*rabkory*), suggesting that they were, perhaps, seen as 'too inquisitive'.[90] Gaza stated that the bureau did not share this view and

85 Ibid., ll. 73–76.

86 TsGAIPD, f. 1012, op. 1, d. 418 l. 103. The exact date is not given, but 1,409 people were noted to be in attendance.

87 *KPSS v rezoliutsiakh*, vol. 4, pp. 161–67.

88 TsGAIPD, f. 1012, op. 1, d. 418, l. 104.

89 Ibid., l. 106.

90 Ibid., l. 109 Workers' – and peasants' correspondents – were grassroots volunteer journalists that reported on various aspects of everyday life for the local and national press. For a fuller discussion, see Jennifer Clibbon, *The Soviet Press and Grass-Roots Organization: The Rabkor Movement, NEP to the First Five Year Plan* (Toronto: University of Toronto Press, 1993).

signalled further disapproval of administrative practice saying that 'we differ with the administration on the question of the fight against bureaucratism. They say there isn't such a problem. We disagree'.[91] The remainder of Gaza's report revolved around the perennial problems of party building like meeting attendance and payment of dues, which Gaza noted had improved significantly along with the general level of the work of the *aktiv*.[92] Predictably, however, the ensuing discussion focused more on administrative failures than party achievements.

Chervinskii stated that management was trying to suppress the *rabkor* movement, including its communist caucus. He then accused the factory administration of dragging its feet on bureaucratism, claiming that the tractor shop employed one white-collar employee for every five workers. To applause from the floor, he added indignantly that the shop-level bureau had informed the administration of the problem but they had chosen to sit on their hands, producing token resolutions without ever putting them into practice. Grachev was then personally attacked by Ruzin for his 'impermissible' treatment of the *rabkory*.[93]

The most comprehensive account of the problems facing the organisation and the factory was, however, given by Ter-Asaturov, a draughtsman at the tractor department. He argued that the low skill level of the membership was the organisation's greatest handicap in its struggle to control the administration and called for the full communisation of the administrative apparatus.[94] Ter-Asaturov went on to argue that persistent problems in political work, like the low-attendance of production conferences by party members and the sluggish rate of party saturation increase, were directly linked to the problem of bureaucratism. He contrasted the approachable manner of managers in 'other factories' with that of KP staff who could never find the time to speak to workers.[95] Bureaucratism was finally condemned in the meeting's final resolution as a symptom of the persistent predominance of old regime specialists in the factory's white-collar staff.[96]

The PPO had by that time been established as a political space concerned chiefly with factory matters, above all, the inevitable tension

[91] TsGAIPD, f. 1012, op. 1, d. 418, l. 109. [92] Ibid., l. 114. [93] Ibid., ll. 117–18.

[94] Ibid., l. 121.

[95] Ibid., ll. 122–23. Ter-Asaturov's description of other factories' directors as having their 'doors open' to workers reflected the popular image of the good red director. See on this Diane P. Koenker, 'Factory Tales: Narratives of Industrial Relations in the Transition to NEP', *Russian Review* 55, no. 3 (1996): 384–411.

[96] TsGAIPD, f. 1012, op. 1, d. 418, ll. 131–32.

between workers and management. The intensity and broad contours of this conflictual relationship were ultimately determined by the Party's economic policy. By emphasising technical and organisational improvements as the key to raising productivity, Rationalisation shifted grassroots party politics towards a more anti-managerial direction, as indicated by Gaza abandonment of the moderate position earlier promoted by himself and Kirov. With respect to labour relations, this foreshadowed the much sharper turn that would take place with the launching of the First Five Year Plan the following year. We will have the opportunity to observe this process more closely in Chapter 3. In terms of the political struggles of the NEP that chiefly concern us here, this policy had more immediate consequences. Towards the end of 1926, party unity was once again shaken by the emergence of a new challenge to the CC, this time from the combined forces of the Zinoviev–Kamenev bloc and their erstwhile opponent Leon Trotsky, who along with the remnants of the Workers' Opposition, came together to form what became known as the United Opposition.

## 2.4 Testing the Organisation

The alliance of these former political opponents against the CC majority was first announced at a joint session of the CC and Central Control Commission in July 1926. This, among other business, expelled Zinoviev from the Politburo on the charge that he had continued his factional activities following his defeat at the Fourteenth Congress, exploiting his position as chair of the Comintern to build support among foreign communist parties while also building parallel organisations with the intention of establishing a second party in the Soviet Union.[97] Possibly in response to this development, Kamenev, Zinoviev and Trotsky expressed regret about their past political differences.[98] The renewed crisis lasted for more than a year, until the oppositionists suffered a final defeat at the Fifteenth Congress which voted to expel the 'active leaders of the Trotskyist opposition' from the Party.[99]

Employing similar political tactics to that of the preceding winter, the revived opposition attacked the CC majority on the grounds that its general line served the interests of the NEP-bourgeoisie and the rural

[97] *KPSS* v *rezoliutsiakh*, vol. 4, pp. 48–54. [98] Halfin, *Intimate Enemies*, p. 228.

[99] The Congress expelled seventy-five members as Trotskyists as well as twenty-three of the 'clearly counterrevolutionary' Sapronov group. *KPSS* v *rezoliutsiakh*, vol. 4, p. 313. Trotsky and Zinoviev had already been expelled by a joint plenary session of the CC and Central Control Commission held in October. Ibid., pp. 249–50.

kulaks at the expense of the working class, therefore compromising the country's path to socialism. This critique was supplemented by charges of organisational malfeasance to the effect that CC loyalists prevented the oppositionists from airing their views.[100]

Sergei Kirov addressed both of these issues when he visited KP on 4 August to report on the decisions of the July CC plenum. The *gubkom* secretary spoke on the familiar problems of the NEP and defended party policy by arguing that the extensive operation of private capital in the economy did not pose a threat to the state-owned, socialist industrial sector. Then, responding to the oppositionists' protests regarding their treatment by the CC majority, Kirov went on to ridicule Zinoviev's and Kamenev's political about-turn in allying with Trotsky and adopting the political positions they had fought him over in 1923.[101] Interestingly, contributions from the floor were largely confined to the second theme of Kirov's report. Grigoriev spoke in favour of the opposition, demanding more intra-party democracy and greater rights for oppositionists to present their views. Kodatskii responded by recognising that there were differences of opinion within the Party but went on to warn against the 'formation of grouplets'. Finally, Kirillov expressed zero tolerance for factionalism, stating that he and other workers from the bench demanded 'a monolithic Party'.[102]

Tensions between the opposition and the CC majority remained high throughout the autumn of 1926. On the first day of October, *Pravda* led with an article which inverted the opposition's criticisms, accusing its members of undermining the country's socialist prospects by breaking ranks just at the time that economic restoration had been achieved and the Party was about to embark on the construction of socialism proper. A month later, the fifteenth all-Union Party Conference condemned the opposition as a social–democratic deviation using revolutionary rhetoric to mask its essentially opportunist policy.[103]

Despite this escalation, however, a KP party meeting held in October to discuss the growing rift in the CC was addressed by none other than Zinoviev accompanied by the former *gubkom* secretary Grigorii Evdokimov and the implacable Sarkis. Zinoviev was given a standard ten-minute time slot as a contributor from the floor, which was then extended, following a vote by hand, by another fifteen minutes. Zinoviev

[100] Daniels, *Conscience of the Revolution*, p. 304. [101] TsGAIPD, f. 1012, op. 1, d. 266, l. 175.
[102] Ibid., l. 176–77. [103] *Pravda*, 1 October 1926; *KPSS* v *rezoliutsiakh*, vol. 4, pp. 108–16.

was not granted a further extension and he was cut off when his extra time ran out by Ivan Gaza, who was chairing the session.[104]

The organisation's attitude towards the opposition remained reasonably accommodative for several months after the Party's all-Union Conference. On 15 January 1927, 1,260 KP communists assembled to hear a report on the latest plenary session of the Comintern executive.[105] By that time, the Party's leadership of the Comintern had emerged as a major issue of contention between the CC majority and the United Opposition, with the oppositionists accusing the majoritarians that their policy undermined the prospects of world revolution.[106] The question notes passed to the presidium from the floor, thus reflected the rank-and-file's interest in both international affairs and their connection to the brewing party crisis. As shown in the following sample, the questions posed suggest that at that stage the rank-and-file still regarded the conflict in the upper echelons of the Party with curiosity rather than any firm conviction either way:

> What party work are the oppositionists doing? Trotsky, Kamenev etc.
>
> Can the opposition mess with the situation in China? How?
>
> What is Zinoviev currently doing? What is his problem with rationalisation? Is he for it or not? What is the difference between socialist and capitalist rationalisation?
>
> What is the dispute over the Chinese and Polish questions?[107]

Six months later, at the next general assembly of KP communists held to discuss international affairs, the mood on the factory floor had become markedly different. The meeting had been scheduled for 9 June to hear a report by *Leningradskaia Pravda* editor Aleksandr Ugarov on the Comintern executive plenum that had taken place in May. By that time, the Comintern's China policy of an alliance between the Communist Party of China and the nationalist *Guomindang* had suffered a catastrophic failure after the nationalists turned on their communist partners in April 1927, killing several thousand in the process. Although the Chinese strategy of the Comintern had played no part in the early rounds of the United Opposition's struggle against the CC majority, the obvious failure of the official policy became a significant source of ammunition for the struggling minority. The May Comintern plenum was the first major

[104] TsGAIPD, f. 1012, op. 1, d. 270, ll. 143–46, cited in Kostiuchenko, *Istoriia*, pp. 252–54.
[105] TsGAIPD, f. 1012, op. 1, d. 418, l. 1.
[106] Isaac Deutscher, *The Prophet Unarmed: Trotsky 1921–1929* (London: Verso, 2003), pp. 233–54.
[107] TsGAIPD, f. 1012, op. 1, d. 418, l. 2.

forum in which the opposition attacked the majority leaders on these grounds.[108]

The meeting that heard the report on the plenum convened under the shadow of dark events that had taken place far closer to home than those of remote China. On 26 May, while the Comintern plenum was in session, the diplomatic crisis between Britain and the USSR, that had been gathering pace since a police raid on the offices of the Soviet diplomatic mission in London two weeks earlier, came to a head. The Baldwin government severed relations with the Soviet Union and cancelled the Anglo–Soviet trade agreement of 1921, thus initiating the 1927 war scare in the USSR.[109] On 7 June, a counter-revolutionary émigré assassinated the Soviet ambassador to Poland Petr Voikov inside the Warsaw central rail station. Voikov was meeting Arkadii Rozengol'ts, the former ambassador to Britain who was on his way to Moscow following the break of relations between the two countries.[110] The same evening, in Leningrad, another group of counter-revolutionaries led by the former White captain Viktor Larionov carried out a bombing attack against a centrally located party club on the Moika river, injuring several party members and successfully escaping to Finland.[111]

The day after the attack, several party organisations demonstrated throughout the country in protest against the growing belligerence of the enemies of Soviet power. In Leningrad, KP communists produced one of the most militant resolutions, vowing to defend the USSR against foreign aggression and denouncing imperialism and 'its faithful servants and minions, social-democrats and socialists of all hues'.[112]

In such circumstances, it should come as no surprise that the benign curiosity towards the United Opposition demonstrated by party activists some months earlier had by that time given way to a much more polarised political climate within the KP organisation. Following Ugarov's report, Tuzhikov, the first contributor from the floor, sought to defend the opposition's line on China, demanding to know why the Party was not supporting a 'soviet line' and going on to argue that the opposition supported cooperation with the *Guomindang* as long as it was 'critical'.[113]

108 Deutscher, *Prophet Unarmed*, pp. 266–80.

109 Jon Jacobson, *When the Soviet Union Entered World Politics* (Berkeley: University of California Press, 1994), p. 222.

110 *Pravda*, 8 June 1927.

111 *Pravda*, 9 June 1927. Larionov later published a memoir account of the attack under the title *Boevaia vylazka v SSSR* (Paris: Bor'ba za Rossiiu, 1931).

112 *Pravda*, 9 June 1927.

113 TsGAIPD, f. 1012, op. 1, d. 418, l. 95.

This hardly inflammatory speech provoked the rage of Ruzin, who denounced Tuzhikov as an oppositionist whose arguments could convince only the politically illiterate. 'The opposition' he argued 'is only offering demagogy. We cannot allow any disunity in our ranks at this stage'.[114]

Some of the speakers that took the floor after Ruzin tried to keep the focus of discussion on the relative merits of the Comintern's China policy, in what might have been an attempt to de-escalate. The inopportune timing of the oppositionists' publication of their differences with the CC majority, however, made such efforts futile. Taking the floor after a speaker had criticised the opposition's radical line on the grounds that China's proletariat was still young, Sharkov told the meeting that the murder of Voikov in Warsaw required every party member to be on alert, while the opposition wanted 'to have a discussion'. Ivan Gaza then took the floor to denounce the 'Declaration of the 84 (sic)' as a 'shameless (*nagleishii*) attack against the Party'.[115]

Gaza's speech seems to have acted as a signal to the more militant opponents of the opposition that the time for restraint was over, for the content and tone of the contributions that followed it are markedly different, with very little to say on Comintern politics but quite vocal in their condemnation of the opposition's factionalism. Thus, Smirnova, a non-KP worker present at the meeting, said the following: 'We don't have oppositionists in our collective. But one must feel for KP, when they have workers running about the shops distributing silly leaflets. The opposition is speculating on our difficulties. Enough!'[116] The question notes attached to the meeting's protocol provide a still stronger indication of the growing impatience of the rank-and-file with the opposition. Out of eighteen *zapiski* in total, thirteen contained questions or statements demanding Trotsky's and Zinoviev's expulsion from the Party.[117]

On 18 August the KP party organisation met again to discuss the results of the joint plenary session of the CC and Central Control Commission that had convened earlier that month to review a Politburo motion to expel the leaders of the opposition from the CC.[118] Following a declaration by the opposition of its unconditional commitment to the defence of the Soviet Union, the party tribunal issued a formal reprimand and concluded its deliberations without taking any further disciplinary action against Trotsky and his allies.[119] By that time, however, the growing schism within the leadership had already become widely known amongst

[114] Ibid., l. 96. [115] Ibid., l. 96 [116] Ibid., l. 97. [117] Ibid., ll. 100–1.
[118] Deutscher, *Prophet Unarmed*, pp. 285–95. [119] *KPSS* v *rezoliutsiakh*, vol. 4, pp. 202–9.

the rank-and-file and could, thus, no longer be contained without a fight. Thus, instead of following the standard format of a main report followed by discussion, the meeting's agenda also included a supplementary report (*sodoklad*) by Grigoriev, a supporter of the opposition.

The meeting protocol indicates that Grigoriev was interrupted by loud heckling from the floor and had to cut his report short after a motion by the presidium to allow him to continue his talk was voted down by the assembly. Tuzhikov faced similar hostility and was also shouted down mid-speech. In this climate, it was an easy task for party loyalists to focus on the opposition's factionalism without having to confront any of the issues that its leaders were trying to wield as political weapons against the CC majority. Almost all of the speakers who took the floor to attack the opposition did so on the basis of its systematic violation of the ban on factions. Unlike past meetings, no energy was expended on arguing on about the wisdom of party policy on China or even the national economy. As one speaker put it, the assembly could not afford to 'lose time arguing about the Party's unity'.[120]

Even those communists who were not comfortable with the way the oppositionists were being treated by the majoritarians could not but condemn violations of party discipline. Such views were expressed by Baranovskii, an old Putilov communist who had left the factory to serve on the Smolensk Control Commission. The party enforcer argued that the oppositionists had the right to present their views to the meeting and distanced himself from attempts to shout them down, stating that their contributions should and would be properly recorded. Nevertheless, he went on to condemn their attempts to bring the issue outside the confines of the Party, 'at train stations etc.' and called on them to respect the rules of discipline.[121]

The meeting concluded with two separate resolutions being put to the vote. The one supporting the CC majority was overwhelmingly carried and consisted of the usual expressions of approval of the Party's general line along with threats of expulsion for unrepentant factionalists. The opposition's resolution fell with only sixteen votes in favour, but its content is worth mentioning here because it demonstrates the extent to which the rift had by that time become irreparable. The motion demanded

[120] TsGAIPD, f. 1012, op. 1, d. 418, l. 148.

[121] Ibid., ll. 150–51. Baranovskii was referring to a possibly spontaneous demonstration held by the opposition at the Yaroslavl' train station in Moscow to protest against the banishment to the Far Eastern town of Khabarovsk of Ivar Smilga, a prominent revolutionary hero who had joined the opposition. Deutscher, *Prophet Unarmed*, 283–84.

not only space in the party press for the expression of its views, but also the recognition of these views as correct and their immediate implementation by the CC.[122] This clause, which could scarcely have done the oppositionists any favours, seems calculated to provoke and can hardly be ascribed to mere political naivety. It seems rather that, despite the purported truce agreed at the top, the tensions that had been generated by the brewing crisis within the KP organisation had by that time become impossible to contain. The oppositionists were no longer seeking to win over the organisation, they were attempting to make their presence as strongly felt as possible before the inevitable showdown. Belying the relatively restrained language of the majority resolution, the question notes attached to the meeting protocol suggest that the majoritarians had also ceased to entertain any notions of reconciliation.[123]

As the conflict at the top reignited in the run up to the Fifteenth Party Congress, KP party meetings also became tenser affairs. On 29 September, the party assembly met again to elect its new leading organs for the following six-month period. The supporters of the opposition put forward a separate slate of candidates for the organisation's bureau. More than its inevitable defeat, it is the composition of the slate that reflects the opposition's isolation within the organisation; only five of the proposed candidates' names were different from the majority-proposed list.[124] The discussion of amendments to the majority slate that followed its confirmation by the meeting also became caught up in the internal party struggle, as allegations about the oppositionist past of some of the candidates came to dominate the process. Even Gaza came under fire, with another candidate stating that he had been a Trotskyist in the past. This elicited a furious response from the *partorg*, who went on to query his accuser about his whereabouts during the Civil War.[125] The last candidate to be reviewed before the final confirmation of the slate was Smirnov, the organiser of the wagon workshop party group mentioned earlier in this chapter. Having been challenged about his oppositionist past, Smirnov took the floor to admit that he had supported the New Opposition in the run up to the Fourteenth Congress but had broken with it at the time of Zinoviev's attack on the CC. He then claimed that he had since been approached by supporters of the United Opposition and asked to sign

[122] TsGAIPD, f. 1012, op. 1, d. 418, ll. 158–59.

[123] One *zapiska* author, for example, wondered: 'Why the devil (*kakogo-zhe cherta*) are they calling for decisions against the opposition while handing out mild punishments. Expel from CC and if necessary from VKP (b).' Ibid., l. 160.

[124] TsGAIPD f. 1012, op. 1, d. 419, l. 77. [125] Ibid., l. 79.

their platform, which he refused. Finishing his response, Smirnov condemned the oppositionists for their attempts to organise non-party workers around their views and stated that, in his view, 'they would not be against an armed coup'.[126]

Tensions inside the KP organisation came to a head after the October plenum of the CC finally expelled Trotsky and Zinoviev from the Party. On the first day of November 1927, the communists of KP assembled once more to hear a report on the decisions of the Party's leading body. The protocol record of the meeting suggests that the last confrontation between majoritarians and oppositionists was extremely acrimonious. Following the main report, Grigoriev and Leontiev took the floor to protest the exclusion of the opposition's views from the party press and argue that workers supportive of the CC majority were not fully informed of the substance of the intra-party dispute. The assembly heard their speeches but went on to deny speaking rights to Oskar Tarkhanov, the organisation's former deputy secretary in 1924–25 and prominent Zinovievite who had since been working as a political advisor in China.[127]

As Tarkhanov was no longer a member of the organisation, the decision was not strictly speaking against the rules. Nevertheless, the reaction of the oppositionists to having one of their ablest allies barred from the meeting was, not surprisingly, to protest. The protocol record notes 'disruption' of the assembly by the oppositionists in response to the decision to bar Tarkhanov, followed by threats of disciplinary action by Antipov, who chaired the meeting. Things in the hall apparently calmed down enough for the meeting to continue only after the assembly ejected Grigoriev following a motion by Ivanov.[128] The latter then took the floor to condemn oppositionist factionalism, stating that Grigoriev did not recognise the authority of the coming Fifteenth party Congress, viewing it instead as 'an all-Russian *aktiv* meeting'. At that, he was interrupted by Mukhin, who blandly confirmed that this was so, to applause from the oppositionists still present. Ivanov then concluded his speech by warning the oppositionists that if it were truly their intention to defy the Party's sovereign body, their only remaining option would be to come out in armed rebellion against the Soviet state.[129]

[126] Ibid., l. 80.

[127] Ibid., l. 96. For a brief sketch of Tarkhanov's eventful life, see M. A. Alekseev et al., *Entsiklopediia voennoi razvedki, 1918–1945 gg.* (Moscow: Kuchkovo Pole, Voennaia Kniga, 2012), p. 769.

[128] TsGAIPD f. 1012, op. 1, d. 419, l. 96.

[129] Ibid., ll. 98–99.

The last major intervention in favour of the opposition came from Ivan Bakaev, the decorated Chekist who had chaired Petrograd's security commission during the Civil War. Bakaev was attending the assembly in his capacity as a member of the Party's Central Control Commission and, unlike Tarkhanov, could not be barred from speaking. In any case, the assembly seems to have heard his appeal for party unity and detailed defence of Trotsky and Zinoviev with considerable interest, as Bakaev was the only speaker to have his fifteen-minute speaking slot extended by an extra ten minutes.[130] Nevertheless, whatever the extent of Bakaev's popularity or rhetorical ability, it was not enough to sway the KP party assembly away from the CC majority. The resolution passed at the end of the meeting approved the decisions of the October plenum and condemned Trotskyism once again.[131] On 29 December, when Sergei Kirov visited the factory to personally deliver the report on the Party's Fifteenth Congress, only one person took the floor to defend the views of the defeated opposition while, with few exceptions, most of the question notes concerning the opposition read more like inquiries about the fate of its leaders as opposed to the indignant denunciations of factionalism and defiant rejections of orthodoxy that been pouring onto the presidium's desk in the previous months.[132]

## 2.5 Conclusion

Two years after it first emerged as a stronghold of Zinoviev's New Opposition, the KP party organisation had been transformed into a pillar of CC loyalism. Given the extent of this transformation, it may be useful here to offer some remarks regarding the implications of the preceding account for our understanding of the place of the primary party organisation in late-NEP Soviet society.

Leningrad communists rallied to the New Opposition because its pro-industrial political platform resonated among workers who felt, with reason, that they were not getting their fair share out of the economic growth generated by the NEP. In order to reintegrate the organisation into the political mainstream, the new regional leadership had to follow a two-pronged strategy based on improving economic performance so as to deprive the opposition of its most potent argument while at the same time rebuilding the party organisation on the basis of the CC majority line, without alienating rank-and-file members who had initially sided with

[130] Ibid., ll.106–7. [131] Ibid., l. 138. [132] Ibid., l. 149.

Zinoviev. These two tasks were almost the sole concern of all levels of the organisation for several months after January 1926. Such efforts notwithstanding, there is little doubt that the economic hardship that had fuelled the party crisis persisted, in less acute form, throughout 1926–27 and it was around this issue that re-emboldened supporters of the opposition agitated after Kamenev and Zinoviev allied with Trotsky in mid-1926, well before Chinese affairs became an issue in the internal struggle. Why then did the resurgent opposition fail to mount a challenge similar to that of 1925–26, even within the confines of the KP party organisation?

We have little reason to doubt the veracity of the oppositionists' claims regarding their exclusion from the press and the suppression of their organisational activities. Neither of these things was sanctioned by either the party Rules or the laws of the Soviet Union. Nevertheless, it would hardly be plausible to suggest that reading articles in *Pravda* would have done more to attract KP communists to the opposition than the visits of such of its luminaries as Zinoviev, Sarkis and Bakaev to the factory grounds. As it was thus possible for leading oppositionists as well as rank-and-file supporters to put their views to the thousand-plus strong KP party assembly, the root causes of the oppositions' defeat must be sought in conditions other than censorship and organisational pressures, even though these constraints certainly limited its ability to constitute itself into a coherent political subject at an all-Union level.

The failure of the opposition should rather be seen as evidence that the response of the new Leningrad leadership to the 1925–26 party crisis was working. As we have seen, the Party's economic initiatives after the Fourteenth Congress were amenable to interpretations that favoured workers on the shop-floor. Putilovite communists could and did argue that cost-cutting and rationalisation were best achieved at the expense of the factory's inflated and poorly performing administration. The June 1927 general assembly of the KP organisation where Ter-Asaturov denounced the factory administration as corrupt bureaucrats took place just as the struggle against the United Opposition was reaching its crescendo. It demonstrated that it was possible to be against the NEP-era industrial establishment while remaining on the side of the leadership. The Party's economic policy in the last years of the NEP not only pulled the rug from under the opposition's feet by declaring industrialisation to be the order of the day, but crucially also gave rank-and-file communists the opportunity to pursue their immediate interests while remaining part of the political mainstream. Thus, it also made it both desirable and possible for former rank-and-file oppositionists to become CC loyalists, depriving the opposition of potential cadres as well as arguments, as demonstrated by the case of Smirnov who, from being a supporter of Zinoviev until December 1925, had by January 1926 become a party organiser in his shop. There is little reason to suggest that this process was peculiar to KP.[133]

Having thus secured the opposition's defeat at the grassroots level, it became easy sport for the CC majority to convincingly ridicule the Trotskyists' claim to represent the genuine views of the rank-and-file and the Party's true Bolshevik spirit, making their defeat at the Fifteenth Congress a foregone conclusion.[134] This outcome had significant implications for the subsequent development of Soviet grassroots politics, especially with regard to their function within the USSR's one-party system. The opposition's refusal to openly reject the Bolshevik Party's monopoly on power and organise itself into a separate political organisation has been cited by many scholars as one of the major factors that contributed to its defeat.[135] By adhering to single-party rule, the argument goes, the opposition locked itself into an irresolvable political contradiction whereby it had to constantly scale back its activities in order to deflect accusations of factionalism by the CC majority. Notwithstanding its merits, this argument still leaves open the question of why the leadership of the opposition never took the decisive step of organisational separation. Although this is usually attributed to the subjective commitment of Trotsky and his allies to the organisational principles of Bolshevism, the account offered here suggests that there was another, equally important factor at play.

We have already seen that the Lenin Levy attracted workers into the Party on the promise of influence and participation in a political system that promoted their class interests. The institutional manifestation of this system in industry was the partnership between management bodies and trade-union committees underpinned by the leadership of both by the Party, the so-called triangle. Party membership gave workers the opportunity to exert political pressure on management while also providing support for their colleagues' demands. This was only possible within the institutional framework of the Soviet party-state, where the Party was fused

[133] For a different Leningrad case study, see Halfin, *Intimate Enemies*, pp. 228–70.

[134] A *Pravda* editorial published shortly after the October plenum remarked snidely that the opposition 'seems to imagine its "influence on the masses" to be growing proportionally to its own menshevisation (*omen'shevichivanie*)'. *Pravda*, 29 October 1926.

[135] See indicatively, Deutscher, *Prophet Unarmed*, pp. 218–19, etc., Halfin, *Intimate Enemies*, pp. 260–61; John Eric Marot, 'Trotsky, the Left Opposition and the Rise of Stalinism: Theory and Practice', *Historical Materialism* 14, no. 3 (2006): 175–206.

with and at every level senior to the state. Appeals to party policy would have been meaningless in a situation where parties alternated in government and public officials, like factory administration staff, could claim to be apolitical. In 1926–27, as economic conditions improved and party policy became more closely aligned to the interests of heavy industry, there was little incentive for communist workers to jeopardise their influence at the point of production by splitting the organisation and every reason for them to react to any initiatives that threatened its unity with negativity, as they did. Rank-and-file oppositionists who, in Leningrad, had until recently themselves been part of the local majority, could hardly have failed to see this.[136]

There were, thus, strong social factors pertaining to the interests of rank-and-file communists, the very constituency that the opposition was hoping to attract, mitigating against full organisational separation. Having established this, the implications of the opposition's defeat can now be more clearly stated. First, the whole process trained the rank-and-file to use party orthodoxy to its advantage and regard challenges to it as threats to its own interests. Second, the outcome taught the central leadership that it could rely on the rank-and-file to see off challenges to its power. In January 1926, the CC had to send some of its most prominent members to win back Leningrad from the Zinovievites factory by factory. A year or so later, it could let Zinoviev visit *Krasnyi Putilovets* while trusting low-ranking functionaries like Ivan Gaza to maintain the rank-and-file's loyalty to the centre. The result was that the KP party organisation never again became a space where party policy could be seriously contested as such. The same was true for the party apparatus more broadly. Zinoviev's Leningrad gambit was the first and last time an opposition had wrenched a major part of the party machine from CC control by mobilising the membership. Although broader at the top, the United Opposition turned out to be much weaker on the ground.

Ultimately, the Lenin enrolment had worked. It had created a mass activist base that the Bolshevik leadership could rely on to promote party policy and see off factional challenges. This suggested that the leadership had succeeded in healing the perceived rift between the Party and the proletariat created during the Civil War. By the same measure, it had also

[136] It seems indeed that concerns about the factional nature of their activities and the attendant dangers of expulsion were common amongst grassroots oppositionists. Halfin, *Intimate Enemies*, p. 253. The return *en masse* of the oppositionists to the Party after the launch of the First FYP demonstrated that Stalin was firmly committed to industrialisation and further underlines this point. Marot, 'Trotsky', pp. 200–6.

rendered irrelevant the introspective debates that had accompanied the launching of the NEP. The membership had rallied to the CC banner, endorsing party policy and fatally undermining oppositionists' claims to represent genuine proletarian sentiment. By the end of 1927 then, the leadership had conclusively defeated all challenges to its management of the NEP and gained the trust of the rank-and-file. The next challenge to the political consensus would not come from an ambitious opposition, but from the CC majority itself.

CHAPTER 3

# *Laying the Foundations*

## *The Rank-and-File and Rapid Industrialisation*

The political battles of the mid-1920s had been fought over the dizzyingly high stakes of the right to determine the future of the revolution. By early 1928 the chief challengers to the CC majority had been comprehensively defeated, with Zinoviev capitulating and the implacable Trotsky exiled to Kazakhstan. With few remaining political obstacles, many in the country must have expected that the victorious leadership would stick to its hitherto successful NEP course of moderate but sustained industrial expansion.

Things turned out rather differently. In addition to condemning the United Opposition, the Fifteenth Party Congress also approved resolutions 'On the directives of the formulation of the Five Year Plan for the people's economy' and 'On work in the village'.[1] Setting the country on the path of comprehensive industrialisation and laying the groundwork for the promotion of collectivised agriculture, these documents were a response to the concerns that had fuelled the oppositionist challenges of the preceding years. Over the course of 1928, a combination of domestic and internal crises induced the leadership to set more ambitious output targets in order to overcome the country's industrial backwardness once and for all. By the time the first Five Year Plan (FYP) was formally adopted by the Fourteenth Congress of Soviets in May 1929, its growth projections implied nothing less than a root-and-branch revolution in the socio-economic life of the Soviet Union.

Stalin himself confirmed as much in a *Pravda* editorial on the twelfth anniversary of the October Revolution, where he described 1929 as the year of the 'great breakthrough on all fronts of socialist construction'. The general secretary argued that the success of the first year of the FYP demonstrated that the party had successfully used the tactical retreat of

[1] *XV s'ezd Vsesoiuznoi Kommunisticheskoi Partii (b). Dekabr' 1928 goda. Stenograficheskii otchet* (Moscow: Gosudarstvennoe Izdatel'stvo, 1928), pp. 1290–317.

the NEP period to launch a full-scale attack on all remaining positions of capitalism in Soviet society. The task ahead consisted in laying the foundations for the complete transformation of the USSR into a socialist society.[2]

The Great Breakthrough article indicated that the uneasy compromises holding the NEP together were no longer in force. Dragging the USSR into the age of metal and mechanisation was going to be a disruptive process, upending the delicate social contract of the 1920s from the factory to the village. As we shall see, the launch of the first FYP triggered the emergence of the last organised opposition amongst the Bolshevik leadership. Unlike, however, what had been the case in the mid-1920s, the chief challenge to the CC line was not dissent in its own ranks but the scale of the task it had undertaken. The plan's ambitious economic goals exacerbated the social tensions of the NEP as the drive to expand capacity and increase labour productivity inevitably strained industrial relations in Soviet factories.

Aware of this, the leadership framed the FYP from the very start as a giant political campaign that would require the deployment of the full efforts and resources of the Party. In April 1929, the Sixteenth All-Union Party Conference issued a political resolution approving the finalised version of the FYP produced by the state planning commission. The resolution noted, however, that the successful implementation of the FYP would face a range of obstacles 'flowing out of the intensity of the plan' and further compounded by the 'intensification of the class struggle and the resistance of capitalist elements'. To overcome these difficulties, it was deemed necessary to promote 'a most great increase in the activism and organisation of the working masses' and channel this force towards increasing industrial production and 'against the bureaucratic degeneration of the state apparatus'.[3]

In response to the challenges of economic dislocation, bureaucratic recalcitrance and social inertia, the Party would have to rally its core constituency of industrial workers to the FYP banner. In practice, this meant that the communist rank-and-file assembled during the NEP would now have to earn its stripes as the vanguard of its class. This was not a straightforward process. Although grassroots communists were, as we have seen, extremely keen to hold managers' feet to the fire, the rapid

[2] Stalin, 'God velikogo pereloma: k XVII godovshchine Oktiabria', *Pravda*, 7 November 1929.

[3] *XVI Konferentsiia Vsesoiuznoi Kommunisticheskoi Partii (b). Stenograficheskii otchet* (Moscow: Gosudarstvennoe Izdatel'stvo, 1929), p. 299.

industrialisation the FYP aimed at entailed the technological and organisational transformation of the labour process while placing extremely high demands on the country's working class. Party activists were, thus, expected to take the lead in implementing a dizzying overhaul of their very social milieu. At the same time, by recasting the Soviet working class, the Party was transforming its own base of support.

Examining the first FYP period from the perspective of the rank-and-file thus involves following two distinct but tightly intertwined processes as they played out on the factory floor: the formation of post-NEP Soviet labour relations and the adaptation of PPO activities to this change. The development and outcome of these processes speaks to the broader issue of the tension in party policy between the demands of ideological purity and technical competence. Accompanied by intensifying attacks on industrial experts and feverish campaigns of labour activism, the launch of the first FYP represented a triumph for the 'reds'. This chapter will show that the activity of the PPO in industrial enterprises tended to institutionalise the 'red', ideological dimension of party policy, transcribing its most radical elements onto the pattern of factory politics. The upshot was that subsequent recalibrations of industrial policy favouring technocratic management were undermined by the very fact of the Party's presence on the factory floor. This grassroots political dynamic became a key element of the industrial relations forged during the FYP, forming the basis of a pugnacious political culture that would define rank-and-file activism for the duration of the period examined in this study. To foreground this discussion, it would be useful here to briefly review the main effects of the FYP on industrial life in the Soviet Union.

## 3.1 The First FYP in Soviet Industry

The primary objectives of the FYP were the construction of large new enterprises and the renovation and expansion of those already in operation. These priorities are reflected in the staggering rates of capital investment anticipated by the plan, with the initial overall target standing at 225 per cent for the five-year period. Long established bastions of Soviet industry were themselves transformed by the FYP, with KP targeted for full-scale refitting.[4] Rapid industrial expansion brought about a sharp increase in the numbers of the industrial workforce, with 10.8 million people entering the

[4] Robert C. Allen, *Farm to Factory: A Reinterpretation of the Soviet Industrial Revolution* (Princeton: Princeton University Press, 2009), pp. 51–55; Carr and Davies, *Foundations*, pp. 314–15, 401–2;

workforce during the FYP, leading to a near doubling of the population of waged labourers from 11.9 million in 1929 to 22.6 million in 1933.[5]

In Leningrad, 133,000 workers entered industry in 1930 alone. Heavy industry grew most of all, with some 46 per cent of all Leningrad workers employed in the metal–electrical sector and machine-builders jumping from 23 per cent to 31 per cent of the total workforce in 1928–32.[6] The workforce of KP more than doubled, reaching a total of about 21,000 around 1931.[7] New arrivals from the countryside accounted for much of this increase, with 55 per cent of trade union members in 1931 being of peasant origin, compared to 9 per cent in 1930.[8] Women also entered industry *en masse*, making up 43.5 per cent of the entire workforce by 1932 compared to 37.1 per cent in 1928; the relative increase was greater in the male-dominated metal industry, from 9.1 per cent to 23.5 per cent.[9]

This was not a smooth transition. The sudden appearance of thousands of keen but inexperienced youths and women on the factory floor was both culturally alien to the patriarchal outlook of an older generation of workers and threatening to their position as relatively privileged, skilled labourers.[10] Contemporary Soviet scholars were aware of these tensions, viewing the latter group as a labour aristocracy with a vested interested in maintaining the pre-FYP state of Soviet industry and, thus, a potential obstacle to socialist construction.[11] Similarly, the influx of new workers from rural backgrounds undermined the status of factories as citadels of grassroots support for the socialist project. Many of the fresh industrial recruits certainly were youthful enthusiasts of the Bolshevik cause wishing to escape rural backwardness and take part in the construction of the bright urban future promised by the FYP. They could, however, just as easily be resentful opponents of the collectivisation drive then in full swing in the countryside.[12]

*Piatiletnyi plan narodno-khoziaistvennogo stroitel'stva SSSR*, 3 vols (Moscow: Izdatel'stvo 'Planovoe Khoziaistvo', 1930), vol 2, pp. 158–59.

5 Wendy Z. Goldman, *Women at the Gates: Gender and Industry in Stalin's Russia* (Cambridge: Cambridge University Press, 2002), pp. 75–77; Melanie Ilic, *Women Workers in the Soviet Interwar Economy: From 'Protection' to 'Equality'* (London: Palgrave Macmillan, 1998), pp. 36–37.

6 *Istoriia rabochikh Leningrada. 1703–1965*, vol. 2 (Leningrad: Nauka, 1972), p. 211.

7 TsGAIPD, f. 1012, op. 1, d. 801, l. 8.

8 *Istoriia rabochikh Leningrada*, p. 213.

9 Ibid., p. 216. Leningrad was representative of the broader Soviet trend, 42 per cent of the Soviet workforce being female after the completion of the FYP. Goldman, *Women at the Gates*, p. 1.

10 Ilic, *Women Workers*, pp. 37–38.

11 Zh. P. Depretto, 'Ofitsial'nye kontseptsii rabochego klassa v SSSR (1920–1930-e Gg.)', *Sotsial'naia Istoria. Ezhegodnik* (2004): 72–90, p. 78.

12 Sheila Fitzpatrick, 'The Question of Social Support for Collectivization', *Russian History* 37, no. 2 (2010): 153–77; David L. Hoffmann, *Peasant Metropolis: Social Identities in Moscow, 1929–1941* (Ithaca: Cornell University Press, 2000), p. 36.

At the same time, the plan's prioritisation of capital investment over the production of consumer goods exerted strong pressures on living standards and shortages in foodstuffs necessitated the introduction of rationing well before the devastating famine of 1932–33. Leningrad was amongst the first places to be hit by the supply crisis and a *gubkom* plenum introduced bread rationing on 23 March 1929, setting the norm at 800 grams per day for workers and 400 grams for white collar staff and dependents.[13] The rationing system often functioned poorly; recurring shortages and the low quality of the food distributed were a source of much discontent that occasionally erupted into acute episodes of industrial unrest.[14] These side-effects of crash industrialisation were offset to a significant extent due to the eradication of unemployment and the integration of women into the labour force, reducing the number of dependents per household. Nevertheless, the pressure on workers' living conditions was significant in terms of both real wages and the disruption caused by the upending of the NEP-era retail network.[15]

Shortages in consumer goods and random variations in the system of remuneration combined to give rise to one of the main features of Soviet industrialisation, the extremely high rates of labour turnover.[16] Along with the deskilling of the now much younger and less experienced working class, high turnover induced directors to over-hire in order to secure their enterprises against the labour shortage, thus compounding the problem and further increasing deskilling in individual enterprises.[17] Things were further complicated by the coexistence of multiple, sharply different types of work-crews throughout the first FYP period. These included radical

[13] Elena Osokina, *Za fasadom 'stalinskogo izobiliia': Raspredelenie i rynok v snabzhenii naseleniia v gody industrializatsii, 1927–1941* (Moscow: ROSSPEN, 2008), pp. 57–58. RGASPI, f. 17, op. 21, d. 2694, l. 6.

[14] The textile dominated Ivanovo Industrial Region seems to have been especially prone to strike action. In 1932, a strike over declining rations developed into a public demonstration attracting at least a few thousand people, significant numbers of which engaged in rioting. Donald Filtzer, *Soviet Workers and Stalinist Industrialization: The Formation of Modern Soviet Production Relations, 1928–1941* (London: Pluto Press, 1986), pp. 83–84; Jeffrey Rossman, 'The Teikovo Cotton Workers' Strike of April 1932: Class, Gender and Identity Politics in Stalin's Russia', *Russian Review* 56, no. 1 (1997): 44–69, pp. 48–52.

[15] L. I. Borodkin, 'Zhizn' v gorode v gody pervoi piatiletki: "uluchshenie material'nogo polozheniia" ili padenie real'noi zarplati?', *Vestnik Istorii i Literatury* (2010): 377–90.

[16] Between May and August 1930, the twenty most important construction projects in the USSR recruited 200,374 workers. Over the same period, 133,031 quit their jobs. Filtzer, *Soviet Workers*, p. 61.

[17] According to the KP administration, the factory was 'making up its full complement of labour power by recruiting and taking on unskilled labour, who gradually settle in and assume the place of skilled workers'. Ibid., p. 58. In the fourth quarter of 1931 alone, the wage fund in Leningrad was overspent by 30 million roubles. *Istoriia rabochikh Leningrada*, p. 211.

grassroots experiments like production communes and collectives, as well as forms of labour organisation inherited from the pre-revolutionary period like that paternalistic *artel'*.[18]

Workers were not the only industrial personnel to be affected by the rapid industrialisation drive. The Soviet forced march to modernity was accompanied by a far-reaching recalibration of the relationship between the state and its industrial cadre of engineers and administrators. We have already seen that communists at all levels of the apparatus had been at best uneasy with the state's reliance on bourgeois specialists inherited from the old regime. The massive expansion of available posts and the reluctance of incumbent industrial cadres to assume responsibility for the fulfilment of seemingly impossible production targets gave the leadership the opportunity to kill two birds with one stone. By launching a broad training programme for a new cohort of engineers and technicians (ITR) drawn from reliable, class-conscious party members and sympathisers, it would become possible to create a new industrial elite that would be both loyal to the Soviet order and on good terms with their workers, while neutralising the influence of the ever suspect bourgeois specialists. Thus, although in 1927 the Party counted less than 300 engineers amongst its ranks, over the period 1928–31 some 15,000 communists were mobilised to engineering and other colleges by party and trade-union organisations.[19]

As the social profile of the Soviet industrial elite changed, so did the attitude of the Bolshevik leadership towards its members. At the start of the industrialisation drive, the press launched an extensive campaign warning about the unreliability of bourgeois specialists and criticising the credulity with which communist executives treated their expert advice. This was initiated in March 1928, when *Pravda* broke the story of the subsequently much-publicised Shakhty affair, where prominent executives of the Donbass mining industry were charged with sabotage at the behest of foreign intelligence.[20] The following year, the leadership stepped up the

[18] The *artel'* was a group of workers headed by an elder (*starshina*) who distributed tasks and pay to members of the group. Hoffmann, *Peasant Metropolis*, p. 33. Production collectives were work units where pay was distributed according to three skill brackets, as opposed to the officially established eight brackets regulating pay. Kenneth M. Straus, *Factory and Community in Stalin's Russia: The Making of an Industrial Working Class* (Pittsburgh: University of Pittsburgh Press, 1998), pp. 147–48. Communes were the most egalitarian type of work unit, with members being paid according to the number of their dependants. Lewis H. Siegelbaum, 'Production Collectives and Communes and the "Imperatives" of Soviet Industrialization, 1929–1931', *Slavic Review* 45, no. 1 (1986): 65–84, p. 65.

[19] Sheila Fitzpatrick, 'Stalin and the Making of a New Elite, 1928–1939', *Slavic Review* 38, no. 3 (1979): 377–402, p. 384.

[20] *Pravda*, 10 March 1928.

pressure on industrial cadres by launching an all-Union campaign of self-criticism (*samokritika*). The campaign sought to tap into the energy of rank-and-file activists by encouraging them to expose 'without regard for personalities' (*ne vziraia na litsa*) all manifestations of bureaucratic obstinance, 'neglect of the interests of the masses and petty-bourgeois complacency'.[21]

By the second half of the FYP, however, it was deemed necessary to rebuild the authority of managerial staff. Stalin signalled this reorientation with a 1931 speech to select executives laying out six conditions for the successful development of Soviet industry. Published in *Pravda*, Stalin's speech stressed technical competence over ideological fervour and encouraged a more benevolent treatment of old regime managers and engineers who had demonstrated their loyalty to Soviet power.[22] Nevertheless, production activism remained a key part of the Party's industrial toolbox. After the launch of the FYP, measured, deliberative forms of workers' participation in management like the production conference gradually declined in prominence. In their place, socialist emulation (*sotssorevnovanie*) and the shock-work movement (*udarnichestvo*) emerged to spur workers to new feats of productivity. Combining sports-like competitiveness with military urgency, 'light brigades' of young workers labouring under red banners to condense the output of multiple shifts into one became a common sight in the plants and construction sites that sprang up during the *piatiletka*.[23]

The Great Break thus involved a bewildering remoulding of social structures. In industry, the upheaval eventually settled into a new form of labour relations that would remain at the heart of Soviet political economy for decades to come. Social historians of Soviet industry developed two main interpretative frameworks to account for this process. Thus, a long-standing tradition has held that Soviet industrialisation was the process by which a new managerial elite consolidated itself as the Soviet ruling class, subjugating the country's neutralised proletariat into a new system of exploitation.[24] By contrast, other scholars pointed out that core features of the industrialisation process, such as the chronic labour shortage that

[21] *KPSS* v *resoliutsiiakh*, vol. 4, pp. 338–42. [22] *Pravda*, 5 July 1931.

[23] Lewis Siegelbaum, 'Socialist Competition and Socialist Construction in the USSR: The Experience of the First Five-Year Plan (1928–1932)', *Thesis Eleven* 4, no. 1 (1982): 48–67.

[24] Filtzer, *Soviet Workers*; Murphy, *Revolution and Counterrevolution*; Jeffrey J. Rossman, *Worker Resistance under Stalin: Class and Revolution on the Shop Floor* (Cambridge, MA: Harvard University Press, 2009); Solomon M. Schwarz, *Labor in the Soviet Union* (New York: Praeger, 1951).

plagued Soviet factories and the multitude of official and unofficial channels for bargaining, provided workers with a degree of workplace power that was inconsistent with the notion of the USSR as an industrial autocracy. Soviet industrialisation became possible through the hammering out of a social contract between workers and the state which was ultimately compatible with the interests of both sides.[25]

Neither framework devoted much consideration to the particular role played by party organisations, except in so far as their leading bodies cooperated (or colluded) with management to keep factories running and the workers in line. In either case, the Party was analytically subsumed under the state administration, irrespective of whether this was conceived of as part of an exploitative ruling class or a less hostile managerial stratum under immense pressure from its superiors. As we will see presently, however, the position of the Party in industry was much more complicated. Far from being a mere element of the administrative apparatus, the Party was a distinct political space whose internal dynamics were determined both by the proletarian composition of its membership and its ideological orientation.

Having spent the last NEP years as both relentless critics of management and trouble-shooters of production, rank-and-file party activists now found themselves confronting rapidly changing realities. Primary party organisations would have to operate within and assimilate a much larger and younger workforce with little experience of factory life within the context of unprecedentedly demanding labour conditions. At the same time, they would have to learn to work closer with a new industrial elite promoted from their own ranks. The initiatives undertaken by the leadership in response to the myriad of problems thrown up over the course of the first FYP served to further complicate an already confused situation. To illustrate the place of these microprocesses in the grander scheme of the Great Break, we need to take a closer look.

## 3.2 Party Activism and Managerial Authority on the Factory Floor

In the first months of 1928, the USSR experienced a spike in labour unrest connected to the negotiation of a new collective agreement in industry.

[25] Chase, *Workers*; Kotkin, *Magnetic Mountain*; Lewis H. Siegelbaum, *Stakhanovism and the Politics of Productivity in the USSR, 1935–1941* (Cambridge: Cambridge University Press, 1988); Straus, *Factory and Community*. For a more detailed account of the literature, see Lewis H. Siegelbaum, 'The Late Romance of the Soviet Worker in Western Historiography', *International Review of Social History* 51, no. 3 (2006): 463–81.

According to secret police reports reaching Stalin's desk in January and February, the main point of contention appears to have been the reform of pay-rates and production norms which undermined the position of skilled workers.[26] An early January session of the Leningrad *gubkom* bureau noted with some concern that the labour disputes in the enterprises of the ship- and machine-building trusts tended to be extremely drawn out, resolving to refer future instances to Moscow.[27]

In the Party's primary organisations, this new wave of industrial unrest contributed to the already volatile political environment generated by two years of factional fighting. Question notes from a KP party meeting held to discuss workers' attitudes towards the new collective agreement indicate that the membership had a mixture of concerns about the new terms of employment. Some were worried that these could play into the hands of hostile forces. One note suggested that communists should be very attentive to the moods of their co-workers and make sure to bring their resentments to the attention of the organisation's bureau. Another particularly alarmed participant inquired whether it was true that recently reported instances of rioting in some Leningrad factories had been instigated 'by the old black-hundreds'.[28] Others, however, were rather keener to register their disapproval of the new agreement. Thus, one note asked the speaker to explain why textile workers at the *Ravenstvo* manufacture had had their pay recalculated at lower wage brackets: 'don't these things lead to strikes?' More candidly, another contributor bluntly stated that the speaker kept 'putting the blame for the strikes on the opposition. But with the pay cuts, I can swear that KP will soon enough have a strike too'.[29]

We have already seen that shop-floor tensions generated by policies like the Regime of Economy played a central role in the development of oppositionist sentiment amongst the rank-and-file and that the ability of CC supporters to address these issues had been key in securing grassroots support for the leadership. When, following publication of the Shakhty affair, the party press began to tell communists throughout the country that managerial staff were not to be trusted, it was thus preaching to the

[26] *Sovershenno Sekretno*, vol. 6, January and February reports.

[27] RGASPI, f. 17, op. 21, d. 2707, l. 1.

[28] The Black Hundreds were a pre-revolutionary ultra-nationalist movement that often engaged in thuggish violence against socialist activists. It is interesting that the note author mentions it here in connection to the strikes as, to the extent that Bolshevik communications linked labour unrest to organised subversion, it was mostly (and reasonably) attributed to Mensheviks, anarchists and other dissident leftists. Reference to this older foe suggests that these rumours drew from an older cultural memory and were independently generated.

[29] TsGAIPD, f. 1012, op. 1, d. 549, ll. 3–4.

converted. After the first press pieces on Shakhty had made the rounds in March, the CC held a plenary session in the second week of April in which it passed a resolution on the political implications of the matter. Significantly, the document criticised communist industrial cadres for the 'blind trust' in the work of old specialists and admonished party organisations not to confine their work to 'formal bureaucratic criticism' of industrial administrations. They were instead instructed to be sensitive to workers' testimonies and seek to actively involve them in 'the leadership of production'. In addition to the promotion of industrial activism in the form of production conferences and wall-newspapers, this would now have to include more intensive recruitment of young workers to training courses leading to executive positions.[30]

Two weeks later, the KP party organisation convened a general meeting attended by roughly 1,000 communist activists and about 100 non-members. The participants heard a report on the plenum by Aleksei Stetskii, a member of the *gubkom* bureau who also sat on the CC. Although the text of Stetskii's speech is not preserved in the archives, the minuted contributions of speakers from the floor are highly illuminative of the way the party rank-and-file received the leadership's signalling of this policy shift. The director Grachev was denounced as a demagogue by Sokolov who complained that the factory's chief executive had attempted to suppress an activist's critical report to the machine-building trust that KP was a part of. This, Sokolov argued, made a mockery of *samokritika*. He then went on to ridicule the incompetence of the factory's technical staff: 'They are refitting the cranes in our workshop and all the workers are laughing. It's obvious that they are doing it wrong, but the specialists won't listen to us.'[31]

Kairov, a worker from the tractor workshop, stated that workers were very concerned about the Shakhty affair and criticised the casual attitude specialists displayed towards their work. He suggested, however, that Grachev was getting too much of the blame, proposing instead to have 'the technical director give a report and grill (*zharit'*) him'. One Lander offered further examples of managerial insensitivity, recounting the story of a foreman – recently promoted from the workers' ranks – whose new invention had been ignored by engineers at a technical conference. Similarly, the superintendent of Lander's shop had flatly refused to speak to the paper produced by its *rabkory*, claiming that he only had to answer to the all-factory paper.[32]

30 *KPSS* v *resoliutsiiakh*, vol. 4, pp. 324–27.
31 TsGAIPD, f. 1012, op. 1, d. 549, l. 10.
32 Ibid., l. 11.

The unreliability of administrative staff was also a major theme in the more than sixty question notes that reached the chair of the meeting from the assembled crowd. One note mused whether 'there isn't an economic counterrevolution going on', when workers criticising the failures of technicians and engineers were threatened with disciplinary measures for inciting 'specialist-baiting'. Posing a question to which its author clearly had an answer, another note read thus: 'We know that our red engineers come out of the higher education institutes insufficiently prepared and certainly weaker than those of old times. Isn't the reason for this that they are taught by old specialists, hostile to soviet power?' A less reserved participant declared the whole factory a 'small nest of sabotage' because of the undue influence of the administration over the party organisation.[33] Predictably, the resolution adopted by the meeting reflected these concerns, proposing that the organisation should work towards getting administrators and engineers to report to workers more regularly.[34]

We cannot know whether the invention of Lander's foreman was dismissed by a condescending *spets* or if it was impractical or simply ineffective. Contributions like Lander's are, nevertheless, indicative of the political gear shift taking place on the factory floor during the wrapping up of the NEP. Although there had been little love lost between workers and managers in the preceding years, the PPO leadership had to some degree attempted to restrain its members and balance attacks on 'bureaucratism' with exhortations to work more and better. With the leadership signalling that it was no longer wise to rely on the available pool of specialist personnel for industrial growth, radicals were free to attack long-resented bosses and supervisors as politically suspect elements.

This tendency was even more apparent at the KP PPO general assembly held on 31 May 1928. At first glance, it would appear that the warning shots fired by the April CC plenum had been sufficient to shake the factory administration into a more cooperative relationship with the workforce. In his political report, Ivan Gaza expressed satisfaction at the improvement of work with specialists. 'Some are truly attempting to rely on workers organisation in the factory for their work.' Of course, he went on, there were others who should be shown the door because 'they see the party organisation simply as a way to improve their material position' and advance their careers.[35] Vigilance against unprincipled careerists was a mainstay of Bolshevik political culture. Gaza's comment did not, therefore, stand out as a particularly grave accusation against white collar staff.

[33] Ibid., l. 16. [34] Ibid., l. 13. [35] Ibid., ll. 28–29.

With respect to factory business, the rest of Gaza's report similarly remained balanced in its demands of workers and specialists. The *partorg* spoke about the perennial problem of labour productivity, noting that unit costs were rising due to the combined rise of wage rates, fuel and raw materials. Against this backdrop, he argued that it was impermissible that stoppages had led to the waste of over 200,000 labour hours. Truancy was also highlighted as an unhealthily common habit amongst KP workers, with Gaza noting that unauthorised absences cost the factory a million roubles yearly. It was particularly embarrassing that, in key shops like the tractor workshop, some 19 per cent of truants were communists. The fact that activists who were not themselves truants did not take the problem seriously was also not reassuring. 'What do party members say about [truancy]? Vodka is bad and must be eliminated.'[36]

Gaza's proposed remedies to the problems catalogued in his report reflected his conciliatory approach. By highlighting issues such as truancy, he was suggesting that party activists could do more to encourage their fellow workers to be more conscientious, thus revisiting the familiar theme of labour discipline. At the same time, he did not fail to mention that workers were losing interest in the factory's performance because their ideas were often ignored by specialists at production conferences; engineers also had a role to play in shaping workers' attitude towards labour. Similarly, Gaza did not delegate responsibility for labour productivity exclusively to workers. Their efforts could only be as effective as the broader organisation of the productive process allowed. This was the purview of the administration and its technical wing, whose performance had not particularly impressed the *partorg*. The continuous stoppages were, according to Gaza, due in large part to the 'incompetence of our shop administrations'. Gaza went on to recount one occasion where self-important engineers had installed inappropriate equipment against the advice of experienced workers. Sure enough, the shop had to revert to the old set-up causing further disruption. This he argued was a symptom of the fact that 'our technical personnel is irresponsible. This is the main problem. They do first and think later. We must demand more from technicians than from workers, their mistakes can cause more damage'.[37]

Gaza's position had not then changed significantly since 1926–27, when he had likewise encouraged workers to be more diligent and managers more sensitive. It is unlikely that the political shift signalled by the April CC plenum had failed to register with the veteran communist. Rather, it is

[36] Ibid., ll. 30–32. [37] Ibid., ll. 34–35.

more plausible that, as head of the factory's PPO, he was attempting to maintain decent working relationships with the administration to minimise disruption. The CC resolution had not demanded something radically different. The leadership had instructed party organisations to supervise industrial cadres more closely, not to purge them from the administrative apparatus.

The rank-and-filers, however, were not as amicably inclined. Khutoretskii from the iron rolling shop was the first to speak after the main report. He started by saying that 'after Shakhty, party members in the shops have begun to sniff out what's going on'. The shop administration and its technical specialists were taking no responsibility for severe planning mistakes, such as the buying of expensive machine tools that could not fit in the shop. The administration continued to employ 'useless cadres', 'like Smirnov', even after the organiser of the shop-level party organisation had recommended their removal. With regard to productivity, 'Grachev is going to call me a demagogue again', said Khutoretskii, but the main reason the factory experienced so many stoppages was the bad state of energy supply.

Liubenko, a communist from the KP saw-mill who rose to speak after Khutoretskii, began his intervention with a direct reference to the director: 'Comrade Grachev is already preparing his pencil and paper . . . despite the fact that I and the comrades who will speak after me will express ourselves softly, within the boundaries of soft *samokritika*'. Grachev's reaction to seeing Liubenko take the floor suggests that the director had had previous experience of dealing with the sawyer, who even in the partial transcript of the meeting found in the archives comes across as particularly cantankerous. His contribution is worth engaging with at some length, as it is particularly instructive regarding the political climate in industry after Shakhty.

A large part of Liubenko's talk consisted of criticising the competence and behaviour of individual engineers as well as the purported reluctance of the KP party leadership to take complaints against them seriously. Thus, he inquired rhetorically whether the case of engineer Veitkhin had been 'investigated to the end', concluding immediately that 'it has not. It has quietly fallen off the agenda'. Liubenko was equally disappointed by the tolerance shown to Freilich, a foreign expert employed by KP. The engineer had apparently expressed the following view about production conferences: 'There's nothing for me to do here. What is there to talk about? And generally, comrade workers, what is it that you talk about?' To make matters worse, technicians and superintendents seemed unperturbed about the fact that 'the opinion of engineer Freilich . . . does not agree with our opinion'. In fact, Liubenko claimed that when he confronted the factory's technical director Sablin about leaving Freilich's views unchallenged, the former responded by saying that 'well, he was being honest'. Clearly, Liubenko argued, this was evidence that the KP party bureau was not exerting sufficient pressure on the communist caucus of the factory administration to ensure that technical staff in a socialist enterprise behaved appropriately.[38]

A skilled agitator, Liubenko swiftly shifted from his criticism of the attitude of individual engineers to the more sensitive question of the broader political reliability of the *spetsy*. 'Comrade Gaza says that our engineers are loyal, more or less. But not long ago, there was an evening meeting of Moskovsko–Narvskii district engineers . . . I was going to speak there and lay out a bunch of problematic issues . . . The chair, Zul' spoke to Grachev and I was asked not to take part.' Not content with suppressing the criticism of concerned activists like himself, Liubenko suggested that bourgeois engineers had also taken to corrupting their communist subordinates. Several young activists who had a glowing record of social and political activism during their study courses had completely dropped out of public life since arriving to work in the factory. This was because the young engineers were 'dependent on the old *spetsy*'. In his conclusion, Liubenko made plain his preferred approach to resolving these problems: 'Given the signals (Shakhty), [our bureau] needs to do a lot more work and take [matters] more seriously. We must demand a far stricter policy to those *spetsy* that do not belong in our factory. Give them a passport: "Kindly clear off".'[39]

The meeting transcript notes that Liubenko's concluding sentence was met with a round of applause, suggesting that his views were not unpopular with the assembled communists. It is not hard to see why this was so. The speaker had skilfully weaved the many grievances held by workers against their immediate bosses into a comprehensive political narrative. The bourgeois *spetsy* were condescending and dismissive of workers' input, but they were abetted in this by the few communist industrial cadres that were meant to supervise them. Freilich was not only a haughty engineer who had no time for production conferences, he was also a foreign expert invited to assist in the factory's development. The Shakhty affair consisted of exactly the same elements: negligent party bureaucrats allowing foreign experts in league with the intelligence services of hostile powers to sabotage

[38] Ibid., ll. 75–77. [39] Ibid., l. 78.

Soviet industry. Liubenko was arguing that managers and the communists colluding with them were violating the principles of conscientious and harmonious cooperation among the three sides of the triangle. His solution for KP was analogous to that of the CC for Soviet industry as a whole: it needed a change of guard.

This thread was picked up by Fedorov, a *Komsomol* member who expressed disappointment at the factory administration and the organisation's leadership in equal measure. Fedorov complained that Gaza and the rest of the bureau had done very little to enlighten the youth about the burning questions of the day, meaning that the KP party was straggling in training the future political leadership of the enterprise. The failings of management were graver still:

> The youth needs and wants qualifications and training. This is a common issue. But we are not helped by management. Grachev is not so sure about the value of the factory vocational school and some industrial cadres want to cut the length of study to two years from three. But we need a cultured worker, a worker [who is a] social activist. ... *We don't yet have the qualifications that industry will need for the five-year plan.*[40]

The sour mood towards management prevalent amongst the organisation was predictably reflected in the question notes, several of which demanded a reduction in the factory's white-collar staff and pressed Gaza and the bureau to get tougher on misbehaving *spetsy*. In this climate, there was little that Grachev could say to convince his comrades that the factory administration was not an incubator of political hostility to socialist development. The last to take the floor, Grachev attempted to defend the administration's record by arguing that problems of labour discipline remained the chief cause of under-performance. He ended up in a shouting match with Liubenko when the latter interrupted his speech with accusations of lying, to which the director responded that 'criticising is easier than doing'.[41]

The Shakhty affair and the CC resolution outlining its political significance had, thus, removed whatever inhibitions restrained the rank-and-filers' anti-managerial sentiments. Combined with the leadership's emphasis on promoting a new generation of cadres, the political conjuncture had emboldened the radicals and isolated the representatives of managerial authority at the party grassroots. In attacking bureaucratism, rank-and-file communists were not breaking party discipline but

[40] Ibid., l. 81, emphasis added. [41] Ibid., ll. 93–94, 96.

implementing CC policy. Significantly, they were to a large extent anticipating rather than responding to leadership initiatives. Communist workers saw the centre shift from a political line demanding tight labour discipline and favouring amicable relations between workers and management, to one calling party members to battle against recalcitrant and politically suspect factory administrations. In a rousing statement issued in June 1928, the CC appealed to all members and working-class sympathisers to unleash the full force of *samokritika* against 'wicked bureaucratism' and 'bureaucratic degeneration' in the state apparatus. The appeal declared that the enormous task of industrialisation could not be completed without the 'supervision and control by the millions-strong masses of the whole of the [state] apparatus . . . clearing out unfit elements'.[42]

Thus, *spetseedstvo*, the anti-intellectualist practice of specialist-baiting that had been the scourge of many an engineer throughout the NEP period, became sanctioned by and institutionalised within the PPO, the very organisation charged with resolving social contradictions on the factory floor. At the same time, the new cadre policy offered opportunities for many ambitious communist specialists who were confident in their ability to replace the incumbents. On the eve of the Great Break, the party collective of Leningrad's Red Putilovite works thus provided the organisational and ideological framework for the formation of an alliance of militant workers and low-ranking technicians that would go on to become the protagonists of the First FYP. This was a critical maturation point in the process of developing the party rank-and-file into an element of the Soviet system of governance.

Simultaneously, the logic of mass supervision of industrial affairs from below expanded the remit of party organisations in the country's enterprises, leading inevitably to them encroaching upon the strictly technical dimension of production which in theory remained within the exclusive competence of management. Even before 1928, the Party had encouraged workers within and beyond its ranks to take an active interest in the productive process, registering their suggestions for improvement through conferences and other channels. Once, however, the exigencies of industrialisation had made the bottom-up control of the state apparatus the chief political priority of party organisations, technical matters such as the ordering of equipment became increasingly more prominent in general meetings and less distinct from the Party's own organisational affairs.

[42] *KPSS v rezoliutsiiakh*, vol 4, p. 339.

Thus, the May KP party meeting where Liubenko quarrelled with Grachev resolved that questions of capital expenditure, labour organisation, unit-costs, etc., were to be discussed at the shop-level cells of the organisation prior to the implementation of any decisions by the *tsekh* administrations.[43] This was in addition to by then familiar resolution items such as promoting production conferences and improving the uptake of workers' suggestions. The new course charted by the leadership was turning industrial party organisations into expanded production conferences. As we will see in Section 3.4, this development would end up playing a crucial part in the subsequent development of Soviet industrial relations. Ignoring the insights of workers' production conferences was one thing; party directives were an altogether different matter. Before examining this question, however, we need first to turn our attention to a more conspicuous consequence of the launching of the FYP; the emergence of a new opposition.

## 3.3 No Right Deviation

Suspicious attitudes towards managers and engineers were a generalised cultural phenomenon of the NEP-era that predated the Shakhty affair. They were also neither confined to the rowdy gatherings of the party rank-and-file nor a peculiar trait of the quarrelsome Leningraders. Delivering his political report to a plenum of the Party's Moscow Committee, the regional secretary Nikolai Uglanov was repeatedly interrupted from the floor because of his equivocation regarding the question of promoting new cadres from proletarian backgrounds. The Moscow chief had mused that rapid worker promotion could swell the bureaucracy with incompetent cadres and insisted that selection should be based on skill rather than social background. The contradistinction between the two left some of the audience unimpressed, with one heckler insisting that 'of the graduates we ought to take those who are from the factory'.[44]

Uglanov would subsequently emerge as one of the main leaders of the Right Opposition, the last publicly declared group of policy dissenters to be formed among the party leadership. Unlike most high-profile oppositionist groups before them, the Rightists did not seek to force a change in party policy but to prevent the leadership itself from doing so. In addition

[43] TsGAIPD, f. 1012, op. 1, d. 549, l. 99.

[44] *Vtoroi plenum MK VKP (b). 31 ianvaria – 2 fevralia 1928. Doklady i rezoliutsii*, cited in Fitzpatrick, 'Stalin and the Making of a New Elite', p. 283.

to Uglanov, the Right was led by Nikolai Bukharin, chief trade-unionist Mikhail Tomsky and head of government Aleksei Rykov. These leading Bolsheviks were united by their opposition to the abandonment of the NEP consensus signalled by the launch of the FYP, wherein the stability of cadres was but one aspect. The group began to cohere when its members successfully opposed increased grain procurement targets in mid-1928 and subsequently warned against the ambitious growth targets of the FYP. Their political activity reached a high point in February 1929, when Bukharin, Tomsky and Rykov sent a common statement to the joint session of the Politburo and the presidium of the Party's Central Control Commission in which they outlined their differences with Stalin's leadership. In April, a CC plenum condemned the 'Right deviation' and by 1930 its leaders had been removed from responsible leadership posts.[45]

In contrast to previous oppositionist groupings, the Rightists never posed a credible threat to the CC majority. They commanded neither the youthful enthusiasm of the various iterations of the Left challenge nor the mass organisational strength of the Zinovievites. Their support, thus, remained confined to some sections of the higher levels of the Moscow party organisation, especially those overlapping with the central state apparatus. To a large extent, this was a corollary of their political line. Support for a moderate status quo is rarely an effective tool for political mobilisation, but the NEP conventional wisdom of appeasing kulaks and relying on bourgeois engineers had been particularly unpopular with the party rank-and-file. Especially in Leningrad, where anti-NEP sentiment had only recently led to a rebellion against the CC, it is hardly surprising that the Rightist political platform attracted marginal support from the membership.[46]

Despite lacking a significant presence amongst the rank-and-file, the emergence of the Right did provide the background for a surge in political activity in the party grassroots. In addition to adopting the enhanced FYP and condemning the Right, the Sixteenth VKP (b) Conference in April 1929 also declared a 'purge (*chistka*) and verification (*proverka*) of members

45 Stephen F. Cohen, *Bukharin and the Bolshevik Revolution: A Political Biography, 1888–1938*, Reprint Edition (Oxford: Oxford University Press, 1980), pp. 277–90; Daniels, *Conscience of the Revolution*, pp. 353–60; *KPSS* v *rezoliutsiiakh*, vol. 4, p. 498. For the statement of the Rightists, see Vladimir Danilov, Roberta Manning and Lynne Viola (eds.), *Tragediia Sovetskoi derevni. Kollektivizatsiia i raskulachivanie. 1927–1939*, 5 vols. (Moscow: ROSSPEN, 1999–2006), vol. 1, pp. 530–37.

46 The only high-profile Leningrad communist to back the Right was Fedor Ugarov, the regional trade-union secretary. He was removed from his post by the *obkom* bureau in late March 1929. RGASPI, f. 17, op. 21, d. 2710, l. 1.

and candidates'. The Conference resolution noted that, although the Party made constant efforts to control the quality of its membership, it had not engaged in a general purge to remove apolitical, careerist and hostile elements from its ranks since 1921, when it had done so upon the victorious conclusion of the civil war. The grave challenges that confronted the USSR on the eve of the 'socialist offensive on all fronts' necessitated that the prompt removal from party ranks of elements that are 'alien to it, harmful to its success, indifferent to its struggle ... linked to the class enemy ... anti-Semites ... Trotskyites ... and supporters of other anti-party groups'. At the same time, the *chistka* was to provide an opportunity for a general review of the performance of party organisations, including the political literacy of their members, the comradely relations communists maintained with each other and the extent to which they remained in tune with the concerns of the non-party masses. To be successful, the purge would, thus, require the full employment of the toolkit of *samokritika*, including mass meetings and the press.[47]

The *chistka* was, thus, conceived as a mass, public campaign of political activism that would energise the rank-and-file in support of the FYP at the same time as removing those elements within the Party that were likely to disrupt its implementation. Significantly, this came after a time of relative calm in terms of the political life of the Party in industry. In the short interval between the final defeat of the United Opposition and the full-scale launch of the FYP, the KP party organisation returned to the familiar business of party building that had been the order of the day in early 1926, perennial conflicts of the rank-and-file with the administration notwithstanding. Like then, the oppositionists and their activities disappeared from the agendas of party meetings and the content of speakers' contributions, even though the question notes surviving in the archives do reflect considerable lingering interest on the part of the rank-and-file.[48] Instead, it was assumed once again that getting on with business would be the best way to return to normality. This is reflected in the figures of disciplinary procedures in the KP PPO. Between September 1927 and May 1928,

[47] *KPSS v rezoliutsiiakh*, vol. 4, pp. 483–90.

[48] This was the case for both sides. Most of the *zapiski* concerning the opposition in 1928 were inquiries about the fate of prominent oppositionists and the prospect of their return to major party posts and can be reasonably assumed to have come from their supporters. At the same time, however, quite a few of the notes reaching the presidiums were raising concerns about the pernicious influence of expelled oppositionists and warning of the possibility that they could provoke workers to riots. TsGAIPD, f. 1012, op. 1, d. 549, ll. 3–4, 19, 96, 214.

there were 121 disciplinary cases which led to 60 expulsions from a total membership of well over 2,000.[49]

Thus, in May 1928, at the first electoral general assembly of the KP party organisation held after the defeat of the United Opposition, Ivan Gaza could declare that the Party was now 'stronger than ever' and that the time had come to fully 'develop party democracy and *samokritika*', while joking that Trotsky had been right about one thing; 'the Party is always right'.[50] Attended by 1,411 delegates and lasting over five hours, the meeting was a milestone in the organisational consolidation of the KP PPO, as demonstrated by the meticulous detail in which the assembly went through its agenda. Gaza delivered the main report on behalf of the bureau which, although predictably focusing mostly on the familiar problems of factory life like truancy and accidents, devoted considerable time to the theme of the organisation's political rejuvenation. Having pronounced the party group to be at the peak of its strength, Gaza went on to praise the activities of the shop-level cells which had achieved record levels of participation and contributions during a recent round of bureau re-elections. The secretary then expressed his ambition to transform the shop-cells into 'genuine political centres on the factory floor', arguing that it was at that level that the rank-and-file membership of the organisation could most effectively exert its influence. This, he went on, would require a careful reorganisation of party meetings in order to ensure that their agendas included only relevant topics that could be meaningfully addressed at their level. In conclusion, Gaza admitted that the KP party organisation was still some way short of achieving this goal and urged his comrades to spare no effort in revitalising the shop-cells.[51]

Gaza's bureau report was followed by an equally long-winded account delivered by a representative of the monitoring commission which had been set up by the organisation's previous general assembly. The commission, composed of eleven experienced communist workers, was charged with the task of checking the bureau's work against directives issued by the *raikom*.[52] The wordy, hard-going document it produced went over the activities of the organisation's leading organ in excruciating detail, dividing it into thirteen major areas of assessment including, among others, agitation, leadership of the *Komsomol* and the communist caucus in the *zavkom*, 'participation in economic life' and 'control of directive implementation'. These were further subdivided into a total of sixty-eight sub-categories.[53]

[49] Ibid., l. 45. [50] Ibid., ll. 41–42. [51] Ibid., ll. 42–45. [52] Ibid., l. 48. [53] Ibid., l. 64.

In itself, this document represents a significant step in the organisational maturation of the KP party cell; only a few months earlier, internal conflict had made it practically and politically impossible to even discuss the organisation's work, let alone set up a functioning monitoring commission on it. The content of the report, however, provides further indication that party life was finally entering a period of stability for the first time since 1926. To be sure, the commission found much that was wanting in the bureau's work, but it commended its members on managing to stick to the agreed work-schedule and successfully resolving tensions between the *zavkom* and the factory administration.[54]

What is more, the problems highlighted by the commission were different to the ones that leading members of the organisation had been complaining about in the early months of 1926. The report mentioned neither attendance nor timely payment of party dues as issues in need of improvement, suggesting that at least some progress had been made in these elementary aspects of party discipline. Instead, the commission representative criticised the outgoing bureau for failing to address the fact that around a quarter of party members in the factory did not have party assignments and suggested that the new leadership should adopt 'no party members without party assignments' as a political slogan. This being a problem that could only be adequately addressed at the shop level, the commission also admonished the incoming bureau that care should be taken to ensure that shop-cells conducted their work in an orderly manner, starting by producing minutes of their meetings.[55]

With the assembly taking place a mere month after the Shakhty affair, the contributions from the floor that followed the commission's report were predictably saturated with attacks on the factory's administrative and technical staff. The political and organisational issues raised by the main speakers were, thus, almost entirely absent from the ensuing discussion, with the speakers being more concerned about Gaza's purported tolerance towards engineers of seemingly dubious loyalty.[56] Nevertheless, the bureau election that concluded the assembly seems to have taken place in an orderly manner, with the exchange of personal accusations that had plagued discussions of candidacies the previous year being notably absent. An element of contestation beyond the confirmation or rejection of candidacies was also introduced to the process, with a slate of thirty-three candidates being put to the vote in order to elect twenty-five full and five candidate bureau members. The election was conducted by

[54] Ibid., ll. 51–52. [55] Ibid., ll. 71–72. [56] See the discussion in Section 3.2.

process of elimination, with the number of abstentions being listed next to candidates' names in the manner of negative votes. Candidates were then ranked according to the number of abstentions, with the three that received the most being disqualified and the next five assuming candidate status.[57]

These were modest but substantial organisational improvements, especially when considered against the backdrop of the smouldering social unrest generated by the grain procurement crisis that struck the country in the end of 1927. The attendant bread shortages and 'extraordinary measures' sanctioned by the CC to secure the amount of grain necessary to feed the cities and the military acted as the prelude to the full collectivisation campaign that marked the Party's complete break with the NEP in 1929.[58] As many employees maintained links with the countryside and food shortages placed considerable pressures on workers just as the country was gearing up for the first FYP, none of these developments could have escaped the attention of the organisation's members. Throughout 1928, the *zapiski* collected at the organisation's assembly meetings reflect growing concern with regard to conditions in the countryside. Thus, when on 8 August CC member Aleksei Stetskii visited the factory to report on the committee's July plenum he received, among others, the following question notes:

> Will we import bread from abroad?
>
> What explains the high tax on peasant livestock?
>
> Why is there a bread crisis now, when in 1924 industry was far less developed and yet there was no crisis?
>
> There have been rumours that supposedly the Ukraine is leaving the Soviet Union and that this is the cause of the bread shortages. If this is not true, and I am convinced it is not, just mention this and confirm [that it is not the case].
>
> I observed the following situation in the village: in the autumn the kulaks bought all the bread, even from the cooperative. And in the spring they sold it no less than five roubles for every *pud'* of rye.

57 Ibid., ll. 25–26.

58 On the 'extraordinary measures', see *KPSS* v *rezoliutsiakh*, vol. 4, pp. 316–17. On the significance of the crisis with respect to collectivisation, see Hughes, *Stalinism in a Russian Province*, pp. 73–91; Alec Nove, *An Economic History of the USSR* (Middlesex: Penguin Books, 1982), pp. 150–53; Lynne Viola et al., *The Tragedy of the Soviet Countryside, vol. 1: The War against the Peasantry, 1927–1930* (New Haven: Yale University Press, 2005); pp. 7–21.

> What concrete measures have been taken for peasants to sow more grain and won't the raising of taxes on the peasant make things worse?
>
> People say that by extraordinary measures the crisis has been overcome but it hasn't as there are queues everywhere. The peasants are saying that we have returned to war communism.
>
> What measures are being taken against peasants who have deliberately reduced the sowing of grain and cotton?[59]

While a stenographic record of Stetskii's responses to the *zapiski* has not been preserved, this sample is by itself indicative of the multitude of views held by KP communists with respect to the rapidly deteriorating situation in the countryside. Ranging from traditional Bolshevik hostility to the kulak through to doubts regarding the economic rationality of the Party's agricultural policies with various shades of bewilderment in between, the attitudes of the rank-and-file were once again divided along the same fault lines as those that split the Party's central leadership. However, although opposition to collectivisation at the top found coherent political expression in the Right Deviation, it never gave rise to a defined factional opposition on the factory floor, in sharp contrast to events in 1925–27. Barring critical comments about the state of agriculture made in the *zapiski*, the rightists did not make their presence felt at KP by stating their views or by being subjected to attacks on account of them.

The first mention of the Right as the chief threat to the Party's unity was made by the chair of the organisation's first delegated conference, held on 18 November 1928.[60] More formulaic than substantial, this denunciation was not a signal for an attack on the rightists, as the conference proceeded without much reference to the brewing internal crisis. The relative calm at the meeting made it again possible for the new leadership slate vote to proceed without much controversy. Reflecting the growth of the organisation, the new body consisted of thirty-five full members and five candidates and became a *partkom* instead of a bureau. The old Putilovite Bolshevik Ivan Alekseev replaced Ivan Gaza – who had been promoted to work in the *raikom* – as party secretary while, reflecting the strategic importance of the enterprise for the FYP, Sergei Kirov himself also took a seat on the committee.[61]

59 TsGAIPD, f. 1012, op. 1, d. 549, ll. 207–11.

60 TsGAIPD, f. 1012, op. 1, d. 550, ll. 2–3. Holding a conference of delegates rather than a general assembly of all party members was an innovation in response to the growing size of the organisation. This practice would be generalised throughout the apparatus as part of a series of organisational reforms. These are discussed in more detail in Section 3.4.

61 Ibid., ll. 64–65; Kostiuchenko, *Istoriia*, p. 288. There were no additions or objections to the slate from the floor for the *partkom* and, although two extra members were added to the control

Instead of dividing the organisation, the attack of Stalin and his allies on the purportedly pro-kulak Bukharin seems to have provided an opportunity for reconciliation with some of the factory's most prominent supporters of the Left Opposition. A month before the first conference, at a meeting attended by Sergei Kirov, the former leading Zinovievist oppositionists Tuzhikov and Kovalevskii formally re-joined the Party, renouncing their erstwhile factionalism.[62] Despite a new crisis brewing at the top, the PPO was overcoming past divisions and proceeding apace with its organisational consolidation.

By that time, the split in the ranks of the leadership coalition that had defeated Trotsky and Zinoviev had already been made public. The Sunday issue of *Pravda* published on 30 September 1928 featured a lengthy article by Bukharin under the rather non-belligerent title *Notes of an Economist*, in which Stalin's erstwhile ally provided an eloquent warning of the destabilising economic effects of the rapid industrialisation course the leadership was about to embark on.[63] Less than three weeks later the rightists suffered their first major organisational defeat, when an extraordinary plenary session of the Party's Moscow Committee and Control Commission called in mid-October by Stalin's supporters amongst the city's activists condemned the rightist leadership of the capital's organisation.[64]

It is not hard to explain the failure of the last in the series of 1920s oppositions to generate much support amongst KP communists. Throughout the internal struggle that had tested the unity of the organisation in the previous years the desirability of industrialisation and the hostile nature of the kulak had never in themselves been matters of dispute. No CC loyalist at KP ever expressed any doubts that the massive expansion of heavy industry was a sound political objective. The CC majority itself had always maintained that the Left Opposition's policies were adventurist and unrealistic on the basis of current circumstances, not of their goals. When these circumstances were declared to be no longer valid and the 'socialist offensive' came to be the order of the day, the effect was not the creation of further division between those who stuck to the moderate outlook of the previous line and those for whom loyalty to the

commission at the suggestion of one of the delegates, this modification seems to have been unrelated to the crisis at the top.

62 TsGAIPD, f. 1012, op. 1, d. 549, ll. 218–19.

63 *Pravda*, 30 September 1928.

64 Molotov replaced Uglanov as Moscow secretary in November. For the struggle between Stalinists and rightists inside the Moscow organisation, see Catherine Merridale, *Moscow Politics and the Rise of Stalin: The Communist Party in the Capital, 1925–32* (London: Palgrave Macmillan, 1991), pp. 47–68.

CC remained paramount. Instead, what had been the only real political cleavage within the organisation disappeared, leading to an even more solid ideological consensus.[65]

The measure of this political achievement can be gauged not only on the basis of the successful reintegration of leftists like Tuzhikov and Kovalevskii into the political mainstream – a process taking place throughout the USSR at the time – but also by the organisation's performance at the various political campaigns that constituted the socialist offensive of the first FYP.[66] The efforts of party activists to promote the productive activism have already been discussed. However, KP communists and their Leningrad comrades more broadly also excelled in campaigns that were not so obviously related to their lives as factory workers. Leningraders made up 12,000 of the roughly 70,000 workers who in 1929 volunteered to be part of the twenty-five-thousanders (*dvatsatipiatitisiachniki*), the contingent of worker activists who left the cities to spearhead the collectivisation campaign in the countryside. KP communists were a significant part of the total number of volunteers, with the actual recruits totalling around 300 and including prominent party members like the chair of the factory's *zavkom* Arkhipov as well as other workers with decades of experience at the bench, including the recently redeemed Tuzhikov.[67]

The performance of the organisation in the 1929 party purge provides an even stronger indication of the KP organisation's successful political consolidation into a stalwart of CC loyalism. As in the rest of the USSR, the campaign at KP was staggered and consisted of several public meetings where party members were examined about the details of their political activities as well as aspects of their personal lives.[68] The first to go through the process at KP were prominent communists who had been selected to serve on the purging commissions of other organisations, including the former secretary Ivan Gaza, the *zavkom* chair Arkhipov and the lathe

65 Even in Moscow, where the rightists had their greatest organisational strength, it seems that the Party's activist base remained lukewarm towards the opposition, suggesting that, unlike previous challengers, Bukharin and his allies failed to connect with the rank-and-file. Ibid., pp. 218–20.

66 On 22 August 1928, the prominent exile Trotskyist Christian Rakovsky issued a declaration in which he urged supporters of the Left Opposition still in the Soviet Union to 'give the Party and the Central Committee full and unconditional assistance in carrying out the plan for socialist construction'. A year later, in July 1929, hundreds of former Trotskyists, including Karl Radek and Ivar Smilga, renounced factionalism and returned to the Party. Marot, 'Trotsky', pp. 189–90.

67 Kostiuchenko, *Istoriia*, p. 324; Lynne Viola, *The Best Sons of the Fatherland: Workers in the Vanguard of Soviet Collectivization* (New York: Oxford University Press, 1989), p. 43. Tuzhikov's pre-opposition Bolshevik credentials had been impeccable, having been a Civil War veteran who had distinguished himself in the operation against the Kronstadt mutineers.

68 Fitzpatrick, *Everyday Stalinism*, pp. 17–20; Getty, *Origins*, pp. 44–47.

operator Aleksander Nikiforov, then serving as secretary at the third mechanical shop cell. They underwent the screening process before thousands of KP workers at a mass, largely ceremonial, meeting held inside the factory's tractor workshop.[69] For the broader membership the purge came a few months later, with the first meetings starting on 1 October and most of the process having been completed by the time of the organisation's fourth conference on 14 November.[70]

Unlike the first screening round, the main *chistka* seems to have been a much more thorough affair. According to the gross figures given in the report prepared for the district control commission, the number of speeches made during the purge amounted to 2,967 and the grand total of questions asked of those examined was 22,313 by 17,815 participants, of whom 5,499 did not belong to the Party.[71] More importantly, the KP organisation performed significantly better than the national average in terms of both the thoroughness of the purge and the incidence of expulsion. By the time the fourth conference met to discuss the results of the campaign, more than 90 per cent of the membership had been examined, with only 4.4 per cent having been shown the door, compared to less than 87 per cent and 11 per cent, respectively, Union-wide.[72]

The report delivered at the conference by the district control commission representative Amosov elaborated further on the different causes of expulsion. Amosov noted that the largest group of the expelled was made up of members who had let their membership lapse by not paying dues or not attending meetings, while drunkenness was also a common cause for ejection from the ranks. 'Concealment of social background' was the most serious offense mentioned in the report, which had claimed 18 out of the total 140 expelled members.[73] Although these were hardly alarming figures, Amosov cautioned against complacency about the presence of hostile elements in the organisation, citing the case of one former member who

[69] Kostiuchenko, *Istoriia*, pp. 298–99. [70] TsGAIPD, f. 1012, op. 1, d. 679, l. 18.

[71] Ibid., l. 141. As the aggregate number of party participants is just under four times that of the total membership of the organisation, it seems that on average each member attended at least three meetings. We have no way of determining the extent of multiple attendance for non-communists but it is improbable that they would have been more likely to attend multiple meetings than Party members, suggesting that the *chistka* attracted significant interest from the broader KP workforce. Overall, the purge of the tractor shop cell seems to have been the most popular, with 2,961 questions asked of 387 screened members.

[72] Ibid., l. 18; Getty, *Origins*, p. 46; T. H. Rigby, *Communist Party Membership in the USSR* (Princeton: Princeton University Press, 1968), p. 178.

[73] TsGAIPD, f. 1012, op. 1, d. 679, l. 18.

'owned three houses and two dachas' and whose father had been 'involved in the shooting of communists'.[74]

Whatever the veracity of the sensational examples used by Amosov to illustrate the dangers of lax recruitment standards, they do not seem to have had much of an impact on the subsequent discussion. While some of the speakers lamented the common practice of not asking many questions as long as members performed the tasks assigned to them, most of the contributions focused on the problem of lapsed memberships as an indication of the failure of the organisation to assimilate new members. Party-building, rather than revolutionary vigilance, was once again the order of the day.[75]

Overall, rather than shrinking and weakening the organisation, the purge largely performed the opposite function, with its many sessions acting as recruitment events as much as disciplinary procedures. During the campaign, the organisation recruited 325 new members, more than double the number of those expelled. A further seventy workers, some of who had spent decades in the factory, triumphantly announced their intention to join the Party by marching into the conference and interrupting the main report.[76] This was possible because, in contrast to the supporters of the New and Left Oppositions, the enemies of the socialist offensive – rightists, kulaks and their minions – never appeared in great numbers amongst KP communists. Although frequently condemned in speeches and resolutions, their activities were rarely if ever directly experienced by the broad party mass in the enterprise and, thus, never generated the vicious infighting that had accompanied the emergence of earlier disputes at the top.[77] The early stages of the first FYP were, thus, a period of consolidation for the party grassroots from which the rank-and-file came out both more united in its outlook and more competent organisationally. This institutional maturation of the PPO would go on to play a crucial role in establishing the main patterns and contours of labour–management relations during this formative period of Soviet industrialisation.

[74] Ibid., ll. 20–21. [75] Ibid., ll. 28–29, 31–33.

[76] Kostiuchenko, *Istoriia*, p. 299; TsGAIPD, f. 1012, op. 1, d. 679, ll. 11–15. Evlampiev, who made the announcement, had been a worker for twenty-seven years, while Kuznetsov, the oldest member of the group, had spent four decades at the bench.

[77] This observation is of course irrelevant to whether the actual intension of the leadership in launching the purge was to rid the Party of oppositionists as has been claimed by Rigby (*Communist Party*, pp. 176–82) among others, or to '"clean" the Party of those who were not full-time, dedicated, honest Party members', as in Getty's (*Origins*, p. 47) more charitable interpretation. For the purposes of the argument developed here, it is enough to note that, for the reasons given, the right opposition never registered a serious presence in the Party grassroots.

## 3.4 *Edinonachalie* and Bacchanalian Counter-Planning

The resolution introducing *edinonachalie*, or one-person management, in Soviet industrial enterprises was adopted by the CC on 5 September 1929.[78] *Edinonachalie* has been the subject of diverging assessments by students of Soviet labour relations, reflecting broader interpretative differences of the industrialisation process. Traditionalist scholarship regarded this as a pivotal moment in the consolidation of a centralised command economy, creating a class of industrial autocrats or 'small Stalins' under the control of the real, life-sized Stalin ruling from the Kremlin.[79] Scholars favouring a social contractual model of Soviet labour took a different view, suggesting that *edinonachalie* was intended to establish proper accountability for the performance of industrial enterprises by clarifying the specific responsibilities and prerogatives of management vis-à-vis the Party and trade-union organisations. The decree did not signal a retreat from the radicalism of *samokritika* but made it more effective by streamlining the nexus of overlapping authorities on the factory floor.[80]

The text itself can support either interpretation. On one hand, the resolution was presented as a response to 'the lack of clear-cut and sufficiently strict demarcation of functions and responsibilities between . . . the director, the *zavkom*, and the party cell', which invariably led to the 'direct interference of party and trade-union organs in the operational work of factory administrations'. As a result of these blurred boundaries, economic problems were addressed 'casually and at times mistakenly' and there were often instances of 'covering-up of errors' from all sides. *Edinonachalie* meant that 'the administration (the director) is directly responsible for the fulfilment of . . . all productive tasks' and 'leads the administrative apparatus and all organisational–technical processes of production'. The director's operational instructions were to be 'compulsory for subordinate management as well as workers, *regardless of the position they occupied in party . . . or other organisations*'.[81]

78 *KPSS* v *rezoliutsiiakh*, vol. 4, pp. 556–62.

79 The term 'small Stalins' belongs to Moshe Lewin. Moshe Lewin, 'Society and the Stalinist State in the Period of the Five Year Plans', *Social History* 1, no. 2 (1976): 139–75, p. 173. A similar conclusion, from different premises, has been drawn by Paul R. Gregory, *The Political Economy of Stalinism: Evidence from the Soviet Secret Archives* (Cambridge: Cambridge University Press, 2010), pp. 268–70. Filtzer, *Soviet Workers* and Murphy, *Revolution and Counterrevolution* develop similar positions.

80 This argument was most elaborately developed in Hiroaki Kuromiya, 'Edinonachalie and the Soviet Industrial Manager, 1928–1937', *Soviet Studies* 36, no. 2 (1984): 185–204.

81 *KPSS* v *rezoliutsiiakh*, vol. 4, pp. 556–57. Emphasis added.

At first glance then, it would seem that the leadership had gotten whiff of the crisis of managerial authority fuelled by political activism on the factory floor, electing to come down on the side of industrial administrations in light of the severe economic challenges posed by the FYP. In terms of the tussle between reds and experts, *edinonachalie* thus appears as a clear point for the latter. The managerialist edge of the decree was, nevertheless, blunted by its insistence that administrative streamlining could not come at the expense of the 'development of the creative initiative of workers' and that correct management was predicated on the ability to combine strict discipline with actively involving workers in 'the administration of production'. The resolution stressed that *edinonachalie* entailed an upgrading of the importance of forms of labour activism like production conferences, the implementation of whose recommendations would now be amongst directors' personal responsibilities. Despite the emphasis placed by the CC on the need to delineate the areas of competence of the three components of the industrial triangle, its instructions to party organisations undermined this intent. Party cells were to keep abreast of every important factory matter and take an active part in the development and implementation of enterprise production plans (*promfinplany*) without, however, 'substituting' themselves for the administration.[82]

Rather than a milestone in the development of industrial authoritarianism, the decree on *edinonachalie* is thus best seen as a directive moulded in the Soviet ideal of good governance: the combination of firm and effective leadership with mass, activist input from below. It is certainly no coincidence that the text of the resolution cites Lenin's *Immediate Tasks of Soviet Power*, the foundational text of Bolshevik thought on institutional design. A closer look at events on the ground can help illustrate this point. During the first half of 1929, the Leningrad *gubkom* bureau was, not surprisingly, particularly concerned about the performance of the region's heavy industry. In a series of resolutions, it highlighted that production continued to be plagued by a multitude of inefficiencies and planning failures. The remedies proposed by the regional leadership did not, however, foreshadow a sharp turn towards managerialism. Instead, they reiterated the standard prescription of using the institutions of labour activism to raise productivity and resolve technical problems in the factory. A bureau resolution on 'Mass agitation on the questions of lowering unit-costs and the organisation of workers' production-related enlightenment' passed on 6 February thus instructed party organisations to employ the tried and

[82] Ibid., pp. 559–60.

tested 'forms of production agitation'. The bureau opined that the industrial apparatus paid 'insufficient attention to production conferences' and recommended that this omission be rectified post haste.[83]

In mid-June, the bureau convened to discuss the progress of the regional *promfinplan* and consider a report by the Leningrad machine-building trust. With some concern, the session noted that plan fulfilment for the half-year period had reached 47.8 per cent, compared to 50.4 per cent the year before. The region had also failed to achieve its 7.8 per cent projected unit-cost reduction over the same period, having managed 5 per cent instead. The bureau instructed industrial authorities to 'force' (*forsirovat'*) an increase in output to match the plan targets, warning, however, that the reduction in unit-costs should not affect product quality. Party organisations were to assist in this task by organising competitions in shops and enterprises aiming to lower the production of faulty output (*brak*).[84]

Things were going slightly better in terms of machine-building, but there were still problems to address. The bureau resolution on the trust report mentioned KP as one of the key achievements of the region's heavy industry, highlighting its production of dredgers for the northern platinum industry and finishing machines for textile works as particularly successful. Nevertheless, the enterprises of the trust were still struggling with deficiencies in their organisation of the work process and there remained much room for improvement in terms of labour discipline. The recommended course of action was once again deemed to be an intensified pace of workers' engagement in the oversight of production under the auspices of the Party. The trust administration was instructed to 'take decisive measures for the timely implementation of the recommendations of production conferences and establish ... commissions for assistance to worker-inventors'.[85]

The conception of activism as a necessary complement to good management was not a rhetorical device confined to the public proclamations of the leadership. It was an operative principle of governance that was reproduced in the directives of the regional body that was responsible for supervising the implementation of party policy. To be sure, it would have been possible for both the centre and the regions to pay lip service to the Leninist principle in policy documents while doing little to enforce it in practice. However, there is little evidence that the regional leadership was gearing up towards an entrenchment of managerial authority at the expense of the powers of party organisations on the factory floor. Quite

[83] RGASPI, f. 17, op. 21, d. 2709, ll. 22–25. [84] Ibid., d. 2710, ll. 47–49. [85] Ibid., ll. 53–55.

to the contrary, during the same period the *gubkom* mandated a restructuring of the party apparatus in industry with the express purpose of raising the role of communist organisations in large factories. The 'Statute on the Factory Party Committee' introduced by the bureau on 26 June recast the bureaus of party organisations as committees (*partkomy*), electable at a yearly enterprise-wide conference of delegates from the shop-cells. Factory committees were to be composed of twenty-five to thirty-five members and hold fortnightly plenary sessions. A bureau of up to ten members including a secretary (replacing the *partorg*) was electable at the plenum and functioned as the organisation's executive organ. The *partkom* had the right to establish its own, unsalaried, instructors to oversee political work in its areas of competence. Crucially, these included 'participation in the productive life of the enterprise on the basis of CC decisions, systematic assistance and control in practice of the implementation of party directives by the industrial apparatus, active participation in the selection of personnel'. At the same time, the shop-cells of enterprise organisations large enough to have a *partkom* were given a status on a par with those of PPOs, gaining the right to send their own delegates directly to the district party conference.[86] Effectively, the *partkomy* of large factories were transformed into parallel, though junior, district committees. The statute, therefore, upgraded the overall standing of large industrial organisations in the party apparatus.

In the months before the introduction of *edinonachalie*, the regional leadership was not only urging greater workers' involvement in management but providing party organisations in the factories with the administrative structures and statutory standing necessary to oversee the work of industrial cadres. Things did not change significantly even after the publication of the decree in September, with the *gubkom* bureau devoting most of its work to matters pertaining to the 'workerisation' of the state apparatus, that is, the promotion of workers to executive positions.[87] This policy was not a Leningrad peculiarity. Party organisations throughout the country were receiving similar signals from the centre. In addition to endorsing the finalised version of the FYP, the Sixteenth Party Conference in April had also declared a bottom-up struggle against bureaucratism in line with the *samokritika* campaign launched a year earlier.[88] In May the CC issued its

[86] Ibid., l. 59. [87] Ibid., ll. 124, 194.

[88] *KPSS v rezoliutsiiakh*, vol. 4, pp. 469–83. It is worth noting here that the new KP party secretary Ivan Alekseev attended the conference as a delegate with consultative voting rights. RGASPI, f. 17, op. 21, d. 2710, l. 8; *XVI Konferentsiia*, p. 326.

decree on the socialist emulation of enterprises as a key tool in the country's quest for industrialisation, urging workers and managers alike to take active part in this new form of production activism.[89] The Leningrad *gubkom* was, therefore, acting according to both the letter and the spirit of central policy when it instructed the party organisations of the *Krasnyi Treugol'nik* and *Bol'shevik* factories to remedy severe delays in their plants' plan fulfilment by promoting socialist emulation.[90]

Events at KP offer a clearer view of the impact of *edinonachalie* on industrial relations in the context of the FYP. They also demonstrate the critical function of party organisations in transforming the *edinonachalie* decree into concrete practice. Party meetings at KP in 1929 did not display the same toxic attitudes towards the factory administration as those of the last NEP years. This was less due to a sudden change of attitude on the part of the rank-and-file than because of the extreme pressures placed on the organisation by the launch of the FYP and its consequences. The mobilisation of party activists for the industrialisation drive, as well as the intra-party crisis over collectivisation, focused factory politics on all-union affairs. General assembly meetings in May and November gathered to discuss and condemn the views of the Right Opposition, thus temporarily displacing the party-management conflict from the centre stage of factory politics.[91]

As a result of the collectivisation drive, however, KP became an enterprise of paramount importance, as the only tractor producing factory in the Soviet Union. This distinction made it possible for the factory's own politics to become embedded in the political struggles taking place at much higher levels. The importance of KP's output for the union-wide collectivisation campaign was not lost on party activists on the factory floor. Although the 1929 general meetings were not stenographed, the *zapiski* included in the protocol records can provide some insight into the way party activists viewed the situation. At the May meeting, one Rassudov bombarded the presidium with notes asking questions about the positions of specific leaders and stating his views on everything from the danger of kulak infiltration in rural soviets to the best way to exploit recently discovered ore deposits in the Lower Volga territory.[92] In one of his

[89] *KPSS v rezoliutsiiakh*, vol. 4, pp. 508–10. [90] RGASPI, f. 17, op. 21, d. 2710, ll. 89–91.

[91] The November meeting was addressed personally by Kirov, who reported on the CC plenum that had taken place on 10–17 of the same month and resolved to remove Bukharin from the Politburo. TsGAIPD, f. 1012, op. 1, d. 675, l. 17.

[92] Present day Saratov and Volgograd regions, more than 1,500 kilometres away from Leningrad. Rassudov had clearly done his homework.

written interventions, Rassudov assured the presidium that the peasantry had realised the importance of the FYP and did not fear collectivisation, but demanded 'to be given all necessary agricultural machines, of which it has very little'.[93]

The entanglement of the permanently strained politics of the factory with the make-or-break stakes of the FYP bode ill for Grachev and his staff. Although KP overfulfilled its 1928–29 target of 3,000 tractors, the factory's beleaguered administration attracted the wrath of the authorities after the enterprise failed to meet a significantly magnified quota of 12,000 for the following year. The prospects of KP's technical leadership had started to look grim already in June 1928 when, during the inauspicious times of the post-Shakhty fallout, a Rabkrin commission visited KP to assess the plant's ability to increase its output from 100 to 250 tractors per month, with a view towards an annual output of 15,000 by 1930. Grachev flatly refused to countenance such a possibility and insisted that any significant increase in output could only be achieved as a result of massive capital investment at KP. Unimpressed by Grachev's demur, the head of the commission, Mikhail Kaganovich, suggested that the director should focus on overcoming the organisational deficiencies plaguing the current capacity of the factory.[94]

Nevertheless, after intense haggling between Grachev, the regional authorities, Rabkrin and the government, the director secured the investment necessary to expand tractor production, while also convincing planning authorities to reduce the factory's quota to more manageable levels. As a result of the new equipment and assistance rendered by other factories however, KP managed to deliver 3,050 tractors in 1928/29, thus exceeding the monthly rate of 250 that Grachev had denied was possible.[95] This unexpected success was a mixed blessing for the plant's administration as, despite leading to a commitment for still greater investment from the centre, it also convinced the proponents of the most ambitious growth targets that KP could do even better. Leading speakers at the Sixteenth Party Conference referred to the KP experience as an example to be imitated throughout the country's fledging tractor industry and predicted that the Leningrad giant would itself scale new heights of output. A CC report on the productive capacity of the Leningrad machine-building trust

[93] Ibid., ll. 9–10.

[94] Clayton Black, 'Answering for Bacchanalia: Management, Authority and the Putilov Tractor Program, 1928–1930', *The Carl Beck Papers in Russian and East European Studies* 1508 (2002), p. 11.

[95] Ibid., p. 12; RGASPI, f. 17, op. 21, d. 2710, ll. 55–56.

published in July indicated that KP should aim for 10,000 finished tractors in 1929/30, a target subsequently confirmed by the VSNKh in October.[96]

This marked the beginning of a cycle of ever-increasing pressures on the factory's administration, which the newly-empowered *partkom* served only to exacerbate. In late 1929, a production-conference at the plant's tractor shop resolved that KP could actually churn out an extra 2,000 units before the end of the second year of the FYP for an annual total of 12,000. In January, with support from the *partkom* and against the protestations of both the shop and the factory administrations, the VSNKh adopted the new figure as KP's official target for 1929/30. After the new revision, KP struggled to meet the tractor production quotas of almost every single month of the plan. Relations between the party organisation and the factory administration were, meanwhile, deteriorating at a rapid pace. Every single delay or stoppage that threatened the plan was met by furious denunciations by party activists of managerial incompetence and refusal to take responsibility in the spirit of *edinonachalie*. Such altercations were not confined to party meetings taking place on the factory grounds but also reached the regional press.[97]

The position of Grachev's administration was rapidly becoming untenable. As each failure generated more criticism, the security services began arresting specialists of suspect backgrounds. During an early June operation, KP lost a number of high-profile engineers and administrators, including the technical director Sablin and the tractor-shop head Ivanov. However, the plant still failed to meet its target output after the removal of the purported saboteurs. On 24 August, Grachev was summoned by the *obkom* to report on the progress of the tractor plan. After hearing his report, the bureau concluded that 'the factory administration of *Krasnyi Putilovets* ... did not demonstrate the necessary foresight, energy and planning flexibility with respect to the tractor-building programme ... leading to the failure of the plan'. A few weeks later, the VSNKh removed Grachev from KP and reassigned him as the director of Stalingrad's new tractor plant. *Edinonachalie* may not have given KP managers the operational control over production that had been its intention, but it did ensure that they had to answer for its outcome.[98]

96 *XVI Konferentsiia*, pp. 23, 31, 55, etc.; RGASPI, f. 17, op. 21, d. 2710, l. 55; Black, 'Answering for Bacchanalia', p. 12.
97 The conflict is narrated in fascinating detail by Clayton Black in ibid., pp. 19–26.
98 RGASPI, f. 17, op. 21, d. 2712, l. 35; Black, 'Answering for Bacchanalia', p. 25.

It is worth noting that the political fight around the KP tractor plan was taking place at the same time as the leadership was launching a new push to promote production activism in support of the FYP. In line with this, the Leningrad region trade-union committee had launched a campaign to recruit 100,000 workers to the shock-work movement. Reviewing the campaign's progress at a session in February, the *obkom* bureau determined that the growth of *udarnichestvo* and socialist emulation in the regional were unsatisfactory, instructing all party and *Komsomol* organisations to achieve 100 per cent participation amongst their members. 'Failure to fulfil this responsibility', announced the bureau directive, 'amounted to desertion from the labour front'.[99]

If production was seen as a battlefield, it followed that the vanguard of the army of labour should be organised in the best possible way to prosecute the war of the FYP. For the leadership, party building remained an integral part of its governance strategy in general and its industrial policy in particular. We have already seen that the 1929 purge acted as a recruitment drive in order to extend the Party's political reach in Soviet society at the outset of the FYP. The campaign to expand Bolshevik ranks did not, however, fizzle out with the *chistka*. On 10 February 1929, the CC issued a resolution 'On Future Work on the Regulation of Party Growth' which declared that the political effervescence generated by the Great Break had created ideal conditions for accelerating the recruitment drive. The directive instructed party organisations to link recruitment to productive activism in support of FYP targets and encourage mass membership applications of shops and work-crews, while insisting implausibly that each candidacy should be individually reviewed.[100] Two weeks later, an *obkom* bureau session concretised the task outlined in the CC resolution by reviewing the progress made in the recruitment campaign. The regional leadership noted that Leningrad communists had not succeeded in stepping up the pace of recruitment at sufficient speed during the previous year, with new entries in 1929 amounting to 16,180 versus 12,480 in 1928. In the first two months of 1930, there had been 'only' 29,000 membership applications, a figure judged to be 'inadequate'. Moreover, new members had increased the relative weight among the membership of workers employed in production from 59.9 per cent to 61.6 per cent, still short of the desired target of two thirds of party members being industrial workers.[101]

[99] RGASPI, f. 17, op, 21, d. 2711, l. 14.
[100] *KPSS v rezoliutsiiakh*, vol. 5, pp. 87–89.
[101] RGASPI, f. 17, op, 21, d. 2711, l. 34.

The Party's goals for quantitative growth and class composition of the membership were clearly bold. Inflating the ranks of workers with party cards was not, however, the peak of the leadership's ambition. Following the *partkom* innovations of a year earlier, the CC embarked on a sweeping reorganisation of the party apparatus in early 1930 with the aim of 'strengthening the party leadership of important focal points of socialist construction' and a stronger participation in the work of the apparatus by the Party's activist base.[102] This involved the creation of a series of new departments at all levels of the apparatus from the CC downwards, but also a further extension of the Party's network of grassroots organisations. In July, the *obkom* issued a new statute on the creation of a further level in the apparatus in the cities of the Leningrad region, the party segment (*partzveno*).

Segments were created as a further subdivision of the shop-cells and were to be organised according to the 'production principle'. This meant that segments corresponded to individual, self-contained elements of the production process in specific enterprises, as long as these involved ten to thirty workers. There could, thus, be party segments in specific work-crews, assembly lines or machines. These new party groups were to elect their own organiser from among their ranks, with the caveat that he or she had to be directly employed in the production element of the segment, rather than in an administrative or technical post. The particular way segments would be embedded in the broader apparatus would depend on the size of the enterprise they operated in and its party organisation. In smaller manufactures they could be directly subordinate to the bureau of the enterprise organisation; in the larger plants that had their own *partkomy*, segments of more than fifteen communists were given shop-cell status, including the right to hold their own general assemblies and elect an executive bureau in addition to an organiser. The tasks assigned to the segments were typical of leadership expectations from the rank-and-file. Thus, a *partzveno* should aim to 'strengthen socialist production and fulfil the productive tasks of a given brigade etc.' and 'rally party members around the implementation of the general line of the Party' while promoting the 'expansion of *samokritika*'. Significantly, the segment and its organiser were expected to keep abreast of developments in the political mood of non-party workers and remain responsive to their demands.[103]

Thus, at the same time as the leadership was insisting on the implementation of the one-person principle of management, it was

[102] Ibid., ll. 8–10. [103] RGASPI, f. 17, op. 21, d. 2712, ll. 18–19.

strengthening the main institutional competitors of managerial authority on the factory floor. There would now be more party members with more opportunities to supervise and troubleshoot production, at the same time as even more workers were attempting to set personal records of productivity as *udarniki*. In this context, it is hardly surprising that KP communists were pushing for greater numbers of what was probably the single most symbolic industrial product of the FYP, the tractor. It is similarly obvious that this necessarily entailed a usurpation of executive authority from the hands of management, as meetings, articles and resolutions denouncing its conservative approach to production proliferated throughout the country. The Party leadership had clearly been aware of this possibility, having already issued an appeal to members and trade-unionists in late January where it warned that plan failures were often directly related to a failure to implement *edinonachalie*, especially with regard to administrations' exclusive operational control over enterprises and their constituent parts.[104]

That the CC nevertheless proceeded to reinforce just those institutions that undermined the authority of industrial cadres reflects the tension inherent in the Party's policy objectives. Promoting managerial authority was a sensible enough policy at a time of tough economic challenges and rapid technological change. However, as long as the leadership believed that input from the managed was a necessary element of good management, they had to make sure that the institutions that made this input possible were adequately equipped to perform their role. In practice, this meant that the communist rank-and-file gained new organisational tools to monitor production, effectively limiting the practical applicability of *edinonachalie*, except in so far as it amounted to the administration getting the blame for missed production targets.

It is then clear from the above that the ultimate effect of the CC initiative was to strengthen the authority of party organisations vis-à-vis the management of industrial enterprises. What remains to be considered is the effect of this grassroots political development on the new industrial relations being created by the launch of the FYP. What were the implications of this assertion of the primacy of politics over specialist authority for the labour–management relationship?

To answer this question, it would be useful to examine the first experience of a KP party conference of Karl Martovich Ots, the factory's new director. Ots presented the main report to the organisation's seventh

[104] *KPSS* v *rezoliutsiiakh*, vol. 5, pp. 76–80.

conference on 2 October 1930, only a week after Grachev's departure. A new appointee, he had a fresh mandate from the country's industrial authorities and the presumed confidence of the corresponding level of the party apparatus. Chairing the meeting, the party organiser Alekseev opened the session by informing those present that the plan had been fulfilled by only 92.1 per cent and the organisation should use the storming quarter (*udarnyi kvartal*) to overcome the persistent problems of truancy, faulty output and labour turnover, using the trusted weapon of *samokritika*.[105] The new director then took the floor to present the factory's production plan for the quarter. He began by stating that fulfilment up until then had in fact been 87 per cent and declared that, in order to fulfil the plan, the factory would have to produce 47 per cent more items than in the previous quarter.[106] Ots conceded that factory output was constrained by the significantly limiting factors that plagued Soviet industry as a whole, like labour shortage and skill depletion. Moreover, the factory's rapid expansion had been disproportionate, with auxiliary shop capacity lagging significantly behind that of main processing shops.[107]

Having indirectly made the point that output could not be immediately increased by further expanding the available workforce, Ots drew the obvious conclusion that the storming quarter target would have to be met on account of an increase in labour productivity. In order to dispel any doubts as to whether this would involve labour intensification and a tightening of discipline, Ots spoke of the labour shortage as 'artificially created', further explaining that he meant this 'not in the literal sense, but in the sense that people do not want to work themselves too hard'.[108] He went on to provide an example of how carelessness and a lax attitude to work were undermining plan fulfilment in the factory's paramount shop:

> It must be said that even now, at a moment when the whole country has its eyes fixed on us ... when everyone's attention is on the tractor shop ... not everyone's attitude to their work is as it should be. There are of course bright examples, but not everyone is like that ... I was there last night at midnight, during shift change, and for 40–50 minutes the place was in a complete mess. Some people were chatting, some benches were being cleaned, and some others weren't.[109]

105 TsGAIPD, f. 1012, op. 1, d. 801, ll. 3–4. 106 Ibid., ll. 6–7.

107 Ots claimed that the factory was going to need about 2,000 extra workers, stating that 'there isn't a single shop that is not hysterically demanding more workers'. According to the director, the growth of the productive capacity of auxiliary shops since the beginning of the FYP had been 15–20 per cent compared to more than 40 per cent for the factory as a whole. Ibid., l. 8.

108 'Liudy ne khotiat potrudit'sia'. Ibid., l. 8. 109 Ibid., l. 11.

From his perspective, the new director was making a perfectly reasonable assessment of the situation. He had limited time to rectify the situation that had cost his predecessor his job, so that the increase in productivity necessary to meet the tractor target would have to be achieved on the basis of existing capital and labour resources. Addressing the chaotic conditions prevalent on the factory floor was an obvious place to start. Not surprisingly, the party members who spoke after Ots were not of quite the same opinion.

The director's report was followed by the presentation of a counter-plan by the factory's temporary control commission (VKK). The reporter, Bolsunovskii, began his contribution on the familiar theme of managerial incompetence:

> It would seem that a counter-plan must be put forward in opposition to something (*chemu-to na vstrechu*), that is, the plan of the administration. But this is not the case because even today, the administration was unable to provide figures on this quarter's plan because it doesn't have them. The VKK was established on June 7 to work out a plan for 1930–31. It was put together in time but as you can see today, neither the administration nor the *zavkom* can present a plan for the whole year.[110]

Bolsunovskii went on to present the counter-plan's adjusted targets. Overall output was projected to be 38.5 million roubles, over the administration's target of 36 million. Labour productivity would rise by 27 per cent, not the 20 per cent forecast by the administration. Bolsunovskii argued that the counter-plan's more ambitious target could be met by eliminating truancy and *brak*. This, he argued, was possible if the Party mobilised all of the factory's public opinion for this goal. To this end, he demanded that the shock-work movement should be expanded to include more workers. By placing responsibility for the plan on the rank-and-file, Bolsunovskii argued, it would be possible to meet the new targets.[111]

The call for higher targets was echoed by Marmel', who argued that even the counter-plan's revised target of 3,600 tractors in one quarter was pessimistic, as the factory could purportedly produce 1,500 per month on average. Marmel', who worked at the old forge shop, argued that it was possible to increase the production of wagons from the seventy-five ordered by the administration to ninety, provided that the shop was relieved from orders for smaller items from other shops which could produce them internally. In order for the required increase in productivity

[110] Ibid., l. 14. [111] Ibid., ll. 15–19.

to take place, the administration would also need to address 'some of the faults of the previous administration', specifically the lack of concern about the shop's ageing equipment which was, according to the speaker, in danger of complete breakdown. Demonstrating considerable skill in Bolshevik rhetoric, Marmel' drove the point home: 'There have been considerable advances ... but we have now come up against what must be called objective conditions. We must get rid of [these] objective conditions comrades.'[112]

Other speakers expressed similar views but were more scathing. Shimkovich admitted that truancy was an important issue but wondered whether management had taken any measures to assist the trade-union in remedying the problem. His contribution is worth quoting at some length:

> Ots told us the story of how he visited the tractor shop and beheld chaos; that people there weren't working, were chatting etc. This will be so tomorrow too. What concrete measures has Ots proposed? None! 75% of absences are because of stoppages ... There are stoppages because of the administration's carelessness ... Regarding planning, there isn't such a thing. If you want to talk about bringing the plan to the worker, then bring it first to the foreman, because he doesn't have it ... You start to work, then the foreman comes and says 'change equipment, work on the engine block.' In half an hour he comes again and says: 'take out the block, work on the cylinder head.' ... If you are going to push the worker about like this, and he earns one and a half rouble per day, then he will say ... 'I better leave, I'll be a drifter (*letun*), but I'll earn more.' Workers get angry at the foreman, but the foreman can't do anything if he doesn't have a task ... Bring the plan to the foreman and after that to the worker, because now ... he doesn't know how many and what kind of items to make.[113]

In his concluding remarks, Ots responded to some of the points raised by the other speakers and answered questions put to him in *zapiski*. One of these asked whether the new director intended to manage the factory from his office, 'like Grachev', or on the factory floor, alongside the communist caucus of the shop. Ots answered that one is only a red director who spends at least four hours per day on the floor and promised to follow that rule. Bolsunovskii used his concluding timeslot to challenge Ots to fulfil the plan: 'We have equipment and contracts, let's fulfil the plan, if you please (*izvol'te vypolniat'*)'.[114]

Whatever the original intent of the decree on *edinonachalie*, Ots's first contact with KP's communist rank-and-file suggests that he had not been

[112] Ibid., ll. 20–21. [113] Ibid., ll. 34–35. [114] Ibid., ll. 39–41.

invested with the powers of an 'industrial autocrat' or 'small-Stalin', certainly not one for whom 'rudeness [was] a virtue'.[115] Instead, according to the stenographic record, Ots comes across as a pragmatic administrator, who, having realised that meeting production targets was only conceivable on the basis of unpopular measures of labour intensification, was trying to secure the support of the institution charged with maintaining the good will of workers both within the factory and society at large. The KP party organisation, however, was not forthcoming with this support. The communist rank-and-file, ever suspicious of management, had not become more open to directorial initiatives since the removal of the previous administration. In fact, it would not be unreasonable to suggest that KP worker-communists experienced the removal of those whom they had for years denounced as incompetent and dangerous as a victory. In this case, the confidence of the rank-and-file in its political power would have been strengthened, as would the conviction that *edinonachalie* did not in any way entail an erosion of workers' control as mediated by the party organisation.[116]

This would account for the confidence with which speakers like Bolsunovskii and Marmel' presented their own suggestions without any significant scale back of the specialist-baiting that had become common currency around the time of the Shakhty affair. It does not, however, explain the specific content of these suggestions. For if in the late NEP-era communist activists were trying to defend against labour intensification by pointing to managerial incompetence as a greater cost to the economy than lax labour discipline, they were now attacking the administration by demanding what seemed conspicuously like *greater* intensification.[117]

The root of this change in rank-and-file attitudes lies in the shift of the boundaries of industrial politics initiated by the launch of the first FYP. During the late NEP period, when the primary objectives of the Party's economic policy were to rationalise production and economise on overhead costs, communist workers had been able to point to the chaotic state

[115] Lewin, 'Society and the Stalinist State', p. 172.

[116] This view could be supported on the basis of the content of the *edinonachalie* resolution itself which criticised management for ignoring the 'productive initiative' of the masses and the 'entirely correct' resolutions of party organisations. Reflecting the political ambiguities of the first FYP era, the resolution also criticised the 'direct interference' of party organisations in the operational work of factory administrations. *KPSS* v *rezoliutsiakh*, vol. 4, pp. 556–57.

[117] Counter-planning commissions invariably discovered 'hidden reserves' allowing higher production rates. In the *AMO-ZiS* automotive plant in Moscow, the counter-planning commission presented a plan for 7,900 cars for 1930–31 in response to the administration's plan for 6,400. Straus, *Factory and Community*, p. 146.

of the managerial apparatus as a more pressing problem than truancy or other labour discipline weaknesses. This was no longer possible by the time Ots took over from Grachev in 1930, as the imperatives of rapid industrialisation left little space for rationalising and economising practices. The industrialisation drive had also made labour intensification inevitable and opposition to it politically hopeless.

At the same time, however, the FYP had opened new possibilities for worker activists. Massive levels of investment made it possible to address long-time structural and organisational problems on the factory floor. By speaking about their potential for greater output, party members like Marmel' were effectively raising the profile of their workshops and attracting attention to real problems, like ageing equipment in the case of the old forge. As well as being detrimental to plan fulfilment, such problems affected workers in more immediate ways. Old equipment was prone to stoppages, which could severely affect the income of workers on piece rates.[118] The often chaotic and cluttered state of factory shops could be and often was a cause of serious, sometimes lethal accidents.[119]

Bolsunovskii's call for an expansion of the shock-worker movement, echoed by other members in their contributions, can be interpreted in a similar manner. Although shock-work was in the last analysis a form of labour intensification, shock-workers were entitled to a range of perks and benefits, like higher rations and priority access to the city's limited housing stock.[120] Thus, Bolsunovskii was able to call for higher targets on the basis of greater efforts on the part of workers, while at the same time effectively pushing for greater access to very scarce consumer goods. In doing so, he was entirely in line with party policy on the shock-work movement which demanded that it should eventually embrace all workers.[121]

This is highly illuminative with regard to the way in which party organisations operated in industrial enterprises like KP. Although composed almost entirely of factory workers who as we have seen were very keen to defend their interests, the KP party organisation was not a trade-union. That is, it was not an organisation charged specifically with protecting the interests of its members in the workplace, as opposed to those of management. It was instead a component part of the All-Union

[118] Siegelbaum, 'Soviet Norm Determination'.

[119] One of the *zapiski* to Ots specifically raised the question of clutter in relation to workplace safety, linking it to two lethal accidents in the iron-rolling workshop. TsGAIPD, f. 1012, op. 1, d. 801, l. 38.

[120] On the housing crisis, see Fitzpatrick, *Everyday Stalinism*, chapter 6.

[121] *KPSS* v *rezoliutsiiakh*, vol. 5, pp. 109–12.

Communist Party whose stated mission was to lead Soviet society in the transition to communism and its task was to oversee this process in the crucial setting of a major industrial enterprise. The organisation derived its authority within the factory from this. Its influence over management was due to the fact that it was embedded in a hierarchy parallel and at every level senior to the state. Furthermore, red directors like Ots owed their positions to their party membership and were thus beholden to the Party as much as to the state economic administration. Because of this, it was essential for factory directors to maintain good relations with their party organisations in order to run their enterprises and keep their jobs. Grachev's permanently tense relations with KP communists, especially after Gaza's departure, earned him a probably unenviable transfer to the less prestigious and likely more uncomfortable Stalingrad tractor plant. Being trusted with the leadership of a new key factory suggested that KP's erstwhile director still had the Party's confidence, but those of his colleagues in other enterprises that had built a less antagonistic relationship with their comrades survived the tribulations of the FYP in their posts.[122]

The nature of this institutional arrangement meant that communist workers who wanted to exert influence in their workplace had to do so primarily in terms of party policy implementation, rather than material demands from management. Nevertheless, the specific character of Marxism–Leninism as an ideology of working-class power ensured that some aspect of party policy could invariably be used by party activists to exert pressure on management. In that regard, the PPO acted as a structural constraint on how far party policy could move in a technocratic direction. As long as the implementation of industrial plans was the business of (some) workers as well as managers, hierarchies were bound to be disrupted and the production process politicised. The ambiguity of the decree on *edinonachalie*, which sought to increase both managerial authority and responsiveness to workers' initiatives, is a case in point. Within the context of the massive industrial expansion of the first FYP, 'bacchanalian planning'[123] became an instrument of pressure in the hands of party activists who sought to secure better remuneration and working conditions by promising greater output.[124]

122 In Moscow, for example, the directors of the automotive *Zavod imeni Stalina* and the metallurgical *Serp i Molot* plants kept their jobs during the first FYP and went on to have long tenures in their factories. Straus, *Factory and Community*, p. 245.

123 The term 'bacchanalian planning' was coined by the economist Naum Jasny to refer to the over-optimistic targets of Soviet planning. Black, 'Answering for Bacchanalia', p. 2.

124 I am not arguing here that party members like Marmel' were being disingenuous in their suggestions. It is not implausible that, assuming extra investment, less *brak* and no other orders,

If, however, the peculiar political ecology of Soviet enterprises placed significant constraints upon the power of management, it also set definite limits to the scope and nature of acceptable labour activism. For the corollary of politically mediated influence in the workplace was that the very institution acting as the instrument of this influence was also responsible for promoting the unpopular aspects of party policy. In fact, it seems reasonable to suggest that the relative power of an industrial party organisation vis-à-vis the administration depended on the extent to which the organisation was successful in mobilising workers' support for party policy as a whole.[125] This placed the party's rank-and-file membership in a rather contradictory position, whereby their role as defenders of their fellow workers' interests was coupled with their task of promoting breakneck industrialisation. It was not always possible to successfully navigate the complexities of this situation.

The tension between the demands of the industrialisation drive and the immediate interests of workers at the point of production put significant strain on the relationship between the Party and its constituents. Throughout the first Five Year plan period, the KP party organisation faced significant difficulties both in mobilising the support of the factory's workers and in maintaining discipline within its ranks. Apart from the perennial problems of labour discipline, party meetings at all levels expressed concern about the declining popularity of production conferences as well as mass campaigns like the subscription drive for the industrialisation bond.[126] Complaints about falling wages became a recurring theme in the *zapiski* of the period and there were at least a few cases where the wisdom of rapid industrialisation was questioned.[127] Curiously, the evidence suggests that collectivisation attracted considerably more negative comments from KP workers than rapid industrialisation, reflecting perhaps the growing presence of former peasants amongst the workforce and the persistence of ties to the countryside even amongst the factory's experienced workers. Reporting on the results of the CC plenum of November 1929, Sergei Kirov received a number of *zapiski* from the floor, some of

the old forge could have produced the extra wagons Marmel' claimed it could. The problem was that, much as with central planning, the optimal conditions on which the projected output of counter-plans were based could not be assumed.

[125] The consistent promotion of KP party organisers to higher posts during this period suggests that their superiors were satisfied with the organisation's performance. Ivan Gaza was promoted to the *raikom* and later *gorkom* leadership and, following his death in 1933, was buried in one of very few personal graves in Leningrad's Field of Mars. *Smena*, November 1940.

[126] TsGAIPD, f. 1012, op. 1, d. 550, l. 25 and d. 710, l. 2.

[127] TsGAIPD, f. 1012, op. 1, d. 675, l. 4.

which were sharply critical of the Party's agricultural policy. One asked if it was true that 'they are taking every last bit of bread from the peasant', while another asked the regional secretary to explain what possible harm could come out of allowing peasants to develop their households.[128]

Nevertheless, despite the resentment that the hardships of industrialisation no doubt generated amongst significant sections of the rank-and-file, the organisation managed to emerge out of this period relatively unscathed. With the exception of some relatively high profile episodes, like an open letter of resignation published by two experienced workers who denounced the Party's industrial policy, a significant weakening of the organisation's rank-and-file core does not seem to have taken place.[129] The purge of 1929, intended among other things to relieve the Party of members who were not strongly committed to the goals of the socialist offensive, made a very small dent on the KP organisation. Of its membership of 3,133, only 143 or less than 5 per cent were expelled. Of these 143, some 47 were automatic expulsions, consisting either of those who had consistently failed to attend party meetings or let their membership lapse by not paying the required dues. A further thirteen were expelled for drunkenness and eighteen for concealing their class background. Even assuming then that the remaining sixty-five were all expelled for open and/or active opposition to party policy, they would still make up a mere 2 per cent of the overall membership.[130]

This small rate of attrition reflects the fact that workers who wished to exert influence in their workspace were in a far better position to do so from within the party organisation than from the outside. We have already seen how worker-communists called on party ideology to draw attention to their concerns within the factory. Party membership did not, however, simply provide a rhetorical space from which to issue demands. At least since the NEP-era, rank-and-file activists had played a central role in resolving the numerous technical problems that came up in the production process. As bottlenecks, stoppages and breakdowns multiplied during the first FYP, so did the initiatives undertaken by workers in response to these problems. This period witnessed the mushrooming of specific work teams (*brigady*) whose task was to resolve such complications. The value of these tug-boating (*buksirnye*) and turnkey (*skvoznye*) brigades as they came to be

[128] Ibid., l. 18.

[129] The letter described industrialisation as 'a heavy burden on the shoulders of the working masses'. Black, 'Answering for Bacchanalia', p. 18.

[130] TsGAIPD, f. 1012, op. 1, d. 679, ll. 18, 141.

known is demonstrated by their official incorporation into the shock-worker movement. Although party membership was not a requirement for participation in these teams, communists were expected to take a leading role in their activities. Very often, party membership came as a consequence of activist engagement, as shock-workers were targeted for recruitment by the party's industrial organisations, sometimes *en masse* as in the case of KP's third mechanical shop.[131] Thus, rank-and-file communists at the time had not only the opportunity to express their concerns in terms that were fully within the contours of government policy, but also the ability to exert a significant level of control over the labour process, by virtue of their role as trouble-shooters and problem-solvers. There was, thus, little incentive for workers to give up this position in order to pursue a strategy of open confrontation with the state.

This goes some way towards explaining the sustained decline in strike and industrial action in the closing years of the NEP and the first FYP. Scholars of Soviet industrialisation have struggled to account for the puzzle of the world's most militant working-class demobilising in the face of one of the most severe campaigns of labour intensification in its history. One of the reasons given for the decline in militancy is the dilution of proletarian solidarity due to the influx of large numbers of peasant youths lacking traditions of labour organisation.[132] In addition, it has been argued that workers were atomised by means of differential remuneration, including material privileges and promotion opportunities for high-performing *udarniki* and so on. To be sure, these factors played their part. Nevertheless, pay differentials had hardly been unknown in Russian industry. The presence in the factories of workers with ties to the countryside was also hardly a novelty in a country where seasonal labour (the *othkod*) had long been a norm.[133]

This prompts us to consider a different explanation for the purported passivity of Soviet workers in the face of crash industrialisation. For the duration of the NEP period, the fate of Soviet industry had been the chief concern of workers of all occupations. Such shocking events such as the near closure of *Krasnyi Putilovets* after the Civil War were a threat to every worker's livelihood. For those who were politically committed to socialism,

[131] TsGAIPD, f. 1012, op. 1, d. 846, l. 5.

[132] Kevin Murphy, 'Strikes during the Early Soviet Period, 1922 to 1932: From Working-Class Militancy to Working-Class Passivity?', in *A Dream Deferred: New Studies in Russian and Soviet Labour History*, ed. Donald Filtzer et al. (Bern: Peter Lang, 2008), 171–92; Filtzer, *Soviet Workers*, pp. 90–100.

[133] Straus, *Factory and Community*, pp. 10–14.

they also represented a grave threat to the future of their revolution. A pro-industrial policy had, therefore, long been a demand of working-class militants. For them, the launch of the FYP was a vindication, as indicated by the return to the Party of former leftist oppositionists. The exhausting labour regime and privations that accompanied rapid industrialisation no doubt disappointed many. Many workers regarded this extreme pressure on their living conditions as a betrayal of revolutionary promises.[134]

Ultimately, the leap in industrial capacity that was the aim of the FYP could only be achieved at the expense of enormous labour exertion and a contraction in consumption. This was never going to be pleasant and for this reason the party leadership presented industrialisation as a military campaign. Nevertheless, by providing a means of direct influence over production and by offering a channel through which to confront management, PPOs by-and-large succeeded in keeping a lid on industrial tensions. There is indeed good reason to suggest that low party saturation was a major factor in cases when smouldering discontent erupted into more serious bouts of social unrest. The textile-dominated Ivanovo region which produced the only major strike wave during the FYP is paradigmatic in that regard. Even there, the rural towns were more prone to industrial unrest than the relatively party-dense regional capital.[135] The activity of communist rank-and-filers in the PPOs diffused tensions and redirected militancy to Party-approved directions. In doing so, it also made the leadership-narrative of the FYP as an enormous collective struggle more plausible. In that regard, the PPOs accomplished their vanguard mission.

## 3.5 Conclusion

As the FYP drew to a close, the rationalising functions of shock-work brigades became more pronounced than the target busting feats they had originally become famous for. As the ranks of *udarniki* expanded to include ever greater numbers of workers, the title came to be little more than a formality. Whole factories could receive the shock-work designation (*udarnye*) during the first FYP period. According to a report given at a meeting of KP's shock-worker foremen, 10,640 of the factory's 15,000 workers were *udarniki* in 1930.[136] Despite the authorities' complaints

134 Aleksei Gusev, 'The "Bolshevik Leninist" Opposition and the Working Class', in *A Dream Deferred: New Studies in Russian and Soviet Labour History*, ed. Donald Filtzer et al. (Bern: Peter Lang, 2008), 153–69, p. 155; Rossman, *Worker Resistance*, pp. 176, 236, etc.

135 Ibid., pp. 231–33.

136 TsGAIPD, f. 1012, op. 1, d. 846, l. 1.

about the phenomenon of pseudo-shock-work (*lzheudarnichestvo*), whereby workers not exceeding or even missing their targets got the title of *udarnik* as well as the attendant benefits, the mass expansion of shock-work ended up having a positive long-term effect on the development of Soviet industry. As the movement grew, the shock-work brigade became synonymous with a stable unit of workers, replacing the multitude of forms of labour organisation that Soviet industry had inherited from the pre-revolutionary period.

The rationalisation of labour organisation, exertion and remuneration that was achieved as a result of the formation of the stable work unit in Soviet enterprises was described by one incisive study of Soviet labour relations as a victory for both workers and the state.[137] Rank-and-file party activists played a decisive role in making this victory possible. At a time of intense social upheaval, communist workers took the lead in organising shock-work brigades by recruiting actual or imagined norm-busters from their shops. Party members also seized every opportunity to argue that disappointing production results were not due to skivers or enemies amongst the workers but because of worn equipment, lack of materials and faulty planning, responsibility for which was invariably laid at the feet of management. Thus, throughout the period of the first FYP, rank-and-file communists acted as a bridge between industrial workers and the state, preventing the opening of a major rift between the regime and its core social constituency. This they achieved by using the authority of their position to cushion the effects of the state's policies on themselves and their co-workers. This authority derived from the fact that they were themselves part of the system, not only as trusted trouble-shooters in the production process, but also as the main ideological conduit between the leadership and the broader population.

By virtue of its engagement in the socialist offensive, the party rank-and-file thus accelerated two distinct but interlocking processes that underlay its development since the Lenin Levy. First, it buttressed its place as a key tool in the political armoury of the leadership. Having first rallied the freshly recruited membership against opponents of the NEP, Stalin's CC was able to redirect the energies of grassroots communists in the struggle against those members of the leadership who wished to preserve the compromise with capitalism. Simultaneously, it wielded their shop-floor power as a cudgel with which to crush the resistance of recalcitrant industrial cadres who questioned the feasibility of the FYP. These twin

[137] Straus, *Factory and Community*, pp. 154–55.

tasks the rank-and-file performed much more readily than its fight against Leftist oppositionists, some of whom were rehabilitated and reintegrated in the process.

At the same time, the relative independence of the party grassroots from the central leadership was reinforced. By mobilising communist workers in support of party policy, the central leadership was inevitably investing them with a degree of political authority that was invariably directed against their bosses in industry. It could not be otherwise. The space of political intervention of industrial party organisations was the factory. Their activity necessarily intersected with that of industrial authorities and thus had the potential to get in their way. Every measure taken to promote grassroots activism thus tended to institutionalise the most radical, 'red' aspects of party policy at its level of implementation. The leadership realised this but was unwilling to take decisive action to remedy the problem. Although creating an industrial autocracy had hardly been the motivation behind *edinonachalie*, rationalising the chain of command by investing managers with exclusive operational authority was a sensible objective that was compatible with the broader participatory principles of Leninism. That central directives continued to complain about party organisations usurping managerial authority demonstrates that they were fully aware of the nature of politics on the factory floor but would not move to constrain the activities of their comrades 'from the bench'. Grassroots communists continued to view the Party's broader socialist project through the lens of their factory experience. Their engagement with leadership directives was thus determined by the industrial relations being constructed by the FYP. As the main contours of party policy changed with the completion of the socialist offensive, the nature of rank-and-file activism would have to adapt but would never become disentangled from its concrete environment. Before proceeding to examine rank-and-file activity after the foundations of socialism had been successfully laid, we must pause to consider a distinct but related question. How did working-class communists come to be sufficiently well-versed in the party's Marxist–Leninist worldview to simultaneously promote its policy and defend their own interests?

CHAPTER 4

# *Marxism and Clean Canteens*
## *Cultural Activism between Ideology and Practice*

The ability of party members to fulfil their vanguard role was predicated upon them having an adequate grasp of Marxist–Leninist ideology, including elementary respect for the norms of Bolshevik organised life. To promote the interests of their shops and colleagues, communist activists had to be sufficiently in tune with the prevailing political winds in order to be able to frame their demands and arguments within the terms of official policy. It was the central role played by the party organisation in the politics of production that drew the rank-and-file into the sphere of politics proper, from the campaign of collectivisation to the defence of the Party's general line against opposition.

While participation in party life did not require a profound grasp of the minute details of Marxist political economy, in order to be an effective activist, one still needed a level of knowledge of Marxism–Leninism that was not imparted by the mere fact of acquiring a party card. It was, thus, expected of party members to devote a considerable amount of time to their self-education or 'working on one's self' in the parlance of the time.[1] The raising of the rank-and-file's level of political–ideological astuteness, as well as its cultural level more broadly, was thus a major aspect of the party building process and the organisation devoted a considerable amount of time and resources to activities that contributed to members' cultural development.[2]

Like most of the Party's initiatives, educational activities were more campaigns than events, seeking to involve broad numbers of non-party

[1] On self-education as an ideological imperative, see Fitzpatrick, *Everyday Stalinism*, pp. 16–17; Andy Willimott, *Living the Revolution: Urban Communes & Soviet Socialism, 1917–1932*. Oxford Studies in Modern European History (Oxford: Oxford University Press, 2016), pp. 34, 162, 167.

[2] Enlightenment, or a general broadening and deepening of mental horizons, was an ambition that the Soviet state had for its entire population. Halfin and Hellbeck, 'Rethinking'; Hellbeck, *Revolution on My Mind*; Hoffmann, *Cultivating the Masses*, pp. 211–37. The point here is that, much like in other areas, communists were expected to lead the way in cultural affairs both as a matter of principle and as a precondition for discharging their other duties.

participants and taking place over extended periods of time. This chapter examines the cultural–educational aspect of party activism and relates this to the functions of the PPO examined in the preceding chapters. It will be shown that the broad range of activities that fell within the scope of the Party's mission of cultural enlightenment gave the latter significant material implications. Because of this, the intensity with which communists engaged in cultural activism was to a significant extent independent of the attitudes prevalent amongst the central leadership, whether with respect to the relative weight attached to the Party's cultural mission or the actual content of the latter. This observation has significant implications that extend beyond the immediate scope of this book onto the broader historiographical debate of Soviet cultural policy in the interwar period. This will be examined in this chapter in greater detail, but it is worth briefly laying out the shape of this debate here in order to better frame the argument.

In broad terms, scholarly interest on Soviet cultural affairs has focused primarily on the question of the relationship between early attempts to transform the cultural landscape by means of ambitious educational and artistic initiatives, and a later turn towards more traditional practices and values. At its core, this debate has been about the extent to which these two periods, roughly delineated by the end of the first FYP, are better viewed as being defined by distinct and mutually exclusive political projects or rather as a more incremental succession of cultural policy that did not signify a sharp political reorientation. Although few scholars would deny that significant changes did take place, there remains a considerable difference of opinion on whether these may be subsumed under a broader continuity.[3]

This concerns the fate of revolutionary culture not only as an element of state policy, but as a broader social phenomenon forming part of the lived experience of millions of Soviet citizens. In the aftermath of the revolution there had been a flourishing of experimental artistic, literary and lifestyle movements that defined cultural life during the first decade of Soviet power. Animated by vast numbers of volunteer activists, this constellation of clubs, reading groups and urban communes had an ambiguous connection to party organisations, their members and priorities not always

[3] See the following sections for further discussion of the relevant scholarship. It is worth noting in passing that that the continuity/retreat dispute overlaps significantly with the modernity/neo-traditionalism debate. Thus, one of the arguments for cultural continuity is Kotkin's account of Stalinism as a socialist civilisation predicated on a rejection of capitalism and tracing its roots to earlier Bolshevism. Kotkin, *Magnetic Mountain*, pp. 1–2.

overlapping. In the 1930s, this multivalent cultural world was transformed into a more homogeneous but still expansive system of party-led activities in education and the arts. This naturally poses the question of continuity and retreat in terms of the experience and implementation of cultural policy at the grassroots level.[4]

This chapter will show that, from the perspective of the party rank-and-file, continuities in both the content and practice of cultural activism were more pronounced than shifts, however conceived. Because the Party relied on the same overworked activists to promote its cultural policy as it did for all of its initiatives, its ambitious plans always came up against the fact that the rank-and-filers could only do so much. In practice, communist workers engaged in the kind of cultural activism they could fit into activities they were already engaged in and which in any case were higher up on their list of concerns. This meant that the familiar matters of factory life invariably took priority over other affairs. The corollary of this is that, when the overall direction of cultural policy did change, its shop-floor manifestation did less so. Cultural activities continued to rank below factory problems in the hierarchy of activists' concerns and the content of those that did clear the bar was not particularly affected by whatever change of policy took place at the top. Ultimately, this meant that the rank-and-file could in practice define the content of Marxist–Leninist ideology – the core subject of their political education – according to their own priorities. The argument offered in this chapter therefore adds a critical analytical layer to the account of rank-and-file activities presented in the preceding chapters (especially Chapters 2 and 3), but also sets the stage for understanding the cataclysmic events that will be treated primarily in Chapter 5.

## 4.1 An Attempt at Cultural Revolution

The period of cultural revolution in the USSR is usually conceived as part of the broader 'socialist offensive' or 'revolution from above' of the first Five Year Plan period and roughly dated from the Shakhty affair in 1928 to Stalin's Six Conditions speech in June 1931. Coinciding chronologically with the party's *samokritika* campaign, it was one of the means towards the end of transforming the Soviet intelligentsia from a remnant of the former

[4] The classic statement of the argument that Soviet revolutionary culture ended with the onset of Stalinism is in Richard Stites, *Revolutionary Dreams: Utopian Vision and Experimental Life in the Russian Revolution* (New York: Oxford University Press, 1989). Andy Willimott's recent work on urban communes takes a more nuanced position, suggesting that early cultural experimentation fed into what became official Soviet culture. Willimott, *Living the Revolution*, p. 133.

ruling class to a new revolutionary leadership with proletarian consciousness.[5] While this is certainly an accurate description for the country as a whole, there is some evidence suggesting that the Party in Leningrad was attempting to pursue more ambitious cultural and political education projects than was the case nationally already upon Sergei Kirov's assumption of the regional leadership.

The resolution adopted at the extraordinary conference of the LPO held in February 1926 after the defeat of the Zinoviev Opposition made specific reference to the cultural underpinnings of the recent party crisis. The document urged members to pay closer attention to the rapidly expanding *Komsomol*, as well as the broader 'non-party mass' in the trade-unions, soviets and co-ops.[6] In the ideologically blurry environment of the NEP, these broader groups of people who had not 'been through the school of class struggle and proletarian organisation' were more vulnerable to falling victim to pessimistic petty-bourgeois mentalities.[7] Motivated by concerns about the politically unhealthy effects of such attitudes on members and their ability to promote party policy amongst the population at large, the new *gubkom* bureau adopted an extensive plan of cultural and educational activities, ranging from organising recreational walks and excursions during the summer period to doing work with national minorities and establishing cultural clubs.[8] Some months later, the bureau reaffirmed its commitment to this aspect of party work, requesting the CC to almost double the budget of its *agitprop* department.[9]

These were not isolated actions. Throughout 1926, the new Leningrad leadership had kept a close watch on the progress of the Party's cultural–educational initiatives, with matters falling within the purview of the *agitprop* department appearing with almost the same frequency as

[5] Sheila Fitzpatrick, *The Cultural Front: Power and Culture in Revolutionary Russia* (Ithaca: Cornell University Press, 1992), pp. 115–18.

[6] RGASPI, f. 17, op. 21, d. 2669, ll. 57–60.

[7] Ibid., l. 57. The notion of *meshchanstvo*, the narrow-minded and self-centred mentality of the petty-bourgeoisie or lower middle class, has a long pedigree in Russian intellectual history. It was counterposed to ideas of selflessness or commitment to a higher purpose already by the pre-revolutionary intelligentsia and naturally entered the discourse of Bolshevik polemics in the mid-1920s on topics ranging from economic growth to sex. On the latter, see Fitzpatrick, *Cultural Front*, pp. 65–70; on *meshchanstvo* more broadly, Timo Vihavainen, 'Meshchanstvo, or the Spirit of Consumerism in the Russian Mind', in *Communism and Consumerism: The Soviet Alternative to the Affluent Society*, ed. Timo Vihavainen and Elena Bogdanova (Leiden: Brill, 2016), pp. 139–60.

[8] RGASPI, f. 17, op. 21, d. 2674, l. 57. The plan was broken down into several categories made up of thirty or forty points.

[9] Ibid., l. 230. The only other request for more funds by the bureau in the same year related to the construction of a hydroelectric power station on the river Svir'. Ibid., l. 204.

economic issues on the bureau's agenda.[10] Only a few days after the LPO's extraordinary conference had confirmed the leadership change, the bureau produced a resolution expressing alarm over the state of the region's workers' and peasants' correspondents' movement (*rabselkor*) and ordering its complete overhaul.[11] Territorial and city-wide correspondents' associations were to be abolished and district committees were instructed to reorganise the movement on the basis of activist circles (*kruzhki*) formed around the wall newspapers (*stengazety*) of specific workplaces, to make sure that published content was more relevant to their readers.[12]

Kirov's bureau also laid out ambitious plans with respect to the LPO's work amongst women, their emancipation (*raskreposhchenie*) being a major pillar of the Party's struggle against cultural backwardness throughout the interwar period.[13] On 23 March, the bureau produced a 'work plan for women workers and peasants' aimed at strengthening the party apparatus amongst women by recruiting to the Party those most actively engaged in public and professional organisations. The document also proposed a thorough review of the state of shop-floor party work amongst women to take place over the following thirty days, with representatives of the *gubkom* to visit district and primary party organisations' meetings and conduct personal interviews with women activists. According to the resolution, the LPO was to intensify its efforts to attract women to literacy circles and increase their presence in technical courses to a level correspondent to that of their presence in the workforce. Mass cultural work amongst women was to be expanded, with a series of activities on topics like 'Marriage and Family' and 'Religion and Worker (*Rabotnitsa*)' planned for the Easter period. In relation to this, the resolution instructed activists to pay particular attention to domestic workers and housewives due to their relative isolation from public affairs and devise appropriate forms of organisation to ensure the establishment of permanent contacts amongst them.[14]

10 Yiannis Kokosalakis, '"Merciless War" against Trifles: The Leningrad Party Organisation after the Fall of the Zinoviev Opposition', *Revolutionary Russia* 28, no. 1 (2015): 48–68, p. 66, n. 70.

11 On the *rabselkor* movement in the NEP-era, see Clibbon, *Soviet Press*; Michael Gorham, 'Tongue-Tied Writers: The Rabsel'kor Movement and the Voice of the "New Intelligentsia" in Early Soviet Russia', *The Russian Review* 55, no. 3 (1996): 412–29; Jeremy Hicks, 'From Conduits to Commanders: Shifting Views of Worker Correspondents, 1924–26', *Revolutionary Russia* 19, no. 2 (2006): 131–49; Jermy Hicks, 'Worker Correspondents: Between Journalism and Literature', *The Russian Review* 66, no. 4 (2007): 568–85; Koenker, 'Factory Tales'.

12 RGASPI, f. 17, op. 23, d. 2674, l. 22.

13 On this, see Fitzpatrick, *Everyday Stalinism*, pp. 139–63; Wendy Z. Goldman, *Women, the State and Revolution: Soviet Family Policy and Social Life, 1917–1936* (Cambridge: Cambridge University Press, 1993); Goldman, *Women at the Gates*; Ilic, *Women Workers*.

14 RGASPI, f. 17, op. 23, d. 2674, ll. 30–34.

Similar issues were a major theme in regional party directives the following year as well. A review of the work of the party organisation of the *Skorokhod* factory identified members' low level of political education as one of the least bright spots of the group's record and instructed its bureau to strengthen its network of party schools, with special attention to women and youth.[15] Cultural and political work amongst women was also the main item on the agenda of a *gubkom* bureau meeting on 16 February 1927 which reviewed the implementation of the relevant work-plan of the preceding year and, noting some modest achievements, set higher targets for the 'promotion of women to leading posts'.[16]

The commitment of the regional leadership to revolutionising the city's cultural life is also reflected in another resolution taken at the same meeting which set out plans for party work amongst 'science workers'. According to the document, the main task of the LPO was to 'attract a broad circle of materialist-minded, loyal to soviet power' scientists and intellectuals to cooperate with the Party in 'a common front against reactionary idealist worldviews'. In order to achieve this goal, the Party would have to strengthen its organisations in educational institutes and ensure that communist scholars were relieved of party assignments to concentrate on their research. At the same time, the resolution stipulated that research should be 'oriented towards the concrete tasks of socialist construction' and that its results should be 'disseminated amongst the masses' in open workshops and public debates.[17]

The preceding examples provide a good picture of the close attention paid to cultural and education affairs by the LPO *gubkom* bureau under Kirov's leadership.[18] A number of reasons can be adduced to account for this. First, cultural experimentation was a major trait of the NEP-period and as the traditional centre of Russian intellectual activity and home of the Revolution, Leningrad could not remain unaffected.[19] Second, as discussed in Chapter 2 and earlier in this section, the new leadership saw the intellectual and cultural development of the party rank-and-file as a key task in preventing the re-emergence of an oppositionist challenge to the

[15] RGASPI, f. 17, op. 23, d. 2675, ll. 8–11. [16] Ibid., ll. 45–51. [17] Ibid,. ll. 51–57.

[18] A note on the copy of the science work resolution sent to the Party CC with the note 'to comrade Stalin' suggests that interest in educational affairs was not limited to the Leningrad leadership. Ibid., l. 51. For an account of Bolshevik attitudes and policy towards higher education in the 1920s, see Michael David-Fox, *Revolution of the Mind: Higher Learning among the Bolsheviks, 1918–1929* (Ithaca: Cornell University Press, 1997).

[19] A detailed account of the northern capital's vibrant cultural life is provided in Katerina Clark, *Petersburg: Crucible of Cultural Revolution* (Cambridge, MA: Harvard University Press, 2010), especially chapters 5, 6 and 8.

CC majority line. Higher education institutions in particular had a complicated role to play in this process, with the Leningrad student body having in the past demonstrated particular vulnerability to the allures of the Left Opposition and the faculty of the city's University having been compromised by its association with the Zinovievites.[20]

A combination of factors relating to contemporary political imperatives and historical precedent thus placed the various aspects of cultural development at the top places of the political agenda of Leningrad's regional leadership. Given the importance attached to this area of party work by the *gubkom* bureau, we should expect the activities of the city's PPOs to reflect similar priorities at least to some extent. This, however, seems not to have been exactly the case. We have already seen that the new leadership of the party organisation at KP was immediately overwhelmed by the problems of production in the enterprise. Despite the commitment of Ivan Gaza's bureau to party building, the strictly political and organisational aspects of party work had to take second place to resolving issues like stoppages, *brak* and wage disputes, all of which had contributed considerably to the success of Zinoviev's supporters in attracting the factory's workers to their cause. Education being the qualitative aspect of party building, it too was put on the backburner.

This is not to say that KP communists did not make any efforts to implement the *gubkom*'s directives. A month after the party assembly that withdrew the organisation's support from the opposition in January 1926, members serving on the *agitprop* committee of the organisation held a meeting to discuss plans and distribute responsibilities for educational work for the following quarter. The resolution produced stipulated that efforts should be made to attract more workers to be *rabkory* while making sure that the existing network of political education should be strengthened by recruiting more workers from the shop-cells to do educational work. During the meeting, Kovsh argued that more attention should be paid to political agitation amongst women. This point was also included in the resolution, which assigned Kovsh the responsibility of coming up with a plan for the relevant work. No other concrete measures were agreed on.[21]

[20] While Zinoviev seems to have made some efforts to generate support amongst the city's students, he did not meet with much success, even though some leading academic staff did take his side. Halfin, *Intimate Enemies*, pp. 193–94; Peter Konecny, *Builders and Deserters: Students, State, and Community in Leningrad, 1917–1941* (Montreal: McGill–Queens University Press, 1999), pp. 103–9.

[21] TsGAIPD, f. 1012, op. 1, d. 272, ll. 1–3.

The underwhelming output of this meeting lies in stark contrast to the ambitious plans produced by the regional bureau a few months later and cited earlier in this section. A similar assessment of educational work at the factory was made by the *agitprop* collegium of the Moskovsko–Narvskii party *raikom* in a review of the organisation's progress on 19 April. The main report was delivered by Kasparov, who outlined the achievements of the organisation in terms of organising courses and study circles on Marxism–Leninism and 'self-education' and promoting press subscription amongst the party rank-and-file and KP's workers more broadly. Kasparov stressed that cultural activities had been more popular amongst non-party members than expected, with around 45 per cent of the entire workforce of 12,000 having participated in one way or another.[22] The libraries organised and maintained by the organisation were amongst its most popular achievements. In February, they had served 4,122 readers, 847 of whom belonged to the party.[23]

Despite these results, however, Kasparov complained that the Party's cultural activism was being undermined by the fact that foremen did not take it into account when assigning shifts, leading to some workers participating irregularly, if at all. This had the effect of keeping the level of discussion at study circles at a very elementary level, a problem compounded by the fact that seventeen out of twenty shop-cell *agitprop* activists had only joined the Party in the last mass recruitment drive of 1924–25.[24] Kondratiev, the communist responsible for *agitprop* at the factory's old smithy, gave his report after Kasparov, noting in a similar manner that shift work and the lack of appropriate premises were posing significant problems to the expansion of shop-floor cultural activism, despite the recent achievement of organising a 'red corner' for the first time. The overall assessment of cultural work at KP given by Levina on behalf of a monitoring committee set up to review the shops' *agitprop* painted an even bleaker picture. In her supplementary report, Levina stated that KP organisation had failed to take advantage of 'the positive peculiarities' of the factory in terms of history and party saturation to establish a strong grassroots *agitprop* network. No work-plan had been produced, the shop-cells remained without leadership from the bureau and the study circles organised were doing poorly both in terms of their curricula and their composition.[25]

Levina's criticisms and the complaints of Kasparov and Kondratiev are very illustrative of the constraints placed by shop-floor realities on the

[22] TsGAIPD, f. 1012, op. 1, d. 264, l. 1. [23] Ibid., l. 2. [24] Ibid., l. 3. [25] Ibid., ll. 4–6.

Party's ambitious plans of cultural transformation. Inexperienced activists had to teach their colleagues things they probably barely understood themselves, more often than not after a long shift at the bench with all the attendant frustrations caused by stoppages and break-downs. Whether members of the Party or not, foremen were more concerned about meeting their production targets than not upsetting the schedule of party study circles with their shift rotas. It is perhaps indicative of both the misunderstanding of the problem and the helplessness of the organisation before it that the only suggestion made by Levina was moving 'towards a system of shop-level *agitprop* assemblies', which was to add a further layer of activity in order to resolve an issue brought about in large part by excessive workloads.[26]

The *raikom* review had a certain urgency about it because, less than two weeks later, the factory would be hosting a major celebration of its 125-year anniversary. The event took place one day before the May Day celebrations on 30 April and seems to have been an enormous success. Thousands of KP workers and other locals assembled at the factory's giant tractor shop which had been converted to a beflagged exhibition of the factory's achievements. An artillery gun and a KP-produced tractor were placed on each side of the meeting's presidium to represent the factory's transition from military to peaceful production under Soviet rule. The main event consisted of a series of speeches by old Putilovites, who recounted their experience of clandestine organisation during the 1905 revolution and WWI, spurring the new generation of workers to new feats of labour and industry. The celebrations were attended by a number of dignitaries, including Sergei Kirov, trade-union, Red Army and Comintern representatives along with delegations from the Communist Party of Germany and the Mongolian People's-Revolutionary Party.[27]

Representatives from Leningrad City Soviet and other factories also addressed the meeting. A worker from *Krasnyi Vyborzhets* drew much applause from the audience after he presented the presidium with a figurine of a tongs-wielding worker representing the readiness of Soviet metalworkers to 'nip the tail of the global bourgeoisie'.[28] The jovial atmosphere was enhanced by the flourishes and tunes played by KP's own choir and orchestra, which also performed a march it had composed

[26] Ibid., l. 6.

[27] This account of the event is based on the description and photographs in Kostiuchenko, *Istoriia*, pp. 239–45.

[28] Ibid., p. 243.

especially for the occasion after Ivan Gaza's closing speech. All of the traits of the new socialist culture envisaged by the Bolsheviks were in evidence at the celebration, including awareness of past sacrifice, optimism for the future and an internationalist outlook tempered with a resolute determination to defend revolutionary gains from the machinations of global imperialism.[29]

It seems unlikely that the KP party organisation, whose *agitprop* activists were struggling to draw up plans for study circles, could have put together such a well organised event. It is rather more probable that, given the high profile of the event and the presence of foreign visitors, the regional leadership had provided at least some material and organisational assistance.[30] Whatever the case, as successful as the anniversary celebration was in its own terms, it does not seem to have provided a boost to KP cultural activism for much longer than its one-day duration. A similarly festive mood was apparent the following evening at the opening of KP's cultural club on the site of an old church across the factory gates, but less than a month later complaints about the persistent weakness of cultural activism re-emerged at party meetings.[31] At the annual electoral assembly of the organisation which met on 27 May, the uninspiring record of the organisation in the *agitprop* priorities set by the *gubkom* was remarked on by a number of speakers. In the main report, Gaza lamented the state of political education, the drop-out rate of which had reached 40 per cent. Little progress had also been made in setting up a *rabkor* collective, as members of the would-be editorial group were at odds with each other on how to proceed. Chervinskii commented that at the tractor department they did not even know who the candidate editors were. Dmitriev complained that *agitprop* was non-existent and cultural activism had been left to its own devices without any leadership from the Party.[32]

[29] These are some of the features of Kotkin's Stalinist civilization. Kotkin, *Magnetic Mountain*, pp. 355–59. It seems that at KP, where the Party had a long and established presence, these cultural traits had already started to take shape some years before the first FYP.

[30] The celebrations had made it to the agenda of the party assembly on 22 April, just a week before the actual event took place. Even then, there was little in the way of concrete task assignment, with a vague mention of the need to get all workers and the family to attend, so as to spend their May Day holiday in an intellectually stimulating manner (*razumno*). Most of the assembly's time was devoted to a speech by Sergei Kirov on the April CC plenum and the mostly economy-related questions that followed it. Even days away from a major event, cultural activism could not compete with the economy for the attention of rank-and-filers. TsGAIPD, f. 1012, op. 1, d. 266, ll. 42–47. On foreign visits to the USSR and the importance attached to them by the Party leadership, see Michael David-Fox, *Showcasing the Great Experiment: Cultural Diplomacy and Western Visitors to the Soviet Union, 1921–1941* (Oxford: Oxford University Press, 2012), especially chapter 3.

[31] Kostiuchenko, *Istoriia*, p. 245.

[32] TsGAIPD, f. 1012, op. 1, d. 266, ll. 63, 70.

It should be noted here that all such mentions of the problems faced by the Party in its mission of enlightenment appeared as afterthoughts within much longer speeches on production problems and disputes. One of the *zapiski* passed to Gaza from the floor complained that he had not said a word about work amongst women in his report. The secretary responded that there were about 300 women in the factory and that a special organiser had been assigned by the *raikom* to lead work with women workers.[33] In a factory of more than 10,000 workers, the otherwise attentive Gaza could only think about the issues concerning specifically the small minority of female employees as being somebody else's problem, despite indications by the *gubkom* that they ought to be taken seriously.[34] The resolution produced at the end of the meeting showed a similar attitude to cultural work more generally, stating that the organisation had to 'increase the political and cultural level of the *aktiv*' but offering little in the way of practical measures to achieve this goal.[35]

The revival of internal political turmoil the following year pushed cultural activism even further down the list of priorities of the organisation. For the duration of 1927, educational activities and the state of *agitprop* were rarely mentioned at party meetings, as the combined strain placed on the organisation by the Regime of Economy and the emergence of the United Opposition left little time for the consideration of other matters. To the extent that the state of activity circles and similar initiatives was discussed, it was usually in the form of complaints by the communists leading them about the lack of support they had received from the bureau.[36]

Even when the state of the organisation's cultural activities was among the main items on meetings' agendas, it was often the case that discussion strayed into the more pressing matters of the factional struggle. Thus, while the annual bureau report delivered by Gaza at the party assembly of September 1927 contained extensive information on the number and attendance of the various *kruzhki* organised by party members, it was

[33] Ibid., l. 69.

[34] Despite CC support, women activists faced considerable difficulty in making their overwhelmingly male rank-and-file comrades take their concerns seriously. This was especially true for workplaces like KP where women made up a very small percentage of the workforce. Goldman, *Women at the Gates*, pp. 33–48; Diane P. Koenker, 'Men against Women on the Shop Floor in Early Soviet Russia: Gender and Class in the Socialist Workplace', *The American Historical Review* 100, no. 5 (1995): 1438–64; Elizabeth A. Wood, *The Baba and the Comrade: Gender and Politics in Revolutionary Russia* (Bloomington: Indiana University Press, 2000), pp. 157–62.

[35] TsGAIPD, f. 1012, op. 1, d. 266, l. 75.

[36] TsGAIPD, f. 1012, op. 1, d. 418, ll. 13, 55, 117–18, 131.

impossible to keep the meeting focused on this topic. The intensification of the leadership struggle during the preceding summer overwhelmed the discussion, leading to calls from the floor to interrupt speakers not addressing the actual business of the meeting or wrap up the assembly altogether.[37]

The information presented by Gaza provides further indication of the organisation's difficulties in implementing the Party's ambitious plans for cultural activism. On the basis of the figures cited by the *partorg*, it appears that KP communists had made considerable progress in setting things up but were not doing as well in sustaining participation. Thus, some form of *agitprop* had reached every single factory employee at least once, with a gross number of over 90,000 having participated in 845 lunch-break discussion sessions (*besedy*).[38] These figures do not, however, provide an indication with regard to the extent of participants' commitment or actual interest in the issues discussed, beyond recording the fact that some sort of discussion took place. Similarly, the numbers given on the membership of mass public organisations appear impressive on the one hand, with the civil defence group OSOAVIAKHIM and the International Association of Aid to Revolutionaries (MOPR) counting 2,082 and 4,799 members amongst the KP workforce, respectively. However, the activist base of these groups was considered to be made up of only 96 and 124 of these members.[39] KP communists had, thus, succeeded in getting several thousands of their comrades and colleagues to demonstrate civic consciousness by signing up to assist in civil defence and support persecuted communists around the world but had failed to ensure that they actually stayed regularly involved in the relevant activities. Participation rates left much to be desired, even amongst those activists specifically charged with the task of overseeing cultural activism in KP, with meeting attendance reaching an average of only 50 per cent for the factory's twenty-nine-member cultural commission.[40]

[37] TsGAIPD, f. 1012, op. 1, d. 419, l. 74. [38] Ibid., ll. 50–51. [39] Ibid., l. 56.

[40] Russian scholars have in recent years produced a number of studies on interwar public activism with a local focus, where difficulties in sustaining high participation rates in the late 1920s emerge as a common theme. See indicatively: A. V. Khlopova, 'Innovatsii v obshchestvennoi zhizni gorozhan viatskogo regiona v 1920–1930-kh godakh', *Sovremennye problemy nauki i obrazovania*, no. 3 (2012): 1–7; Olga Nikonova, 'OSOAVIAKhIM kak instrument stalinskoi sotsial'noi mobilizatsii (1927-1941 gg.)', *Rossiiskaia Istoriia*, no. 1 (2012): 90a–104; Olga Nikonova, *Vospitanie patriotov. Osoaviakhim i voennaia podgotovka naseleniia v ural'skoi provintsii (1927–1941 gg.)* (Moscow: Novii Khronograf, 2010); Elizaveta Palkhaeva and Natal'ia Zhukova, 'Deiatel'nost' obshchestvennykh organizatsii Buriatii (vtoraia polovina 1920-kh gg.)', *Vestnik Buriatskogo Gosudarstvennogo Universiteta*, no. 7 (2005): 96–100.

This puts into perspective some of the other achievements claimed by Gaza. According to the report, there were 380 *rabkory* at KP, writing for no less than 8 factory-wide and 15 shop-level papers. While there is no reason to doubt that these numbers are real, we may question the extent to which these papers were produced with any regularity. Even if there was enough going on at KP to justify the existence of eight separate publications covering the entire enterprise, one third of the *rabkory* editorial groups had never met.[41] This suggests that the ambitious cultural plans of the new Leningrad leadership notwithstanding, the KP party achieved mixed results in putting them into practice. *Rabkor* groups and *kruzhki* for various activities had been set up and large numbers of KP workers had indeed been attracted to them. On the other hand, a large part of the membership of these groups likely existed only on paper, leaving overworked and poorly qualified activists to run them with little assistance from the organisation's leadership.

This trend would persist even as the cultural revolution began to gather momentum the following year. On 13 March 1928, the *obkom* held a joint meeting with the secretaries of primary party organisations of the city's Vasileostrovskii and Moskovsko–Narvskii districts, thus including KP's Gaza. The regional *agitprop* department had prepared an extensive report on the progress of the Party's enlightenment mission which warned that cultural development lagged significantly behind economic growth throughout Leningrad. Despite significant achievements in setting up adult education institutes and similar activity groups, the report indicated that library work and the literacy campaign had slowed down considerably in the preceding year, in the latter case leading to significant dropout rates.[42] This is of course consistent with the account of KP cultural activism given in this chapter; whether students or instructors, the Party's overworked activists could just not keep up with everything expected of them.

This would not change significantly in the years of the first FYP. Despite the Party's determination to create a new, thoroughly proletarianised intelligentsia through cultural class struggle, the flurry of new initiatives promoted during the Cultural Revolution ended up considerably tempered by the constraints of time and resources. As the collectivisation

[41] TsGAIPD, f. 1012, op. 1, d. 419, l. 52.

[42] Over the preceding three years, 63,000 people had received literacy training in the city of Leningrad, but around 14 per cent had shown signs of relapse (*retsidivizm*). RGASPI, f. 17, op. 21, d. 2693, ll. 8, 15.

and industrialisation campaigns got underway, the *obkom* began to devote increasingly more time to coming up with stop-gap measures to resolve supply bottlenecks and acute shortages than proletarian enlightenment.[43] The Party's educational mission did continue, but it was now subordinated to the more pressing tasks of providing the population with the skills needed to run an industrial economy. Thus, an *obkom* plenum resolution issued in February 1931 demanded that 'clubs and cultural centres be transformed into places of technical education'.[44]

As might be expected, primary party organisations felt the strain of the socialist offensive more directly than the *obkom*, leading to a proportional shift of rank-and-file attention even further away from cultural activism than had been the case during the Regime of Economy period. As we saw in Chapter 3, during the first FYP KP communists got involved – among other things – in the 25,000ers campaign, the 1929 purge and the shock-work movement, all against the backdrop of bitter conflicts with the factory administration over the tractor target assigned by the government. It should be hardly surprising then that cultural and educational activities appear in KP party records from this period primarily with reference to their failure or absence, if at all.[45] In fact, what was perhaps the greatest success of the organisation in terms of *agitprop* in this period had taken place several months before the launch of the FYP in February 1928, when the factory's *rabkor* publications were consolidated to form the *Krasnyi Putilovets* paper.[46] The paper went on to become an established part of factory life and played an important role in the ouster of the factory's director Grachev a couple of years later.[47] *Putilovets* also became the main medium for KP's *litkruzhkovtsy*, the group of primarily *Komsomol* amateur poets and writers among the factory's workers.[48] Nevertheless, the *rabkor* movement was only one of many initiatives through which the Party was attempting to transform daily life, few of which would thrive during the FYP.[49]

43 For example, the first item of business of the first *obkom* plenum in 1929 was supplying Leningrad's population with 'necessary foodstuffs'. RGASPI, f. 17, op. 21, d. 2694, ll. 3–6.

44 RGASPI, f. 17, op. 21, d. 2697, l. 19.

45 TsGAIPD, f. 1012, op. 1, d. 675, ll. 6–8, 18–20; d. 679, ll. 29, 32–35; d. 710, ll. 2–4.

46 TsGAIPD, f. 1012, op. 1, d. 549, l. 39.

47 For the role of the paper in the conflict, see Black, 'Answering for Bacchanalia'.

48 Kostiuchenko, *Istoriia*, pp. 311–12. The promotion of literary pursuits amongst the country's working-class youths was a key aspect of the Party's cultural policy during the cultural revolution. On this, see Lynn Mally, 'Shock Workers on the Cultural Front: *Agitprop* Brigades in the First Five-Year Plan', *Russian History* 23, nos. 1–4 (1996): pp. 263–75.

49 The strength of rural traditions amongst the millions of peasant internal migrants was a major obstacle to the promotion of the Party's cultural initiatives. Hoffmann, *Peasant Metropolis*, chapter 6; Straus, *Factory and Community*, pp. 69–83. I have deliberately set this issue aside here to focus on

KP communists were not entirely indifferent to their organisation's failures on the cultural front. The more conscientious amongst them demonstrated strong concern about this crucial aspect of party building even at the height of the industrialisation drive. The last person to take the floor during the discussion of the purge campaign results in November 1929, Trutnev warned that the campaign had revealed that 'many of our communists are captives of cultural–political darkness'. He went on to wonder:

> Is it possible for a communist without elementary knowledge to exert influence over alien and even hostile forces amongst us? Is it possible for a superintendent who is a cultural–political invalid [sic] to lead work on the balance of class power etc.? Before everything else, we must study, study and study.[50]

Like the *obkom*, Trutnev believed that the low educational level of the rank-and-file posed a threat to the Party's ability to perform its leadership role, both in terms of running production and forestalling political opposition. Whatever the views of Trutnev's comrades, however, they did not view the matter with the same urgency. Neither the question notes nor the main speaker's closing remarks expressed similar concerns. This trend continued for the remainder of the first FYP period and besides the occasional lecture on ideology, cultural activism retreated into the background.[51]

Transforming a giant machine-building plant into a beacon of culture was always going to be a tall order. This was doubly so within the context of the first FYP, with shop-floor conflict and chaotic work schedules placing severe limits on the scope of activities not directly related to production. Against this backdrop, the successful setting up of *Krasnyi Putilovets* and a writers' collective were no mean feats. At the same time, however, the organisation failed to establish a reliable, functioning network of educational and cultural activities to free the rank-and-file from the bonds of cultural darkness, as Trutnev might have hoped. Like most

the specifically institutional constraints of cultural revolution, namely its reliance on a group of extremely busy activists.

50 TsGAIPD, f. 1012, op. 1, d. 679, ll. 32–33.

51 The industrialisation drive interfered even with these simple activities, as the transformation of the factory into a giant construction site meant that there was little unoccupied space left in the factory. Kostiuchenko, *Istoriia*, pp. 303–8. Even when space was found, the chaotic state of the enterprise could cause other disruptions. Thus, a group activity titled 'Bolshevism was tempered and grew stronger in the struggle against which enemies?' held in early January 1931 was interrupted by a power failure. TsGAIPD, f. 1012, op. 1, d. 922, l. 5.

aspects of the socialist offensive, the attempt of KP communists at cultural revolution yielded mixed results.

## 4.2 Not So Great a Retreat

Following the completion of the first FYP, the party leadership embarked on a campaign of all-round consolidation that was marked by a more moderate approach to most aspects of policy. In industry, technical competence came to be valued more than shock-work and managerial authority started to be promoted over *samokritika*, if not always consistently so.[52] A similar attitude of going slower and taking stock led the Party to freeze recruitment and shift through its vastly expanded membership in the 1933 purge.

Disillusionment with the results of earlier rounds of radical experimentation also motivated a series of reversals on the cultural sphere. The Soviet 1930s witnessed among other things the rehabilitation of Russian history, the reintroduction of traditional methods of schooling and the promotion of traditional family values.[53] Avant-garde tendencies in literature and music were condemned in favour of purportedly more accessible themes inspired by tradition and everyday life.[54] Famously, Stalin started to become the subject of increasingly magniloquent public adoration which cast his leadership in patriarchal terms, not entirely unlike those used to praise the Tsars.[55] Above all, the multitudinous forms of experimental lifestyles and collectives abundant in the 1920s were absorbed into a mainstream culture defined by the Communist Party and its youth wing.[56]

The Russian exile sociologist Nikolai Timasheff interpreted these developments in terms of a 'Great Retreat' from the Soviet revolutionary project, inspired by a realisation on the Bolsheviks' part that their

[52] This recalibration in economic policy is examined in more detail in Chapter 5.

[53] David Brandenberger, *National Bolshevism: Stalinist Mass Culture and the Formation of Modern Russian National Identity, 1931–1956* (Cambridge, MA: Harvard University Press, 2002); Fitzpatrick, *Everyday Stalinism*, pp. 152–63; Goldman, *Women, the State and Revolution*, pp. 296–344; Hoffmann, *Stalinist Values*, pp. 96–110.

[54] Vera S. Dunham, *In Stalin's Time: Middle Class Values in Soviet Fiction* (Durham: Duke University Press, 1990); Fitzpatrick, *Cultural Front*, pp. 183–89; Boris Groys, 'The Birth of Socialist Realism from the Spirit of the Russian Avant-Garde', in *The Culture of the Stalin Period*, ed. Hans Günther (London: Palgrave Macmillan, 1990), pp. 122–48.

[55] Jeffrey Brooks, *Thank You, Comrade Stalin! Soviet Public Culture from Revolution to Cold War* (Princeton: Princeton University Press, 2001); Sarah Davies, 'Stalin and the Making of the Leader Cult in the 1930s', in *The Leader Cult in Communist Dictatorships*, ed. B. Apor and J. Behrends (London: Palgrave Macmillan, 2004), pp. 29–46.

[56] Willimott, *Living the Revolution*, p. 156.

experiment had failed.[57] It is not the purpose of this account to examine Timasheff's argument in depth, but it should be noted that the view from the ground suggests less of an about-turn than is implied in the notion of a great retreat.[58] This seems to be due to a misrepresentation of the actual state of affairs under the status quo ante. As indicated in Section 4.1, there are strong reasons to doubt the extent to which the Party had succeeded in implementing its cultural programme by the time this was purportedly abandoned at the end of the FYP.

The same combination of ambitious plans for cultural projects and sobering realities on the ground is reflected in the activities of rank-and-file communists throughout the 1930s. The first couple of years after the completion of the first FYP the LPO's first order of business was to address the crises generated by the upheaval of the Great Breakthrough, with the food and housing shortages caused by famine and in-migration being the most pressing issues.[59] Thus, resolutions addressing problems in housing construction and the distribution of rations dominated the agenda of *obkom* plenary sessions in 1932–34.[60] Even then, however, the regional leadership remained sufficiently concerned with the cultural state of the LPO to keep the pressure on the lower party organs regarding the educational dimension of their work.

In October 1934, at one of the last plenums before Kirov's murder, the *obkom* voted on a lengthy resolution regarding the 'ideological arming' of Leningrad communists. The document noted a number of weaknesses in the Party's ideological work, including predictably that organisations were not affording it the appropriate amount of attention. The resolution went on to state that cultural awareness was a necessary precondition for the performance of the Party's vanguard role, listing 'science, art and literature' among the main subjects that the good communist ought to be conversant in. Such broad general knowledge would enhance the ability of rank-and-filers to participate actively in the party's discussion and decision-making

57 Nicholas Sergeyevitch Timasheff, *The Great Retreat: The Growth and Decline of Communism in Russia* (New York: E. P. Dutton & Company, Inc., 1946), pp. 349–71. Also from exile, Leon Trotsky concluded that the revolution had been betrayed based on similar observations. Leon Trotsky, *The Revolution Betrayed* (Mineola: Dover, 2004).

58 For a more detailed discussion of Timasheff's work in light of recent research, see Michael David-Fox, Peter Holquist and Alexander Martin (eds.), 'Ex Tempore Stalinism and "The Great Retreat"' [special section], *Kritika: Explorations in Russian and Eurasian History* 5, no. 4 (2004), pp. 651–733.

59 The deterioration of rations had been the main cause of the unrest at Ivanovo region in April 1932, of which Kirov as a Politburo member must have been aware of. Rossman, 'Teikovo Cotton Workers'. For the housing crisis, see Fitzpatrick, *Everyday Stalinism*, pp. 46–50.

60 RGASPI, f. 17, op. 21, d. 2698, ll. 14, 25, etc.; d. 2699, ll. 3–6, 71, etc.; d. 2700, ll. 1–12, 29–36, 39–43, etc.

processes, while at the same time enabling them to relate party policy to real every-day issues.[61]

During the same period, KP communists attempted to get their own cultural activism up to the standards of the *obkom*. The ninth conference of the organisation held in April 1932 heard a report from Aleksandr Ugarov, head of the cultural department (*kul'tprop*) of Leningrad's city party committee (*gorkom*). The hour-long talk concerned the 'tasks of Marxist–Leninist education in the factory' and its content is indicative of both the importance attached to this task by the leadership and the difficulties faced by the rank-and-filers trying to implement it.[62]

Ugarov began his talk by reiterating the importance of educational activities as an 'enormous part of party work' without which it would be impossible to 'resolve the fundamental questions of socialist construction' and 'craft a successful foreign policy'.[63] In order to stress his point, the *gorkom* functionary referred to the case of a kolkhoz in Valdai district, where the local party organisation's relaxed attitude towards ideological instruction had allowed former kulaks to assume leading posts. According to Ugarov, after predictably distributing most of the collectivised animals to their own households, the kulaks went on to cancel the Party's educational initiatives.[64] The moral of the story was that only the class enemy stood to benefit from an abandonment of the Party's educational mission, a lesson especially apposite in the case of KP's own organisation, where youth of peasant origin made up a large part of its massively expanded membership, around half of which had only candidate status.[65]

During his talk, Ugarov received a note from the floor suggesting that educational sessions should be treated in the same way as labour discipline, with 'truancy' controlled by means of appropriate disciplinary sanctions. This prompted the *kul'tprop* to warn against 'administrative attitudes' towards the Party's cultural activism, arguing that the process of assimilating recent recruits and improving the abilities of old ones was necessarily a protracted one that required patience.[66]

Ugarov's report provides a succinct overview of leadership views on party education, but it is the ensuing discussion that offers a glimpse into the way these were received by the rank-and-file. Of course, nobody disagreed in principle with Ugarov's take on educational activities; the problem was one of implementation. Fratkin, one of the members of the editorial group of *Krasnyi Putilovets*, complained that factory affairs took

[61] Ibid., ll. 70–75. [62] TsGAIPD, f. 1012, op. 2, d. 439, l. 7. [63] Ibid., l. 9.
[64] Ibid., ll. 14–15. [65] Ibid., ll. 20–21, 58. [66] Ibid., ll. 27–28.

up all of the organisation's time, with shop cell meetings often having to hear extensive reports on the progress of their production plans. This left little time for discussing even such prominent political affairs as Party Conferences, let alone questions of cultural activism. According to Fratkin, wall-newspapers were little more than complaints forums, reporting that 'this or that guy is a self-seeker, truant, etc.' but not much of substance.[67] Similarly, Sobolevskii stated that at the factory's turbine department, around two thirds of the Party's members and candidates were not involved in any kind of educational activity.[68]

Deviatkin brought up the perennial issue of the organisation's failure to devote sufficient time to work among women, noting that this had not even been mentioned in the report, to supportive cries of 'that's right!' from the floor.[69] Krasnopolina, a delegate from the KP's *Komsomol*, warned that the state of education amongst the factory's youth was such that some members lacked basic political knowledge and even thought that 'the *Komsomol* is the vanguard of the Party'. She went on to argue that party members had failed to provide adequate leadership to the youth, with not a single one of the tractor department's shop cells having devoted any time to reviewing *Komsomol* work. Seizing on Ugarov's point regarding the vulnerability of young people to bourgeois ideology, Krasnopolina stated that the factory *Komsomol* had attempted to put together a series of events dedicated to the life of youth before the revolution, but very few party members had agreed to help out. The youth representative closed her contribution by urging the organisation to pay as much attention to education as it did to production, drawing applause from the floor.[70]

Much like their comrade Tutnev some years earlier, activists like Deviatin and Krasnopolina were genuinely worried by their organisation's substandard performance in cultural activism and education. In this, their views were entirely in line with those of the Party leadership as expressed by Ugarov and the *obkom* resolutions cited. Like the leadership, concerned activists could do little more than reiterate the significance of the Party's cultural mission. The resolution produced at the end of the conference itself merely recorded the many weak spots of educational work, without stating any concrete plan of action to remedy them.[71]

[67] Ibid., ll. 39–41.
[68] The exact numbers were 173 out of 268 and 56 out of 83 for members and candidates, respectively. Ibid., l. 54.
[69] Ibid., l. 64. [70] Ibid., ll. 72–75. [71] Ibid., l. 84.

It is hard to gauge the extent to which these complaints reflected real indifference to cultural activism on the part of large numbers of the party rank-and-file or the unrealistic expectations of those who voiced them. To be sure, even with the best of intentions, it is not hard to imagine why experienced workers would be keener to get on with the business of making tractors and turbines than offering history lessons to the young. Solving problems of production was simply a higher priority, affecting both remuneration and personal safety for everyone involved.

On the other hand, warnings against ideological laxity notwithstanding, there was quite a lot of party-educational work going at KP at the time. Shortly before the organisation's conference, the *partkom* had organised a competition between the numerous party study groups operating in the factory. One of the best was run by Krasnoshevskii, a 1930 recruit who had spent twenty years working at the factory. Krasnoshevskii's group had an attendance rate of 72 per cent and had organised a small campaign of looking into the state of consumer services available to workers of the tractor department's erecting shop, as an assignment in connection with the relevant resolution of the October 1931 CC plenum.[72] Significantly, the group had managed to recruit five new members to the Party during its activities. Similar achievements were reported by the *partkom* for the other winning groups, all of which were awarded literary book-coupons.[73] The *partkom* awarded similar prizes to some instructors dispatched to the enterprise from the Leningrad Province Communist Academy (LOKA), the prestigious party-affiliated educational institute that had been supervising the organisation's cultural mission for the preceding couple of years.[74]

In light of these achievements and the fact that KP communists were receiving specialised assistance from the Party's own higher learning institute, it may be tempting to view the alarm expressed regarding the state of cultural activism by some of the speakers at the conference as misplaced or exaggerated. It is more likely, however, that what was at play had once again more to do with a divergence of priorities than an absolute lack of interest about cultural matters in some quarters. In a still primarily male factory, the even more male party membership struggled to take women's issues sufficiently seriously, even though it was a male communist who

72 The plenum had issued a resolution 'On the expansion of Soviet trade and improvement of workers' provisioning'. *KPSS v rezoliutsiakh*, vol. 5, pp. 366–69.

73 TsGAIPD, f. 1012, op. 2, d. 432, ll. 85–94.

74 These seem to have been awarded on the basis of the achievements of their students. Ibid., ll. 92–96.

raised the issue.[75] Even young communist workers were probably more concerned with everyday matters than ideological education specifically targeted to their age group. The advantage of the consumer services related activities organised by groups like Krasnoshevskii's was that they touched on issues that were of primary concern to every worker in the factory, perhaps more so for the minority of women.[76]

Other initiatives of cultural activism that met with success during the same period lend further support to this reading. Perhaps the most extensive and elaborately planned of these was a competition for the best canteen (*stolovaia*) held over two months in September 1933. The competition involved the setting up of a seven-person commission to investigate the performance of the factory's canteens in terms of cleanliness, speed of service, the food's calorific value and responsiveness to complaints. Apart from visiting twelve canteens and interviewing users and staff, the commission also conducted two 'night raids' to ensure appropriate standards were maintained during the night shifts too.[77] The results were announced at a meeting attended by 100 representatives from the Party, trade-union, *Komsomol*, administration and canteen commissions (*stolovye kommissii*). Speakers at the event demonstrated all the traits of Bolshevik militancy, including *samokritika*, denunciations of incompetence and mutual admonition to strive for better results.

Delivering the report, the commission member Potikov classified the *stolovye* in groups of 'bad', 'good' and 'best', enumerating the achievements and failures of each to the audience. Thus, amongst the 'bad' ones, canteen No. 29 of the rolling-mill shop had failed to make planned renovations, did not provide tea and had been the subject of rat and cockroach infestations for which nothing was being done. No. 5 of the tractor department's smithy was also a poor performer, with Potikov stating that there was 'no discipline in the canteen', as reflected by the numerous broken forks, flies in the kitchen and two kilograms worth of wasted

75 Exact numbers for women in the workforce and membership are not easy to determine for 1932 due to the chaotic state of record keeping in the aftermath of the first FYP. However, in January 1934, immediately after the 1933 purge (see Chapter 5), there were about 6,000 women amongst KP's 30,000 workers, or 20 per cent of the workforce. Just under 400 of them were in the Party, then numbering 3,233 members, or just over 12 per cent. TsGAIPD, f. 1012, op. 2, d. 1012, l. 1.

76 Acquiring the goods available through the state trade network and restricted market outlets remained a task primarily performed by the female members of Soviet households. Fitzpatrick, *Everyday Stalinism*, pp. 54–58; Osokina, *Za Fasadom*, pp. 189–214.

77 TsGAIPD, f. 1012, op. 2, d. 623, l. 1–2.

cabbage. On one occasion, the poor planning at No. 5 had led to lunch being delayed for two hours.[78]

'Good' canteens were not necessarily free of such problems, but their committees demonstrated an attitude conducive to improvement. Thus, canteen No. 32, serving the factory's construction workers, had been on schedule with its repairs and was regularly meeting the target of 1,033 calories per meal, while smooth service ensured that there were no queues. However, No. 32 had had wastage (*brak*) amounting to eighteen kilograms of potatoes and been the subject of complaints about cockroaches. What saved No. 32 a 'bad' assessment was that its committee was 'conducting a struggle' (*vedet bor'bu*) against these failures.[79] In the same way, it was the efforts of its committee that won canteen No. 34 the best assessment in the competition. This *stolovaia* had not only exceeded its calorific target on two separate samplings and never been infested by any critters, but its committee had been on such good terms with staff that they had even managed to organise the production of a wall-newspaper for the canteen.[80]

Closing his report, Potikov encouraged those canteens that were 'lagging behind' to strive to 'transform themselves into leading, exemplary canteens' by the October celebrations.[81] In the discussion that followed, speakers addressed issues overlooked by the report in similarly militant terms. Belokurova, a trade-union representative, criticised the poor oversight exercised by some committees, noting that at canteen No. 28 – which had not been part of the competition – the committee had failed to realise that the canteen's auditor, one Solov'ev, was working with expired credentials. As a result, Solov'ev almost made off with the till before trade-union activists 'unmasked' (*razoblachili*) him.[82] Martianov, the committee chairman of canteen No. 17 took the floor to criticise the non-rounded prices that canteens had to charge leading to complaints when workers were short-changed because of the low availability of single kopek coins.[83] Other speakers complained about the familiar problems of bad planning, interference by outsiders and substandard performance by some activists. In his closing remarks, the chair of the meeting Zhukov suggested that the issues that had not been resolved through the competition could be taken up during the upcoming round of the 1933 purge.[84]

There is something slightly comical in associating one of the Party's most exalted procedures of political introspection with the performance of canteens, as there is in the notion of a 'struggle' against cockroaches. In

[78] Ibid., ll. 3–5. [79] Ibid., l. 6. [80] Ibid., ll. 7–8. [81] Ibid., l. 8. [82] Ibid., l. 11.
[83] Ibid, l. 15. [84] Ibid., l. 19.

connection with such quotidian things as calorie measurements, the use of language charged with revolutionary pathos certainly has an incongruous ring to it. It nevertheless accurately reflects the importance attached by the participants to the issues discussed.[85] With famine spreading through the country and the availability of food at state trade and market outlets severely restricted, the network of canteens operating at factories and other public institutions had become a primary means of subsistence for the Soviet people.[86] Making sure that their canteens were clean, efficient and wasting no food was thus a matter of more than cultural importance for KP workers. This is not to say, however, that any cultural dimension was absent from the campaign. Promoting habits of personal and communal hygiene had been a strong theme of the Bolsheviks' ongoing campaign to 'cultivate the masses' since the early years of Soviet power and remained part of the Leningrad *obkom* cultural agenda throughout the interwar period.[87] One of the most proudly proclaimed aspects of KP's extensive renovation during the first FYP had been the building of shower-rooms on the factory premises.[88] Moreover, promoting a 'cultured' attitude towards consumption, including food, emerged as a major aspect of state policy regarding the provision of goods in the 1930s.[89]

At the same time, involvement in the campaign should not be mistaken for a disingenuous hijacking of a party initiative by workers attempting to draw attention to their concerns. Party policy foresaw and presupposed public involvement in the retail sector both as a means to generate information on quality and uncover malfeasance.[90] Indeed, less than a year after the KP competition, an *obkom* plenum criticised the state of public catering with respect to the sanitary standards of canteens as well as the nutritional value and even presentation of meals offered. The regional leadership also instructed party and trade-union organisations to ensure

85 In earlier years, bread and the overcoming of hunger had been important parts of Russian revolutionary politics and discourse. See Lars T. Lih, *Bread and Authority in Russia, 1914–1921*, (Berkeley: University of California Press, 1990); Mary McAuley, *Bread and Justice: State and Society in Petrograd 1917–1922* (Oxford: Clarendon Press, 1991) and, of course, Peter Kropotkin, *The Conquest of Bread* (London: Penguin Classics, 2015).

86 Osokina, *Za fasadom*, pp. 150–55.

87 Hoffmann, *Cultivating the Masses*, chapter 2; RGASPI, f. 17, op. 21, d. 2700, ll. 41, 111; d. 2707, l. 26.

88 Kostiuchenko, *Istoriia*, p. 307.

89 Julie Hessler, *A Social History of Soviet Trade: Trade Policy, Retail Practices, and Consumption, 1917–1953* (Princeton: Princeton University Press, 2004), pp. 198–215; A. Randall, *The Soviet Dream World of Retail Trade and Consumption in the 1930s* (London: Palgrave Macmillan, 2008), pp. 134–57.

90 Ibid., pp. 112–33.

the greatest possible 'participation of the masses' in overseeing the public catering network.[91]

This raises an interesting point regarding Soviet cultural activism and the role of party activists therein. In the absence of widely available marketed goods, participation in party-led campaigns of involvement in and oversight of the state retail network became an important means of exercising control over consumption. In the same way that communist activists took an active and often aggressive interest in production as a precondition for gaining a degree of control over the conditions of their labour, cultural activism offered them a degree of control over what they got in return for it. In the years of famine, nutritious food was the most important form of remuneration but, even then, the 'cultural' services offered through factory-based structures included theatre tickets, day care services and tourism, including highly desirable but rare trips abroad.[92]

At the same time, the *ipso facto* politically charged character of party activism made consumption into a means of ideological hegemony. Thus, in a late 1933 interview with the KP *partkom*, a 46 year old non-party shock-worker called Boroda reported that his life was especially hard in terms of accommodation and access to food, but that he could bear the hardship in the knowledge that 'if not us, then our children will live well' and that 'in capitalist countries they live worse'.[93] During the first FYP, Boroda had been one of the country's exceptionally productive *udarniki* who had been rewarded with a cruise around Europe on the ship *Abkhazia*. The travellers had had time to observe the plight of workers in depression-era Europe and Boroda returned to KP to tell his fellow workers that the idle shipyards of the city of Kiel resembled the state of Russian industry in the Civil War year of 1918.[94]

For the remainder of the decade, cultural activism in the factory proceeded along similar lines. The first conference of the organisation to be held after the Party's seventeenth Congress met in March 1934 with an agenda dedicated to party educational work.[95] Despite significant improvements in terms of the numbers of members and candidates

[91] RGASPI, f. 17, op. 21, d. 2700, ll. 39–43.

[92] Filtzer, *Soviet Workers*, pp. 174–75; Diane P. Koenker, *Club Red* (Ithaca: Cornell University Press, 2013), pp. 89–115. The multitude of services offered by and at factories has prompted Kenneth Straus to describe the Soviet factory as a community organiser. Straus, *Factory and Community*, p. 212. In keeping with this metaphor, the argument offered in this chapter is that the Party was the community organiser of the factory as a community centre.

[93] TsGAIPD, f. 1012, op. 2, d. 628, l. 2.

[94] Ibid., l. 1.

[95] TsGAIPD, f. 1012, op. 2, d. 939, l. 5.

participating in educational activities, the familiar themes of competing priorities and work overload dominated the discussion. Thus, although the *partorg* Tiutin noted in his report that over three quarters of communists were engaged in some form of study, the progress of more than half of participants was assessed as 'satisfactory' and 'unsatisfactory' and only a third or less were 'good' or 'excellent'.[96] Even worse, basic literacy and numeracy skills amongst the membership left much to be desired, with Tiutin jokingly commenting that, although everyone was Russian, 'when it comes to an exam in the Russian language, you couldn't tell if we were French or some other people'.[97]

The scarcity of basic mathematical skills was a particularly sensitive issue, given their importance for comprehending and monitoring the progress of production plans. One of the last to speak at the conference, the factory director, Ots, described party education as a necessary condition for economic progress.[98] Pichugina, a KP communist on secondment to the regional higher party school (*komvuz*) made the same point more blatantly, stating that workers who studied at the *komvuz* learned 'the language of political economy and dialectical materialism without mistake' but had trouble using fractions and percentages. Pichugina went on to attack both Ots and Tiutin for failing to take adequate interest in the kind of training provided to future production cadres at the *komvuz*.[99]

Other speakers highlighted the persistence of religious attitudes amongst older workers as well as the familiar problem of lack of interest in women's issues as areas in need of improvement.[100] The variety of loosely related matters discussed at the conference may seem to indicate that the speakers were talking past each other, but is better viewed as a reflection of the vast scope of activities that fit under the label of party education. The blurry contours of the subject-matter continued to make it hard to discuss any concrete issues regarding the broad range of activities that constituted party education, beyond the problem, common across the board, that there simply was not enough time to get everything done. In the end, the most concrete measure taken by the conference in that respect was to instruct the organisation to extend its educational reach by taking activities beyond the factory and into workers' own apartments, an innovation in cultural activism apparently pioneered by the second mechanical

[96] For example, of the 619 people studying 'political literacy', 304 were 'satisfactory', 149 'unsatisfactory', 132 'good' and 33 'excellent'. Ibid., l. 14.
[97] Ibid., l. 91. [98] Ibid., ll. 73–75. [99] Ibid., ll. 51–57. [100] Ibid., ll. 59, 92.

shop-cell.[101] In its habitual manner, the party organisation resolved to remedy its overwhelming workload by expanding its activities.

Home visits seem to have become a regular component of the organisation's cultural activism after the conference, with collected minutes of interviews at workers' apartments appearing as separate entries in the archival catalogue.[102] References to home interviews conducted by communists of the second mechanical shop made at the March conference suggest that their content was fairly balanced between the concerns of everyday life ('why are light industry products of low quality?') and the broader political awareness expected of engaged Soviet citizens ('why, precisely speaking, are such contradictions developing in the Far East?').[103] In addition to being a means of strengthening the rank-and-filers' links with their non-party colleagues, home visits also became a way by which the organisation monitored the private behaviour of its own members in order to ensure it met the cultural standards expected of communists. Activists visited the homes of their comrades to hold what seem to have been similar to counselling sessions, offering help to those struggling with alcohol and advising on marriage problems ranging from how to relate to a religious or non-communist spouse to more serious cases of domestic violence.[104]

Though not necessarily attributable to such innovations, cultural activism as a whole seems to have risen in prominence in the period after the Party's seventeenth Congress. In the years leading up to 1937, the organisation began to hold regular educational activities on specialised topics in addition to the long-running study circles. These included lessons on party history, shop-floor discussions on developments regarding the Spanish Civil-War and what seems to have been an exceptionally well-planned conference on Marxist theory held over two days in March 1936.[105] The transcript of the conference – which was one of the very few party educational activities to have been fully stenographed – indicates that by the mid-1930s factory communists had acquired substantial knowledge of Marxism that went considerably beyond concurrent party slogans. The event's agenda included extensive presentations on 'Utopian Socialism', 'The Dictatorship of the Proletariat as an instrument for the

101 Ibid., ll. 96–98.
102 TsGAIPD, f. 1012, op. 2, d. 1012. Unfortunately, these files were not accessible on the grounds that they contained personal data.
103 TsGAIPD, f. 1012, op. 2, d. 969, ll. 16–18.
104 Ibid., l. 59; TsGAIPD, f. 1012, op. 2, d. 1051, ll. 45–46.
105 TsGAIPD, f. 1012, op. 2, dd. 1171, 1172, 1242.

construction of a classless society' and 'The Socialist State' by members of the factory's shop-cells.[106] These well-crafted talks were followed by equally erudite discussions during which speakers disputed some of the most minute points of the original presenters. Thus, Miliutin of the third mechanical shop took issue with the account of pre-Marxist socialism offered by Markin of the energy shop on the grounds that it underestimated its 'influence on the development of the revolutionary worldview of the proletariat'. This was apparently because Markin had focused on Étienne Cabet's Icarian movement instead of Robert Owen's attempts to create working-class led industrial communities.[107]

A year later, the organisation began its descent into the delirium of denunciation and 'unmasking' which will be examined in more detail in Chapter 5. For the purposes of the present discussion, it is important to highlight the fact the mass repression of 1937–38 was accompanied by renewed calls for educating the membership on the part of the leadership. Meeting in June 1937 as the violence was reaching a crescendo, the sixth conference of the Leningrad *obkom* – since 1935 under the control of Stalin's close ally Andrei Zhdanov – adopted a resolution noting with alarm that the 'paramount task' of Marxist–Leninist education among the ranks was 'in an extremely unsatisfactory state'. Linking this policy failure with the perceived infestation of the Party with enemies, the resolution went on to instruct district committees and PPOs to adopt a number of measures for ensuring the personal involvement of all members in educational activities.[108]

The result of this process on cultural activism amongst the party grassroots was a forceful resurgence of interest in the service provision aspects of the new socialist culture being built by Soviet workers. Thus the first conference of the Kirov factory party organisation held in April 1938 saw the interim *partkom* that had emerged during the previous year come under sustained attack with regard to the factory's housing-building plan. The most biting criticism came from Sitarzh, a communist who worked as a trade-union representative at the factory's dormitories (*obshchezhitiia*). Sitarzh began her intervention by saying that the new *partkom* had done a good job in putting production in order but had forgotten about the other side of party work, namely 'concern about people, the creation of conditions for people, the nurturing of people who live and study and do great things'.[109]

[106] TsGAIPD, f. 1012, op. 2, d. 1171, l. 1.
[107] Ibid. ll. 35–38.
[108] RGASPI, f. 17, op. 21, d. 2690, ll. 25–26.
[109] TsGAIPD, f. 1012, op. 2, d. 1467, l. 162.

She went on to attack by name everyone involved in some capacity in the factory's housing development programme for having failed to demonstrate such concern, to applause and encouraging cries from the floor. Sitarzh demanded of the new director Viktor L'vov to 'find the money' to build a new club at one of the dormitories and went on to attack Maliutin, the culture and propaganda organiser of the *partkom*, for his lack of concern about the provision of cultural services like film screenings to the dormitories.[110] Maliutin attempted to respond to Sitarzh's criticisms by stating that other party members had been successful in performing their cultural enlightenment duties without complaints, but he was interrupted by cries of 'she is right!' from the floor and a member of the presidium dryly commenting that listening to Maliutin, 'one could think that a club is not even necessary'.[111]

As a result of Sitarzh's efforts, L'vov promised to reserve part of the factory's budget for renovations at the dormitories.[112] During the discussion of the resolution draft at the end of the conference, Sitarzh also demanded that a point be added instructing the *partkom* to build a school for the children of factory workers. Many pointed out that this was a matter for the city authorities and not the Party but, at that point, the chair of Leningrad Soviet who was attending the conference announced that he would see to it that the issue was forwarded to the relevant agencies, to applause from the floor.[113]

## 4.3 Conclusion

Regardless of when it was that the promised school materialised, Sitarzh's efforts to get it built demonstrate the very material implications of some aspects of the Party's mission of cultural enlightenment. Indeed, a few months later, the seventh conference of the Leningrad *obkom* highlighted housing and public utilities construction as a central element of the province's economic targets for the third FYP, suggesting that the issues raised by Sitarzh where not confined to the Kirov factory.[114] The remaining three years between the first conference and the German invasion of the USSR, Leningrad communists would continue their cultural activism along much the same lines as described in this chapter, with the only major difference being the much stronger emphasis placed on the promotion of civil-defence and paramilitary training as appropriate 'leisure'

110 Ibid, ll. 166, 169. 111 Ibid., l. 177. 112 Ibid., l. 276. 113 Ibid., l. 322.
114 RGASPI, f. 17, op. 21, d. 2691, l. 43.

activities.[115] On that note, it is possible to offer some concluding comments on the KP/Kirov organisation's efforts to transform the factory into a socialist cultural site.

The Party's cultural activism can be divided into two main periods corresponding roughly to what cultural historical scholarship has identified as the cultural revolution accompanying the first FYP and the subsequent establishment of Stalinist culture. The picture that emerges from observing the activities of the factory's communist activists on the cultural front is one that suggests more continuity than is implied in the twin concepts of revolution and retreat. This is because, on the one hand, the poorly educated and extremely busy rank-and-file lacked the ability to affect revolutionary changes in the cultural sphere and, on the other, the rehabilitation of traditional values in Soviet public culture did not in any way diminish the extent of cultural activism that was taking place on the factory floor. Paradoxically, the intensity with which the KP/Kirov party organisation pursued its mission to cultivate the masses seems to have only increased after the national leadership 'retreated' from its revolutionary cultural ambitions.

The reason for this development is that the recalibration at the top confirmed what had always been the case at the bottom. As we have seen, the new Leningrad regional leadership under Sergei Kirov took a great interest in the development of cultural activism as a means of promoting the rank-and-file's political astuteness and preventing the re-emergence of pro-opposition views. In between implementing the Regime of Economy and fending off oppositionists, however, the party grassroots at KP did not rush to respond to the *gubkom*'s repeated calls for expanded intellectual horizons, except in so far as these translated into the provision of much desired services. As crash industrialisation followed by famine further squeezed the already pressed living standards of industrial workers, these services increased in importance, providing further incentive for activists to become actively involved in supervising their quality and provision. Although of course not attributable solely to this, the Union-wide shift in cultural policy towards less ambitious goals reflected the adoption of a more instrumentalist logic which required that cultural activism was directed towards the achievement of concrete policy objectives. When the securing of adequate standards of service quality became such an objective, communist workers responded actively and creatively. In famine

[115] TsGAIPD, f. 1012, op. 2, d. 1467 l. 81; TsGAIPD, f. 1012, op. 2, d. 2192, ll. 1–9; Kostiuchenko, *Istoriia*, p. 409.

conditions, 'battling cockroaches' and preventing potato waste were more pressing matters than studying party history.

None of the above goes to say that the rank-and-file did *not* engage with the more party-ideological aspects of their cultural mission. Marxist study circles were organised and joined by thousands of rank-and-filers and the progress of their studies was a frequently raised issue at the organisation's meetings by *partkom* members and concerned activists alike. Organising shop-floor newspapers, amateur writing clubs and political theory conferences was not a mean task in a giant machine-building plant increasingly staffed by barely literate former peasants. The frequent complaints about the state of cultural activism and party education in the factory thus seem to be more indicative of unrealistic expectations than anything else.

Finally, it is worth reiterating that there was nothing in the actions of the rank-and-file that went against the tasks set by party directives. The range of activities that fell within the scope of the Bolsheviks' cultural mission was so broad that every member of the factory's workforce could find something to relate to. Naturally, most party members gravitated towards the issues that affected their lives most directly, so that cultural activism on the KP/Kirov factory floor came to be primarily focused on matters of consumption and the provision of services. Conversely, those aspects of cultural activism that were of interest to fewer activists were marginalised in party discussions. This was the permanent problem of those seeking to promote activities regarding women's issues. One suspects that it was also the reason why some activists felt so disappointed by their comrades' performance in Marxist education. In terms then of the historiographical debate regarding the fate of the Soviet Cultural Revolution, what this chapter has shown is that the presence of the PPO provided party policy with a certain ideological and practical continuity even when the leadership engaged in what appear to be political about-turns. This is because, whatever the specific content of the Party's cultural policy, rank-and-file communists would be called upon to implement it in practice. Although party members obliged, they inevitably gravitated towards those aspects of cultural policy that were more readily relatable to their everyday concerns. Because of the worker-oriented nature of Marxist–Leninist ideology, there was always some campaign or part thereof that was of interest to KP/Kirov workers, making it possible for grassroots communists to engage actively with the Party's cultural enlightenment project even if they did so partially and intermittently.

The point here is that, in cultural affairs as much as in industrial policy, Marxist–Leninist ideology was sufficiently flexible that the varied signals and decrees emanating from the centre could always be selectively interpreted and partially implemented. In this area of party work also, the rank-and-file could thus pursue its own agenda while still remaining within the boundaries of the political mainstream. With this in mind it is easier to comprehend the process of political interaction between the leadership and the rank-and-file described in the preceding chapters. The centre relied on the vigorous presence and active engagement of party activists to promote its policies to the broader masses. Engaging the activists in a comprehensive programme of Marxist–Leninist education and a curriculum of cultural activities was intended on one hand to provide them with the skills necessary to lead their colleagues, that is to perform their vanguard role. One the other hand, and no less important from the leadership's point of view, solid ideological instruction inoculated the rank-and-file against views and attitudes that opposed the general line of the Party. Expanding the range of cultural and educational activities was, as we saw, an immediate concern of Sergei Kirov when he took over the city's organisation after the fall of Zinoviev.

This educational process was conducted in the same manner as other party business, that is through the organisation of campaigns involving the rank-and-file. Those whom the leadership sought to educate thus got to be in charge of the process of their education. There were concrete benefits of this state of affairs for the leadership, as it meant that its political message could reach a potentially larger party audience. The successful deployment of the rank-and-file against the opposition in the late 1920s is one indication of this. Nevertheless, the same Bolshevik discourse that kept the bulk of party activists on the side of the Central Committee was also what transformed the policy of *edinonachalie* into a target on the back of managerial personnel throughout Soviet industry at a time when the leadership was trying to build up their authority. The longer the reach of the leadership in delivering its message, the less control it had over its actual content. As the focus of CC declarations shifted from matters of administration and competency to those of state security and sabotage, this trade-off would end up giving the conflict between party activists and the administration a lethal dimension.

CHAPTER 5

# *Democratisation and Repression*

When the time came for delegates to the Seventeenth Congress to hear the general secretary's concluding remarks, Stalin rose to the podium to decline his ex officio right to have the last word at the Party's sovereign body. To thunderous applause from the floor, he told the audience that the responses to the CC main political report had demonstrated 'the complete unity of views of our party leaders ... on all questions of party policy', suggesting a hitherto unknown 'ideological–political and organisational firmness of the ranks of our Party'. There had been no objections to the CC line and there was, therefore, no need for the general secretary to respond.[1]

The so-called Congress of Victors convened in late January 1934 to review the results of the Socialist Offensive and outline the Party's political tasks with respect to the second FYP, already underway since the preceding year. It had the distinction of being the first such event since the revolution to not devote any of its time to the discussion of the views and activities of an organised opposition. The successful construction of the foundations of a socialist economy during the first *piatiletka* had demonstrated in practice that the CC had charted a true course, leading all honest oppositionists to recant and return to the fold. In Stalin's words, it seemed that there 'was nothing left to prove and, apparently, no one left to beat'.[2] Socialism had been built; the Party would now have to make it work.

In essence, this entailed a reorientation away from the expansionary, quantitative goals of rapid industrialisation towards a focus on the qualitative outcomes of policy. With regard to industry, this meant that if the goal of the first FYP had been nothing less than the complete transformation of the USSR's productive base, the second FYP would face the slightly less ambitious but still formidable task of bringing the products of the industrialisation drive to bear on production. What an early account

[1] Stalin, *Sochinenia* 13, p. 381. [2] Ibid., p. 346.

called the 'good years' of Soviet industrialisation saw a relative decline in the production of capital goods and armaments and a proportional increase in investment in the consumer goods sector. A series of good harvests made possible the phasing out of rationing by late 1934, signalling a broader relaxation of the extreme pressures on livelihoods demanded by the industrialisation drive.[3]

Aiming at the consolidation of the achievements of rapid development of the preceding period, the Party's industrial policy included plans for significant changes to workplace and labour organisation in order to rationalise the production process. With respect to shop-floor level labour relations, the most significant aspect of the Party's industrial policy was its renewed emphasis on technical competence and organisational efficiency, which in turn implied greater managerial authority and responsibility (*edinonachalie*) as well as the side-lining of some of the more conflictual forms of shop-floor activism – like counter-planning – in favour of a tightening of labour discipline. This shift in outlook amongst the leadership had already been signalled by Stalin in an important speech to industrial executives delivered in 1931.[4] November 1932 saw the introduction of new labour legislation that strengthened the position of management, making it possible to dismiss workers for one day's unjustified absence and transferring control of workers' ration books from consumers' cooperatives to enterprise administrations.[5] The resolution passed by the CC plenum of January 1933 formalised the new direction of industrial policy, declaring the second FYP to be one of 'mastering' (*osvoeniie*) and 'organised consolidation' of the new enterprises created by the previous FYP.[6] Thus, the Seventeenth Congress resolution on the second FYP positing the 'completion of the technical reconstruction of the people's economy' as a precondition for the 'raising of the material and cultural living standard of workers and peasants' was confirming a political reorientation already underway for some time.[7]

[3] Fitzpatrick, *Everyday Stalinism*, p. 6; Naum Jasny, *Soviet Industrialization, 1928–1952* (Chicago: University of Chicago Press, 1961), p. 142; Osokina, *Za Fasadom*, pp. 229–32.

[4] This listed six new conditions within which Soviet industry was developing and an equal number of tasks that needed to be tackled. Amongst these were the limitation of labour turnover, the training of technical cadres from the ranks of the working class and, importantly, a more conciliatory approach to old regime specialists who had demonstrated their loyalty to Soviet power. *Pravda*, 5 July 1931.

[5] The extent to which this latter provision was an integral part of labour policy or an improvised measure in response to the 1932–33 famine has been disputed by Robert Beattie, 'A "Great Turn" That Never Happened: A Reconsideration of the Soviet Decree of Labor Discipline of November 1932', *Russian History* 13, no. 1 (1986): 235–57, p. 250.

[6] *KPSS* v *rezoliutsiiakh*, vol. 6, pp. 17–18.

[7] Ibid., pp. 106, 120.

Although the renewed focus on technical skill and competence indicated a move away from dramatic, military-style campaigns in the economic field, the successful construction of the foundations of socialism encouraged the leadership to pursue no less ambitious goals in the political sphere. These included a series of sweeping reforms embracing both the Communist Party and the Soviet state. In 1935, Stalin headed a commission composed of the Party's most illustrious leaders to draft a new constitution for the country with the express aim of democratising the Soviet electoral system and reflecting the revolutionary social transformation that the USSR had undergone since the Great Break. The following year, the Party launched a mass public consultation campaign encouraging all Soviet citizens to comment on and recommend amendments to the draft.[8] In early 1937, a CC plenum resolved to shake up the party and trade union apparatuses by extending the Soviet democratisation campaign to their own ranks.[9]

Predicated on the premise that the toughest challenges to the USSR's march to communism had been overcome, the campaigns for democracy nevertheless unfolded against the backdrop of overlapping campaigns of repression gradually gaining steam over the same period. In what remains the most iconic aspect of these, several prominent former oppositionist leaders, including Kamenev, Zinoviev and Bukharin, were condemned to death between 1935 and 1938, after publicly confessing to shocking crimes against the state in three sets of highly publicised trials in Moscow. Furthermore, although the early years of the second FYP saw a decline in repression in terms of arrests and convictions, in mid-1937 the secret police unleashed a wave of mass operations against suspected enemies, leading to roughly two million arrests and 680,000 executions in one of the most violent episodes of the twentieth century.[10]

The dissonance between the noble pronouncements of democratisation and the violent elimination of political opponents led to a long tradition of

[8] J. Arch Getty, 'State and Society under Stalin: Constitutions and Elections in the 1930s', *Slavic Review* 50, no. 1 (1991): 18–35; Ellen Wimberg, 'Socialism, Democratism and Criticism: The Soviet Press and the National Discussion of the 1936 Draft Constitution', *Soviet Studies* 44, no. 2 (1992): 313–32.

[9] Getty, *Practicing Stalinism*, pp. 211–12; Wendy Goldman, 'Stalinist Terror and Democracy: The 1937 Union Campaign', *The American Historical Review* 110, no. 5 (2005): 1427–53.

[10] J. Arch Getty, Gábor T. Rittersporn and Viktor N. Zemskov. 'Victims of the Soviet Penal System in the Pre-War Years: A First Approach on the Basis of Archival Evidence'. *The American Historical Review* 98, no. 4 (1993): 1017–49; Peter H. Solomon, *Soviet Criminal Justice under Stalin* (Cambridge: Cambridge University Press, 1996), pp. 230–46; Robert Thurston, *Life and Terror in Stalin's Russia, 1934–1941* (New Haven: Yale University Press, 1998), pp. 1–10.

scholarship dismissing the democratisation campaigns as an elaborate piece of political theatre on the part of the regime, variously motivated by a desire to ingratiate itself with public opinion in liberal democracies or improve relations with its own subjects within the context of a rapidly deteriorating international environment.[11] Archival evidence, however, told a different story. The leadership collectively and Stalin personally invested considerable time and effort to design and promote the reforms and had to press hard against resistance from the party-state apparatus in order to get their way. This lent support to interpretations of the campaigns as a genuine though abortive attempt at institutional renewal, motivated by a desire to leverage popular mobilisation in order to dislodge corrupt party barons from crucial nodes of the Soviet state.[12] On this reading, mass repression was the product of the inauspicious confluence of mounting security fears and pent up social tensions, creating an explosive mix of denunciations and scapegoating, as exhortations to expose corrupt bureaucrats blurred into a hunt for enemies and wreckers. Grassroots political mobilisation generated targets for repression, leading to a rapid proliferation of victims and perpetrators in Soviet society.[13]

Primary party organisations were key engines driving this process, providing the institutional framework in which the social tensions of the mid-1930s could become entangled with the political initiatives of the leadership. PPO records thus offer a unique vantage point for following the gradual transformation of ordinary, if tense, social conflict into a lethal political crisis. They also demonstrate the significant extent to which the party rank-and-file remained a distinct actor deriving its understanding of the repressions from its own lived experience as filtered through its political outlook, in this way placing its own mark on events. In industry, this experience consisted primarily of workplace conditions and the permanently tense relations between workers and managers.

[11] Robert Conquest, *The Great Terror: A Reassessment* (Oxford: Oxford University Press, 2008), p. 79; Solomon, *Soviet Criminal Justice*, p. 191; Adam B. Ulam, *Stalin the Man and His Era* (London: I. B. Tauris, 2007 [1973]), p. 402.

[12] Getty, 'State and Society'; Samantha Lomb, *Stalin's Constitution: Soviet Participatory Politics and the Discussion of the 1936 Draft Constitution* (London: Routledge, 2017); Olga Velikanova, 'Stalinist Moderation and the Turn to Repression: Utopianism and Realpolitik in the Mid-1930s', in *The Fate of the Bolshevik Revolution: Illiberal Liberation, 1917–1941*, ed. Lara Douds, James Harris and Peter Whitewood (London: Bloomsbury Academic, 2020), 141–54.

[13] Getty, '"Excesses Are Not Permitted"'; Goldman, *Terror and Democracy*, pp. 133–62; Harris, *Great Fear*.

## 5.1 Management and Labour in the Second FYP

As we have seen, during the early phase of the second FYP, the Party's industrial policy was recalibrated to reiterate the main principles underlying the managerialist elements of *edinonachalie*, namely the pursuit of productive efficiency through discipline and clear delineation of responsibilities in the workplace. The new priorities stressed by the central leadership were promptly reflected in the business agenda of the Leningrad *obkom* bureau sessions.

In the first half of 1933, the leadership of the northern capital heard reports and passed resolutions on a number of matters relating to the broader goal of improving product quality in industry. On 25 March, the bureau issued a set of guidelines regarding 'Measures to implement the January CC plenum resolution on raising the quality of production', noting with disapproval that most sectors had not achieved a breakthrough in terms of qualitative indicators and that there had been individual enterprises where the quality of output had declined. The resolution warned that the bureau held enterprise and trust directors 'personally responsible for this completely unacceptable situation' and went on to list a number of recurring administrative failures that were compromising production quality throughout Leningrad industry. It concluded by instructing party and trade union organisations to reorient the focus of production conferences towards generating recommendations for improving the quality of output.[14] A month later, the regional leadership reviewed the progress of trade unions in pursuing this goal, directing lavish praise in the direction of machine-builders. Their achievements in reorganising productive activism to reflect the focus on qualitative improvements were declared to be examples worthy of imitation for organisations operating in all industrial sectors.[15]

In late May, the bureau heard reports from the director and party secretary of the *Svetlana* incandescent lamp manufacture, whose innovations in labour organisation and measures to rationalise administration stood as true 'examples of Bolshevik struggle for the fulfilment of economic–political tasks'. *Svetlana* had completed its production quota for the first FYP in a staggering two and a half years, during which time it had mastered the production of more than 100 lightbulb and vacuum tube types that the USSR previously had to import. The factory continued to

[14] RGASPI, f. 17, op. 21, d. 2717, ll. 26–28. [15] Ibid., ll. 89–90.

overfulfill its plan targets, having produced 111.3 per cent of assigned output by the end of the first quarter of 1933.[16]

The bureau noted that *Svetlana*'s outstanding success was due to its implementation of a 'technical industrial–financial plan' (*tekhpromfinplan*), which provided the enterprise with 'enormous advantages in the organisation of production and the mobilisation of all internal resources'. According to the report, the chief benefit of the *tekhpromfinplan* consisted in that it had provided the enterprise with a 'technically grounded and internally agreed plan of work as much for the factory as a whole as for every individual work-crew'. This made it possible to rationalise norm-setting and improve accounting at all levels of the productive process. At the same time, by further concretising assigned tasks, it facilitated 'mass control' on the workers' part of correct implementation of technical directives. Politically, this amounted to nothing less than every communist now having an enhanced ability to 'carry out the vanguard role in relation to non-party workers'.[17]

It is unclear from the bureau records whether the *tekhpromfinplan* amounted to a considerable innovation on the mere *promfinplany* used by Soviet enterprises to organise production or if *Svetlana's* management had been exceptionally competent in drawing up a workplan that reflected the principles of rationalisation and streamlining on which planners had been insisting for some time. Whatever the case, the excitement with which the Leningrad leadership welcomed this report reflected the new priorities of the second FYP. *Svetlana* was not only overfulfilling its targets, but also saving the USSR precious foreign exchange reserves by import substitution in a critical technological sector.[18] It had succeeded in doing so by rationalising the work process and raising productivity, an objective that the Party leadership had been pursuing since at least the mid-1920s. By the same token, *Svetlana* and its party organisation had made it easier for rank-and-file communists to further the Party's political objectives.

Such a combination of technical competence with political commitment being the desired outcome of the party-state institutional set-up in industry, the case of *Svetlana* was naturally seen as a model for the type of labour–management relations that could best drive forward the goals of

[16] Ibid., l. 116. [17] Ibid., l. 117.

[18] Vacuum tubes were essential components of radio receivers and transmitters at the time. Mastering their production thus represented a major technological breakthrough for the Soviet economy, securing domestic supply for its telecommunications industry. I am indebted to Stamatis Zafiropoulos for highlighting the significance of vacuum tubes in the technological context of the early–mid twentieth century.

the second FYP. The bureau thus instructed a number of key Leningrad enterprises to imitate the lightbulb manufacture and begin working according to a *tekhpromfinplan*. The streamlined efficiency and harmonious industrial relations reported by *Svetlana* were, however, not easily reproduced. Quality considerations had preoccupied KP party meetings well before the *obkom* bureau began to promote the bulb-makers' managerial innovations as the way forward for Leningrad industry. The new imperatives of the second FYP were reflected in the eleventh conference of the KP party organisation which met on 26 March 1933 to discuss the progress of the factory's production plan.

Delivering the main report, the factory director, Karl Ots, spoke of the achievements of KP during the first FYP, praising the factory's tractor and turbine departments for the progress made in the 'mastering' of new technology. As might be expected, however, there were a number of problems in production that demanded the organisation's attention, including rising unit costs and the familiar problem of stoppages, which had amounted to 2.9 per cent of worktime for the reviewed period. He went on to single out the metallurgical and first mechanical shops as facing particularly challenging tasks regarding the organisation of production in the coming period.[19]

In contrast to the organisation's seventh conference of 1931, party members from the shops did not attempt to deflect the director's criticisms by means of a comprehensive attack on managerial incompetence. Instead, they focused on the achievements of their shops and attributed problems to factors beyond their control. Studenikin, from the old forge, claimed that the shop had made great steps in combatting the extent of faulty output. This, he suggested, was achieved by means of campaigns by the *Komsomol* group of the shop which worked hard to promote orderliness in the workplace and the rationalisation of the working day. At the same time, workers who were producing high amounts of *brak* were brought under the supervision of more experienced employees. As a result, it was claimed that, in one case, a worker who produced sixty-five kilograms of faulty forged pieces the previous month had since produced no *brak*.[20]

Things in the steel-making shop were going less smoothly. Berlin, a delegate from the shop, deflected criticism about the pace of plan fulfilment by pointing out that the whole factory experienced supply problems.

[19] Ots did mention, however, that this was a significant improvement over the 4.8 per cent of time lost in 1931. TsGAIPD, f. 1012, op. 2 d. 616, ll. 4–6.

[20] Ibid., l. 38.

Stoppages at the shop were due to the fact that it was impossible to keep the furnace in constant operation without a reliable supply of magnesite. Berlin went on to criticise the bad state of account keeping in the factory which made it impossible to produce reliable inventories stating bluntly that the extent of useless paper-pushing at KP had become ridiculous ('*do smeshnogo dokhodit*'). The steel shop representative ended his contribution by demanding that Ots make good on his promises to reduce white collar staff and warning that if such plans did not go through, it would not be possible to speak of victories at the next conference.[21]

The morning session of the conference was concluded with a greeting from the 4th Turkestan Division of the Red Army, delivered by Kasin, a communist KP worker who was then serving at one of the division's rifle regiments. Before leaving the platform, Kasin reminded conference delegates that red soldiers around the country expected Putilovites to fulfil all CC resolutions regarding the mastery of technology and the elimination of *brak*.[22] The conference reconvened for its evening session a few hours after Kasin's greeting. Titov, from the turbine department, took the floor to report on the progress made by the department and respond to some of the criticisms made in its direction by members of the administration. Titov claimed that, in 1928 prices, productivity at the department had risen by 6 per cent while unit costs per turbine had been decreased by 30 per cent. In response to comments made by a member of the administration to the effect that the turbine department did not 'pay enough attention' to its set tasks, Titov returned the criticism:

> The leadership of our factory does not take into account the enormous importance of turbine production. If you are aware of the state of Leningrad industry . . . then you should know what kind of strain Leningrad's power stations are currently under. You are aware that Moscow power stations were attacked by wreckers and this speaks volumes about the importance of our production . . . Comrade Ots suggests that the turbine department should take care of its instruments. But the department is making its own instruments because of the lack of special equipment.[23]

Meiulans, a delegate from the metallurgical department, spoke along similar lines. Although he accepted that the department had been performing very badly and made up a significant part of the factory's overall *brak* and losses, he questioned whether the factory administration paid enough attention to metallurgy:

[21] Ibid., ll. 39–41. [22] Ibid., l. 45. [23] Ibid., l. 50.

> ... I must tell comrade Ots, the government and Party have issued a declaration calling for a turn to metallurgy but, so far, the administration has not done so ... The supply of materials is unsystematic. We only get help from the administration, particularly Ots, only when the factory shuts down. Then Ots himself gets this or that material necessary for metallurgy.[24]

After a few more contributions and another guest speech by a military officer reminding Putilov workers of the significance of the factory for the USSR's defence, Ots took the floor to deliver his concluding remarks. The director responded personally to Titov, stating that he protested too much. The turbine department had plenty of support, as demonstrated by its 400 hundred strong administrative apparatus. Rather than complaining, Ots went on, they should 'kindly work' (*izvol'te rabotat'*). Responding to Meiulans's complaints, Ots commented that if he turned his face to the metallurgical department, he would be turning his back on turbines. He would, therefore, not turn in any direction but get on with work, as should every factory department.[25]

The resolution passed at the conference was, in the habitual manner, a compromise document including references to all problems of factory life that had been highlighted during the discussion.[26] In this respect, there was nothing particularly new about the organisation's eleventh conference. It is this absence of significant change, however, that is of particular interest here, as this grassroots-level continuity was being maintained within the context of a significant recalibration of industrial policy at the top. At the same time as CC resolutions and the stricter labour legislation enacted by the government were signalling a shift towards a more productivist outlook on the part of the central leadership, the basic contours of factory-level party politics remained essentially the same as they had been since the beginning of the period examined here. The red director tried to get communist workers – nominally his comrades, but functionally his subordinates – to work harder and also convince their colleagues to do so too in order to meet the factory's persistently elusive targets.

As they had done consistently since the NEP period, communists from KP's shops responded by pointing out that they were already working hard enough, accomplishing significant feats in production. Whatever problems there were in fulfilling the factory's production plan were either due to

[24] Ibid., l. 66. [25] Ibid., ll. 81–84.

[26] The resolution included points about strengthening *edinonachalie*, raising workers' qualifications and improving the supply of goods through the enterprise stores. Ibid., l. 106.

economic factors beyond anyone's control, like the high cost of raw materials, or due to managerial incompetence, like bad book-keeping. What had changed were the terms in which the rank-and-filers made their case. This was a development similar to that of five years earlier, when the launch of the first FYP had closed off the possibility of openly opposing labour intensification, while at the same time enabling a frontal assault on managerial authority through the *samokritika* campaign. Now, the more technocratic orientation of the second FYP period necessitated the moderation of anti-managerial attitudes and specialist-baiting but also made possible a defence of shop interests articulated along the lines of a more business-like focus on achievements and possibilities of improvement in production.

Regardless of the political winds prevalent at the top, the nature of the party organisation as a political space where the conflicting interests of labour and management confronted each other remained essentially unchanged. This conflict was not predicated upon any of the centre's political initiatives, but on the economic realities of a rapid industrialisation drive which, even at its most moderate pace, put extreme pressure on workers while also making huge demands of managerial personnel.[27] What could, however, be affected by policy shifts was the relative intensity of this conflict on the factory floor. As the good will of the central leadership towards administrative staff was heavily dependent on economic performance, the truce between management and workers was as precarious as the sustenance of satisfactory output rates across Soviet industry.

The remaining years of the second FYP would place this truce under new stress. Although a number of economic indicators were improving in 1934, the breakthrough in labour productivity expected by the country's

[27] It may be objected here that rapid industrialisation was itself a political initiative of the Party leadership. The debate on whether this was a case of reckless adventurism or the only available response to an increasingly hostile international environment in an unfavourable economic conjuncture has a long pedigree and is beyond the scope of this monograph. For opposing views see Allen, *Farm to Factory*; R. W. Davies, 'The Economic History of the Soviet Union Reconsidered', *Kritika: Explorations in Russian and Eurasian History* 11, no. 1 (2010): 145–59; Gregory, *Political Economy of Stalinism*; Alec Nove, *Was Stalin Really Necessary?: Some Problems of Soviet Economic Policy* (London: Routledge, 2012). For a recent contribution on the international context of industrialisation, see Oscar Sanchez-Sibony, 'Depression Stalinism: The Great Break Reconsidered', *Kritika: Explorations in Russian and Eurasian History* 15, no. 1 (2014): 23–49. What is significant here is that the industrialisation drive was at the time already an economic reality that was beyond the scope of political debate even at the top, unlike the numerous campaigns initiated by the Party leadership in relation to it.

leadership had yet to materialise.[28] The plan foresaw that over 40 per cent of industrial growth for the 1932–37 period would be due to an increase in output per worker, in sharp contrast to the investment-led growth of the first FYP.[29] The persistence of the familiar problems of the Soviet production process, however, cast doubts on the feasibility of such ambitious improvements.[30] Combined with increased pressure from the industrial and defence commissariats for more investment, the unsatisfactory pace of labour productivity growth convinced the leadership to abandon the financial restraint of the original plan for a significantly larger investment budget for 1936.[31]

Besides the pressure placed on enterprise administrations by the progressive intensification of the plan, the emphasis placed by the CC on workers' cultural and material welfare posed further challenges for bosses throughout industry. Responding to the centre's instructions, the regional leadership in Leningrad began to display greater initiative in investigating and punishing cases of negligence or corruption adversely affecting workers' remuneration as well as their physical and mental health. On 30 January 1934, the *obkom* bureau issued a strongly worded public warning to the directors of a number of heavy industrial enterprises. The executives, including KP's Karl Ots, were threatened with party disciplinary action and legal sanctions if their factories continued to lag behind the repair schedule for tractors attached to their Workers Service Points (*Obsluzhivaiushchie Punkty Trudiashchikhsia, OPS*).[32] Created in 1932 as part of the Soviet state retail network, *OPS* were consumer good outlets attached to and serving the workers of particular enterprises. The larger ones acted themselves as parent enterprises to a number of subsidiaries, including of course state farms.[33] Having replaced a director who had failed to provide enough tractors for the USSR, Ots now found that his

[28] In the iron industry for example, the First FYP revised optimal target of 10 million tons smelted in 1932–33 was finally met in 1934. Allen, *Farm to Factory*, p. 93. Similarly, a good harvest in 1934 made possible the abolition of bread rationing in 1935.

[29] R. W. Davies and Oleg Khlevnyuk. 'Stakhanovism and the Soviet Economy', *Europe–Asia Studies* 54, no. 6 (2002): 867–903, p. 876.

[30] At KP, the party organisation's fourteenth conference held in March expressed concern at the factory's failure to fulfil its plan for February and called all workers to 'battle against *brak*'. TsGAIPD, f. 1012, op. 2, d. 939, ll. 103–5.

[31] Davies and Khlevniuk, 'Stakhanovism and the Economy', p. 874; Mark Harrison and R. W. Davies, 'The Soviet Military–Economic Effort during the Second Five-Year Plan (1933–1937)', *Europe–Asia Studies* 49, no. 3 (1997): 369–406.

[32] RGASPI, f. 17, op. 21, d. 2719, l. 9.

[33] *KPSS* v *rezoliutsiakh*, vol. 5, pp. 421–27; Osokina, *Za Fasadom*, pp. 163–67.

position was being threatened because he could not keep his own factory's tractors running.

Ots's administration and the factory's trade union organisations attracted the attention of the *obkom* again the following year. On 30 April 1935, a bureau session passed a resolution naming the enterprise along *Krasnyi Treugol'nik* and other pillars of Leningrad industry as being guilty of persistently and intentionally short-changing workers when paying wages. The bureau admonished those guilty of such malpractices that their behaviour amounted to 'forgetting on the part of the factory organisations ... of their direct responsibilities before the worker' and created a commission of its members to determine the concrete persons responsible and propose appropriate disciplinary measures to be published in the press. The bureau revisited this issue the following month, issuing formal reprimands to the chairs of the trade union committees of three enterprises and threatening all directors caught cheating workers out of earned wages with criminal prosecution.[34]

Although reflective of the shift in priorities inaugurated by the Second FYP, these interventions by the bureau should not be seen as a signal that the regional leadership was about to abandon industrial cadres to the whims of their party organisations. For the Leningrad chiefs as much as for the CC, the ideal form of industrial relations remained the harmonious coordination outlined in the decree of *edinonachalie*, where the political interventions of communists facilitated the diffusion of tensions generated in a productive process firmly under the operational control factory administrations. When overeager party committees got carried away and became too permissive of disruptive activities by workers, the *obkom* intervened to restore order.

One occasion for such intervention arose in early summer 1935, when the committee of Leningrad's Volodarskii district alerted the regional leadership that the machine-building plant *Bol'shevik* was in the throes of a serious crisis, due to the disconcerting inclination of its director, comrade Ruda, to a style of management relying on 'over-administration' (*pereadministrirovanie*) and bureaucratism. Responding to the *raikom*, the bureau noted that the behaviour of director Ruda had been 'incompatible with the principles of Bolshevik *edinonachalie* in a socialist enterprise'. However, it went on to rebuke the district leadership for having failed to control the activity of the factory's party organisation. The communists of *Bol'shevik* had crossed the line of acceptable criticism by casting aspersions on Ruda's

34 RGASPI, f. 17, op. 21, d. 2721, l. 46; d. 2722, l. 70.

political loyalties. To resolve the situation, the *obkom* bureau assigned its member Vasilii Shestakov to visit the factory and address an assembly of its party activists.[35]

Regardless, however, of the leadership's commitment to achieving the elusive balance between operational efficiency and ideological scrupulousness, the economic objectives of the mid-1930s ultimately increased the vulnerability of industrial executives to pressure from their party organisations. Shifting the emphasis to qualitative indicators of output did not in any way curtail the ability of the party rank-and-file to blame factory administrators for failures. Meanwhile, by insisting on improvements on living standards at a time when individual enterprises bore significant responsibility for provisioning their workforce, the leadership effectively created a new opportunity for administrations to fail and attract the wrath of their party groups.

The Stakhanovite movement of super-productive workers emerged within this context, less than two months after the Politburo meeting on 28 July 1935 had approved the new investment plan for the following year. Although Stakhanovism had antecedents in the shock-work movement of the first FYP, the initiative for this specific form of labour activism seems to have belonged to Konstantin Petrov, the party organiser of the Central Irmino mine in the Donbass where Aleksandr Stakhanov performed his legendary shift on 2 September.[36] The mobilising potential of Stakhanov's feat was quickly grasped by the leadership, who made sure it received maximum publicity in the national and regional press. Stakhanovism grew rapidly over the next few months and, by November 1935, the movement had gained such prestige that the First All-Union Conference of Stakhanovite Workers was attended by the full Politburo and addressed by Stalin.

In the spirit of the second FYP, Stakhanovism emphasised technical competence over physical exertion. It thus differed from earlier forms of labour activism in that it made aspiring Stakhanovites more dependent on external factors. These included the provision of favourable working conditions by their superiors and the competent performance of auxiliary tasks by their fellow workers. This increased the potential for workplace tensions, as auxiliary workers resented the prestige and benefits awarded to Stakhanovites for what they saw as a collective effort, while most foremen were probably less than keen to take on even more responsibilities in order to provide their subordinates with the opportunity to earn sometimes

[35] Ibid., ll., 236–37. [36] Siegelbaum, *Stakhanovism*, p. 69.

double their own wages. There were, thus, good material reasons for many workers and foremen to be against Stakhanovism just as there were good reasons for many workers to aspire to Stakhanovite status. This was precisely the kind of conflict of interests that the presence of the Party on the shop floor was intended to mediate.[37]

Indeed, Stakhanovism at the Kirov works does not seem to have become immediately popular amongst the Party's rank-and-file. The protocols of a number of shop-level party meetings held in the autumn of 1935 suggest that leading communist workers were frustrated by their comrades' under-performance and general lack of interest in the movement. At a meeting of the cold-stamping shop organisation, the party secretary reported that the leading Stakhanovite brigade was that of the wheel-builders, whose foreman was not a communist, while the shop's trade-union representative complained that some communists had even mocked Stakhanovism.[38] The party group of the second mechanical shop described the pace of the movement as extremely unsatisfactory and instructed its members to popularise Stakhanovism amongst workers by publishing the higher earnings of Stakhanovites and work with the shop's administration to review the pay of auxiliary personnel and expand the progressive piece rate system.[39] Similar concerns were raised at the metallurgical construction shop, with the superintendent Kulichkin admonishing communist activists to give Stakhanovism the attention it deserved.[40] This view of the movement's predicament was not one shared by all party activists.

A number of communist workers attending these meetings objected to accusations of indifference, arguing instead that whatever problems there were in the development of Stakhanovism in their shops was, predictably, the fault of their superiors. At the metallurgical shop, Alekseev argued that foremen bore prime responsibility for the obstacles faced by Stakhanovism such as the lack of clear pay rates and the existence of 'boring paperwork' which put workers off the movement. Alekseev further claimed that foremen avoided popularising the movement, stating that he had been awarded a bonus of twenty-five roubles for rationalising his work time but this was done 'somehow secretly, without telling anyone about it'. Another participant at the meeting, Bobrov, supported Alekseev, citing the example of the smith Alekhanov, who was not listed as a Stakhanovite despite regularly exceeding production norms. Parfenov concurred that

[37] For an overview of the sources of opposition to Stakhanovism, see ibid., pp. 190–204. For foremen in particular, pp. 165–68.

[38] TsGAIPD, f. 1012, op. 2, d. 1051, l. 42. [39] Ibid., l. 163. [40] Ibid., l. 58.

foremen did not understand Stakhanovism and were holding it back for fear that, if workers exceeded production norms, foremen would get fined for overspending their wage budgets.[41] Skokov, a worker of the shop's second shift, expressed the argument implicit in his comrades' contributions in a more succinct manner, stating that 'the essence of the Stakhanovite movement consists in raising the productivity of labour power . . . The system of labour remuneration in our department does not stimulate the raising of labour productivity'.[42]

Discussion sessions in other shops were conducted along very similar lines, with the timidity of foremen and issues of remuneration providing the common theme on which the speakers developed their contributions.[43] This peculiar form of buck-passing is a familiar process that can be traced at least as far back as attempts to economise and rationalise production in the NEP era. It is worth noting, however, that this is here taking place at the very bottom of the party and factory hierarchies. This is not a case of departmental representatives defending their shops' particular interests vis-à-vis the factory administration, but of rank-and-file workers negotiating their terms of employment with their immediate superiors, a negotiation made possible because of the political imperative of supporting the development of Stakhanovism. Less than two months after the publication of Stakhanov's record, party activists at the Kirov works were already warning about what we now know were the main constraints on the growth of Stakhanovism, the opposition of foremen and auxiliary workers.

The different terms in which this problem was framed with respect to foremen and auxiliary workers is worth considering shortly. Shop-floor party organisations seem to have viewed auxiliary workers as potential allies of Stakhanovism that could be enticed to support the movement if they were given adequate material incentives to do so. In contrast, foremen and superintendents were seen as being responsible for the development of the movement by virtue of their position, so that failure to promote Stakhanovism was presented more in terms of dereliction of duty than a problem which could be resolved by taking appropriate measures. Nobody

[41] Ibid., l. 59. [42] Ibid., l. 60.

[43] One of the main points made by the speakers at the cold-stamping shop meeting for example was that foremen and administrative staff must eliminate stoppages. Ibid., ll. 43. Apart from being a significant obstacle to the overfulfilment of norms, stoppages were also a threat to the income of any worker on piece-rates. Since 1932, workers were paid one-half or two-thirds (depending on sector) of their norm rate for periods of inactivity if they were not responsible for the stoppage and not at all if they were. Siegelbaum, *Stakhanovism*, p. 103.

proposed that foremen should be enticed to support Stakhanovism with material benefits. Much like the all-factory party conference, shop-level party meetings provided communist workers with an institutional space where they could articulate their interests and those of their colleagues and that they did so in terms of politically grounded demands from their superiors, in this case foremen and superintendents. The industrial party organisation functioned in much the same way at all enterprise levels. Communist workers like Skokov were letting their superintendents know that, unless they were provided with reasonable working conditions and attractive pay rates, they would not be able – or willing – to exceed their production norms and they would, therefore, not achieve Stakhanovite status. As every party member knew from experience, such a failure in policy implementation could draw the attention of their superiors, themselves reasonably worried about catching the eye of the authorities who, even during the most specialist-friendly phase of the second FYP, never quite stopped being on the lookout for recalcitrant officials.[44]

This practice took on a darker dimension as the Stakhanovite year of 1936 was succeeded by the mass repressions of 1937. The social tensions that had been accumulating in industry over the preceding years fuelled the hunt for enemies that swept Soviet society. However, they were not on their own sufficient to turn accusations of incompetence into suspicions of sabotage. To explain the conflagration, we need to turn our attention to a distinct process transforming rank-and-file communist politics at the same time as the second FYP was failing to change the fundamental contours of industrial relations within which they were embedded.

## 5.2 Another Purge

By the end of the first FYP, the political health of the KP party organisation was once again becoming a matter of concern for the leadership and *aktiv*. Success at the campaigns of 1929–32 had come at the cost of increasing neglect of the qualitative aspects of party building, as the need to keep up with the growth of the workforce had led to mass recruitment amongst the ranks of *udarniki* and other promising young workers. Assimilating the new communists proved to be a significant challenge for

[44] Despite signalling a more technocratic orientation in the Party's industrial policy, the January 1933 CC resolution did not fail to inform party organisations that 'merciless battle against all manifestations of opposition to party policy by the class enemy' was a necessary condition for the success of the plan. *KPSS v rezoliutsiakh*, vol. 6, p. 21.

the organisation. According to a report delivered at the ninth KP party conference by Aleksandr Ugarov, then chief of the culture and propaganda department of the Leningrad city committee, some 47 per cent of its total strength in April 1932 was made up of candidate members.[45] Of the 650 delegates that had been elected to hear and deliberate on Ugarov's report, 380 had joined the Party from 1928 onwards, 95 of whom had done so in 1931 and 17 in the four months of 1932.[46] In an attempt to remedy the growing levels of political inexperience within the organisation, the *partkom* had resolved that all new party secretaries of shop-level cells should undergo an intensive training course consisting of a total of twenty-four hours of study and including topics ranging from technical aspects of the production process to more abstract notions like 'the vanguard role of communists'.[47] The extent to which that programme was implemented remains unclear, as do its immediate results. Only a few months later, the *partkom* had to provide guidelines to its own members regarding the adequate preparation and timely submission of materials pertaining to items on its order of business. It seems then that organisational competence was a skill in short supply even above the shop level.[48]

The ability of the inexperienced, expanded communist rank-and-file to exert influence on the young former peasants that made up a large part of the industrial workforce following the FYP had become a major worry for the Party. In early 1933, the leadership decided that the circumstances called for a new purge campaign, announcing its decision in an article signed by the CC and published in *Pravda* in April. Noting that the Party had almost doubled in size by acquiring 1,400,000 new members over the previous 2.5 years, the front-page piece declared that the speed of recruitment had once more allowed the – by then proverbial – 'alien elements' that were 'careerists', 'double-dealers' and 'self-servers' to contaminate the membership. At the same time, it was highlighted that a number of 'conscientious' comrades remained 'unfamiliar with the programme, Rules and main resolutions of the Party'. They were, thus, unable to actively promote party policy. Thus, in addition to being an opportunity for the Party to demonstrate its integrity before the public by cutting loose the corrupt and the 'morally rotten', the purge was also meant to act as a means to gauge the political literacy of new communists and to provide them with an opportunity to raise their 'ideological level' within the context of a structured, mass campaign.[49] It was, thus, an attempt at

[45] TsGAIPD, f. 1012, op. 2, d. 432, ll. 20–21. [46] Ibid., l. 101.
[47] TsGAIPD, f. 1012, op. 1, d. 940, ll. 1–2. [48] Ibid., l. 8. [49] *Pravda*, 29 April 1933.

political consolidation following a period of disciplinary relaxation and ideological confusion, much like those that had followed the opposition crises of the 1920s.

The first meetings of the campaign at KP began in the first week of June and most of the purging process had been completed by the end of October, with the exception of some busy commissions which exhausted the November deadline set by the CC. A total of 5,324 full and candidate members of the Party underwent the scrutiny of their comrades and co-workers under the oversight of twelve shop-level purge commissions. As in the whole of the USSR the expulsion rate was significantly higher than in 1929, with 779 members excluded from the organisation according to the report given in its twelfth conference on 15 November 1933.[50]

In contrast to 1929, records of the public meetings of the 1933 purge at KP have been preserved in the organisation's archival collection, making possible a more direct examination of the purge campaign on the factory floor. The purging process consisted of a brief political–autobiographical statement given by the member under review followed by a number of questions asked by the commission and those present at the meeting. These were subsequently followed by contributions from the floor, after which the commission could pronounce its verdict. No specific limitations were stipulated with respect to the number of questions or contributions, with some of the more controversial cases taking up several hours.

The purge meeting protocols suggest that the higher rate of attrition was an effect of the indiscriminate recruitment of the previous couple of years much more than of any revival of oppositionist activity. In fact, while instances of past factional scheming were brought up by suspicious or curious participants at the purge sessions, these were in themselves neither sufficient grounds for disciplinary sanctions nor did they elicit a particularly inquisitorial style of interrogation from the commissions. One comrade, Shchagin, from the turbine shop-cell for example, for whom the only biographical information recorded is that he had a party penalty (*vzyskanie*), was asked by one commission member about his participation in the 1925 opposition. Shchagin responded that he was 'politically uneducated' at the time and that he no longer held such views. The commission member pressed on, asking Shchagin about his views on a 'newly emerging class'. Shchagin responded that he had 'believed the ITR to be a new class,

[50] TsGAIPD, f. 1012, op. 1, d. 955, ll. 1, 22; Kostiuchenko, *Istoriia*, pp. 437, 442. The national expulsion rate was 16 per cent, only marginally higher than that of KP. Rigby, *Communist Party*, p. 202.

but [was] more or less past this' following the clarification of the Marxist concept of class by one comrade, Sinev. In order to determine the extent of Shchagin's grasp of the party line, the commission went on to ask him 'what is the error of the Trotskyist view?' Shchagin responded correctly that Trotskyites were mistaken on the question of the peasantry and about 'socialism in one country'.

Despite his past, Shchagin seems to have been a conscientious worker. Comrade Tomason took the floor to speak in his favour after the end of the question session, saying that 'Shchagin doesn't have much education, but by his proletarian instinct always does the right thing'. Kostia Karimov, the secretary of the first mechanical shop cell who served on the commission also took Shchagin's side on the basis that he was 'a devoted worker' and therefore 'must stay in the Party'.[51] Such leniency regarding ideological infractions was also applied with respect to more recent events, as shown by the case of Ekaterina Ivanova, a 21 year-old candidate member who worked as a polisher. Ivanova, who was of peasant stock, gave satisfactory responses to a number of general political knowledge questions but was cornered by the commission about some limited commercial activity she seems to have engaged in at some point since her recruitment. In response to a commissioner's inquiry on whether she thought it 'appropriate (*k litsu*) for a party candidate to sell products on the market', Ivanova could only answer that she had been 'in a tight spot'. However, neither the circumstances nor the very fact of Ivanova's transgression were of much interest to her comrades and colleagues, who cared about her skill as a worker much more than any ideological infraction. Thus, after the end of questioning, one comrade, Shatsman, took the floor to deliver a fiery defence of the young polisher's record. Having reminded those present that Ivanova was an *udarnitsa*, Shatsman concluded that 'if everyone worked like her, we'd have a lot less *brak*'. The applause that followed Shatsman's defence sealed the positive outcome of Ivanova's review.[52]

Ivanova's and Shchagin's purge sessions were by no means atypical of the 1933 *chistka* at KP. The purge protocols contain numerous examples of communists under review receiving spirited defences by their comrades, as well as non-party participants, on the basis of their good record as workers. It is worth pointing out here that, strictly speaking, these arguments were for the most part irrelevant to the actual transgressions or failures that party members were grilled about; Ivanova's skill as a polisher

[51] TsGAIPD, f. 1012, op. 1, d. 958a, l. 8. [52] Ibid., l. 18.

was not in any way connected to her trade activities or to the question of their political permissibility. But as the purge campaign had been framed in broad ideological terms demanding ruthlessness towards self-seekers but clemency to those of pure intention, without stipulating concrete grounds for expulsion or demotion, it was up to the rank-and-filers to interpret these political imperatives.

At a time of rapid industrial expansion and technological change accompanied by rising levels of waste, stoppages and industrial accidents, skill at one's specialty and a good work ethic were far more valued qualities by shop-floor communists than the ability to distinguish between minute conceptual details or to adhere to political principles that were not directly related to factory life. It must be stressed again that, in conducting the purge in this way, the rank-and-file was neither hijacking nor being disingenuous about the campaign in any meaningful sense. The main duty of the industrial party organisation was to create and maintain appropriate political conditions for the realisation of the Party's ambitious industrial plans. In this sense, a skilled communist with a sound work ethic was also the 'committed in practice to the cause of the working-class' communist that the CC directive had explicitly shielded from the purge.[53]

Who then was not? From the available evidence, it seems that the penalty of expulsion was reserved for those who were politically entirely ignorant, as well as those who demonstrated a gratuitously careless attitude towards their work and had a very bad reputation amongst their colleagues and/or subordinates. The questions asked by the purge commissions to gauge the general level of communists' political awareness seem to have been deliberately designed to weed out only the completely clueless, ranging from the ludicrously obvious but not uncommon 'Who is Stalin?' to the bizarre 'When will Lenin rise from the dead?' asked of one Antipenko at the factory's electrical shop.[54] Even so, ignorance was not by itself a punishable offense, as even elementary mistakes were overlooked if the reviewee was a sufficiently capable worker. Irina Lebedkina, a 38-year-old drill press operator who had failed to progress from candidate status despite having joined the Party in 1927, stated that Stalin was the highest party organ before changing her answer to 'the Party Congress' after some

[53] *Pravda*, 29 April 1933.

[54] TsGAIPD, f. 1012, op. 1, d. 985b, l. 30. The protocol does not report any response by Antipenko who, having already answered a number of more reasonable questions about his payment of subscription dues, must have been completely dumbstruck by the last one.

thought. Lebedkina's co-workers remarked that she produced no *brak* and, therefore, 'must stay in the Party'.[55]

The reverse was not true, however. There are several cases of members whose past political credentials had been impeccable but fell afoul of the purge because of their attitude towards work and their colleagues. V. I. Pavloskii, a stoker-crew foreman with voluntary service in the Red Army and former agent of the OGPU, was deprived of membership after he was denounced as a 'bad and careless *brigadir*' in the contributions of his co-workers.[56] Most expulsions were, nevertheless, due to a combination of political and work-related irresponsibility, with persistent absence from party meetings and truancy or drunkenness at work emerging as the most common issues.[57] The most high-profile of such expulsions was that of the assistant superintendent of the electrical shop, Mironenko, whose examination lasted over six hours and had to be extended over two sessions. Mironenko, who seems to have been despised as a rude bureaucrat, was also discovered to have concealed his social origin when entering the Party in 1930 and was purged as a class-alien element after it was revealed that his kulak father had owned thirty-five horses and employed around forty labourers.[58]

Much then like the 1929 campaign, the *chistka* of 1933 had very little to do with internal political opposition. It was instead an attempt to ensure that the party membership maintained at least a tolerable level of political awareness as well as some understanding of and identification with the goals of party policy, after the immense pressures of the first FYP had caused political education to be neglected at a time of mass recruitment. The inevitably vague CC directives emanating from Moscow and demanding a separation of the wheat from the chaff, were implemented in practice by the KP communist rank-and-file as a mass examination of professional competence and collegial behaviour. At the purge meetings held in the shops of the enterprise, skill and work-ethic emerged as the ultimate markers of political reliability. The ability to confront and resolve the myriad of production-related problems thrown up during the socialist offensive had overtaken unreserved support for rapid industrialisation as the defining quality of a good communist.

We saw in Chapters 2 and 3 that the events of the late 1920s entrenched the status of the party organisation as a distinct locus of power on the factory floor, first by teaching the rank-and-file to draw links between its

[55] Ibid., d. 985a, l. 19. [56] Ibid., d. 985b, l. 22. [57] See e.g., ibid., ll. 21, 43–45.
[58] Ibid., l. 150; Kostiuchenko, *Istoriia*, p. 442.

own workplace demands and party policy and, second, by eliminating internal divisions which threatened its political legitimacy. The purge of 1933 also consolidated the strength of the organisation on the factory floor, but it did so in a slightly different way which would turn out to have significant consequences for the future. Apart from training a new cohort of party activists in the ways of mass *samokritika*, the purge's focus on and reward of technical competence also equipped communist rank-and-filers with the arguments and rhetoric they would need in order to confront the administration in the less voluntarist political environment of the second FYP.[59] By the same token that skill and competence became equivalent to political loyalty, incompetence or mere failure could now be framed in terms of duplicity, leaving administrative staff particularly exposed in the climate of individual responsibility promoted by *edinonachalie*.

## 5.3 Vigilance and Verification

While in 1933 the conflicts surrounding the identification and removal of the disloyal remained within the boundaries of relatively benign administrative sanctions, a year later things started to take a darker turn when, in the evening of 1 December 1934, Leonid Nikolaev shot Sergei Kirov dead inside the headquarters of the Leningrad Party Organisation at Smolny. A pivotal event in Soviet history, the Kirov murder and its connection to the mass repressions that followed a few years later have been the subject of much debate since the 1930s, with the weight of scholarly opinion currently against earlier speculation suggesting a Stalinist conspiracy.[60] Neither the motives of the murderer nor the effects of his act on the outlook of Stalin and the leadership are of import to this account. It is, however, necessary to briefly consider the impact of the murder of the Leningrad party chief and regular visitor at KP on the factory's own party organisation.

59 Several contributors at a meeting of purge commission members from all shops held in 1933 noted that labour discipline and output quality had increased during the campaign, while the main speaker suggested that the *chistka* had made it harder for the administration to 'hide behind the organisation', forcing it to assume greater responsibility for production. TsGAIPD, f. 1012, op. 1, d. 955, l. 20.

60 Åsmund Egge, *Zagadka Kirova: ubiistvo, razviazavshee stalinskii terror* (Moscow: ROSSPEN, 2011); J. Arch Getty and Oleg V. Naumov, *The Road to Terror: Stalin and the Self-Destruction of the Bolsheviks, 1932–1939* (New Haven: Yale University Press, 2002), pp. 140–47; Matthew E. Lenoe, *The Kirov Murder and Soviet History* (New Haven: Yale University Press, 2010) all favour the lone gunman view of the murder. The only post-archival scholarly study that remains open to the provocation theory is Amy W. Knight, *Who Killed Kirov?: The Kremlin's Greatest Mystery* (New York: Hill and Wang, 2000).

News of the murder spread quickly to KP and the first meetings to discuss the fateful event took place just after the end of the factory's evening shift, only a few hours after Kirov's death.[61] These produced a resolution, published the following morning, which denounced the 'vile hired murderer', praised Kirov and called members and workers to 'close ranks around the Party'.[62] In the late afternoon of 2 December, KP workers marched to the Taurid Palace where Kirov's body lay in state. Having paid their final respects, party members and supporters returned to the factory to hold funerary meetings and discuss the implications of the party chief's death. Karl Ots, the factory director, led one such meeting at the third mechanical shop. Ots opened the gathering with the solemn declaration that 'Kirov has been killed. Kirov is no more. He is dead.'[63] According to the stenographic record, everyone present stood up at this point, following which Ots proceeded to give a political appraisal of the murder. The bottom line of the director's speech was that Kirov's death was a form of punishment for the Party's under-estimation of the class enemy, a sign that 'the many tales regarding the end of difficulties, that our enemies recognise us as a great power . . . that the class struggle is over that we can live quietly, have not been proven right'.[64]

A number of contributions from the floor followed Ots's opening remarks, mostly consisting of short expressions of indignation and the occasional declaration of intent to join the Party or *Komsomol* as a militant response to the crime. However, the change in political outlook within the organisation brought about by the shocking event was best captured by a longer speech made by Matveev, an old Putilovite communist worker. Matveev wondered how it had been possible, at a time when 'the final class struggle' was approaching, for a class enemy to find his way into Smolny when one needed a permit to enter even the factory's workshops. He went on to add his own political appraisal of the murder which different slightly, but significantly, from that offered by Ots:

> At the morning meeting I looked at people's faces and read on those faces that they wanted to go and fall on (*brosit'sia*) that enemy. Who is that [enemy]? It is all those who are in the enterprises and waste-producers (*brakodely*) and machine-tool breakers (*stankolomy*), loafers, all truants, all

[61] Kirov entered Smolny at 4.30 pm and was shot shortly thereafter. Matthew E. Lenoe, 'Fear, Loathing, Conspiracy: The Kirov Murder as Impetus for Terror', in *The Anatomy of Terror: Political Violence Under Stalin*, ed. James Harris (Oxford: Oxford University Press, 2013), 195–215, p. 197.

[62] *Krasnyi Putilovets*, 2 December 1934 cited in Kostiuchenko, *Istoriia*, p. 462.

[63] TsGAIPD, f. 1012, op. 2, d. 952, l. 2. [64] Ibid., l. 5.

> those who mess up our socialist construction. Look, on the Neva there is a monument to Peter I. He was a great reformer. He is preparing to charge (*brosit'sia*) into Europe but old Russia in snake form holds him by the leg. Thus we must fall on our enemies.[65]

The resolution produced by the organisation in the hours after the murder and the speech made by Ots later in the day of its publication approached Kirov's murder in similar terms that would have been squarely within the mainstream of the Party's political thought at the time. The victorious construction of socialism pronounced by the Party's Seventeenth Congress in January and the USSR's accession to the League of Nations in September of the same year had taken place against the disturbing backdrop of Japan's occupation of Manchuria in 1931 and the Nazis' assumption of political power in Germany in 1933. The murder of Kirov must have served as an indication that no economic or political success could guarantee security in the current international context, making a call for unity and vigilance a reasonable, if formulaic, response under the circumstances.

Matveev's understanding of the situation was different. Not content with a mere call of unity in the face of the enemy, the old communist also stated his views on who the enemy actually was. In this his views differed considerably from those of Ots. For, instead of placing the murder within the framework of the menacing foreign threat, Matveev drew the attention of his comrades to enemies within not just the country but the very factory. The defeated class enemy, 'old Russia', had struck against the Party just as it was preparing to confront its enemies from abroad. It was not only those who were willing to resort to terrorism and murder that were enemies within. Matveev explicitly branded as enemies all those who were in anyway related to failures in production, attributing malicious intent to a broad range of problems ranging from truancy to equipment breakdowns. In line with Matveev's analogy, the party organisation had to fall on these enemies just as the Bronze Horseman tramples the snake of Russian backwardness under hoof.

Although preceding the mass violence of 1937 by more than two years, Matveev's speech foreshadowed the character of the terror as a campaign driven in large part by the misperception of failures or accidents as hostile acts. What makes it particularly striking is that it was not prompted by anything Matveev could have seen in the press. Although Stalin's

[65] Ibid., ll. 17–18.

suspicions appear to have settled on Zinovievites almost immediately after the murder, it was not until a couple of weeks later that supporters of the old Leningrad boss would be formally blamed for the crime.[66] The articles that appeared in *Pravda* the day after the murder described the killer as 'sent' or 'planted' (*podoslannyi*) by the class enemy, suggesting a foreign angle.[67] Matveev's identification of the incompetent and the indifferent with the class enemy was, therefore, an independent conceptual act. Significantly, neither Matveev nor any other speaker had anything to say about the Zinoviev or any other opposition; it had not after all been a matter of concern within the organisation since the end of the 1920s. Although then Kirov's murder was viewed as an attack on the Party, Matveev's speech provided an interpretation in distinctly new terms. His interpretation of the meaning of the murder was derived from his own experience as a worker and a Bolshevik. Thus, when Stalin and the leadership subsequently pointed to the enemy within as the main threat to the security of the Soviet state, they were echoing an already existing current of popular thinking which they themselves almost certainly shared.[68]

Pressure on former oppositionists started to build in party organisations throughout the country after Zinovievites in league with Whites were declared to have masterminded the murder.[69] Even so, vigilance with respect to the perfidious activities of oppositionists would emerge as a secondary theme at the meetings held as part of the renewed campaigns of organisational consolidation that were launched the following year. On 10 February 1935, the party organisation of what was now the Kirov plant held a general but closed meeting to take stock of the results of the discussions held around the confidential letter sent to party organisations nation-wide by the CC on 18 January. The letter had reiterated the allegations, placing the 'Leningrad centre' that had organised the murder under the tutelage of a 'Moscow centre' that was, therefore, morally complicit in the crime, condemning the Zinovievites in no uncertain terms

[66] *Pravda*, 17 December 1934. [67] *Pravda*, 2 December 1934.

[68] On the social roots of the pervasive belief in conspiracies in the interwar USSR, see Gábor T. Rittersporn, 'The Omnipresent Conspiracy: On Soviet Imagery of Politics and Social Relations in the 1930s', in *Stalinist Terror: New Perspectives*, ed. John Arch Getty and Roberta Thompson Manning (Cambridge: Cambridge University Press, 1993), 99–115.

[69] William Chase. 'Scapegoating One's Comrades in the USSR, 1934–1937', in *The Anatomy of Terror: Political Violence under Stalin*, ed. James Harris (Oxford: Oxford University Press, 2013), pp. 267–71; Lenoe, 'Fear, Loathing, Conspiracy', p. 206.

as 'the most traitorous, the most contemptible of all factional groups in the history of our Party'.[70]

Kostia Karimov, by then a *partkom* member, delivered the main report. Karimov started his speech with some typical invocations of the need for revolutionary vigilance at a time of intensifying class struggle and, in the spirit of the CC letter, went on to warn that the Party's enemies were everywhere and would use any available means in their desperate struggle to undermine socialist construction. As an example, he cited the one million rouble loss suffered by the Institute of Workers' Provisions, allegedly a result of the activities of the convicted Tolmazov who had been employed there.[71] Karimov went on to admonish his comrades to shed the habit of overlooking social origins and political pasts in favour of workplace achievements, mentioning the case of one comrade, Reviakin, 'who although not a bad communist or a bad superintendent, gave a bonus (*premiroval*) to a class alien and then made a theory about it, saying that bonus payments are not related to class'. According to Karimov, Reviakin failed to realise that 'working well is a method of class struggle on the part of kulaks who have entered our Party'.[72]

It would be stretching credulity to suggest that Karimov seriously held this view, having observed him advocating for fellow communists precisely on the basis of their work record less than two years earlier. In fact, only a few minutes later he would return to the familiar theme of a strong work ethic as a marker of political reliability, stating that the activity of party members, especially their performance in production, would have to be reviewed in a number of shops as 'the vanguard role in production of our communists' was the main indicator of good party character (*partiinost'*).[73]

Similarly contradictory views were also expressed by other speakers. Ter-Asaturov, the engineer who would succeed Ots as factory director a year later, declared that it would be best to rid the factory once and for all of alien elements, which he nevertheless equated with those who were not working correctly. According to Ter-Asaturov, two mechanics at the second mechanical shop had been found to disorganise production and been subsequently discovered to be class aliens. Nevertheless, 'from the point of view production ... they probably worked better than the previous mechanic'. Ter-Asaturov admitted that if they had not been alien elements, their work could have been deemed satisfactory but in light of

[70] *Izvestiia TsK KPSS*, 1989, No. 8. [71] TsGAIPD, f. 1012, op. 2, d. 1036, ll. 1–3.
[72] Ibid., l. 6. [73] Ibid., l. 8.

the circumstances the administration 'had to remove them immediately'. He promptly went on to contradict himself as follows:

> On the other hand, we have instances in the shops of people who had been White non-commissioned officers but then spent ten years in the Red Army and have proven themselves in production. And what should we do? Let them be or remove them immediately? Of course it would be good if these workers were our own (*nashi*), but at the present day it is undoubtedly necessary to leave them at work, but in the name of vigilance, some workers do not understand this issue, and begin to surround them in such an atmosphere in which a worker can't work.[74]

Even those militant speakers who did not see any reason to urge restraint could not quite decouple the question of one's political attachments from that of their performance at work. Speaking immediately after Ter-Asaturov, Sokolov from the cast iron shop warned that the careful approach suggested by previous speakers could 'lead to problems'. Among such problems Sokolov counted the activities of the planning department of his shop, which was staffed by people who were 'difficult to trust'. After some further speculation that the problems created at his foundry by the suspicious planners were derailing the plan elsewhere in the factory, Sokolov eventually came to the topic of Zinovievism with reference to one Gusev. A 'double-dyed Zinovievite', Gusev was apparently a serial 'wrecker' who had somehow managed to be classed as a shock-worker and get 'a shock-worker's rations card and receive a good sum of money'. Having nearly beaten up some worker who called him out, Gusev was eventually fired but, until that time, Sokolov claimed, 'everyone was pampering (*laskali*) him' and gloating that they were thus creating 'nice conditions'.[75]

Karimov, Ter-Asaturov and Sokolov were all responding to a political signal from the centre by interpreting it in terms that were comprehensible to themselves and their audience, while at the same time drawing attention to those issues to which they assigned the greatest priority. Karimov, an experienced communist with years of shop-floor experience as a fitter, understood that if communists did not behave as model workers they could scarcely expect to induce their non-party colleagues to do so. An engineer with responsibility for plan fulfilment, Ter-Asaturov was probably more concerned about holding on to skilled and capable workers than about their pre-revolutionary past. As senior members within the context

[74] Ibid., ll. 28–29. [75] Ibid., l. 31.

of the organisation, both Karimov and Ter-Asaturov demonstrated their vigilance by warning that performance should not be mistaken for loyalty, but they had both barely finished their sentences before declaring that performance was in fact the most important form of loyalty.

By contrast, Sokolov's concerns could be easily expressed in the language of vigilance, so that he did not have to qualify his condemnation of Gusev with any calls for caution. According to Sokolov, Gusev was a bad worker, a wrecker, allowed to pretend to be an *udarnik* because of the organisation's softness. He, thus, undermined both the interests of the factory and the authority of the Party amongst non-party workers, having access to shock-worker privileges at a time of renewed concern about the availability of staples.[76] For Sokolov, Gusev's Zinovievism seems to have consisted entirely in his bad qualities as a worker.

It is worth noting at this stage that the CC letter that provided the occasion for this meeting did not mention 'wrecking' or sabotage as activities that the minions of the Leningrad and Moscow centres should be expected to engage in. The letter had denounced the Zinovievites as an unprecedentedly treacherous faction but had failed to provide any indication as to what kind of activities their devious henchmen might get up to. Thus, Karimov and the other speakers were of their own accord linking the question of the presence of political enemies with that of problems in production. It is unclear if they were doing so in an attempt to respond to views that had been expressed by workers like Matveev in the weeks since Kirov's murder, or if they themselves genuinely believed that production was under threat because of the presence of hostile elements in the factory. In either case, Zinovievism was not evoked here as a concrete oppositionist political platform. Within the framework of an industrial party organisation, politics was about making the factory run smoothly and fairly. If the nebulous menace of Zinovievism could account for such shocking tragedies of high politics as Kirov's murder, it made sense for grassroots communists to associate it with the multitude of problems they experienced on the factory floor. Party activists at KP needed no prompting to attribute production failures to bad bosses and inconsiderate colleagues; these had always been the main target of invective in the PPO. When the

[76] The abolition of bread rationing on 1 January 1935 had been the cause of much worry amongst workers in Leningrad and the USSR, as the attendant wage raises failed to immediately catch up with prices. See Sarah Davies, *Popular Opinion in Stalin's Russia: Terror, Propaganda and Dissent, 1934–1941* (Cambridge: Cambridge University Press, 1997), pp. 27–29; Osokina, *Za Fasadom*, pp. 238–39; Lesley A. Rimmel, 'Another Kind of Fear: The Kirov Murder and the End of Bread Rationing in Leningrad', *Slavic Review* 56, no. 3 (1997): 481–99.

leadership began to frame Zinovievism as the epitome of political iniquity, it was an obvious move for the rank-and-filers to adopt the term to brand the villains of their own social context.

As Kirov's murder receded into the past, the notion of an organised political threat broadly related to Zinovievism gave way to the older and more vaguely defined idea of the presence of alien elements amongst the ranks. The corollary of this was that at the grassroots level, the indeterminacy of the purported threat made it even less distinguishable from the ever-present problems of industry. Thus, the Union-wide verification of documents campaign launched in May 1935 quickly got entangled with the numerous other challenges faced by party organisations during that period, not least of which was the launching of the Stakhanovite movement later in the year. Protocol records from meetings held in the factory's shops in late 1935 indicate that the verification campaign was rarely discussed, even when it appeared on the meetings' agendas, with speakers often admitting that they were failing to give it the required attention. When they did talk about it, Kirov communists more often than not linked the need to confirm the reliability of party card holders to specific failures in plan fulfilment which, in light of their comrades' presence where they occurred, were seen as inexplicable.[77]

It is worth devoting some space to considering the verification campaign (*proverka*) here, as it provides substantial insight into the multiple crises coalescing in the mid-1930s. Concerns about membership accounting and the quality of record keeping induced the leadership to freeze recruitment at the launch of the 1933 purge and, by October 1934, had crystallised into a decision to conduct a large-scale documentation of active members. On 13 December, the CC instructed regional organisations to review and improve their methods of record-keeping and report on the results. The regions were less than keen to comply, with several *obkomy* failing to even respond to the directive. This prompted the CC to send out instructors to the straggling regions to inspect local document handling practices on site. The emissaries discovered instances of shocking disregard for proper accounting practices and document security, including hundreds of unregistered active communists, cases of expelled members retaining their

[77] For example, at a meeting of the wood processing shop cell held on 8 October to discuss the potential presence of hostile elements in the Party, Egorov decried the fact that communists had allowed faulty chairs to be sent to a retail outlet (*univermag*) urging vigilance. TsGAIPD, f. 1012, op. 2, d. 1051, l. 40.

credentials and casual attitudes towards the keeping of blank party cards, which were often found lying about in party offices.[78]

Having spent a considerable part of the first half of 1935 in fruitless exchanges with the regions, the CC resolved to relaunch verification as a centrally coordinated all-Union campaign. In mid-May, a secret letter 'On Disorders in the Registration, Distribution and Safekeeping of Party Cards and on Measures for Regulating this Matter' was dispatched to all party organisations, lambasting the state of record keeping in the entirety of the apparatus from PPOs to the CC. The letter declared a verification of the entirety of the Party's membership to be the only way in which the chaotic state of the apparatus could be brought to order. This was to take the form of individual assessment of every single card-carrying member by the *raikom* bureaus, in a process that was expected to last no more than three months. The concluding section of the letter left no room for doubt as to the seriousness with which the CC regarded the *proverka*, threatening to expel regional and district secretaries who failed to pursue the campaign with appropriate vigour.

Such vigour turned out to be in short supply and the CC had to push repeatedly for the campaign to remain on schedule, while also taking disciplinary action against the most obstinate heel-draggers.[79] A plenary session of the CC held in late December heard a report from Nikolai Yezhov in his capacity as head of the Department of Leading Party Organs, in which he admitted that the verification had still not been carried out in its entirety. Effectively conceding that the *proverka* had been unsuccessful, Yezhov announced an almost identical campaign of 'Exchange of Party Documents' to be conducted over 1936.[80]

The failure of the party apparatus to run what on the face of it was a simple accounting exercise was certainly a serious disappointment for the leadership. More disturbing still, however, was the fact that the process had confirmed some of the suspicions that had motivated the verification in the first place. Yezhov's report stressed the fact that the process had uncovered serious malpractice with respect to recruitment in numerous organisations, whose alarming lack of 'Bolshevik vigilance' had resulted in party cards ending up in the hands of the wrong people, including sworn enemies of the Soviet state.

[78] Getty, *Origins*, pp. 58–62.
[79] For a detailed account of the verification process and its eventual fizzling out, see ibid., pp. 68–78.
[80] *Pravda*, 26 December 1935.

Evidence from Leningrad is indicative of such failures at the local level, even though the province was amongst the model performers in terms of the *proverka*. Under the leadership of Andrei Zhdanov, who had succeeded Sergei Kirov after the latter's murder, Leningrad carried out the verification on schedule and with a small rate of attrition.[81] During the course of the campaign, however, the *obkom* discovered cases of severe incompetence and disturbing dereliction of duty by party officials. Thus, despite having issued clear instructions regarding the proper procedure to be followed during the verification immediately after the circulation of the CC letter, the *obkom* bureau had to intervene a few weeks later and annul the results of the process in a number of districts where it had already been completed. Inspections had shown that the verification of individual members had in several cases been partial or merely rubber-stamped, casting doubts about the extent to which district-level officials took the campaign seriously. Such worries were compounded by the cavalier disregard for document security often observed at district party offices, which raised serious concerns about the integrity of the procedure more broadly. The bureau ordered a rerun of the whole verification process in the worst performing districts, making sure to inform the affected PPOs that the ordeal had to be repeated because of the ineptitude of their *raikomy*.[82]

In line with events in the rest of the country, the Leningrad verification brought to light long-festering cases of corruption and serial malpractice that threatened to fatally undermine the authority of the Party amongst its constituents. Such revelations were more alarming to the regional leadership than the familiar ineffectualness of the apparatus, but they also highlighted the significant extent to which administrative failures overlapped with and exacerbated the social tensions party policy was trying to diffuse. On 26 June, the bureau reviewed the findings of an investigation of two suicides committed by workers in the rural Starorusskii district. Both suicides had been esteemed activists. Efremov, a warehouseman at the state farm *Stal'*, had held party membership since 1928 and Arsent'eva, a worker at the *Parfinskii* plywood factory, had distinguished herself as a shock-worker. The inquiry had shown that negligence and callousness on the part of their superiors had in both cases been key factors in driving the workers to take their own lives.

The bureau deemed Efremov's suicide to have been 'the result of the heartlessly bureaucratic treatment' he had experienced from the leadership of the *sovkhoz*. Efremov had been facing material hardship for some time,

[81] RGASPI, f. 17, op. 21, d. 2702, l. 5. [82] Ibid., d. 2722, ll. 191–93.

while also struggling with his warehouse accounting tasks due to his low level of education. His bosses and comrades not only made no effort to lend him assistance, but also threatened him with criminal prosecution. The circumstances surrounding Arsent'eva's death were even more disturbing. The investigation had established that the decorated *udarnitsa* had killed herself after having been sexually assaulted by the superintendent of her shop, Vasilii Chernov, and subsequently slandered by his brother as a prostitute. Chernov had a reputation as a sleazy boss who often used his position to take sexual advantage of his subordinates. Despite the fact that both brothers were party members, the secretary of the *Parfinskii* organisation took no measures against them.[83]

In both cases, the *obkom* bureau identified deeper and more alarming dimensions to the villainy of the local leadership. The administration of *Stal'* often delayed workers' wages, a practice that certainly contributed to Efremov's hardship. The party committee had not only failed to hold the farm's managers to account, it had also gratuitously neglected its own fundamental responsibilities, having organised very little in the way of political meetings, conferences and other forms of 'mass party work'. Although scarcely comforting to the regional leadership, the identity of *Stal's* party organiser went some way towards explaining such egregious dereliction of duty. *Partorg* Dobashin was 'the son of a large landowner, [had in the past been] expelled from the Party [and] dismissed from trade union work with a reprimand for idleness'. Murkier still was the aftermath of Arsent'eva's suicide. Although both of the unfortunate woman's tormentors stood trial and were convicted, they inexplicably kept hold of their party cards and remained at large for a month and a half. The regional review court then quashed their convictions in what the bureau resolution described as an instance of 'criminal short-sightedness'. To make matters worse, the Starorusskii district committee had been impermissibly torpid in its response to the suicides, being content with taking the local leaders at their word without carrying out a thorough investigation involving the rank-and-file.[84]

The bureau resolved to issue formal reprimands to the district committee instructor who handled the case and the party secretary of *Parfinskii.* It also took the extraordinary step of dissolving the factory's party committee and placed the organisation under the direct control of the district. Dobashin was removed from his post and referred for (re)expulsion. The *raikom* secretaries were admonished that their failure to expose 'the

[83] Ibid., l. 149. [84] Ibid., l. 150.

scandalous facts' taking place at *Parfinskii* amounted to a dereliction of duty. They were instructed to expose and bring to justice the persons responsible for the overturning of the Chernovs' conviction, while also carrying out an energetic campaign of *samokritika* to revitalise 'the mass party work of the organisation, cultivating a sensible, loving (*liubovnoe*) attitude towards living people'. To the same end, the trusts to which *Stal'* and *Parfinskii* belonged were instructed to take immediate measures to eliminate wages arrears and commit funds to the improvement of housing and services for workers. These measures were to be overseen by the regional trade union committee and supported by a press campaign managed directly by the *obkom*.[85]

It is unclear whether the investigation into Arsent'eva's and Efremov's suicides in the midst of the verification drive was coincidental. Whatever the case, the details of the case and the outcome of the inquiry are highly illustrative of the way in which the bottom rungs of the party apparatus provided the point of convergence for the multiple crises brewing in the mid-1930s. Economic hardship had in both cases been the underlying cause of the two workers' desperation, leading the bureau to respond by instructing local authorities to improve living conditions and liquidate wage arrears.[86] The proximate cause was found to be callousness and abuse by superiors. That such phenomena plagued the apparatus was of course no news. Party resolutions had been condemning 'wicked bureaucratism' for at least a decade. In the context of the Union-wide verification campaign, however, this familiar, if troublesome, issue assumed a new dimension. The negligent secretary of Efremov's PPO had turned out to be a class enemy who had conned his way into the Party. It was scarcely surprising that his record of political work had been underwhelming. More alarmingly still, the infamous Chernovs had not only retained their party cards even after receiving a court conviction for their crimes, but also evidently had a patron powerful enough to get these convictions overturned.

It was certainly bad enough that the Chernovs and Dobashins lurking within the apparatus were blackening the Party's name amongst its core constituents. The verification had, however, demonstrated that such bad apples were not exactly rare, raising the question of what other executive posts had been usurped by the incompetent, the corrupt and the outright

[85] Ibid., l. 151.

[86] In Arsent'eva's case, the assumption was presumably that Chernov would not have been in a position to exploit his subordinates if the latter had had sufficient economic security.

hostile. Thus, having started as an exercise in good book-keeping, an administrative counterpart to the mass-political campaign of the 1933 purge, the *proverka* ended up casting serious doubts on the reliability of the party-state apparatus at a time when the leadership was beginning to or had already set in a motion a number of ambitious policy initiatives that had been made possible by the completion of the first FYP. By means of the purge, the leadership had been able to leverage the activity of sympathisers and the rank-and-file to drive unreliable elements out of sensitive party and state posts, while also legitimating a new grassroots leadership by making it undergo a mass process of public accountability. The verification demonstrated, however, that it had been possible for plenty of the intended targets of the purge to escape detection. Worse, it had shown that the local instances of the party apparatus could close ranks around individual members to shield them from deserved punishment.

The response of the Leningrad bureau to the *Starorusskii* muddle foreshadowed the way the Party would address the smouldering organisational crisis uncovered by its recent bout of administrative introspection. By ordering a mass political campaign involving the local rank-and-file and publicising it in the press, the regional leadership was in effect redeploying the tools of the purge on a more limited scale. This move indicated that if the Party could not trust its local executives, it was willing to mobilise the mass membership against them. Two years later, the same process would be launched on an all-Union scale.

## 5.4 Party Revival, State Violence

When the public consultation campaign for the 1936 Constitution was launched, the Party leadership had already been issuing unequivocal signals of its intention to mobilise the Soviet people in order to expose and dislodge unfit elements from the state apparatus. A few months before the publication of the draft, Stalin gave an interview to American journalist Roy Howard where he predicted that the multi-candidate elections stipulated in the new basic law would arm the people against corrupt officials. 'Have you improved housing . . .? Are you a bureaucrat? Have you helped to make . . . our lives more cultured?' would be some of the issues candidates would be grilled on by their constituents according to the general secretary.[87]

[87] *Pravda*, 5 March 1936.

By that time, however, the crisis generated by persisting social tensions and organisational disarray was being compounded by a precipitous deterioration in the international environment. Hitler's efforts to construct an international anti-communist coalition, further Japanese encroachments into China and the subsequent outbreak of the Spanish Civil War all served to convince Stalin and the leadership that an international military conflagration was imminent. In this context, NKVD investigations became particularly concerned with uncovering spy rings and other subversive elements in the party-state apparatus that could be exploited by the enemy in the event of a military invasion of the USSR.[88]

In the autumn of 1936, and as the public discussion on the draft Constitution was gathering pace, Nikolai Yezhov replaced Genrikh Yagoda as head of the NKVD. Yezhov's appointment came shortly after the arrest of the deputy commissar of heavy industry, Georgii Piatakov, in September 1936 and an explosion in the Kemerovo mines in Siberia that cost the lives of ten workers. Having already emerged as the Party's chief inquisitor in the preceding years, Yezhov had long sought the top security job in the USSR. Although his appointment was not prompted by the Kemerovo explosions, their coincidence was reflective of the convergence of the social and political crises. The highly publicised trial of former oppositionists and managerial staff in the mines as wreckers who had deliberately caused the explosions was followed less than three months later by the trial of the Parallel Anti-Soviet Trotskyist Centre, the second Moscow Trial which condemned Piatakov to death.[89]

Thus, by the end of January 1937, the Party leadership was issuing unequivocal signals that problems in production were the malicious work of enemies and saboteurs who inhabited the party-state apparatus. It did so in the midst of an expansive drive for democratic reform that it had framed as a far-reaching anti-corruption campaign. And by entrusting the security apparatus to the most relentless conspirator-hunter among its ranks, it had finally locked into the place the conditions that led to the explosion of state violence that swept the country in subsequent months. Rank-and-file communists had needed no special tutelage to attribute everyday crises to foul-play. Their constant stream of complaints about incompetence and corruption certainly filtered upwards and likely played its part in convincing the leadership that something was gravely amiss in the Party and the

[88] Harris, *Great Fear*, pp. 143–45; William Chase, *Enemies within the Gates?: The Comintern and the Stalinist Repression, 1934–1939*, 1st ed. (New Haven: Yale University Press, 2001), chapter 4.

[89] Goldman, *Terror and Democracy*, pp. 95–109.

state apparatus. Yezhov's appointment marked that critical turning point when pervasive social tensions began to be treated as problems of state security. State violence thus became a seemingly appropriate response to the mass of denunciations that were already a permanent feature of grassroots politics.[90]

This fateful policy shift occurred just as the development of Stakhanovism in industry had kicked off a new spell of shop-floor tensions. As we have seen, the Stakhanovite movement was launched as an effort to raise the productivity of labour across Soviet industry by providing workers with a complex set of material and moral incentives in the form of higher wages, improved access to consumer goods, publicity and prestige. In this respect, it was substantially similar to efforts to improve productivity through labour activism in the first FYP. Unlike *udarnichestvo*, however, Stakhanovism emerged at a time when specialist-baiting was officially discouraged and technical competence was overtaking the ability to 'storm' as the defining feature of the model worker. However, the mistrust of workers towards the administration was not produced by the political signals emanating from the centre but had been a permanent feature of industrial relations on the factory floor at least since the beginning of the period examined in this book. It was the scale of this mistrust, as well as the way in which it could manifest inside the party organisation that the political initiatives of the leadership determined.

This is consistent with the views of a number of scholars who have argued that Stakhanovism provided the background to repression in industry by creating multiple opportunities for conflict between workers and management, which fed into the waves of denunciation that fuelled the terror.[91] Following the Union-wide trend, 1937 at the Kirov works saw allegations of blocking Stakhanovite initiatives turn into accusations of wrecking and industrial sabotage. During a meeting of the factory's third mechanical shop, a recent promotee named Vetiutnev came under fire for

[90] On Yezhov's strong belief in an expansive conspiracy of foreign intelligence and former oppositionists and his efforts to convince more sceptical members of the Politburo (including Stalin), see J. Arch Getty and Oleg V. Naumov, *Yezhov; The Rise of Stalin's 'Iron Fist'* (New Haven: Yale University Press, 2008), pp. 185–202, 212, 222.

[91] Goldman, *Inventing the Enemy*, pp. 81–139; Goldman, *Terror and Democracy*, pp. 55–94; Siegelbaum, *Stakhanovism*, p. 249, etc.; Robert Thurston, 'The Stakhanovite Movement: The Background to the Great Terror in the Factories, 1935–1938', in *Stalinist Terror: New Perspectives*, ed. J. Arch Getty and Roberta Manning (Cambridge: Cambridge University Press, 1993), 142–60. See also Roberta Manning, 'The Soviet Economic Crisis of 1936–1940 and the Great Purges', in *Stalinist Terror: New Perspectives*, ed. J. Arch Getty and Roberta Manning (Cambridge: Cambridge University Press, 1993), 116–41 for an account linking the repressions to economic problems.

allowing 'wrecking' to take place in the shop. One Kotliarenko warned party members that there were many enemies of the people in their factory and accused Vetiutnev of underestimating the threat of wrecking while letting the Stakhanovite movement fizzle out without leadership. Spitsa, a worker who took the floor after Kotliarenko, suggested that part of the blame for the shop's failures should be attributed to the factory's new director, Ter-Asaturov, who, having placed Vetiutnev at this post, did nothing to check up on the shop's progress. 'Essentially', he went on, 'willingly or not, everything has been done so that the plan would not be fulfilled'. Spitsa finally claimed that nothing had been done to improve the workplace and wondered if this was because 'they' could not or did not want to do so. His rhetorical question elicited a quick response from the floor with an unnamed participant interrupting to state in no uncertain terms that it was because they did not want to.[92]

Given the conflictual nature of factory politics we have observed so far, it is hardly surprising that party members like Spitsa seized the opportunity provided by the changing political climate to launch attacks against the administration. What is worth noting here, however, is that, as demonstrated by the shop meetings of October 1935 discussed in this chapter, party activists had already identified the main potential obstacles to the then nascent Stakhanovite movement in the usual suspects of bureaucratic administrators and foremen at a time when the Party leadership was still committed to a technocratic orientation in its industrial policy. This suggests that in spite of the promotion of professionalism and managerial authority by the leadership for at least a few years, the outlook of rank-and-file party members had not changed substantially since the first FYP.

Much as had been the case with the introduction of *edinonachalie* into the factory, party members manipulated a political initiative which the leadership had hoped would rationalise the work-process and raise productivity to improve their position as workers with respect to the administration. The technical expertise required to make Stakhanovism work thus ended up making it possible to hold experts and foremen responsible for its failures, just like the authority bestowed upon directors by *edinonachalie* ended up making them responsible for failures in plan fulfilment. In both cases, it was the activity of communist workers in their capacity as enforcers and trouble-shooters of party policy that undermined the

[92] TsGAIPD, f. 1012, op. 2, d. 1060, l. 1. Mikhail Ter-Asaturov, the young draughtsman who we saw earlier arguing for the communisation of the administration had by that time replaced Karl Orts as director.

position of managerial staff and made them targets for the authorities. Once the Party began looking for wreckers rather than solutions to industrial problems, political discourse on the factory floor changed seamlessly from allegations of incompetence to accusations of sabotage, as exemplified in Spitsa's statement that consciously or not, as if it made no difference, his shop's plan was being sabotaged.

The ubiquitous presence of wreckers thus acted as the main point of reference against which the mass campaign of repression that marked Yezhov's NKVD tenure was waged in industrial enterprises. If, however, the perceived need to root out saboteurs provided the rationale for the hunt for enemies, the mechanism by which repression spread through industry was on the face of it a much more benevolent initiative. Apart from the *Yezhovshchina*, 1937 also saw the leadership double down on the democratisation campaign initiated by the launch of the draft Constitution. The confluence of repression and democratisation was starkly manifest in the CC plenary session held in February–March 1937.

The plenum has long been known as a prelude to the Third Moscow Trial, devoting the first part of its business to interrogating Bukharin, the erstwhile leader of the Right Opposition, about his links to the alleged conspiracy uncovered by Yezhov's investigations. After Bukharin was escorted out of the conference hall by armed NKVD officers, the focus shifted on leading CC functionaries without an oppositionist past. Zhdanov took the floor to announce that the multi-candidate elections by secret ballot that formed the spearhead of the Soviet democratisation campaign would be extended to the party apparatus. Supported by Stalin, Zhdanov made no bones of the fact that the ultimate aim was to break up corrupt cliques in the apparatus and raise the legitimacy of the leading party bodies by forcing them to reconnect with the rank-and-file.[93] What amounted to a revival and amplification of the old *samokritika* campaign – Zhdanov used this exact term – at a time when any production failure could be potentially viewed as an intentional compromising of state security, provided the explosive mix of circumstances that fuelled the spread of repression throughout industry.

[93] In what appears to have been a spontaneous idea, Nikolai Shvernik intervened to suggest that the same process be extended to the trade union apparatus. Goldman, 'Stalinist Terror and Democracy', p. 1434. For cliques as a target of both elections and repression see Getty, 'Rise and Fall', pp. 66–85; Harris, *Great Fear*, pp. 158–80; James R. Harris, 'The Purging of Local Cliques in the Urals Region, 1936–7', in *Stalinism: New Directions*, ed. Sheila Fitzpatrick (London: Routledge, 1999), pp. 262–85.

Regional party chiefs throughout the country attempted to protect their fiefdoms by stalling or deflecting the campaign of democratisation. Being in firm control of the Leningrad apparatus, Zhdanov moved quickly to ensure that the campaign would not fizzle out on his own turf. Thus, a week after the end of the CC plenum where he had first announced the campaign, the Leningrad chief gave an almost identical report to a session of the Leningrad *obkom*, where he harshly denounced the established practice of cadre appointment instead of election, declaring 'long-term democratisation' to be the order of the day. The plenum then passed a resolution requiring all primary party organisations to begin holding their electoral meetings by 1 April and stipulating that reports on the work of outgoing *partkomy* were to be presented at every gathering. There would be no stalling in Leningrad.[94]

Promptly complying with the directive, the Kirov factory party organisation held its own meeting over three days from 15 to 17 April 1937. In line with the plenum resolution, the organisation held a non-delegated general assembly of party members, with over 2,500 communists congregating at the fifth mechanical shop to hear the main report.[95] The *partkom* secretary Aleksei Tiutin painted a worrisome picture about the political state of the enterprise, stating that there were over 1,000 expelled former members still in employment, 'a whole army' of whom at least 37 had been Trotskyite–Zinovievites. Drawing attention to the dangers posed by the relaxation of vigilance, Tiutin attacked comrade Sviatogorov, the head of the factory's inventors' club, who loved to 'write reports and a brag about his achievements' but had apparently failed to notice that his group had become the home of several enemies of the people.[96]

Tiutin's report extended over three hours and took up the entire time of the assembly's first session. Despite the secretary's attempts to appear sufficiently self-critical about the work of the *partkom* in supporting political participation and promoting revolutionary vigilance, the following day's issue of the factory newspaper *Kirovets* carried a less than ringing endorsement of his report: 'The report of comrade Tiutin insufficiently mobilises to struggle, to the liquidation of weaknesses in party work, because of its weak *samokritika* and insufficient political acuteness.'[97]

If Kirov communists had needed a definitive indication than a full-scale *samokritika* campaign was on the agenda, the *Kirovets* leader provided just

[94] RGASPI, f. 17, op. 21, d. 2703, ll. 3–5. [95] Kostiuchenko, *Istoriia*, p. 535.
[96] TsGAIPD, f. 1012, op. 2, d. 1385a, ll. 1–2.
[97] *Kirovets*, 16 April 1937, in Kostiuchenko, *Istoriia*, p. 535.

that. Tens of party members registered to speak before their comrades that evening, with the agitated audience often interrupting with heckles, applause or laughter. Rybakov attacked both the party organiser of the second mechanical shop who had apparently gotten in trouble with the police for some financial offense and the *partkom* which had attempted to hide this from the shop-cell. He then attacked Ter-Asaturov for having spent only 14 per cent of the assigned housing fund since becoming director, showing that 'he cares more about plan-fulfilment, than about those who fulfil the plan'.[98] Speranskii criticised the *partkom* practice of appointing so-called Varangian organisers – that is outsiders who did not have the confidence of the shop-cells – noting that its choice for the cast iron shop had, after Kirov's murder, been found to belong to 'a Trotskyist gang'.[99]

A perennial issue, housing was also one of the lines of attack employed by Spitsa who, having started his speech with an attack on the *Kirovets* editor, Antselovich, for being lukewarm about *samokritika*, went on to warn that workers were spending thousands of roubles on temporary accommodation while the factory administration remained indifferent. Spitsa had exceeded his timeslot, but several voices from the floor demanded that the presidium allow him to continue. Buoyed by his comrades' support, Spitsa pressed on:

> I know of instances when a shop is not fulfilling its programme and comrade Ter-Asaturov, by secret order, illegally, gives the ITRs forty, twenty thousand in bonuses. Why, I ask? 'They insisted, what can you do, I had to give it'/laughter, applause/ ... We then put this issue before Tiutin, and Ter-Asaturov's explanation satisfied [him].[100]

The accusations of favouritism, suppression of criticism and plain indifference kept piling on the party and factory apparatuses as speakers succeeded each other on the podium. The *partorg* of the first mechanical shop, Nikolai Es'kov, emerged as one of the most skilled wielders of *samokritika*, beginning his contribution with an extensive apology concerning a recent bout of heavy drinking he had been seen to engage in after an *aktiv* meeting. Es'kov then spoke extensively on a number of problems demonstrating the lamentable state of party work, including the *Kirovets* editor's disdain of *samokritika*, the almost non-existent accounting of members – an affliction which, according to Es'kov, extended to the *raikom* – and, chiefly, the habitual neglect of duty by *partkom* members,

[98] TsGAIPD, f. 1012, op. 2, d. 1326, ll. 15–16. [99] Ibid, l. 23. [100] Ibid., ll. 41–43.

only four of whom had bothered to turn up at its last session. Before standing down, Es'kov also attacked the *partkom* and Tiutin in particular for their careless attitude towards party members. A distinguished old worker, 'auntie Niusha' Moiseeva, had been suffering from a chronic illness but with the exception of Es'kov, none of the organisation's officials had so much as paid her a visit, despite Es'kov's attempts to get Tiutin to organise support for the sick woman. 'Is this a way to treat people?' wondered the *partorg*, to applause from the audience.[101]

Having thoroughly thrashed the factory's party leadership in their speeches, the communists of the Kirov plant reassembled the following day to elect a new *partkom*, with forty-four candidacies proposed for the committee's eleven seats. Notwithstanding the attacks of the previous day, the incumbents Tiutin, Ter-Asaturov and Antselovich were successfully returned to the committee, joined by mostly new additions like Es'kov.[102]

Within the next few months, the newly-elected *partkom* would be decimated by arrests as the democratisation campaign initiated at the general assembly spilled over into the mass repression spreading through the country. Although it is not possible to examine the succession of denunciations and arrests in detail, the available evidence indicates that the dynamics of the process were similar to that in other major enterprises.[103] In spite of complaints to the contrary during the assembly, *Kirovets* seems to have acted as a major facilitator of repression, publishing denunciations and egging on its readers to provide more 'exposures', with Tiutin coming once more under fire for attempting to keep a lid on the campaign.[104]

In the summer of 1937, production failures relating to Kirov's armaments building plans attracted the attention of both NKVD officers and the military representatives present in the factory. A number of arrests were made amongst managerial staff, while Ter-Asaturov himself started coming under intense pressure for his suspect staff appointments. During a shop-cell meeting, Spitsa, who as we have seen was rather suspicious of Ter-Asaturov's soft treatment of underperforming ITRs, questioned the

101 Ibid., ll. 17–23. 102 Kostiuchenko, *Istoriia*, p. 536.

103 TsGAIPD, f. 1012, op. 1, dd. 1121, 1122, 1124, 1164 containing reports on moral–political moods, membership statistics and the special folder (*osobaia papka*) which only appears in the archival catalogue in 1937, were not available for examination by non-citizens of the Russian Federation in December 2014.

104 Kostiuchenko, *Istoriia*, p. 538. Factory newspapers were playing a rather similar role in Moscow enterprises as the time. Wendy Goldman. 'Small Motors of Terror: The Role of Factory Newspapers', in *The Anatomy of Terror: Political Violence under Stalin*, ed. James Harris (Oxford: Oxford University Press, 2013), pp. 240–62.

wisdom of the director's appointment of Boris Vetiutnev as head of the factory's artillery department, as he purportedly displayed a very relaxed attitude towards *brak*.[105]

Vetiutnev was arrested on 29 June 1937 and tried by the Military Collegium of the Supreme Court of the USSR on 25 August. He was shot the same day.[106] Similar fates would befall many other employees of the factory, both party members and non-partyists. By the end of 1937, three members of the *partkom*, including Ter-Asaturov, would be arrested by the NKVD and subsequently shot. When the mass violence campaign was finally wrapped up in the final months of 1938, almost 300 of the factory's employees had been executed, over a quarter of whom were communists.[107]

In an incisive account, one of the most perceptive researchers of repression in industry argued that, in effect, 'the party organisations devoured themselves'.[108] Although capturing the staggering scale of state violence of 1937, this formulation is not entirely accurate. Lethal as it was, the quantitative effect of the *Yezhovshchina* on the Kirov party organisation was in fact well below the incidence of expulsion during the 1933 purge and probably not much higher than the low rates of 1929.[109] A different

[105] TsGAIPD, f. 1012, op. 1, d. 1060, l. 1.

[106] *Vozvrashchennie Imena. Knigi pamiati Rossii* (hereafter *VI*). Online at http://visz.nlr.ru/person, last accessed 20 July 2016.

[107] My examination of the electronic version of the *Leningradskii Martirolog* available at *VI* showed that 285 Kirov employees were executed during the period 1937–38. They ranged from the director Ter-Asaturov to unskilled workers (*chernorabochie*) and even a couple of sports coaches employed by the factory. A significant number of the arrests took place in the autumn of 1937, suggesting that they were part of the mass operations. Eighty of those executed were communists at the time of arrest, but a few more had been members of the Party at some other point in the past. Ibid., 20 July 2016. This is consistent with the findings of quantitative studies of repression in Leningrad noting that Party members tended to be over-represented amongst the arrested and/or executed. See, for example, Getty et al., 'Victims'; Denis Kozlov, 'The Leningrad Martyrology: A Statistical Note on the 1937 Executions in Leningrad City and Region', *Canadian Slavonic Papers* 44, no. 3–4 (2002): 175–208.

[108] Goldman, *Inventing the Enemy*, p. 252.

[109] It has not been possible to determine the exact number of Party members expelled without being arrested or arrested without being executed. The continuation of recruitment during 1937–38, as well as the review and annulment by the *partkom* of around sixty cases as unfounded after January 1938, further complicate the calculation. In fact, from the available evidence, the 3,454 strong membership of 1 April 1937 seems to have declined by only fifty members by August 1938. Kostiuchenko, *Istoriia*, pp. 534, 541; TsGAIPD, f. 1012, op. 2, d. 1478, l. 12. In any case, assuming that, in line with the all-union trend, about as many arrestees were convicted to sentences other than death as were executed, we should expect a minimum of 160 expelled (because repressed) communists or 4.6 per cent of the total. Even double that would be significantly lower than the ~15 per cent expulsion rate of 1933.

study by the same author reported similar rates in major Moscow factories.[110]

Certainly, the disappearance of known colleagues and comrades cannot but have had a psychological impact that cannot be conveyed by statistical observations. Nevertheless, it is important to bear in mind that many, if not most, of those who perished did so because they were denounced by their comrades on the basis of suspicions that, albeit mostly unsubstantiated, were nonetheless real. As we saw in Section 5.3, the notion that production failures amounted to sabotage had hardly been alien to members of the organisation before it became standard discourse in the national press.

At the same time, however macabre, the emergence of vacancies made possible the promotion of a new cohort of party members and distinguished workers to posts of greater significance. Es'kov was the only elected member of the 1937 *partkom* to be returned in 1938, this time as secretary.[111] Viktor L'vov, until 1937 a superintendent at the blast furnace shop, briefly replaced Tiutin as *partkom* secretary, then became factory director and before the end of 1938 had become head of the short-lived People's Commissariat of Machine Building.[112] Even some who were subjected to denunciation managed through luck or effort to shake off the charges and end up in a better position than prior to 1937. Such was the case of Iakov Kapustin, who was expelled, reinstated, elected to the *partkom* and then left the factory to head the *raikom*.[113] In total, around 500 technicians, engineers and Stakhanovites were promoted to higher posts in 1938.[114] The storm of 1937 certainly shook the Party's foundations, but they did not come loose.

## 5.5 Conclusion

Mass repression was the macabre denouement to a phase in Soviet political development that had begun on rather auspicious terms. With the toughest challenges of socialist construction behind it, the leadership felt confident enough to launch a series of policy initiatives aiming to defuse social tensions by improving living standards and enhancing economic efficiency,

110 At the *Dinamo* factory, for example, the rate was 11 per cent, equal to the all-Union expulsion rate for the 1929 purge. Goldman, *Terror and Democracy*, p. 245.

111 TsGAIPD, f. 1012, op. 2, d. 1467, l. 9.

112 Unlike Ter-Asaturov, Tiutin had been transferred to work at *Uralmashzavod*. Kostiuchenko, *Istoriia*, p. 541.

113 Ibid., p. 539; TsGAIPD, f. 1012, op. 2, d. 1954, l. 123.

114 Kostiuchenko, *Istoriia*, p. 542.

while also increasing the accountability and responsiveness of the state apparatus. How such unobjectionable reform schemes ended up converging into a cataclysm of state violence has been one of the most enduring questions in the field.

The activity of the party grassroots goes a long way towards explaining the social dynamics of repression and, therefore, the process by which so many individuals who were far removed from positions of power became targets of a lethal security sweep. The PPO provided an institutional interface between state and society that allowed the conflicts and tensions of everyday life to become entangled with the political crisis brewing at the apex of the party-state apparatus. Essentially the same mechanism had been at work when the leadership struggles of the 1920s had been refracted through the factory politics of the party rank-and-file. A decade later, the perception of a mortal security threat had replaced disingenuous factionalism as the chief danger threatening the unity of the leadership and the survival of the Soviet state. The same actions, omissions and attitudes that had previously been attributed to incompetence, complacency or political indifference now appeared as calculated, malicious sabotage against the USSR.

The stabilisation of industrial relations that had been amongst the priorities of the Party's economic policy for the second FYP thus met a sticky end in 1937 in a violent conclusion to a process which, although initiated with benign intent, was badly suited to promote industrial peace. In the end, from the workers' point of view, Stakhanovism went much the same way as *udarnichestvo*, with the ever-expanding ranks of the movement making Stakhanovite status progressively less meaningful with respect to remuneration and benefits.[115] In its short heyday, however, Stakhanovism gave rise to a new round of *spetseedstvo* which, for a different set of reasons, turned bloody.

Social tensions accumulating since the early days of industrialisation provided the combustible material that allowed mass repression to spread through Soviet factories. Interpreting the terror in industry simply as a violent re-enactment of workplace tensions would, however, leave us with an incomplete picture. Conflicts over work conditions did not automatically transform into denunciations once the leadership started looking for enemies. The politicisation of production was a more long-term process inherent in the presence of party organisations in industry. This process received a boost when, upon completion of the first FYP, the leadership ordered a mass campaign of political introspection to expose those who were unworthy of party membership. Rank-and-file communists and

[115] Siegelbaum, *Stakhanovism*, pp. 280–81.

sympathisers took active part in the 1933 purge, demonstrating a distinctive understanding of political loyalty that was inextricably linked to competence and reliability in the workplace.

One year later, after the shocking murder of their leader, Leningrad communists were associating Kirov's killing with the same forces of 'Old Russia' that were holding back industrial development. When the leadership pointed at Trotskyites and Zinovievites as the moral instigators of the murder, the rank-and-file began to associate Trotskyism with the lazy, the incompetent and the corrupt. They were probably not surprised when the verification campaign revealed that a good number of these everyday villains had concealed suspicious personal backgrounds. In this context, it did not require an enormous leap of faith to believe that the multitude of technical failures and personal indignities that plagued workers' lives were in fact embedded in a pernicious plot against Soviet power.

Primary party organisations thus provided the framework for the maturation of the political, as well as the social preconditions for mass repression. This was a process that remained distinct and often anticipative of developments within the leadership, even though the latter naturally maintained the initiative in this process. Stalin and the Politburo were in a position to unleash successive campaigns of productive rationalisation, Party purification, mass democracy and ultimately sweeping repression. These waves of political mobilisation did not, however, animate an inert mass of foot-soldier activists. Party organisations had a political life that extended beyond the mobilisation campaigns of the leadership. Each campaign found rank-and-file communists already active in the business of monitoring and troubleshooting production while also engaging in the party-building tasks of recruitment, agitation and education. The leadership campaigns were thus refracted through the prism of the concrete tasks of the party organisations putting them into practice – in industry almost invariably associated with production – while also leaving an imprint on the way they subsequently functioned.

The repressions of 1937 did not disrupt this process. In the years that followed 1937 and as the leadership began to place the country on a war footing, the fusion of democratic impulse with state violence and spy fever had left its own mark on grassroots communist politics which nonetheless continued to function within the institutional contours of the PPO. With the Soviet state beginning to gear up for its long-expected showdown with the capitalist world, its renewed – because decimated – executive cadre would have to learn how to work with the unflagging militancy of their subordinates.

CHAPTER 6

# *Party Activism on the Road to War*

By early 1938 it had become clear that repression was getting out of hand. Whereas in earlier months the leadership had been willing to sign off on regional requests to raise the prescribed limits for arrests and executions, accumulating reports of systematic slander, score-settling and busybody accusations connected to large numbers of convictions were sufficiently worrying for the Politburo to signal a retreat. In January, *Pravda* carried a CC resolution 'On the mistakes of party organisations regarding expulsions of communists from the Party, on the formal-bureaucratic treatment towards those expelled from VKP (b), and on measures for the elimination of these faults.'[1]

The directive condemned the malignant practices of 'mass expulsions' and 'slander' in no uncertain terms. Such 'false vigilance' was denounced as an essentially counter-revolutionary phenomenon, an enemy tactic intended to demoralise party ranks by destroying honest communists and an insidious form of 'political wrecking in party organisations'. Party organisations were instructed to complete all outstanding appeals against expulsions within three months while implementing a ten-point set of measures to combat the deleterious effects of 'over-vigilance' (*perestrakhovka*), including the provision that members facing disciplinary action should not be dismissed from their jobs before their appeal had been reviewed. Although it took care to note that state security was still threatened by enemies within the apparatus, the CC resolution signalled that the leadership intended to restrain the torrent of denunciations. Indeed, accusations of slander and police misconduct featured prominently during the last wave of repression that saw the fall of nearly a thousand NKVD officers for violations of socialist legality.[2]

[1] *Pravda*, 17 January 1938.

[2] The Soviet Procurator's Office received some 600,000 complaints of such violations in 1938. On this and the so-called purge of the purgers more broadly, see Lynne Viola, *Stalinist Perpetrators on*

The end of mass repression coincided roughly with the launch of the third FYP in 1938. The rapidly deteriorating international environment led to an enormous increase of the relative weight of the arms industry in the economy, both in terms of investment and labour employment.[3] At the same time, a massive expansion of the armed forces during this period led to a renewed intensification of the labour shortage that had plagued the Soviet industrialisation effort from the beginning.[4]

These economic realities and the extent to which the repressions of 1937 had destabilised industrial administration throughout the country induced the Party leadership to embark once more on a campaign to raise the authority of specialists and administrators accompanied by a number of measures to enforce stricter labour discipline on the factory floor. There is consensus amongst historians of Soviet labour that the third FYP period saw the introduction of the harshest labour legislation to date. The bundle of laws was initiated with a December 1938 joint resolution of the government, CC and trade-union executive 'On Measures to Regulate Labour Discipline, Improve the Practice of State Social Security and Combat Malfeasance in that regard' which introduced a new set of fines and administrative penalties for truancy and other breaches of labour discipline. It culminated in the June 1940 law making it illegal for workers to quit their jobs and transforming personnel transfers into purely managerial affairs. In October, a decree of the Presidium of the Supreme Soviets created the State Labour Reserves, giving the government the right to mobilise up to one million youths for vocational training. Upon its completion, they were to be attached to specific enterprises for a period of four years.[5] As the international conflagration was gathering pace, labour in the Soviet Union was effectively militarised.

Industrial executives were amongst the main victims of state repression, as denunciations by their subordinates urged by the press to unmask saboteurs had been instrumental in providing targets for the security

*Trial: Scenes from the Great Terror in Soviet Ukraine* (Oxford: Oxford University Press, 2018), p. 168.

[3] In 1938, 3 out of 8.5 million industrial workers were employed in the armaments industry. Filtzer, *Soviet Workers*, p. 128. For a discussion of the economic effects of the prioritisation of defence see Andrei Markevich, 'Planning the Supply of Weapons', in *Guns and Roubles: The Defense Industry in the Stalinist State*, ed. Mark Harrison (New Haven: Yale University Press, 2008), pp. 107–10.

[4] The number of serving military personnel trebled from 1,433,000 in 1937 to 4,200,000 in 1941. Manning, 'The Soviet Economic Crisis of 1936–1940', p. 132.

[5] Straus, *Factory and Community*, pp. 91–92; *Resheniia Partii i pravitel'stva po khoziaistvennym voprosam. 1917–1967 gg. Sbornik dokumentov za 50 let.* (Moscow: Politizdat, 1967), 3 vols, vol. 2, pp. 665–72, 774–75.

apparatus. At the same time, the hunt for enemies in the Soviet factory took place against the background of a reinvigorated challenge to managerial authority in the form of Stakhanovism. From a certain perspective then, the winding down of the terror and the redoubling of efforts to enforce labour discipline seemed to dovetail into a pivoting move away from the promotion of activist participation and towards a retrenchment of established hierarchies. Thus, according to one of the most astute scholars of Soviet industry the Party's post-1937 labour policy represented a closing of ranks with management and a return to 'the status quo ante'.[6] This is perhaps true but, as we saw in previous chapters, the pre-Stakhanovite ancien régime in the Soviet factory was hardly one where labour discipline reigned and the ground shook under the director's footsteps, notwithstanding the best efforts of some of the bossier industrial executives.[7] The previous pro-managerial initiatives of the Party had had partial success in suppressing some of the most extreme cases of industrial strife, but had never really transformed the party organisation into a disciplinary instrument. The evidence suggests that this state of affairs did not change substantially after 1937.

Similarly, the embarrassing climbdown from contested elections to the soviets, as stipulated by the 1936 constitution, did not herald a complete reversal of course on the democracy campaigns. Rather, the leadership doubled down on its efforts to shake up the party apparatus, ordering a rerun of internal party elections in 1938 after finding the results of the 1937 ballots to have yielded underwhelming rates of renewal in the leading organs. In 1939, Andrei Zhdanov initiated a public consultation on proposed changes to the Party Rules which would come under review at the Eighteenth Congress. Echoing earlier discussions on the draft constitution, the discussion around the Rules likewise raised a broad range of parallel matters regarding the duties and rights of members, the ideological dimensions of political participation as well as the perennial issue of responsive and effective leadership by party office holders.[8]

[6] Siegelbaum, *Stakhanovism*, p. 264.

[7] That the earth should shake when a director enters the factory is a phrase often attributed to Lazar M. Kaganovich when it was in fact said by his elder brother, Mikhail M. Kaganovich, at a major conference of industrial executives organised by the People's Commissariat for Heavy Industry in 1934. Moshe Lewin, *The Making of the Soviet System: Essays in the Social History of Interwar Russia* (New York: The New Press, 1994), p. 25; Siegelbaum, *Stakhanovism*, p. 34. Regardless of its provenance, the phrase was scarcely descriptive of reality on the shop floor.

[8] Yiannis Kokosalakis, 'The Communist Party and the Late 1930s Soviet Democracy Campaigns: Origins and Outcomes', in *The Fate of the Bolshevik Revolution: Illiberal Liberation, 1917–1941*, ed.

As earlier, these policy shifts at the apex of the apparatus generated a flurry of activity at the bottom. Focusing on the last years of grassroots party work before the war, this chapter makes the following historiographical points. First, by formalising accountability checks and whistleblowing practices that had long been established functions of party activism, the new rules laid the groundwork for key post-war political initiatives such as anti-corruption campaigns and reviews of officials' personal conduct. More limited in scope than party purges, these techniques of governance sought to tap into the grassroots enthusiasm generated by the mass campaigns of the 1930s, while remaining within the bounds of bureaucratic predictability.[9] The archival record suggests that this mode of politics had begun to function on the ground before the war's outbreak. Its further development after Soviet victory is, thus, best understood as a continuation of a long process of institutional maturation, rather than an innovation responding specifically to wartime and/or post-war challenges.

Second, as this chapter will show, the leadership's pursuit of stability did not entail a retreat from its commitment to grassroots communist political activity as a fundamental part of the toolkit of Soviet power. In official pronouncements and rank-and-file discussions alike, the two goals were understood to be complementary. Thus, primary party organisations retained their role as key policy conduits and, crucially, had their institutional position strengthened in the new Party Rules. Their members continued to exert considerable influence in their immediate social environment as a core element of the governance of the Soviet system. On the eve of the gravest existential challenge in its brief history, the Soviet Union continued to function on the efforts of activists as well as professional administrators.

## 6.1 Democratisation, Party Building and the Winding Down of Repression

Concern about the consequences of slanderous accusations and 'over-vigilance' had been building up in some quarters of the leadership for some time before the January 1938 CC plenum. In early December 1937, the Leningrad *obkom* bureau discussed the results of an inquiry into the

Lara Douds, James Harris and Peter Whitewood (London: Bloomsbury Academic, 2020), 77–92, pp. 85–90.

[9] Cohn, *High Title of a Communist*; Gorlizki and Khlevniuk, *Substate Dictatorship*, pp. 328–30; Stotland, *Purity and Compromise*, pp. 104, 136–37, 170; Yekelchyk, *Stalin's Citizens*, especially chapters 5 and 6.

handling of 'evidence' regarding the purported wrecking activities of M. I. Safonov, the second secretary of the Kingisepp okrug committee. The review showed that Safonov had been removed from his post after the regional newspaper *Krasnoe Znamia* published a bundle of unsubstantiated accusations by local communists accusing him of a number of suspicious practices undermining party policy. The bureau dismissed the allegations as 'baseless and slanderous' and cautioned the authors of the claims while firing the editor of *Krasnoe Znamia* for permitting their publication.[10]

The bureau resolution offers no hint as to whether Safonov was reinstated or assigned to a different party post. There being no indication that he had been expelled from the Party as a result of the wrecking accusations, it is probably safe to assume that he had not suffered a fate worse than a temporary loss of income.[11] As in the case of the Kirov communist Iakov Kapustin, Safonov's vindication shows that it was possible to survive the maelstrom of denunciations and that there were at least some efforts by the leading party organs to put some boundaries on the arbitrary nature of the repression. There were, however, only so many cases that could be individually reviewed by party bodies with sufficient clout to dismiss accusations in the atmosphere of generalised suspicion engulfing the country. A better clue regarding the impact of the terror on the party-state apparatus is provided by the protocol records of the bureau session held on the last day of 1937. These included more than seventy pages listing hundreds of names of new appointments approved by the bureau, ranging from prominent industrial executives to obscure cadres like the chair of Leningrad's 'barber shop, bathhouse and launderette workers' union'.[12]

The destabilising consequences of the sudden, undirected shake-up of the apparatus caused by the repressions was undoubtedly a key factor in motivating the January CC resolution condemning false vigilance, as indicated by its prohibition of sacking cadres before the completion of disciplinary proceedings. Nevertheless, a reading of this as a unidimensional manoeuvre of bureaucratic retrenchment would be rather difficult to square with the Party's subsequent practice.

Sometime in March 1938, the Leningrad *obkom* bureau undertook a review of the directive's implementation in the region, which predictably uncovered copious instances of negligent or purposefully flawed

[10] RGASPI, f. 17, op. 21, d. 2731, l. 5.

[11] In the conditions of mass repression, the expulsion of communists was often a precursor to their arrest.

[12] RGASPI, f. 17, op. 21, d. 2731, ll. 11–82.

application of its actionable clauses. The city committee of Pskov and *raikoms* of Luga, Borovichi and Novgorod appeared to have performed exceptionally poorly, prompting the bureau to issue a resolution in which local activities to promote the CC resolution and clarify its political implications were pronounced unsatisfactory. More than one third of members in Luga's seventeen PPOs had not attended any events regarding the danger of false vigilance, while there had been several occasions where a discussion of the January plenum had not appeared on meeting agendas.

Other party organisations had attempted to dispense with the discussion as a mere formality, scheduling it as the last item on meeting agendas or passing abstract resolutions condemning careless denunciations without adequately describing concrete cases of unfounded expulsions. More worryingly still, the committees were found to have been reluctant to vigorously 'expose ... careerists, slanderers and the *perestrakhovshchiki*'. Pskov attracted special rebuke for failing to ensure the prompt publication of restitutions in the regional press, thus failing to properly restore the stained reputations of honest party members. In response to these shortcomings, the bureau ordered a rerun of party meetings on the plenum and promised to reinvestigate the performance of the local committees at a later date.[13]

The bureau's insistence on the full involvement of the rank-and-file in the implementation of the CC resolution was consistent with the established Bolshevik practice of mobilising the membership to promote policy initiatives. To some extent, this may have been a sensible response to the fact that, if not most, then at least a significant number of denunciations within the Party originated in the grassroots. Convincing overzealous communists to moderate their 'unmasking' activities was one way to stem the tide of allegations that had overwhelmed the apparatus. If, however, buttressing the apparatus and reinforcing existing chains of command had been the primary objective behind the January CC resolution, Zhdanov and the Leningrad leadership were going about this in an oddly circuitous way. Promoting public discussion of malpractice and rerunning meetings effectively undermined the authority of local leadership groups by drawing attention to their failings. Putting an end to mass meetings and instructing district level organisations to conduct the repression campaign in a more directed manner – in tandem with the security apparatus and with less input from the rank-and-file – would seem to have been a more appropriate course of action.

[13] Ibid., ll. 116–17.

The Leningraders' prescription of the standard Bolshevik treatment of mass discussion to troubleshoot the implementation of the directive on false vigilance rather suggests that the party leadership remained as committed as ever to the task of dislodging corrupt and incompetent officials from key posts, concerns about stability notwithstanding. The measures put forward by the January plenum to combat the activities of malicious slanderers and careerists were intended to block the further saturation of the apparatus by elements of dubious ideological commitment. Moreover, rather than providing incumbent apparatchiks with the means to defend themselves against their subordinates, the resolution limited their range of options. Responding to denunciations with one's own set of allegations was a standard defensive tactic in the conditions of the terror and a key mechanism by which the scale of repression snowballed. Constraining the casual exchange of accusations was a way to separate the signal from the noise generated by years of successive anti-corruption campaigns. The objective remained to strengthen the Party by ensuring that the apparatus remained responsive to the input of the rank-and-file.[14]

This political intent becomes more apparent if we consider that, around the same time as the Leningrad *obkom* was reviewing the region's performance in combating false vigilance, the Politburo was concluding that the political health of the Party would benefit from a further shake up of the apparatus. On 29 March, the CC published a resolution ordering a repetition of party elections, having found the preceding year's polls to have been severely compromised by the activities of stalling bureaucrats. The party press began a sustained, months-long promotion of the campaign, publishing a torrent of critical reports on the failure of regional and district committees to ensure the integrity of the 1937 contests. Particular opprobrium was reserved for local organisations that had not secured high levels of participation by the rank-and-file in the process. In Leningrad, Zhdanov moved with typical haste with the *obkom* bureau issuing instructions that elections to the region's leading party organs were to take place from 13 April to 25 May.[15]

By ordering a rerun of elections a year after they had been launched at the February–March 1937 plenum, the leadership was acting to prevent bureaucratic inertia from scuppering its reform agenda, establishing the new practices as a norm in the Party's political life. Similarly, the speed

[14] On deflection by denunciation, see Goldman, *Inventing the Enemy*, pp. 81–139.

[15] *Pravda*, 15, 24 April 1938; *Pravda Severa*, 27 November 1938; RGASPI, f. 17, op. 21, d. 2731, l. 129.

with which party organisations were expected to complete the process was likely motivated by an intent to keep local chiefs off balance, preventing the reconstitution of the cliquey 'family-circles' that had long been in the centre's crosshairs. The evidence suggests that local organisations made considerable efforts to adhere to the strict instructions of the *obkom* on the proper procedure for running the polls. This was not always a straightforward affair. The stipulation that elections were to be by secret ballot and contested by multiple candidates turned out to be a challenge given the Party's long practice of direct appointments and slate voting. Established, well-functioning party organisations such as those operating in large industrial enterprises appear to have gone through the process with little incident, electing their committees, bureaus and delegates to the higher organs in full compliance to the rules laid down by the leadership.[16]

Things went less smoothly in organisations that were smaller, less active or more transient in terms of the composition of their memberships. Party organisations operating in the Baltic Fleet for example seem to have struggled to find communists willing to stand for party office, in some cases listing candidates even after they had originally been barred due to suspicious connections.[17] Be that as it may, the campaign seems to have enjoyed some degree of success. Reports from PPOs and district committees indicated reasonably high levels of renewal in leading posts, including the ousting of recalcitrant local chiefs such as Pskov's first secretary S. N. Epifanov.[18]

Administrative and institutional hurdles notwithstanding, the Party's experiment with elections was moving apace and yielding acceptable results. We will subsequently return to the concrete experience of this process at the party grassroots. In order, however, to gain a better understanding of the contours of the leadership's plans for political reform, it is first necessary to spend some time considering its next moves. The drive to rejuvenate the Party's political life did not peak at the 1938 elections. Rather, the campaign served as a means to boost the more mundane but still vital activities associated with the all-important task of party building. As in the past, the two main elements of this process were the recruitment

[16] In the archival records of the Kirov PPO, for example, minutes from the electoral meetings note the time that the ballot box was sealed. The same files also contain the original ballot papers, which list at least two candidates.

[17] Rossiiskii Gosudarstvennyi Arkhiv Voenno-Morskogo Flota, RGAVMF, f. r-852, op. 5, d. 15, 25–29.

[18] RGASPI, f. 17, op. 21, d. 2731, l. 179.

of new members to the Party's ranks and the political education of all communists, whether freshly minted or experienced activists.

On 14 July 1938, the CC issued a resolution on 'The Progress of Induction of New Members to the Party'. The document noted that, following the resumption of recruitment in late 1936, the Party had received 348,435 statements of intent to join, accepted 141,132 candidacies and promoted 81,533 candidates to full membership. The vast majority of all applications had been received and reviewed since January 1938, clogging the apparatus and creating a backlog of some 180,000 unprocessed membership requests. The CC instructed all lower instances of the party apparatus to speed up the review process for new applicants and candidates, verify the correct formulation and timely issuing of party documents and, above all, ensure the immediate involvement of new members in party life. Underscoring the gravity of this task, the resolution explicitly named the worst stragglers among the Party's regional organisations and summoned their chiefs to the CC to explain their tardiness.[19]

Important as it was, the finetuning of recruitment practices came a distant second to political education in the priorities of the leadership. Although regular study and engagement with the intellectual universe of Marxism–Leninism had always been an essential aspect of party membership in principle, 1938 saw a surge in ideological activities connected with the publication in September of the *History of the All-Union Communist Party (Bolsheviks): Short Course.* Drafted by a group of party historians and then heavily edited personally by Stalin, the *Short Course* aspired to provide a master narrative of Bolshevism from its foundation through to the October revolution and the successful construction of socialism. It was intended to provide a unitary, accessible account of key stages in the evolution of the Party along with the appropriate political conclusions in order to facilitate the ideological education of the membership.[20]

There is no space here to enter into the fascinating debate on what the themes accentuated in the *Short Course* signified for the maturation of Marxism–Leninism as state ideology. What is significant for this account is that Stalin and the leadership took the dissemination of the text and the digestion of its content by the rank-and-file extremely seriously. On 11–12 October, the Politburo convened in a special session to hear a report by

[19] *KPSS v rezoliutsiiakh*, vol. 7, pp. 30–32.

[20] David Brandenberger and Mikhail Zelenov, *Stalin's Master Narrative: A Critical Edition of the History of the Communist Party of the Soviet Union* (New Haven: Yale University Press, 2019), pp. 1–10.

Andrei Zhdanov on 'the formulation of party propaganda in the press in connection with the publication of the [Short Course]'. The session was attended by the secretaries of major *obkomy* who shared their experiences of the progress of establishing an expansive network of reading groups for grassroots members to study the textbook. Although the quantitative results of this effort had been impressive, with study circles mushrooming throughout the country and involving ever more thousands of members, its actual educational efficacy was the subject of more than a little doubt. Reading groups were often hastily put together, resulting at best in a large turnover of participants and often enough in their dissolution after the first session. The quality of instruction also left much to be desired, with poorly prepared instructors being unable to answer questions from some of the more engaged students of party history. These shortcomings were subsequently denounced as 'amateurism and disorganisation' in a lengthy CC resolution published on 14 November and bearing the same title as Zhdanov's Politburo report.[21]

The Leningrad secretary had of course had ample opportunity to acquaint himself with the weaknesses of party building well before the publication of the *Short Course* and the subsequent Politburo meeting. Under Zhdanov, the party organisations of the northern capital and the surrounding province had been stepping up recruitment efforts well before the CC published its July resolution. Similarly, the *obkom* had been actively promoting educational activities aiming to raise the level of members' political astuteness since the completion of the spring electoral campaign. These included study circles and reading groups on various key themes of Party history that would later appear as chapters in the *Short Course.* The regional leadership reviewed the ideological work of subordinate district and city committees regularly throughout 1938, pouring predictable scorn on those local leaders who found the promotion of sound Marxist–Leninist education to be a task of secondary importance.[22]

Concrete action for the advancement of party building remained, however, within the purview of the Party's primary organisations. It is, thus, worth returning to the Kirov factory floor to take a closer look at the obstacles facing party policy on the ground. Although the increased emphasis placed on political education by the *obkom* ensured that the

[21] Rustem Nureev, 'Kratkii kurs istorii VKP(b) v krivom zerkale partiinoi propagandy (materialy zasedania politbiuro 11 i 12 Oktiabria 1938 g. kak istoricheskii istochnik)', *Zhurnal Institutsional'nykh Issledovanii* 3, no. 1 (2011): 83–92; *O postanovke partiinoi propagandy v sviazi s vypuskom 'Kratkogo kursa istorii VKP(b)'* (Moscow: Gospolitizdat, 1938), p. 6.

[22] RGASPI, f. 17, op. 21, d. 2704, ll. 5, 13, 15–16; d. 2732, l. 111.

Kirov PPO leadership made sustained efforts to ensure that the Party's ranks remained filled with devoted communists, a multitude of factors conspired to make this a complicated task. By late summer 1938, only two thirds of Kirov's over three thousand communists were engaged in some sort of study circle or reading group. Still more worryingly, attendance rates at established circles had registered a steady decline from 84.1 per cent in January to under 50 per cent by July. Considering the tendency of irregular attenders to quietly drop out, only about a third of the membership could be said to be engaged in serious, systematic study of Marxism–Leninism.[23]

The underlying causes of such disappointing results were discussed at a mass gathering of Kirov party activists convened on 15 August 1938. The main report 'On the growth of the Party and political education' was delivered by Iakov Kapustin who, after his brief expulsion, now served on the Kirov *partkom*. Kapustin began by bluntly stating that the performance of the PPO on both aspects of party building had been unsatisfactory. In terms of recruitment, he noted that, over the preceding three months, recruitment efforts had yielded a mere fifty-three new candidates and thirty-four promotions to full membership. The replenishment of party ranks was moving so slowly that, at least in one shop, the Party had no presence at all. He went on to wonder: 'Is it possible that in the Kirov factory, with 14,000 people, stakhanovites, 902 candidates ..., 4,000 *komsomoltsy* ... we couldn't find good [communists]?'[24]

In Kapustin's view, the root cause of the organisation's failure to grow at a satisfying pace lay with the rather timid attitude towards management demonstrated by certain communist activists in responsible posts. A *raikom* bureau review of the milling-cutter shop of the factory's third machine-building shop had revealed that 'the party group as such (*kak takovaia*) did not work, it copied the methods of the administration'. These consisted in the 'theory' that some degree of faulty output in the shop was inevitable. Having accepted this to be true, the organisation made no effort to mobilise workers around troubleshooting the shop's production process. Communists thus remained invisible and failed to attract their keenest colleagues to the Party.[25]

There is little reason to doubt the accuracy of Kapustin's analysis; we have already seen that the Party's tendency to address problems in production by getting workers actively involved in their resolution was a major source of its prestige on the factory floor. A group of communists

[23] TsGAIPD, f. 1012, op. d, d. 1478, ll. 12–13. [24] Ibid., ll. 5–7. [25] Ibid., l. 9.

failing to act in this way were, thus, not likely to inspire new members to join party ranks. In mid-1938, however, there were other obstacles to the expansion of the membership, to which Kapustin could only refer obliquely. Having outlined the reasons why party building efforts were stalling, he went on to describe a few cases of mistargeted recruitment. 'I would like to show that sometimes it is best not to accept [someone] into the Party. For example, the party organiser of the smithy comrade Matveev himself gave a recommendation to Kiiazovich whose brother-in-law has been expelled from Leningrad. One of his brothers has been arrested and another has been fired from the factory.'[26]

Having had the misfortune to personally experience the paroxysm of denunciations and arrests, Kapustin may have had misgivings about the extent to which the suspicions swirling around Kiiazovich's family members had any bearing on his worthiness as a potential comrade. As the CC had not yet signalled an unequivocal end to the hunt for enemies, he was obliged as a *partkom* member to warn his comrades that they should remain vigilant about hostile elements attempting to insinuate themselves into the PPO. It is indicative of the disarray in the apparatus caused by mass repression that activists were expected to expand the ranks of communists while trying to keep a growing number of people out of the Party.

Kapustin then moved on to the state of political education, making a number of observations that had much in common with the main points of the subsequent CC directive on the *Short Course* and party propaganda. Kapustin recounted a number of incidents reflecting the 'bad organisation' and amateurish quality of educational work. A three-person study group on the history of the Party during the civil war was set up by one comrade Alekseev. The group reconvened for a second session, but only one of the original students was present; different people took the remaining two places. This turnover continued until the group stopped meeting altogether. Alekseev had been obviously trying to lead a three-person study group on Party history without much regard for the stability of its composition.

Although this was a prime example of carelessness and poor planning, Kapustin argued that one should not be too quick to judge Alekseev. Lacking experience and presumably overwhelmed by other party assignments, he had approached the *partkom* for assistance but was not given any useful instructions on how to run his study group. Neither were the group's members to take full blame for their unconscientious attitude to

[26] Ibid., l. 10.

the study of Party history. Kapustin remarked that even those groups that were run by seasoned organisers failed to keep their members' attention because they were extremely dull: 'In comrade Trofimov's group at the die shop, [teaching] is impossibly boring. I visited comrade Trofimov's group with the *raikom* secretary. For three quarters of the time only comrade Trofimov speaks, the students are not prepared. It's pure toadying (*alliluishchina*).'[27]

Kapustin listed a litany of other ways in which the Kirov PPO was failing in its mission of political enlightenment before opening the meeting to contributions from the floor. These painted a more mixed picture of the organisation's party building activities than the main report and reflect the way in which the priorities of the rank-and-file converged with those of the leadership, even as they remained distinct. Focusing on the progress of recruitment, Berlin expressed some concern about the organisation's lack of growth but attempted to dismiss Kapustin's security-related alarmism. 'There are good people in our shop, but we are all ifs and buts with respect to recommendations [as if it were] better not to give than to give [a recommendation]. In my view, it's the opposite: if you gave five and were mistaken once, then it's not so bad.' Berlin went on to argue that it was much worse for the organisation to let potentially good comrades slip from its hands. He then expressed his regret for having failed to recruit his Stakhanovite colleague Artamonov to the Party, despite sustained efforts. In a most succinct expression of rank-and-file values, Berlin went on to describe Artamonov's worth as a potential comrade as follows: 'If he is good in production, then he is dedicated to the cause of socialism, dedicated to our Party'.[28]

Petrov, from the second machine-building shop, informed the assembly that the study group on 'current affairs and the international situation' that he was part of met regularly and had a stable composition of around thirty participants. These ranged from young *komsomoltsi* to seasoned Bolsheviks well into their sixties. The leader, one Orshanskii, was 'always well prepared' and did not just talk at the students. As a result, argued Petrov, the group had become a centre of party building activity. Its members had gained a better understanding of the importance of party recruitment in its broader political context and were, thus, both more motivated and more effective in attracting new members.[29]

Others were less impressed by the organisation's performance. Andreev, an activist from the steel casting shop, complained that there was no form

[27] Ibid., ll. 15–16. [28] Ibid., ll. 30–31. [29] Ibid., ll. 21–23.

of party education running amongst the steel-casters. He then decried his comrades' lack of interest in serious party work, claiming that many of them 'do nothing' and seem to think that 'they are in a spa town' (*sic*). Their idleness was not entirely their own fault, however. Andreev stated that, having joined the Party in 1932, he spent several years as a candidate before finally being promoted to full membership a few months earlier. The organisation had not shown any interest in his political development since then. 'I don't know why they haven't once asked me what work I am engaged with, what I know. I have finished the fourth group [course] but I don't know where to go after. The party organisation is not interested.' Andreev warned that such careless attitudes were putting off young workers who were approaching the Party with genuine interest only to be disappointed on their first contact with the apparatus.[30]

Andreev's thread was picked up by the youth organiser, Fedotov, whose contribution also focused on the harm caused to young workers' relationship with the Party by the disorganised state of educational work. Fedotov spoke at length about the dearth of adequately trained party members who were capable and willing to lead *Komsomol* study groups in the factory's three machine-building shops. 'At the first machine-building shop there are twenty-two party members, only Yakubovich was available, no one else can lead. This is nonsense.' Keen to embarrass some of the worse shirkers, Fedotov went on: 'Goncharov is here in the room. Apparently, on the fourth [of this month] he wasn't prepared, so he wasn't allowed to lead the study session. On the tenth, Babaev asked to be relieved. This is a shameful attitude towards studying.' To make things worse, Fedotov argued that Kapustin was well aware of this situation but the *partkom* was sitting on its hands.[31]

After the speakers had had their turns, a final resolution incorporating the main points raised was passed by the assembly. Kapustin then returned to the podium to make a couple of announcements that provide a further hint as to the nature of the organisation's troubles with party building. First, over the course of the following week, party organisations in the Kirov district were to undergo an exchange of party documents, as thousands of party cards had been signed by secretaries who had since been 'exposed' as enemies of the people. In the factory, roughly 2,000 cards were compromised in this manner, meaning that some two thirds of the membership would have to go through the trouble of acquiring new ones. Second, Kapustin announced that only a few months after the April party

[30] Ibid., l. 24. [31] Ibid., ll. 42–43.

elections, Kirov's *partkom* had lost three out of its eleven members who had been promoted to other posts. It was about to lose a fourth one, who happened to be the one responsible for culture and propaganda work.[32]

There are a number of interesting points that can be made on the basis of this brief review of party-building initiatives in 1938. First, it is clear that having signalled its intent to moderate the scale of repression, the leadership nevertheless pressed ahead with its plans to shake up and revitalise the party apparatus. The repetition of party elections was intended to prevent the reconstitution of corrupt cliques controlling organisations and maintain the pressure on party officials from below. The renewed focus on recruitment and educational push culminating in the publication of the *Short Course* were meant to strengthen the Party by expanding its ranks and ensuring that members were steeped in Bolshevik political culture. Second, despite the priority accorded to these initiatives at both the central and regional level, the repressions had sent the apparatus into such a tailspin that even robust organisations like the Kirov PPO had trouble attracting new members and running routine courses of political education. Leading cadres were whisked away to fill more senior posts while grassroots activists wasted time getting new credentials and thought twice about recommending their colleagues for party membership.

Finally, the outcome of the leadership initiatives remained to a large extent determined by the internal dynamics of the PPO. As a member of the local leadership, Kapustin was trying to strike a balance between shop floor realities and the demands of the party line. Rank-and-filers like Berlin, however, remained more interested in reinforcing the organisation with eager workers who, in their view, could not possibly make bad communists. Every experienced activist could agree that political education was a core element of party life, even if its correct organisation remained an elusive goal. As both Fedotov and Petrov indicated, well-run study circles could make the difference between effective recruitment and membership loss. High quality ideological work allowed party freshers to gain a better understanding of the significance of party membership and provided them with the skills to take part in PPO life and, crucially, take the Bolshevik message to their colleagues. It was, thus, imperative for the leading party organs from the CC to the district and primary party committees to make party building activities relevant to the concerns of its grassroots members.

By the time the CC held its plenary sessions on recruitment and propaganda in July and November, respectively, the leadership must have

[32] Ibid., ll. 75–76.

had a clear picture of the worrisome state of party building. This explains the urgency of the measures to address the situation, with their combination of threats and encouragement to regional and local party officials. At the same time, a parallel development was creating the conditions for a return of party life to a more predictable course. Sometime in the spring of 1938, Nikolai Yezhov began to lose Stalin's confidence. In April, the Commissariat of Water Transport was added to his portfolio. In August, Lavrentii Beriia became his deputy at the NKVD and went on to replace him as commissar in December. From the moment of his deputisation, Beriia turned the repressive apparatus inwards, launching the so-called purge of the purgers against Yezhov's men.[33]

The leadership thus renewed its commitment to party building activities at the same time as it put an end to mass repression. The concomitance of these initiatives was not fortuitous. Yezhov's appointment to the NKVD had followed a series of frustrated attempts to revitalise the Party apparatus by weeding out venal and negligent officials who were systematically remiss in their duties. Mass violence had ensued after the anti-corruption drive merged with security concerns and struck the Party via proliferating rounds of denunciations within the context of the democratisation campaign launched by Zhdanov in 1937. Repression against the apparatus had been a blunt tool used to remove those nefarious forces that were sabotaging the Party's mission. It made sense for it to be reined in once it had become clear that it was undermining core party work even in established, robust organisations like the Kirov PPO.

What is more significant for this account, however, is that the leadership did not limit itself to a reiteration of the principles of party building, in an attempt to take the damage done to the apparatus in its stride and a return to the status quo in party life. Instead, it went on to launch yet another ambitious attempt to reinforce and institutionalise the political transformations of the preceding years in a new set of Party Rules. Such fundamental reform could only be enacted by a Party Congress.

## 6.2 The Eighteenth Congress and New Party Rules

The agenda for the Eighteenth Party Congress was finalised at a CC plenum held in January 1939. In addition to Stalin's main political report, the main items on the agenda were a report by Molotov on the third FYP

[33] *Pravda*, 9 December 1938; Getty and Naumov, *Yezhov*, pp. 10–12; Viola, *Stalinist Perpetrators*, p. 4.

launched the previous year and a set of 'Amendments to Party Rules' to be introduced by Zhdanov. In early February, *Pravda* published Zhdanov's proposed changes in the form of a long list of theses followed by an editorial arguing that the need to update the Party's governing statutes was grounded in the far-reaching transformation of Soviet society effected by the construction of socialism. The leader piece declared that no organisational form is eternal and that 'flexibility is a Bolshevik virtue', a clear reference to the party-building resolutions of the early 1920s.[34]

In response to the new tasks posed by the maturation of Soviet socialism, Zhdanov proposed a number of reforms to the Party's apparatus with the intention of rendering it more flexible and responsive to the pace of an advanced industrial society. In addition to streamlining the departments of the Party's central and regional committees, Zhdanov's theses also proposed a set of measures to consolidate the achievements of the preceding years' campaigns in terms of internal democracy and members' rights. The most significant of these were the abolition of differential recruitment on the basis of social origin, the abolition of the mass purge as an acceptable organisational practice, the return to the principle of electability for responsible posts and the strengthening of PPOs operating in productive units.[35]

Zhdanov proposed the abolition of the four, class-based recruitment categories and their correspondingly different lengths of candidate membership in favour of a year-long candidate period applicable to all prospective members (I.1). The reasoning was that differential recruitment had been introduced in the NEP-era in order to create a barrier to party membership for non-labouring elements of the population. As the successful construction of socialism was leading to a gradual erasure of class distinctions among social groups, there was little reason for the Party to be particularly suspicious of any one these.

Similar grounds were offered for the formal ban on mass party purges (I.3). Purges were a defensive measure introduced in the 1920s to allow the Party to expose and rid itself of socially hostile elements whose power was otherwise growing due to the market-based nature of the NEP (3.a). What is more, they had proven in practice to be incompatible with a careful, attentive approach to the rights of individual members (3.b) and had been shown to be of limited effect against the true, double-dealing enemies of

[34] *Pravda*, 2 February 1939.

[35] *Pravda*, 1 February 1939. In the following paragraphs, Arabic numerals in brackets refer to Zhdanov's theses, while those preceded by Latin numerals refer to the specific amendments proposed to the Party Rules.

the Party (3.c), leading instead to the mass expulsion of 'passive members', honest communists who for some reason or other had not been able to keep up with party activities (3.d).

The abolition of the purge was part of a broader set of measures intended to enhance the quality of the Party's political life by buttressing members' rights (2, 4). The theses proposed an amendment to the relevant Rules section to include specific mention of rights 'thought to be self-evident' but hitherto absent from party statutes. These included, among others, the right of members to criticise any party official at party gatherings (2.a), to elect and to be elected to party organs (2.b) and to appeal for any issue to any party instance up to and including the CC (2.d). In addition to these provisions, the theses stated that the new Rules would have to reflect the successful measures introduced by the Party since the introduction of the new Soviet constitution, 'ensuring the consistent implementation of democratic practice' (6). These included the ban on voting by slate in favour of individual candidacies (III.11.a), mandatory secret ballots (III.11.b) and the obligation of city and district level committees to organise regular assemblies of party activists to ensure accountability and responsive leadership (III.12).

The document concluded with a section on PPOs, noting their crucial role as the Party's point of contact with the masses and as the conduit through which communists performed their vanguard role. Experience had shown, it was argued, that party work had been most successful where PPOs had successfully connected political work with their 'struggle for the successful completion of production plans, the improvement of the state apparatus' and 'the development of the Stakhanovite movement'. By contrast, according to Zhdanov, party work had suffered where primary organisations had become mere agitation vehicles or attempted to substitute management by assuming operational control of production (12). In order to strengthen the role of PPOs in production, they were to be given the statutory right to control (oversee) the work of enterprise or farm administrations (IX.21). To further encourage the political activity and ideological development of the rank-and-file, the right to form elected bureaus was extended to department level organisations of at least fifteen members (IX.24).

After the publication of Zhdanov's theses, the CC initiated a broad ranging mass discussion of the proposed amendments, modelled largely on the public consultation of the draft constitution a few years earlier. District committees and PPOs throughout the country were instructed to organise activist meetings and return detailed reports of the feedback offered by the rank-and-file. Central and regional party media reported closely on the progress of deliberations among the party grassroots, often attacking local officials who failed to stir up sufficient interest and engagement in their organisations.[36]

Though most communists would have voiced their opinion on the amendments at such meetings, party members could also publish short articles addressing issues on the Congress agenda in the party press. Pre-Congress bulletins carried by *Pravda* contain several such contributions, indicating that members responded vigorously to the leadership initiative. Despite the customary praise heaped upon the leadership in many of these pieces, most took issue with at least some aspect of the proposed amendments. In addition to being a rather good indication of what issues the leadership wished to highlight, these bits of comradely criticism also offer valuable insight into the priority concerns of the rank-and-file.

Democratising the apparatus and ensuring that party members were adequately protected from bureaucratic capriciousness were almost universally applauded as political goals of vital importance. Several speakers and authors recommended additional concrete measures to safeguard members' rights. A communist from Kirov city suggested that the rules should stipulate that party organisers should bear personal responsibility for the reprimands they signed off on. One Gulin, from Sverdlovsk, recounted his personal experience of having been thrice expelled and reinstated to the Party in the last ten years and recommended that the misapplication of disciplinary measures be designated a disciplinary offense in itself. Such sentiments were echoed by demands to further clarify the appeals procedure and formalise the obligation of higher party organs to respond to members' requests.[37]

Similar levels of interest were generated by the proposed enhancement of the statutory rights of PPOs. Not surprisingly, Zhdanov's suggestion that primary organisations be given the right to control the work of enterprise administrations was the subject of a large volume of letters from party members asking for further elaboration as to how this would affect the principle of *edinonachalie*. Many contributors went further, arguing that even more powers should be devolved to the PPOs. Thus, a joint letter by political officers serving in the Baltic Fleet proposed that PPOs should have the right to lift disciplinary sanctions without district

[36] *Krasnyi Sever*, 17 February 1939; *Pravda*, 7 February 1939; *Pravda Severa*, 11 February 1939; *Vostochno-Sibirskaia Pravda*, 15 Februrary 1939; RGASPI, f. 17, op. 21, d. 2705, l. 3; d. 2733, l. 62.

[37] *Pravda*, 7, 8, 12, 13, 17 February 1939.

committee clearance. One Oreshkin from the town of Shchelkovo in Yaroslavl' argued that, in order for PPOs to be able to exercise control in industry without bureaucratic meddling, they should be given the right to go over the head of enterprise administrations and directly address any level of the state apparatus.[38]

Extending the powers of PPOs and buttressing members' rights may, thus, have enjoyed obvious popularity with the rank-and-file, but the same was not true for another of the substantial amendments to the rules proposed by Zhdanov's theses. The relaxation of recruitment standards proposed by the Leningrad chief aroused the suspicions of several contributors to pre-Congress deliberations conducted in the party press. A worker from a safe-making factory in Kiev suggested that recommendations for new members should come from communists with a minimum of five years in the Party, rather than the three stipulated in the theses. One Klimovich wrote against an amendment of the definition in the Rules of a member from someone who has 'mastered the party programme' to someone who accepts it. This, he argued, would lead to a decline in the average level of political astuteness within the Party. Such was the blowback created by the suggestion to do away with class-based differential recruitment that three Leningrad party secretaries had to pen a joint article defending the measure. Their intervention was clearly insufficient as, a few days later, *Pravda* published an article by the leading party intellectual and Party Control Commission member Emel'ian Iaroslavskii, who defended the single-path recruitment procedure on similar grounds to Zhdanov's theses.[39]

The discussion of Zhdanov's theses on amending the Party Rules was the most extensive act of self-reflection that the Bolsheviks had engaged in since the polemics surrounding the opposition struggles of the 1920s. Throughout the USSR, grassroots communists spoke at meetings and wrote to the press to weigh in on questions touching upon the very substance of their vanguard mission, such as their role in production and the rigidity of the boundary demarcating the Party from the broader masses. It is scarcely surprising that large swathes of the membership applauded and sought to advance an initiative strengthening the institutions closest to it while also offering protection from the arbitrary whims of despised bureaucrats whom they often held in contempt. By disputing the purported relaxation to recruitment standards, the rank-and-filers also

[38] *Pravda*, 17, 19 February, 9 March 1939. [39] *Pravda*, 7, 8, 12 February 1939.

indicated that they viewed party membership as something valuable and worth protecting from incursions by elements unfit or hostile.

This is not to say that the party rank-and-file uniformly supported one part of the amendments and rejected another. There was in fact at least some grassroots opposition to the abolition of the purge, as indicated by calls that the measure should be retained for use in particularly problematic organisations. Opposition to the relaxation of recruitment procedures was likewise not universal. One Red Army political officer, for example, argued that members serving in the military should have the right to provide recommendations to party candidates after only six months rather than a full year, because 'people get to know each other better in military conditions'. Several other contributors asked for further simplification of the induction process, including drastic measures such as the abolition of the pre-membership category of 'sympathisers' in favour of an expanded population of candidate members.[40]

This should not surprise us. As we have seen in previous chapters and will have occasion to observe again shortly, the notion that the Party was besieged by enemies who often sneaked into key posts was not alien to the rank-and-file. There is little reason not to expect that some of its members would feel uncomfortable with the Party being deprived of a crude but formidable means of dislodging hostile elements from its ranks. Similarly, that a section of the rank-and-file would be in favour of further simplifying the recruitment process is entirely consistent with what we know about the process of party building on the ground. If party activists measured the political reliability of their colleagues in terms of their skill and work ethic, it made sense for them to want to dispense with red tape and recruit to the Bolshevik family those who they, better than anyone, knew to be good and virtuous.

Such variations in outlook notwithstanding, the contributions to the pre-Congress deliberations indicate that the rank-and-file backed those measures which reinforced the position of PPOs vis-à-vis the state apparatus and gave their members greater control over recruitment, whether their intention was to limit entry or to throw open the gates. As for the leadership, its intentions were made clear in Zhdanov's theses, *Pravda* editorials and in the speeches subsequently delivered by its members at the Congress itself.

That the latest round of purging had put the stability of the apparatus in danger was obvious enough, as was the fact that the spiralling rounds of

[40] *Pravda*, 4, 11, 19 February 1939.

denunciations had condemned large numbers of innocent people, while also providing real enemies with cover for their nefarious activities. This renunciation of mass repression came from no less an authority than security chief Lavrentii Beriia, who condemned the generalised misperception of incompetence as sabotage. Both Stalin and Zhdanov argued in their own addresses that purging was a relic from an earlier era when the ubiquitous presence of members of the former exploiting classes made socialism in the USSR much more precarious. Enemies still existed, of course, but they were petty traitors and foreign agents who could be individually dealt with by the security organs. The norm would, henceforth, be stability rather than shake-ups.[41]

Stable and reliable governance was also served by the abolition of differential recruitment. We have already seen that the leadership had been trying for years to raise the authority of industrial and other executives, only for its efforts to be repeatedly frustrated by the persistent suspiciousness of the party rank-and-file. By abolishing differential recruitment, the Party was signalling a shift in its political culture towards a more inclusive direction. At the same time, it extended its potential control over highly skilled specialists by attracting them to its ranks, while also encouraging its sympathisers to pursue executive careers, as there would no longer be a trade-off between professional advancement and political participation. Zhdanov provided a theoretical grounding for this policy in his speech, arguing that the new Soviet intelligentsia was a product of the country's socialist system and bore no relationship to its bourgeois predecessor. It would be absurd, he argued, for the Party to have liberated the working class from the shackles of exploitation only to then penalise those of its members who had risen to positions of prominence in their own state.[42]

A large part of Congress business was conducted in a similarly theoretical key, as the main speakers advanced complex arguments in order to ground the leadership's policy initiatives in Marxism–Leninism. In his own contribution, Zhdanov argued that 'forms of organisation are determined by practical tasks'. He reminded delegates that amendments to the Rules had followed all major social and political developments such as the introduction of the NEP and the completion of the first FYP, reflecting

[41] *XVIII S'ezd Vsesoiuznoi Kommunisticheskoi Partii (b): Stenograficheskii Otchet* (Moscow: Gosudarstvennoe Izdatel'stvo Politicheskoi Literatury, 1939), pp. 32–36, 144, 515–20.

[42] Ibid., p. 515–20.

the Party's efforts to adapt to the varying tasks posed by different phases in the transition to communism.[43]

Stalin himself devoted a significant part of his main political report to 'theoretical questions', arguing that the social transformation effected by the construction of socialism required a thorough re-evaluation of the relationship between Party, state and society, an intellectual task so vital that the general secretary described it as a continuation of Lenin's *State and Revolution*. The amendments to the Party's Rules were part of this re-evaluation. They were also a necessary condition for strengthening the Party for the challenging tasks that lay ahead, including the imminent showdown with the capitalist world that party intellectuals were already framing as a 'Second Imperialist War'.[44]

It would be facile to dismiss these arguments as ex post facto rationalisations of organisational reforms inspired by bureaucratic pragmatism. For, although a stable and predictable internal political environment was certainly one aim of the amendments, the leadership made it emphatically clear that it was not going to tolerate a limitation of the scope of grassroots activism as its prize. Speaking about the proposed enhancement of the status of primary organisations, Zhdanov declared that 'PPOs are the flower of our enterprises . . . [shining] a Bolshevik projector on productive life' and that those who doubted the compatibility of *edinonachalie* with PPO control 'understood nothing of *edinonacalie*'. Zhdanov suggested that sceptics should look to the primary organisation of the Kirov works to see a model combination of quality political work with constructive oversight of production.[45]

Still more indicative of the leadership's commitment to the Leninist vision of a politically engaged rank-and-file was the fact that it made it abundantly clear that there would be no back-tracking with regard to the proper conduct of party elections. Zhdanov told Congress delegates that, in order for the Party to be able to perform its vanguard role, it was essential that 'all party organs become electable . . . that accountability of party organisations before the party rank-and-file becomes fully activated'. A thinly veiled threat followed. According to Zhdanov, the February–March 1937 CC plenum had exposed the fact that regional leaders had been 'violating the Party Rules with impunity' precisely in order to escape

[43] Ibid., p. 512.

[44] Ibid., p. 34; Evgenii Varga, 'Kapitalizm nakanune pervoi i vtoroi imperialisticheskikh voin', *Bol'shevik* 13 (1939): 11–20.

[45] *XVIII S"ezd VKP (b)*, pp. 533–35.

accountability. The democratisation campaign had been launched in order to remedy this situation. The success of this initiative consisted in the fact that the renewal rate in the composition of party committees after the internal elections of the previous year ranged from 35 per cent to 60 per cent. Many of the regional and local party officials who made up a large part of the delegate body knew well enough that they owed their positions to this clearing out. They were being warned that, the ban on purges notwithstanding, the leadership had no intention of shielding party functionaries from the disapprobation of the rank-and-file.[46]

This was not an idle threat. The leadership took a keen interest in the implementation of Congress directives intended to generate greater political participation on the part of the rank-and-file. Where district- and city-level party committees failed to organise activist assemblies or ignored their recommendations, higher party organs could and did intervene to discipline or remove the main culprits. What is more, Stalin and his allies did not backtrack from their commitment to multicandidate elections in the Party. Records from Zhdanov's Leningrad region indicate that party elections continued to take place at regular intervals after their first pronouncement at the February–March 1937 CC plenum, up to the very eve of the German invasion of the Soviet Union in June 1941. The evidence suggests that the multi-candidate rule was observed. In very small organisations, such as those operating on the ships of the Baltic Fleet, this led to situations where reluctant nominees had their names put on ballot papers against their will due to the lack of members willing to take up responsible posts. In some of the more populous organisations, such as those of large industrial enterprises, elections were more complicated affairs. As stipulated by the new rules, they held delegated conferences to elect their leading organs, thus having to run multi-tier contests. The integrity of these conferences was guaranteed by mandate and accounting commissions elected by the delegates as the first order of business, adding a further layer of procedure.[47]

It should then be clear from the preceding discussion that the period that followed the crescendo of mass repression in late 1937 did not in any way involve a decline of leadership interest in matters of ideology and political reform. On the contrary, it is during this period that some of the

[46] Ibid., pp. 526–27.

[47] RGASPI, f. op. 21, d. 2736, ll. 30, 80. RGAVMF, f. r-852, op. 5, d. 15, ll. 25–29, 42, 111; op. 6, d. 24, ll. 117, 123; op. 8, d. 19, ll. 1–2; TsGAIPD, f. 1017, op. 1, d. 1287, ll. 161–63, 173–75; op. 2, d. 1467, ll. 13–15, 332, 337; d. 1954, ll. 1–2, 9.

most ambitious projects of party building were launched and institutionally codified in the new set of Party Rules. This is grounds enough to reject an interpretation of the democratisation campaigns as a political smokescreen for a strike against unreliable elements in the party-state apparatus. Repression and democratisation were overlapping but distinct processes, the latter of which outlived the former. Indeed, the electoral regulations introduced by the Eighteenth VKP(b) Congress were further concretised in a 1941 CC resolution and would remain a significant element of the Party's mode of internal governance in the post-war period, constraining the power of regional bosses while enhancing the position of the rank-and-file.[48]

The introduction of the new rules, thus, marked the culmination of a long process of institutional experimentation that had begun with the Revolution. On one hand, this had sought to work out the right relationship between the Party and the state apparatus. On the other, to strike the right balance between the Party's own executive and supervisory tasks; what Stalin had some ten years earlier described as the combination of professionalism with revolutionary fervour. After several years of violent upheaval, the synthesis of grassroots activism with technocratic competence remained the desired goal of party policy. The PPOs had never had their statutory rights so clearly defined before, nor had they been given such explicit political backing. At the same time, the third FYP launched in 1938 brought alongside it the introduction of iron-fisted industrial legislation, effectively militarising labour. How did this fit with the empowerment of PPOs ordained by the Eighteenth Congress? To answer this question, we must return to the factory floor.

## 6.3 Discipline, Control and *Edinonachalie* in the Third FYP

The first all-factory conference of the Kirov PPO was held over seven days from 19 to 25 April 1938 as part of the second wave of the party democratisation campaign launched in February–March 1937. Its proceedings are highly illuminative of the impact of the campaign on rank-and-file politics and, thus, provide a good indication of the kind of political environment in which the harsh measures of the third FYP would have to be implemented.

In line with the resolution of the January 1938 CC plenum, one of the main themes of the conference was the denunciation of slanderers who had

[48] Gorlizky and Khlevniuk, *Substate Dictatorship*, pp. 60–61, 78–85.

purportedly been responsible for the expulsion of honest communists as well as the rehabilitation of their victims. Indeed, Nikolai Dmitrievich Es'kov, the former *partorg* of the first machine-building shop who was now the organisation's acting secretary, spent at least a few minutes of his opening contribution on this subject.[49] Nevertheless, Es'kov insisted that the significant delays in plan fulfilment the factory was experiencing yet again were to a large extent due to the perfidious activities of a 'trotskyite–bukharinite gang of fascist agents' that had been allowed to operate by enemies within the *partkom*, such as the purged former director Ter-Asaturov.[50]

If the intention of the leadership had been to rebuild the authority of administrative personnel and limit the extent of industrial strife, it failed to communicate this to the Kirov plant organisation. For, although it could be argued that rehabilitating a relatively high-profile victim of the purge would have been politically difficult, it is harder to explain Es'kov's attacks on the plant's *new* director, Viktor Konstantinovich L'vov. The acting secretary went in almost the same breath from blaming the disgraced – and executed – Ter-Asaturov for production failures to accusing L'vov of not taking decisive measures to improve a series of problems he was perfectly aware of.[51]

Es'kov's criticisms were relatively mild, however, in comparison to the attack launched against L'vov and other members of the administration by a rank-and-file member named Fedorova. Fedorova made a scathing, lengthy speech in which she accused by name several members of the administration of demonstrating inappropriate lifestyles and making questionable use of socialist property. Her contribution captures several of the themes of grassroots party politics examined in this book with rare clarity and is, thus, worth quoting at some length:

> Let's take for example the use of our light transport. Things there are like, I do not want to say there exists still the Ter-Asaturov method, but our method is similar to the old method ... Our *ZiS* cars are assigned to engineers etc. but they are mainly used by their wives and families. Zal'tsman's wife lives opposite the House of Soviets and we know that one hour of such a car costs 80 roubles. Well just before the New Year she

[49] TsGAIPD, f. 1012, op. 2, d. 1467, ll. 37–45.

[50] Ibid, ll. 23–24. Among other things, the purged party members were said to be guilty of 'putting the brakes on the Stakhanovite movement'.

[51] Ibid, l. 24. Problematic areas included a full list of the labour-organisation improvements that Stakhanovism was predicated on, like 'organising technology properly' and 'correct organisation of remuneration policy'.

> used the car for four hours in order to go round every market to find herself a fir tree. I think that we should take into account here that we do not elect engineers to the party committee in order to give such examples to the non-partyists who are observing us ... And yourself comrade L'vov. When we elected a new *partkom* we screened everyone carefully. Ter-Asaturov turned out to be an enemy of the people. He spent 160,000 roubles from the public purse to decorate his apartment. And L'vov's wife calls a car and our enterprise pays the driver's overtime ... And then you can see cases like for example N. V. Volkov, whose heart bleeds about work, he asks for a car to get him to Smolny to sort out fuel supply problems, and they tell him that all the cars are assigned. Turns out there are no cars for such cases but there are for wives ... You get decent salaries, hire a taxi and drive your wives around ... This is nothing to laugh about comrades and if it isn't wrecking then, at the very best, it is bad management ... And our party committee says that there must be pure *samokritika* without fear or favour. Well then, wherever you look, disgraceful things are happening.[52]

Fedorova's intervention linked managerial incompetence to political malevolence but also something more fundamental; failure to be a good communist. Embezzlement of factory property was doubly reprehensible when there were committed activists who devoted serious efforts to fix pressing problems, only to be thwarted by the brazen indifference of their superiors. This was an ethical, rather than strictly technical or political criticism. Similar views underlay warnings to previous directors against spending their time locked up in their offices. Fedorova and her comrades were not challenging the office of director as such or even the privileges attached to it. They were admonishing fellow party members and officials of the Soviet state who failed to live up to their implicit reciprocal commitment to the construction of socialism.

This is consistent with the findings of scholars of Soviet subjectivity showing communist ethics were an important element in interactions among individuals and in their encounters with the state.[53] Within the context of the PPO, however, discursive appeals to communist ethics carried special weight because they touched upon the addressee's moral right to membership and evoked the possibility of expulsion. Fedorova's speech was so powerful because it combined a moral appeal with a thinly disguised and credible threat of state violence. This was only possible because of the institutional status of the Party as the supreme guide of state power at all levels of the apparatus. It was all the more effective

[52] Ibid., ll. 95–98.

[53] See, for example, the striking letter to Marfa in Kotkin, *Magnetic Mountain*, 218–19.

because it was being made in the context of a mass campaign initiated by the leadership and encouraging the rank-and-file to expose those who were failing to live up to the demands of party membership.

Other contributions were not as vitriolic as Fedorova's, but she was not alone in expressing disapproval of managerial behaviour. What is more, although the stenographer recorded several outbreaks of laughter amongst the audience, it is unlikely that the engineers and administrators attacked by Fedorova viewed the parallels she drew between their behaviour and that of their recently departed predecessors as attempts at humour. After all, the acting head of the *partkom* had also warned the director against neglecting his duties, a point he reiterated responding to a *zapiska* during his concluding remarks a few days later. The note, as read out by Es'kov asked: 'Will cars remain out in the open to rust and have their alternators etc. stolen by whoever feels like it? Will a garage be built?' Es'kov responded that this was a question for L'vov, one which he in fact got many times but kept dodging. The acting secretary then admonished the director that leaving tractors to rust in the rain was not only bad management but also a negative influence on 'workers' moral–political moods'.[54]

The political climate prevailing amongst the rank-and-file at the peak of the party-democratisation campaign thus remained antagonistic to management for familiar reasons. The situation was compounded by the deep suspicions regarding the political steadfastness and moral integrity of party members in leading posts raised by the repressions. Competence and rectitude where thus the key qualities by which the conference delegates nominated candidates for the *partkom*. The nomination process consisted simply in delegates putting forward candidates' names. Those who accepted the nomination then rose to speak and answer questions about their professional and political activities.[55]

It is indicative of the ability of the rank-and-file to exercise and act upon its own judgement that candidates with suspicious pasts and/or associations could make it to the *partkom* on their merit as communist cadres, only weeks after the last Moscow trial. It was this conference that elected Kapustin to the PPO leadership after his doubtlessly harrowing acquaintance with the security services. Similarly, when one delegate interrogated the *partkom* nominee Grigorii Ivanov about the fact that his brother was

[54] TsGAIPD, f. 1012, op. 2, d. 1467, l. 312.

[55] A total of twenty-eight names were put forward. Ten of them declined the nomination, citing inexperience or health reasons preventing them from taking up leadership positions. There were, thus, eighteen candidates for the eleven-strong *partkom*. Ibid., l. 8

serving a sentence of hard labour, he was defended by acting secretary Es'kov on the basis of his record as a shop-cell organiser. Stukalov, whose membership record had been stained by expulsion in 1936, was highly praised as a deeply conscientious comrade by a delegate who stated that 'he treats every communist like a human being . . . he talks, he warns, he tries to remedy the weaknesses of every person', a fact reflected in the '100 per cent production success rate' of his shop. Proven dedication could also be a substitute for experience. When the candidacy of Feodosia Stepanenko was challenged by a delegate on the grounds that she had only been in the Party for one year, she was defended by Es'kov who praised her for having been amongst the first Stakhanovites in the factory. Her communist zeal was further demonstrated by the fact that she was extremely committed to her self-education, 'persistently hacking away at the granite of science' even though she had children and had only been semi-literate when she joined the Party.[56]

Party democratisation thus reinforced the prevalent political culture of the PPO, but we cannot infer from this a directly proportionate decline in managerial authority. Despite the blistering attacks on the administration by Fedorova and other speakers, the *partkom* nomination of factory director Viktor L'vov was met with applause from the floor and there were no objections to his candidacy. Neither should we assume, however, that the political effervescence generated by the campaign could be simply shrugged off by industrial executives. Indeed, there is good reason to believe that L'vov's personal authority derived less from his job than his status as one of the factory's most senior communists, having joined the Party in 1918.[57]

This becomes clearer if we consider subsequent events at the Kirov plant. In line with the all-Union trend, wrecking accusations became rarer after 1938. However, conflicts between workers and industrial cadres did not disappear, even as they became non-lethal in their intensity. They reverted instead to the familiar manner of buck-passing and mutual accusations of incompetence.[58] This detente notwithstanding, however, there are strong indications that managerial authority at Kirov remained severely constrained, even as the state was introducing progressively tighter labour legislation in anticipation of the coming war.

[56] Ibid., ll. 344, 350, 354, 358–61. These candidates were all elected to the *partkom*. [57] Ibid., l. 9.

[58] This is demonstrated in the protocols of several production and Stakhanovite conferences held in late 1938 and 1939. Ibid., dd. 1099, d. 1707.

By 1939 the Kirov works once again had a new director in Isaac Moiseevich Zal'tsman, the former head engineer of the factory who had been a subject of Fedorova's criticism a year earlier.[59] Zal'tsman's administration came under intense scrutiny during a rare stenographed session of the *partkom* that took place on 25 September 1939 on the subject of a recent fire in one of the factory's warehouses.[60] Zal'tsman's contribution to the meeting was limited to a short introductory speech in which he affirmed that fire safety was a 'cardinal matter of factory work'.[61] Following this, Vladimir Drabkin, the *zavkom* chair, invited the head of the factory's fire brigade, Iushkov, to report on the incident. Iushkov prefaced his report by stating that he, along with the factory's trade union group, had tried to put pressure on administrators that 'did not implement our measures' and had even brought that matter to the attention of the NKVD.[62] He then went on to give a detailed account of the fire's development and, after rejecting a number of possible scenarios, left open the possibility of sabotage. The members of the committee who spoke after Iushkov, including the secretary, vice secretary and a superintendent who had been assigned to investigate the issue, all agreed that sabotage was the most likely cause of the fire.[63] Drabkin then suggested that the supervision of the implementation of safety measures be assigned to himself personally. The *partkom* accepted his self-nomination and went on to pass a resolution criticising the factory administration for 'not devoting sufficient attention' to the factory's water supply, 'despite repeated warnings from the *partkom*'.[64]

Whether the matter was pursued further is unclear, but Zal'tsman remained in his post, reflecting what was by then a much more benign attitude towards industrial cadres on the part of the authorities. What is interesting about this episode, however, is that it also demonstrates the

[59] L'vov was removed from the factory in 1938 to take up the short-lived post of People's Commissar of Machine Building, abolished in 1939. Zal'tsman was promoted from shop superintendent to head engineer sometime during or immediately after the purges of 1937. TsGAIPD, f. 1012, op. 2, d. 1467, l. 26. He, therefore, had less than two years' experience in that post before becoming director. Such dazzling rates of promotion were by no means atypical during this period, both due to the decimation of the ranks of industrial cadres by the repressions and the massive expansion of technical positions which had reached a ratio of 110 per 1,000 workers in 1940 from 70.5 per 1,000 in 1936. Kendall E. Bailes, *Technology and Society under Lenin and Stalin: Origins of the Soviet Technical Intelligentsia, 1917–1941*, Reprint ed. (Princeton: Princeton University Press, 2015), p. 289.

[60] *Partkom* sessions were normally minuted in the form of protocols, not transcripted. This transcript is entitled 'Transcript to Protocol No. 80'. TsGAIPD, f. 1012, op. 2, d. 1688, l. 1. The stenographer's presence suggests that the fire attracted the attention of higher powers.

[61] Ibid., ll. 1–3. [62] Ibid., l. 3. [63] Ibid., ll. 8–19. [64] Ibid., ll. 24–27.

extent to which the Party's function as an instrument of political control persisted even during a time when the leadership was signalling and effecting a pro-managerial line. Despite this political turn at the top, the immediate response of the *partkom* to a potentially important problem was to blame the administration. For Drabkin, this was also an opportunity to strengthen the status of the *zavkom*, usually thought of as the weak part of the power 'triangle' of Soviet enterprises.[65] That the *partkom* secretary at the time was a CC-appointed organiser (*partorg TsK*), Vladimir Stepanovich Efremov, may or may not have moderated the attack on Zal'tsman but Efremov himself said nothing in the director's defence, instead joining in the criticism of the other members.[66] This was hardly a resolute defence of managerial authority. Evidently, whatever operational prerogatives were granted to the administration by the principle of *edinonachalie* could be waived by the *partkom*.

A few months later, Zal'tsman's status within the factory would suffer a further blow when the organisation's second all-factory conference, held in February 1940, did not elect him to the new *partkom*, despite his candidacy.[67] The election took place after two days of discussion in which remarkably little was said about labour discipline despite the conference taking place a mere week after the Red Army Winter War breakthrough of 11 February. Although the factory's obligations towards the war effort figured prominently in Efremov's main report, the problems he identified in production were primarily organisational in nature and, therefore, easily framed as administrative failures.[68] Thus, Buter, the open-hearth shop delegate who took the floor immediately after the secretary, could complain: 'We are so close to the front, but we have stoppages because of the lack of mazut oil, despite there being some in the factory.'[69] Babaev, the secretary of the party bureau of the second machine-building shop, went a bit further, saying that 'comrade Zal'tsman is a young director, he needs to be helped at work. For this reason, it was necessary to demonstrate the director's shortcomings ... Not a word was said about him ... Comrade Efremov will have to speak about this in his closing remarks'.[70] A similar

[65] It is worth mentioning here that, with membership dating from 1917, Drabkin was one of the oldest Bolsheviks in the factory and certainly the most senior communist elected to the 1938 *partkom*. Ibid., d. 1467, l. 8. That the weak part of the triangle was led by a member whose prestige in the PPO was likely unmatched suggests some sort of intention to maintain a balanced relationship amongst the institutional pillars of the factory.

[66] Ibid., d. 1688 l. 22.

[67] Ibid., d. 1954, l. 9.

[68] Among these were intra-factory transport, construction and the organisation of labour and wages. Ibid., d. 1688, l. 28.

[69] Ibid., l. 72.

[70] Ibid., l. 84.

note was struck by a tractor department delegate, Vinokur, who accused both Zal'tsman and Efremov of never visiting his shop.[71]

As very busy people engaged in wartime production, these speakers could have been excused for being somewhat out of tune with the new political mainstream cementing managerial prerogatives. The same cannot be said about the contribution of our familiar Iakov Kapustin, who was attending the meeting in his new capacity as secretary of the Kirov district committee. Kapustin criticised Zal'tsman's 'method' and admonished Efremov that a CC organiser should closely supervise the director of such an important enterprise.[72] Using rhetoric that was indistinguishable from that of the decade-old *samokritika* campaign and to much applause from the floor, Kapustin added:

> We must sweep all of our departments with a party broom *(partiinoi metloi)*. Comrades say that … the system is too cumbersome, there are many spongers of various kinds, many inspectorates, who do nothing, but get money. Is it not time then to go through the whole apparatus with a party broom and clear out people who get money illegally? … For this is a disgrace – the office has turned into its own kind of department, with a superintendent, a deputy and a ZiS car. Shouldn't we go round these departments and clear out some people from there with an iron party broom?[73]

With this being the political tone of the conference, it is not difficult to see why Zal'tsman would fail to get elected to the committee. Why then would a member of the *raikom* actively incite anti-managerial feelings at a time generally seen as the apogee of Soviet industrial authoritarianism? It may be that Kapustin's long past as a worker in the factory had made him inclined to take a hard line against the administration when problems arose. If this were so, then his was by no means an isolated case as many low-ranking *apparatchiki* of the time had spent considerable time as workers at the bench. We need not assume, however, that Kapustin was demonstrating initiative that was at odds with party policy. The right of PPOs to control their factory administration had been enshrined in the new Party Rules. Zhdanov himself had presented the activities of the Kirov organisation as a model for factory politics. While still secretary at Kirov, Kapustin took up the task of broadcasting his know-how throughout the apparatus, authoring an article on PPO control for the Party's flagship theoretical journal.[74]

71 Ibid., l. 89. 72 TsGAIPD, f. 1012, op. 2, d. 1954, ll. 128–29. 73 Ibid., l. 132.

74 Iakov Kapustin, 'O kontrole pervichnykh partorganizatsii na predpriiatiiakh', *Partiinoe Stroitel'stvo*, no 5 (1939): 37–40.

Although we have no reason to doubt the urgency with which the leadership approached the task of putting industry on a war footing, it never seemed to think of party activism as being counter-productive to this goal. Throughout the third FYP, the Leningrad *obkom* conducted regular reviews of the economic performance of industrial enterprises throughout the provinces, invariably attributing plan failures to the lax control exercised by party organisations over production.[75] As late as February 1941, the Eighteenth VKP (b) Conference sought to expand party control over industry by creating new secretarial posts at the city and regional levels to oversee specific industrial sectors. At the same time, it instructed party organisations to establish 'permanent control over the work of enterprises' and 'increase the masses' labour activism in every possible way' while also expanding socialist competition.[76] The CC proceeded to call for a new Union-wide competition on 16 June 1941.[77]

Even then, on the eve of the war, the Party leadership remained firm in its conception of party activism as complementary to its objective of establishing order within industry. Kapustin's behaviour becomes more comprehensible in this light. If the enterprise was lagging behind in its production plan and if Kapustin's task was to remedy this by, among other things, inducing the party organisation to be more active in its involvement in production matters, there was no better way to do this than by attacking management for taking advantage of its privileges while also doing a poor job. For the past fifteen odd years, greater party involvement in production had meant precisely that.

Combined with the heightened labour shortage, the persistence of Party-promoted activism on the shop floor after successive political blows to managerial authority made the enforcement of labour discipline an uphill struggle. Zal'tsman's contribution to the Kirov plant organisation's third conference held in May 1941 is indicative of the extent to which this was the case at this major factory. Zal'tsman began his report by going over some familiar problems like stoppages and the practice of fake Stakhanovism, citing the case of one shop which had purportedly recorded more than 500 Stakhanovite records in one day.[78] He then went on to touch on labour discipline problems in a curiously roundabout way, beginning by offering an apology about his past rudeness and pledging

[75] RGASPI, f. 17, op. 21, d. 2732, ll. 111; op. 22, d. 1622, ll. 63–66, 116.
[76] *KPSS v rezoliutsiiakh*, vol. 7, p. 192.
[77] Ibid., p. 209. Although this campaign would be disrupted by the German invasion of the USSR six days after its publication, the CC renewed it the following year, pp. 283–300.
[78] TsGAIPD, f. 1012, op. 1, d. 1287, ll. 102–5.

to take into account the criticism he had received on that score. This, Zal'tsman suggested, was a matter of workplace culture and, in order to get better at it, he would require help from the organisation. 'Help', went on the director, 'I consider to be the following: our factory needs to pay more attention to questions of discipline ... order and implementation'.[79]

This was the most Zal'tsman was willing to insist on the priority of raising labour discipline. In fact, the director went on to say that, while truancy was a problem, it was mostly one caused by the inexperience of new recruits, who should not be treated too harshly. The director went so far as to argue that his administration was being 'over-vigilant' in the implementation of labour-discipline regulations:

> I am obliged to say that there are incidents of over-vigilance (*perestra-khovka*). For example, worker Vasiliev's wife died and he came to work in distress. At the shop ... he was declared drunk and prosecuted. I signed the relevant order myself. Only the next day was the matter cleared up and the order annulled. In the same shop ... worker Zhernovskii was not informed that his day off had been moved from the 27th to the 30th. He was working a nightshift [on the 26th] and he didn't come to work on the 27th. The superintendent reported him for prosecution but attached a document confirming that Zhernovskii's truancy was not his fault /laughter/. Comrades, we must fight against such over-vigilance in the most decisive manner.[80]

It is worth recalling here that the term 'over-vigilance' had a pedigree in the Bolshevik vocabulary, having been specifically denounced as an enemy practice by the January 1938 CC plenum. Whether Zal'tsman was consciously using it to underscore the seriousness of the problem he was considering or merely reaching for a familiar word signifying too much of a good thing is unclear. Whatever the case, Kirov's director was discussing labour discipline in terms suggesting he was concerned by its overabundance. Less than two months before the German invasion of the USSR, the director of one of the country's most strategically important enterprises was still far from the fearsome, 'little Stalin' figure sketched in the literature on Soviet industrialisation.

## 6.4 Conclusion

The period following the winding down of mass repression in mid-1938 and extending up to the German invasion of the USSR in the summer of

[79] Ibid., l. 108. [80] Ibid., ll. 112–13.

1941 has attracted relatively modest scholarly interest. Lacking the cataclysms that shook the country in the first two thirds of the 1930s, the years of the third FYP are remembered less for domestic Soviet developments than for the country's diplomatic and military manoeuvring in the run up to the Second World War.

The preceding account has offered a corrective to this tendency. Rather than being the mere aftermath of a paroxysm of mass repression or the conclusion to a decade-long process of mounting authoritarianism in industry, this period was marked by some of the most intense bouts of party activism, fostered by the leadership seemingly at cross-purposes with its broader authoritarian posture. Policy initiatives aimed at strengthening industrial chains of command and bringing order to the unruly Soviet workplace were introduced alongside an intensification of the party democratisation campaign encouraging rank-and-file communists to ensure the proper functioning of their organisations and to take ownership of the work of their factories. The mass discussion on the proposed amendments to the Party's Rules spurred activists to think and talk about the rights and duties of membership while highlighting barriers to the exercise of both.

By ratifying the amendments, the Eighteenth Congress buttressed the rights of individual members and reinforced the institutional status of their chief channel of influence, the PPO. These moves were ill-suited to the promotion of ham-fisted authoritarianism in industry, as evinced by the Kirov director's warnings of the dangers of disciplinary 'over-vigilance'. At the same time that labour legislation became progressively militarised, the exercise of managerial authority remained embedded in the industrial primary party organisation and constrained by its internal dynamics. Successive waves of activist mobilisation and institutional reform favouring the rank-and-file had turned the PPO into a less than co-operative partner for the factory administration. Such was the political dynamic that the Eighteenth Party Congress formalised as the right of industrial PPOs to control the work of factory administrations.

Two main points can be made on this basis. First, with regard to the development of Soviet production relations, it seems clear that the labour laws of 1938–40 were neither the capping stone in a process of industrial enserfment initiated with the first FYP nor a panicked retreat to familiar modes of economic management after a brief period of experimentation. Harsh penalties for truancy and other breaches of labour discipline were introduced without any measures being taken to contain the chief antagonist of managerial authority on the factory floor, namely the primary party organisation. Instead, the end of the 1930s found the PPO strengthened and with its anti-managerial political culture intact. The experience of Isaac Zal'tsman is instructive here. The young engineer first gained a leading post in the factory during the cataclysm of mass repression and soon attracted the hostility of militant Kirov communists. A couple of years later, invested with nearly dictatorial powers by the new labour laws, the young director could still be excluded from the factory's party committee and have his administration threatened with 'the iron party broom' by a senior Leningrad party secretary who had only recently left the very same enterprise.

The combination of strong executive authority with a political framework supplementing its functions and constraining its power had been the modus operandi of Soviet industry throughout the period examined in this monograph. In this sense, the last years of the 1930s saw a maturation of this institutional arrangement rather than a departure from its framework. This brings us to the second point. The tension between *edinonachalie* and activist participation in administration extended beyond the factory gates. This institutional dualism formed the basic blueprint of socialist governance laid out by Lenin in the *Immediate Tasks of Soviet Power* in 1918. The introduction of new labour legislation and Party Rules is, therefore, best seen as an instalment in the long process of working out the post-revolutionary relationship between Party, state and society. Initiated upon the Bolshevik capture of power, this process was punctuated by various institutional reforms and policy initiatives, including the ban on factions, the Lenin Levy, purges, Stakhanovism, democratisation and mass repression. These events and campaigns had long lasting effects that were incorporated in the broader process of Soviet state-building, the construction of socialism. None of them, not even the violent cataclysm of 1937–38, signified an end to institutional experimentation. Major reform and fine-tuning continued until the Nazi onslaught posed a new set of challenges to the Soviet system.

# *Conclusion*

## *The Vanguard Concept As a Promising Category for Historical Research*

A recent, global account of the history of communist parties in political theory and governing practice has argued that the path taken by the Bolsheviks under Stalin's leadership represented a break with their past as a party of ideas and their transformation into an instrument of policy implementation. It was a triumph, as it were, of organisational expediency over ideology.[1] This monograph has presented a different view. For the Bolsheviks, the Party had always been an agent of revolutionary social transformation rather than a mere association of individuals sharing certain political principles. Its structure and mode of operation were determined by the demands of the revolutionary process. Freedom of discussion, political rights and democracy were not ends in themselves but means to a transformation of world–historical scale that would render them redundant by erasing the distinction between state and society and the class structures on which it rested.

On this point, all Bolsheviks agreed. Even Trotsky, Stalin's subsequent arch-rival, spared no effort arguing that every principle was conditional upon revolutionary expediency. Initiated by Lenin and carried through by Stalin, the post-Civil War transformation of the Bolsheviks into what would become the All-Union Communist Party certainly entailed a narrowing of a broad spectrum of revolutionary ideas into the concrete political project of the construction of socialism. Dubbed 'Stalinism' by its opponents, this was no less ideologically driven than any of the oppositionist platforms that challenged it during the 1920s. The combination of 'Russian revolutionary fervour' and 'American professionalism' saw the Party grow into a mass organisation present in every social setting, from its natural habitat in the industrial enterprises of big cities to the less familiar world of the Soviet countryside.

[1] McAdams, *Vanguard of the Revolution*, pp. 178–82.

For as long as the leadership remained committed to its revolutionary ideology and pursued revolutionary policies, the Party remained an agent of revolutionary change. During the period examined in this monograph its members engaged in feats of labour while cajoling and pushing their colleagues to transform Soviet industry. They became a powerful competitor for authority on the factory floor, monitoring plan fulfilment while advocating for workers' interests. The rank-and-file also played an active part in its own formation. Grassroots communists were keenly involved in the process of party building, both in its mundane everyday form of recruitment and education and in its more dramatic instances such as the purge and democratisation campaigns. In all these processes party activists were not merely carrying out directives relayed to them by their superiors. They interpreted, concretised and manipulated often contradictory policy initiatives and by the same token affected their outcomes.

There are significant implications following from this for our conceptualisation of the history of the Soviet Union and international communism. This book began with a discussion of the problem of state–society relations for historical scholarship on the Soviet Union in the Stalin period. The argument made was that the issue highlighted by J. Arch Getty in the late 1980s regarding the fuzzy boundaries between state and society in the USSR had been obscured by the exponential growth of empirical research after the opening of the archives. Remaining unaddressed, the binary conception of state and society as distinct and competing entities continued to structure the field, broadly dividing research into state–political and social–cultural, even as the growing popularity of the indeterminate intellectual approach known as the 'linguistic turn' purported to deconstruct concepts of social structure.[2]

This did not so much negatively affect the quality of the research outputs produced in either category as complicate the task of relating them to each other. If pre-1991 totalitarianism and revisionism had a clear-cut mode of communication in often heated disagreement, after the opening of the archives had given both sides cause for celebration it became less clear where their successors stood relative to each other. How did confirmation of Stalin's commitment to building a true classless society influence the much more detailed picture of everyday life that emerged from the archives? What did this new appreciation of the multiplicity of forms of everyday people's interactions with the state, 'the little

[2] Mark Edele, 'Soviet Society, Social Structure, and Everyday Life: Major Frameworks Reconsidered', *Kritika: Explorations in Russian and Eurasian History* 8, no. 2 (2007): 349–73, p. 351.

tactics of the habitat', have to contribute to research about the nature of the ideologically derived 'grand strategies of the state?'[3]

Attempts to classify the Soviet system as a distinctive modernisation project or neo-traditional society generated very interesting empirical insights but ultimately failed to develop into fully-fledged theoretical frameworks. This was to a large extent due to their mutual compatibility; it was perfectly possible to view the pioneering welfare projects of the USSR as modernising policy initiatives, while at the same time recognise that the persistence of informal patron–client networks reflected the failure of the Bolshevik endeavour to overcome the Russian past. There was, thus, no obvious reason why the concepts of modernity or neo-traditionalism had any particular heuristic value beyond serving as descriptors of different features of the Soviet system.

This prompted some more theoretically inclined researchers to suggest that the time of competing and mutually exclusive research frameworks had come to an end. The fall of the USSR and the archival revolution had made it possible to treat the findings of all scholarly traditions that had been part of the field's history as having mutually contributed to the incremental development of its collective wisdom. Scholars like Gábor Rittersporn, Mark Edele and Jean-Paul Depretto argued that this made it possible to start the business of theorising from scratch, by deploying the resources of different traditions of classical sociology in order to make sense of the field's massively expanded source base and eventually come up with a new theoretical understanding of the USSR's social structure.[4]

There is much to agree with in this view; the mutual appreciation of the relative merits of formerly competing research agendas has been one of the most positive effects of the archival revolution on the field's development since 1991. Nevertheless, several years after this conceptual reboot was first announced, we are still not any closer to developing a theory of Soviet social structure or a conceptual framework of the history of the Stalin period. It would seem that the 'quicksand society' described by Moshe Lewin resists theorisation, if only for the fact that the structures it produced were too transient for their conceptualisation to be of any use.

[3] Kotkin, *Magnetic Mountain*, titles of parts I and II, respectively.

[4] Jean-Paul Depretto, 'Stratification without Class', *Kritika: Explorations in Russian and Eurasian History* 8, no. 2 (2007): 375–88; Edele, 'Soviet Society, Social Structure, and Everyday Life'; Gábor T. Rittersporn, 'New Horizons: Conceptualizing the Soviet 1930s', *Kritika: Explorations in Russian and Eurasian History* 2, no. 2 (2001): 307–18.

This monograph has shown that it is possible to side-step this problem in the study of Soviet state–society relations by focusing on an institutional feature of the Soviet political system, a structure that does not need to be theoretically derived. The Communist Party and its primary organisations were stable features of the Soviet system for the duration of its existence and rank-and-file communists are easily distinguishable from the rest of society by virtue of their party membership. What makes the study of the Party especially illuminating with regard to the relationship between state and society is that mediating this relationship had been its core task from its inception as an institution. If the ultimate goal of the Bolshevik project was to create a state in which 'every kitchen-hand' could govern, it was the task of the vanguard party to make this a reality by getting as many people involved in the business of running the state as possible.[5]

The way this was to be achieved was leading by example. Communists were expected to be the first to take part in both the government's far-reaching policy initiatives and the everyday business of keeping the country running. The role envisaged already in the mid-1920s by the leadership for the organisations of their rank-and-file comrades was that of administrative trouble-shooter, educator and liaison with the broader public. Party activists were, thus, involved in the minute details of daily administration as much in the factories, where they were permanently in search of solutions to problems like bottlenecks and faulty output, as in less obviously proletarian environments like farms, offices and military units. In this sense, vanguardism consisted in recruiting a section of society to become a non-professional arm of the state. On this definition and based on the evidence presented here, grassroots communists certainly lived up to their title in the interwar period.

This state of affairs differed significantly from that described by the concept of political mobilisation, primarily because it was permanent. Certainly, the various campaigns initiated by the leadership can be seen as attempts to mobilise the rank-and-file in order to achieve specific objectives. However, the indeterminacy of the tasks set and the ubiquity

[5] 'Every kitchen-hand must know how to govern' (*kazhdaia kukharka dolzhna umet' upravliat' gosudarstvom*) is a phrase often attributed to Lenin. In 'Uderzhat li bol'sheviki gosudarstvennuiu vlast'?' Lenin actually wrote that 'We are not utopianists ... We know that ... not every kitchen-hand can engage in governing the state now ... We demand that training in the affairs of government is led by the most conscious workers ... that it begins without delay ... to involve all workers, all poor peasants'. *PSS* 34: 229–339, p. 315. The implication remains that a state run by non-professionals was a desirable goal for the Bolshevik leader. Vladimir Maiakovskii later included the first version of the quote in his poem *Lenin*, from which the epigraph of this monograph is taken.

of everyday crises in the Soviet interwar period meant that the rank-and-file was constantly active in some way or other. Unlike specific campaigns which the leadership could call off or reverse, the party rank-and-file was a permanent structure of the Soviet system. The vanguard could not – or would not – be switched off as long as the leadership remained committed to Marxism–Leninism and the role it assigned to the Party.

Organised in the PPO, the party rank-and-file thus formed a distinct element of the Soviet political system in its formative period. It functioned according to its own dynamics which had to be taken into account by other actors, including the state apparatus, district and regional party committees and, ultimately, the top leadership. It thus affected the way in which other cleavages of Soviet politics operated. Thus, in the perennial tension between 'reds' and 'experts', the PPO was by its very function always 'red'. Whatever the balance between the ideological and technocratic aspects of party policy was at any given time, the fact that it would have to be implemented at least in part through the efforts of activists placed a definite limit on how technocratic any piece of policy could be.

Ultimately, the value of studying the communist rank-and-file lies in the fact that party organisations were the institutional link between the state and society at large, a locus in the Soviet system where the two overlapped. They were the site of interaction between grand strategies and little tactics. The party organisation as vanguard was an ideologically imbued institutional structure, operative for as long as the central leadership was committed to the theoretical principles that ascribed to it a leadership role over its social setting. At the same time, because party organisations were composed of ordinary people, their social setting determined the nature and effects of their ideologically motivated activities.

Thus, KP/Kirov communists were industrial workers whose efforts were primarily directed towards addressing the issues confronting themselves and their colleagues in their giant machine-building plant within the context of Soviet industrialisation. Their understanding of concepts like class struggle, *samokritika* and, ultimately, their own vanguard role were always inflected through the prism of labour–management conflicts and the permanent pressure exerted on their living standards. This is perhaps most clearly reflected in the fate of the Party's ambitious cultural enlightenment programmes which the scarcities of time and things largely limited to the supervision of the quality of services.

Be that as it may, it is neither helpful nor accurate to view the activities of the rank-and-file in an instrumentalist manner. The activities of communist workers examined in the preceding chapters were not such that could be considered disingenuous by either themselves or the leadership. Their involvement in factory affairs was both expected and desirable as far as the leadership was concerned, even if the outcome thereof was more often than not at odds with what was sought. As the rank-and-filers could thus get what they wanted whilst acting largely within the letter and spirit of party policy, there is little reason to suggest that they did not do so in good faith. The upshot was that, as their party membership inevitably drew them into political affairs extending beyond the factory gates, their participation was no less keen than it was with respect to the issues of immediate concern to them as workers. This also made it possible for the rank-and-filers to view their own concerns through the prism of broader political issues, including the ever more threatening security environment. Fires, accidents and plain selfishness were, thus, understood in terms of sabotage or 'Zinovievism' by some communists, years before the leadership came to publicly adopt a similar outlook.

Although, however, the centralist principle on which the Party operated meant that similar kinds of activities would be attempted wherever there were communists present, we should expect their outcomes to differ depending on the conditions in which these activities took place. It is the ubiquity of the Party's presence combined with the variation of Soviet social conditions that makes the appreciation of the PPO as a specific element of state–society relations a useful substitute for a theoretical framework of the same. If one of the purposes of theory is to make the findings of empirical research comparable and applicable across research projects, then further study of the party rank-and-file can provide a similar service.

Useful insight can be gained by comparing the picture of rank-and-file activism emerging from the account offered in this study with that of the party grassroots in workplaces that were smaller, less party-saturated, where women made up a greater part of the workforce, or any combination of these conditions. We may further expect rank-and-file activism to have had a different impact in rural areas, where the insistence of the Party on recruiting chiefly amongst proletarian village elements like farmhands and shepherds deprived it of members during the NEP era and can hardly have placed it in a strong position to launch its aggressive campaign of collectivisation in the late 1920s. As we saw in the preceding chapters, the leadership of Leningrad province was much more concerned about the performance of party organisations in the small cities and towns of its remote rural hinterland than that of model PPOs like KP/Kirov.[6]

The party rank-and-file may also serve as the object of diachronic comparisons. This study has traced the contours of party activism from the NEP-era to the outbreak of WWII and argued that these remained remarkably stable for the duration of this period. It is unlikely, however, that things continued thus for much longer, as the war killed and displaced significant numbers of communists, destroying some party organisations while forcing others to operate underground for the first time after two decades of monopolising political power. While the activities of party activists during WWII would in themselves be a fascinating subject for research, the effects of the war on the place of the rank-and-file in the Soviet system after the USSR's victory are perhaps more relevant to the issues that have been examined here. The available evidence suggests that the party's budgetary expenditures on ideology, its privileged domain of activity, collapsed during the war and, despite a brief revival, declined consistently in the post-war period.[7] Combined with a contemporaneous strengthening of the state apparatus vis-à-vis the Party, this could have had a significant impact on the activities of primary party organisations and their effect on state–society relations.[8] This is a question worth exploring, as are similar issues emerging with respect to other major milestones in the Soviet Union's history, like the response of the grassroots to destalinisation and perestroika. Thus, in an entertaining anthropomorphic metaphor, one scholar described the post-Stalin USSR as a middle-aged revolution seeking comfortable retirement.[9] Red flags and demonstrations still abounded as tropes and rituals of Soviet power, but neither the leadership nor the broader population was as invested in the radical social transformation that officially remained the Party's *raison d'être*. How did party activism change in the transition to this new context? And how did PPO dynamics themselves contribute to this transformation?

[6] Isabel Tirado, 'The Komsomol's Village Vanguard: Youth and Politics in the NEP Countryside', *The Russian Review* 72, no. 3 (2013): 427–46, p. 442; Samantha Lomb, 'Personal and Political: A Micro-History of the "Red Column" Collective Farm', *The Carl Beck Papers in Russian and East European Studies* 2404 (2016).

[7] Belova and Lazarev, *Funding Loyalty*, pp. 17–18.

[8] Edward D. Cohn, 'Policing the Party: Conflicts between Local Prosecutors and Party Leaders under Late Stalinism', *Europe–Asia Studies* 65, no. 10 (2013): 1912–30; Daniel Stotland, 'The War Within: Factional Strife and Politics of Control in the Soviet Party State (1944–1948)', *Russian History* 42, no. 3 (2015): 343–69.

[9] Amir Weiner, 'Robust Revolution to Retiring Revolution: The Life Cycle of the Soviet Revolution, 1945–1968', *The Slavonic and East European Review* 86, no. 2 (2008): 208–31.

Perhaps more interestingly, the communist rank-and-file can serve as a comparative tool for state–society relations between different twentieth-century socialist states. Some version of the vanguard party principle was applied by all states that declared themselves to be on the socialist path. Despite their organisational similarities, these parties came to power in very different circumstances and had to 'lead' the way to socialism in different conditions. Thus, Chinese and Cuban communists alike came to power by means of guerrilla warfare in conditions of economic backwardness. They both developed Marxism–Leninism in ways inspired by their national intellectual traditions. Nevertheless, in contrast to the Chinese communists who had spent years establishing base areas in the countryside before their victory, the Communist Party of Cuba numbered only 55,000 members a decade into its rule, less than half the membership of the Leningrad Party Organisation in the period examined in this monograph.[10] In most of Eastern Europe, formerly strong communist parties that had been destroyed by Nazism and war were brought to power by the might of Soviet armour and began building their links with society in entirely different conditions to those of the Bolsheviks. Nevertheless, scholars working on the social history of the East and Central European socialist states have highlighted similar patterns of grassroots activism to the ones examined here.[11] The reproduction of the institutional form of the Leninist concept of the vanguard party in different historical conditions thus provides a promising lead for comparative research in state–society relations, as a component part of the emerging historiography of international communism.

10 Stephen A. Smith, 'Introduction: Towards a Global History of Communism', in *The Oxford Handbook of the History of Communism*, ed. Stephen A. Smith (Oxford: Oxford University Press, 2014), p. 18; Peter Zarrow, *China in War and Revolution, 1895–1949* (London: Routledge, 2005), chapter 16.

11 Eszter Bartha, 'Welfare Dictatorship, the Working Class and the Change of Regimes in East Germany and Hungary', *Europe–Asia Studies* 63, no. 9 (2011): 1591–610; Jan De Graaf, 'The Occupational Strikes in the Dąbrowa Basin of April 1951: Stalinist Industrialization against the Traditions of the Polish Working Class', *International Labor and Working-Class History* 98 (2020): 22–42; Padraic Jeremiah Kenney, *Rebuilding Poland: Workers and Communists, 1945–1950* (Ithaca: Cornell University Press, 1997); Marek Sroka, '"Soldiers of the Cultural Revolution": The Stalinization of Libraries and Librarians Hip in Poland, 1945–1953', *Library History* 16, no. 2 (2000): 105–25; J. B. Straughn, '"Taking the State at Its Word": The Arts of Consentful Contention in the German Democratic Republic', *American Journal of Sociology* 110, no. 6 (2005): 1598–650; Maciej Tymiński, 'Apparatchiks and Enterprises: The Case of the Warsaw Region in 1950–1970', *Europe–Asia Studies* 72, no. 8 (2020): 1277–304; Dorothee Wierling, 'Work, Workers, and Politics in the German Democratic Republic', *International Labor and Working-Class History* 50 (1996): 44–63.

# *Bibliography*

## Archival Collections (*Fondy*)

RGASPI – Russian State Archive of Social and Political History
f. 17: *Tsentral'nyi Komitet KPSS*
RGAVMF – Russian State Archive of the Navy
f. r-852: *Divizion Linkorov*
TsGAIPD – Central State Archive of Historical-Political Documents
f. 1012: *Partiinyi Komitet Proizvodstvennogo Ob'edineniia 'Kirovskii Zavod'*

## Published Sources and Secondary Literature


Albert, Gleb J. '"Comrade Speaker!" Zapiski as Means of Political Communication and Source for Popular Moods in the 1920s'. *The NEP Era: Soviet Russia 1921–1928* 8 (2015): 43–54.

Alekseev, M. A., A. I. Kolpakidi and V. Ia. Kochik. *Entsiklopediia voennoi razvedki, 1918–1945 gg.* Moscow: Kuchkovo Pole, Voennaia Kniga, 2012.

Allen, Barbara. 'Alexander Shliapnikov and the Origins of the Workers' Opposition, March 1919–April 1920'. *Jahrbücher Für Geschichte Osteuropas* 53, no. 1 (2005): 1–24.

*Alexander Shlyapnikov, 1885–1937: Life of an Old Bolshevik.* Leiden: Brill, 2015.

Allen, Robert C. *Farm to Factory: A Reinterpretation of the Soviet Industrial Revolution.* Princeton: Princeton University Press, 2009.

Andrle, Vladimir. *A Social History of Twentieth-Century Russia.* London: Edward Arnold, 1994.

Armitage, David and Sanjay Subrahmanyam, eds. *The Age of Revolutions in Global Context, c. 1760–1840.* London: Palgrave Macmillan, 2009.

Bailes, Kendall E. *Technology and Society under Lenin and Stalin: Origins of the Soviet Technical Intelligentsia, 1917–1941.* Reprint ed. Princeton: Princeton University Press, 2015.

Ball, Alan M. *Russia's Last Capitalists: The Nepmen, 1921–1929.* Berkeley: University of California Press, 1990.

Bandera, V. N. 'Market Orientation of State Enterprises during NEP'. *Soviet Studies* 22, no. 1 (1970): 110–21.

Bartha, Eszter. 'Welfare Dictatorship, the Working Class and the Change of Regimes in East Germany and Hungary'. *Europe–Asia Studies* 63, no. 9 (13 October 2011): 1591–610. https://doi.org/10.1080/09668136.2011.611647.

Bartolini, Stefano. *The Political Mobilization of the European Left, 1860–1980: The Class Cleavage*. Cambridge: Cambridge University Press, 2007.

Beattie, Robert. 'A "Great Turn" That Never Happened: A Reconsideration of the Soviet Decree of Labor Discipline of November 1932'. *Russian History* 13, no. 1 (1 January 1986): 235–57. https://doi.org/10.1163/187633186X00098.

Belkin, G. 'Formy Chastnoi Promishlennosti'. In *Chastnyi kapital v narodnom khoziaistve SSSR*, edited by A. M. Ginzburg, 217–49. Moscow: Promizdat, 1927.

Belova, Eugenia and Valery Lazarev. *Funding Loyalty: The Economics of the Communist Party*. New Haven: Yale University Press, 2013.

Black, Clayton. 'Answering for Bacchanalia: Management, Authority and the Putilov Tractor Program, 1928–1930'. *The Carl Beck Papers in Russian and East European Studies* 1508 (2002).

'Manufacturing Communists: "Krasnyi Putilovets" and the Politics of Soviet Industrialization, 1923–1932'. Dissertation, Indiana University, 1996.

'Party Crisis and the Factory Shop Floor: Krasnyi Putilovets and the Leningrad Opposition, 1925–26'. *Europe–Asia Studies* 46, no. 1 (1 January 1994): 107–26. https://doi.org/10.2307/153033.

'Zinoviev Re-examined: Comments on Lars Lih's "Populist Leninist"'. *The NEP Era: Soviet Russia, 1921–1928* 2 (1928): 25–38.

Bogushevskii, Vladimir. 'O derevenskom kulake ili o role traditsii v terminologii'. *Bol'shevik*, no. 9–10 (1925): 63–64.

Borodkin, L. I. 'Zhizn' v gorode v gody pervoi piatiletki: "Uluchshenie material'nogo polozheniia" ili padenie real'noi zarplaty?' *Vestnik istorii i literatury* (2010): 377–90.

Borodkin, L. I. and E. I. Safonova. 'Gosudarstvennoe regulirovanie trudovykh otnoshenii v gody nepa: formirovanie sistemy motivatsii truda v promyshlennosti'. *Ekonomicheskaiia istoriia: Obozrenie* 5 (2000): 23–46.

Bossenga, Gail. 'The Nobility's Demise: Institutions, Status, and the Role of the State'. *The American Historical Review* 124, no. 3 (1 June 2019): 942–49. https://doi.org/10.1093/ahr/rhz314.

Brandenberger, David. *National Bolshevism: Stalinist Mass Culture and the Formation of Modern Russian National Identity, 1931–1956*. Cambridge, MA: Harvard University Press, 2002.

Brandenberger, David and Mikhail Zelenov. *Stalin's Master Narrative: A Critical Edition of the History of the Communist Party of the Soviet Union*. Critical ed. New Haven: Yale University Press, 2019.

Brooks, Jeffrey. *Thank You, Comrade Stalin!: Soviet Public Culture from Revolution to Cold War*. New ed. Princeton: Princeton University Press, 2001.

Brovkin, Vladimir. *Russia after Lenin: Politics, Culture, Society*. London: Routledge, 1998.

Brown, Richard D. 'Microhistory and the Post-Modern Challenge'. *Journal of the Early Republic* 23, no. 1 (2003): 1–20. https://doi.org/10.2307/3124983.

Carr, E. H. *The Interregnum 1923–1924*. Baltimore: Penguin Books, 1969.

*Socialism in One Country*. Vol. 1. New York: Macmillan, 1958.

Carr, E. H. and R. W. Davies. *Foundations of a Planned Economy*. Vol. 1. 3 vols. London: Macmillan, 1969.

Chase, William. *Enemies within the Gates?: The Comintern and the Stalinist Repression, 1934–1939*, 1st ed. New Haven: Yale University Press, 2001.

'Scapegoating One's Comrades in the USSR, 1934–1937'. In *The Anatomy of Terror: Political Violence under Stalin*, edited by James Harris, 267–71. Oxford: Oxford University Press, 2013.

*Workers, Society and the Soviet State: Labor and Life in Moscow, 1918–29*. Champaign: University of Illinois Press, 1987.

Chernev, Borislav. *Twilight of Empire: The Brest–Litovsk Conference and the Remaking of East-Central Europe, 1917–1918*. Toronto: University of Toronto Press, 2017.

Cherniaev, V. Iu. *Piterskie rabochie i 'Diktatura Proletariata': Oktiabr' 1917–1929*. Saint-Petersburg: Russko-Baltiiskii informatsionnii tsentr BLITs, 2003.

Chernova, O. A. 'Deiatel'nost' professional'nykh soiuzov po razresheniiu trudovykh konfliktov na predpriiatiiakh tsentral'nogo Chernozem'ia v 1920-e gody (po materialam kurskoi i voronezhskoi gubernii)'. *Nauchnye vedomosti. Seriia istoria, politologiia, ekonomika, informatika* 16, no. 19 (2010): 188–96.

Clark, Katerina. *Petersburg: Crucible of Cultural Revolution*. Cambridge, MA: Harvard University Press, 1995.

Clibbon, Jennifer. *The Soviet Press and Grass-Roots Organization: The Rabkor Movement, NEP to the First Five Year Plan*. Toronto: University of Toronto Press, 1993.

Cohen, Stephen F. *Bukharin and the Bolshevik Revolution: A Political Biography, 1888–1938*, Reprint ed. Oxford: Oxford University Press, 1980.

Cohn, Edward. *The High Title of a Communist: Postwar Party Discipline and the Values of the Soviet Regime*. 1st ed. DeKalb: Northern Illinois University Press, 2015.

'Policing the Party: Conflicts between Local Prosecutors and Party Leaders under Late Stalinism'. *Europe–Asia Studies* 65, no. 10 (1 December 2013): 1912–30. https://doi.org/10.1080/09668136.2013.848644.

Conquest, Robert. *The Great Terror: A Reassessment*. Oxford: Oxford University Press, 2008.

Daniels, Robert V. *The Conscience of the Revolution: Communist Opposition in Soviet Russia*. Cambridge, MA: Harvard University Press, 1960.

Danilov, Vladimir, Roberta Manning and Lynne Viola (eds.), *Tragediia Sovetskoi derevni. Kollektivizatsiia i raskulachivanie. 1927–1939*, 5 vols. Moscow: ROSSPEN, 1999–2006.

David-Fox, Michael. *Crossing Borders: Modernity, Ideology, and Culture in Russia and the Soviet Union*. Pittsburgh: University of Pittsburgh Press, 2015.

*Revolution of the Mind: Higher Learning among the Bolsheviks, 1918–1929*. Ithaca: Cornell University Press, 1997.

*Showcasing the Great Experiment: Cultural Diplomacy and Western Visitors to the Soviet Union, 1921–1941*. Oxford: Oxford University Press, 2012.

David-Fox, Michael, Peter Holquist and Alexander Martin (eds.), 'Ex Tempore Stalinism and "The Great Retreat"' [special section]. *Kritika: Explorations in Russian and Eurasian History* 5, no. 4 (2004): 651–733.

Davies, R. W. 'The Economic History of the Soviet Union Reconsidered'. *Kritika: Explorations in Russian and Eurasian History* 11, no. 1 (2010): 145–59.

Davies, R. W. and Oleg Khlevnyuk. 'Stakhanovism and the Soviet Economy'. *Europe–Asia Studies* 54, no. 6 (2002): 867–903.

Davies, Sarah. *Popular Opinion in Stalin's Russia: Terror, Propaganda and Dissent, 1934–1941*. Cambridge: Cambridge University Press, 1997.

'Stalin and the Making of the Leader Cult in the 1930s'. In *The Leader Cult in Communist Dictatorships*, edited by Balázs Apor and J. Behrends, 29–46. London: Palgrave Macmillan, 2004.

Davies, Sarah and James Harris (eds.). *Stalin: A New History*. Cambridge: Cambridge University Press, 2006.

*Dekrety Sovetskoi vlasti*, 18 vols. Moscow: Politizdat, 1957–89.

Depretto, Jean-Paul. 'Ofitsial'nye kontseptsii rabochego klassa v SSSR (1920–1930-e gg.)'. *Sotsial'naia istoria. Ezhegodnik* (2004): 72–90.

'Stratification without Class'. *Kritika: Explorations in Russian and Eurasian History* 8, no. 2 (2007): 375–88.

Deutscher, Isaac. *The Prophet Unarmed: Trotsky 1921–1929*. London: Verso, 2003.

Douds, Lara. *Inside Lenin's Government: Ideology, Power and Practice in the Early Soviet State*. London: Bloomsbury Academic, 2018.

Dunham, Vera S. *In Stalin's Time: Middle Class Values in Soviet Fiction*, New ed. Durham: Duke University Press, 1990.

Dzerzhinskii, Felix Edmundovich. *Izbrannye proizvedeniia v 2-kh tomakh*, Vol. 2. 2 vols. Moscow: Izdatel'stvo Politicheskoi Literaturi, 1967.

Edele, Mark. *Debates on Stalinism*. Manchester: Manchester University Press, 2020.

'Soviet Society, Social Structure, and Everyday Life: Major Frameworks Reconsidered'. *Kritika: Explorations in Russian and Eurasian History* 8, no. 2 (2007): 349–73.

Egge, Åsmund. *Zagadka Kirova: ubiistvo, razviazavshee stalinskii terror*. Moscow: ROSSPEN, 2011.

Eliseeva, I. I. and E. I. Gribovaia. *Sankt-Peterburg, 1703–2003: Iubileinyi statisticheskii sbornik*. Saint-Petersburg: Sudostroenie, 2003.

Emdin, Ia R. 'Polozhenie Truda v Chastnoi Promishlennosti'. In *Chastnyi kapital v narodnom khoziaistve SSSR*, edited by A. M. Ginzburg, 206–16. Moscow: Promizdat, 1927.

Fender, Stephan. *The Global Perspective of Urban Labor in Mexico City, 1910–1929: El Mundo al Revés*, 1st ed. New York: Routledge, 2020.

Filtzer, Donald. *Soviet Workers and Stalinist Industrialization: The Formation of Modern Soviet Production Relations, 1928–1941*. London: Pluto Press, 1986.

Fitzpatrick, Sheila. *The Cultural Front: Power and Culture in Revolutionary Russia*. Ithaca: Cornell University Press, 1992.

*Everyday Stalinism: Ordinary Life in Extraordinary Times: Soviet Russia in the 1930s*. New York: Oxford University Press, 2000.

'Ordzhonikidze's Takeover of Vesenkha: A Case Study in Soviet Bureaucratic Politics'. *Soviet Studies* 37, no. 2 (1985): 153–72.

'The Question of Social Support for Collectivization'. *Russian History* 37, no. 2 (2010): 153–77.

'Stalin and the Making of a New Elite, 1928–1939'. *Slavic Review* 38, no. 3 (September 1979): 377–402. https://doi.org/10.2307/2496711.

Gerwarth, Robert. *November 1918: The German Revolution*. Oxford: Oxford University Press, 2020.

Getty, J. Arch. '"Excesses Are Not Permitted": Mass Terror and Stalinist Governance in the Late 1930s'. *The Russian Review* 61, no. 1 (2002): 113–38.

*Origins of the Great Purges: The Soviet Communist Party Reconsidered, 1933–1938*. Cambridge: Cambridge University Press, 1987.

*Practicing Stalinism: Bolsheviks, Boyars, and the Persistence of Tradition*. New Haven: Yale University Press, 2013.

'Pragmatists and Puritans: The Rise and Fall of the Party Control Commission', *The Carl Beck Papers in Russian and East European Studies*, no. 1208 (1997).

'The Rise and Fall of a Party First Secretary: Vainov of Iaroslavl''. In *The Anatomy of Terror*, edited by James Harris, 66–84. Oxford: Oxford University Press, 2013. https://doi.org/10.1093/acprof:oso/9780199655663.003.0005.

'State and Society under Stalin: Constitutions and Elections in the 1930s'. *Slavic Review* 50, no. 1 (1991): 18–35. https://doi.org/10.2307/2500596.

'State, Society, and Superstition'. *The Russian Review* 46, no. 4 (1987): 391–96. https://doi.org/10.2307/130292.

Getty, J. Arch and Oleg V. Naumov. *The Road to Terror: Stalin and the Self-Destruction of the Bolsheviks, 1932–1939*. New Haven: Yale University Press, 2002.

*Yezhov; The Rise of Stalin's 'Iron Fist'*. New Haven: Yale University Press, 2008.

Getty, J. Arch, Gábor T. Rittersporn and Viktor N. Zemskov. 'Victims of the Soviet Penal System in the Pre-War Years: A First Approach on the Basis of Archival Evidence'. *The American Historical Review* 98, no. 4 (1993): 1017–49. https://doi.org/10.2307/2166597.

Gimpel'son, E. G. *Sovetskii rabochii klass 1918–1920 gg.: sotsial'no-politicheskie izmeneniia*. Moscow: Nauka, 1974.

Ginzburg, A. M. (ed.). *Chastnyi kapital v narodnom khoziaistve SSSR*. Moscow: Promizdat, 1927.

Ginzburg, Carlo, John Tedeschi and Anne C. Tedeschi. 'Microhistory: Two or Three Things That I Know about It'. *Critical Inquiry* 20, no. 1 (1993): 10–35.

Goldman, Wendy Z. *Inventing the Enemy: Denunciation and Terror in Stalin's Russia*. Cambridge: Cambridge University Press, 2011.

'Small Motors of Terror: The Role of Factory Newspapers'. In *The Anatomy of Terror: Political Violence under Stalin*, edited by James Harris, 240–62. Oxford: Oxford University Press, 2013.

'Stalinist Terror and Democracy: The 1937 Union Campaign'. *The American Historical Review* 110, no. 5 (1 December 2005): 1427–53. https://doi.org/10.1086/ahr.110.5.1427.

*Terror and Democracy in the Age of Stalin: The Social Dynamics of Repression*. Cambridge: Cambridge University Press, 2007.

*Women at the Gates: Gender and Industry in Stalin's Russia*. Cambridge: Cambridge University Press, 2002.

*Women, the State and Revolution: Soviet Family Policy and Social Life, 1917–1936*. Cambridge: Cambridge University Press, 1993.

Gorham, Michael. 'Tongue-Tied Writers: The Rabsel'kor Movement and the Voice of the "New Intelligentsia" in Early Soviet Russia'. *The Russian Review* 55, no. 3 (1996): 412–29.

Gorlizki, Yoram. 'Ordinary Stalinism: The Council of Ministers and the Soviet Neopatrimonial State, 1946–1953'. *The Journal of Modern History* 74, no. 4 (2002): 699–736.

Gorlizki, Yoram and Oleg V. Khlevniuk. *Substate Dictatorship: Networks, Loyalty, and Institutional Change in the Soviet Union*. New Haven: Yale University Press, 2020.

Graaf, Jan De. 'The Occupational Strikes in the Dąbrowa Basin of April 1951: Stalinist Industrialization against the Traditions of the Polish Working Class'. *International Labor and Working-Class History* 98 (2020): 22–42. https://doi.org/10.1017/S0147547919000322.

Gray, Marion W. 'Microhistory as Universal History'. *Central European History* 34, no. 3 (September 2001): 419–31. https://doi.org/10.1163/156916101152959181.

Gregory, Paul R. *The Political Economy of Stalinism: Evidence from the Soviet Secret Archives*. Cambridge: Cambridge University Press, 2010.

Groys, Boris. 'The Birth of Socialist Realism from the Spirit of the Russian Avant-Garde'. In *The Culture of the Stalin Period*, edited by Hans Günther, 122–48. London: Palgrave Macmillan, 1990.

Gusev, Aleksei. 'The "Bolshevik Leninist" Opposition and the Working Class'. In *A Dream Deferred: New Studies in Russian and Soviet Labour History*, edited by Donald Filtzer, Wendy Z. Goldman, Gijs Kessler and Simon Pirani, 153–69. Bern: Peter Lang, 2008.

Hainian, Liu. 'The Struggle for Human Rights by the Communist Party of China (1921–1949)', Institute of Law of the Chinese Academy of Social Sciences website, available at: www.iolaw.org.cn/global/en/new.aspx?id=44851, last accessed 9 February 2019.

Halfin, Igal. *Intimate Enemies: Demonizing the Bolshevik Opposition, 1918–1928*. Pittsburgh: University of Pittsburgh Press, 2007.

*Red Autobiographies: Initiating the Bolshevik Self.* Herbert J. Ellison Center for Russian, East European, and Central Asian Studies. Seattle: University of Washington Press, 2011.

*Stalinist Confessions: Messianism and Terror at the Leningrad Communist University*, 1st ed. Pittsburgh: University of Pittsburgh Press, 2009.

Halfin, Igal and Jochen Hellbeck. 'Rethinking the Stalinist Subject: Stephen Kotkin's "Magnetic Mountain" and the State of Soviet Historical Studies'. *Jahrbücher Für Geschichte Osteuropas* 44, no. 3 (1 January 1996): 456–63. https://doi.org/10.2307/41052991.

Harris, James R. 'Discipline versus Democracy: The 1923 Party Controversy'. In *The Fate of the Bolshevik Revolution: Illiberal Liberation 1917–1941*, edited by Lara Douds, James Harris and Peter Whitewood, pp. 115–17. London: Bloomsbury Academic, 2020.

*The Great Fear: Stalin's Terror of the 1930s*, 1st ed. Oxford: Oxford University Press, 2016.

*The Great Urals: Regionalism and the Evolution of the Soviet System*. Ithaca: Cornell University Press, 1999.

'The Purging of Local Cliques in the Urals Region, 1936–7'. In *Stalinism: New Directions*, edited by Sheila Fitzpatrick, 262–85. London: Routledge, 1999.

Harris, Jonathan. *The Split in Stalin's Secretariat, 1939–1948*. Lanham: Lexington Books, 2008.

Harrison, Mark and R. W. Davies. 'The Soviet Military–Economic Effort during the Second Five-Year Plan (1933–1937)'. *Europe–Asia Studies* 49, no. 3 (1 May 1997): 369–406.

Hatch, John B. 'The "Lenin Levy" and the Social Origins of Stalinism: Workers and the Communist Party in Moscow, 1921–1928'. *Slavic Review* 48, no. 4 (1 December 1989): 558–77. https://doi.org/10.2307/2499783.

Heilmann, Sebastian, Elizabeth J. Perry, Jae Ho Chung, Nara Dillon and Nara Fewsmith. *Mao's Invisible Hand: The Political Foundations of Adaptive Governance in China (Harvard Contemporary China Series): 17*, Illustrated ed. Cambridge, MA: Harvard University Press, 2011.

Hellbeck, Jochen. *Revolution on My Mind: Writing a Diary under Stalin*. Cambridge, MA: Harvard University Press, 2009.

Hessler, Julie. *A Social History of Soviet Trade: Trade Policy, Retail Practices, and Consumption, 1917–1953*. Princeton: Princeton University Press, 2004.

Hicks, Jeremy. 'From Conduits to Commanders: Shifting Views of Worker Correspondents, 1924–26'. *Revolutionary Russia* 19, no. 2 (2006): 131–49. https://doi.org/10.1080/09546540600970773.

'Worker Correspondents: Between Journalism and Literature'. *The Russian Review* 66, no. 4 (1 October 2007): 568–85. https://doi.org/10.1111/j.1467-9434.2007.00459.x.

Hoffmann, David L. *Cultivating the Masses: Modern State Practices and Soviet Socialism, 1914–1939*, 1st ed. Ithaca: Cornell University Press, 2011.

*Peasant Metropolis: Social Identities in Moscow, 1929–1941*. Ithaca: Cornell University Press, 2000.

*Stalinist Values: The Cultural Norms of Soviet Modernity, 1917–1941*. Ithaca: Cornell University Press, 2003.

Hoffrogge, Ralf. *Working-Class Politics in the German Revolution: Richard Müller, the Revolutionary Shop Stewards and the Origins of the Council Movement*. Leiden: Brill, 2014. https://brill.com/view/title/20956.

Holquist, Peter. '"Information Is the Alpha and Omega of Our Work": Bolshevik Surveillance in Its Pan-European Context'. *The Journal of Modern History* 69, no. 3 (1 September 1997): 415–50. https://doi.org/10.2307/2953592.

*Making War, Forging Revolution: Russia's Continuum of Crisis, 1914–1921*. Cambridge, MA: Harvard University Press, 2002.

Hooper, Cynthia. 'Terror from within: Participation and Coercion in Soviet Power, 1924–1964'. Dissertation, Princeton University, 2003.

Hughes, James. *Stalinism in a Russian Province: A Study of Collectivization and Dekulakization in Siberia*. London: Palgrave Macmillan, 1996.

Iarov, Sergei. 'Predposilki Konformizma: Prekrashchenie zabastovok v Petrograde v 1917–1925 gg.' *Sotsiologicheskii Zhurnal*, no. 2 (2007): 109–47.

Ilic, Melanie. *Women Workers in the Soviet Interwar Economy: From 'Protection' to 'Equality'*. London: Palgrave Macmillan, 1998.

Isaev, A. *Bezrabotitsa v SSSR i bor'ba s neiu (za Period 1917-1924 g.g.)*. Moscow: Voprosy Truda, 1924.

*Istoriia rabochikh Leningrada. 1703–1965*. Vol. 2. Leningrad: Nauka, 1972.

Iudina, Taisiia. 'Profsoiuzy kak instrument regulirovaniia obshchestvennykh otnoshenii v SSSR v 1920-e gg. (Na primere kontsesii "Gruzinski Marganets")'. *Vestnik RUDN, seriia 'Istoriia Rossii'*, no. 1 (2011): 58–65.

Jacobson, Jon. *When the Soviet Union Entered World Politics*. Berkeley: University of California Press, 1994.

Jasny, Naum. *Soviet Industrialization, 1928–1952*. Chicago: University of Chicago Press, 1961.

Jones, Mark. *Founding Weimar: Violence and the German Revolution of 1918–1919*. Cambridge: Cambridge University Press, 2016.

Kapustin, Iakov. 'O kontrole pervichnykh partorganizatsii na predpriiatiiakh'. *Partiinoe Stroitel'stvo*, no 5 (1939): 37–40.

Kelly, Catriona. 'What Was Soviet Studies and What Came Next?' *The Journal of Modern History* 85, no. 1 (1 March 2013): 109–49. https://doi.org/10.1086/668800.

Kenney, Padraic Jeremiah. *Rebuilding Poland: Workers and Communists, 1945–1950*, 1st ed. Ithaca: Cornell University Press, 1997.

Khlevniuk, Oleg. 'Top Down vs. Bottom-up: Regarding the Potential of Contemporary "Revisionism"'. Translated by Aaron Hale-Dorrell and Angelina Lucento. *Cahiers du monde russe. Russie – Empire russe – Union soviétique et États indépendants* 56, no. 56/4 (1 October 2015): 837–57.

Khlevniuk, Oleg, Liudmila P. Kosheleva, A. V. Kvashonkin and Larisa A. Rogovaia (eds.). *Bol'shevistkoe rukovodstvo. Perepiska. 1912–1927*. Moscow: ROSSPEN, 1996.

Khlopova, A. V. 'Innovatsii v obshchestvennoi zhizni gorozhan viatskogo regiona v 1920–1930-kh godakh'. *Sovremennye problemy nauki i obrazovania*, no. 3 (2012): 1–7.

Kiselev, S. M. 'Kredit v sisteme narodnogo khoziaistva SSSR'. *Planovoe khoziaistvo* no. 2 (1925): 22–38.

Knight, Amy W. *Who Killed Kirov?: The Kremlin's Greatest Mystery*. New York: Hill and Wang, 2000.

Koenker, Diane P. *Club Red*. Ithaca: Cornell University Press, 2013.

'Factory Tales: Narratives of Industrial Relations in the Transition to Nep'. *Russian Review* 55, no. 3 (1 July 1996): 384–411. https://doi.org/10.2307/131791.

'Men against Women on the Shop Floor in Early Soviet Russia: Gender and Class in the Socialist Workplace'. *The American Historical Review* 100, no. 5 (December 1995): 1438–64. https://doi.org/10.2307/2169865.

*Republic of Labor: Russian Printers and Soviet Socialism, 1918–1930*. Ithaca: Cornell University Press, 2005.

'Urbanization and Deurbanization in the Russian Revolution and Civil War'. *The Journal of Modern History* 57, no. 3 (1 September 1985): 424–50.

Kojevnikov, Alexei B. *Stalin's Great Science: The Times and Adventures of Soviet Physicists*. London: Imperial College Press, 2004.

Kokosalakis, Yiannis. 'The Communist Party and the Late 1930s Soviet Democracy Campaigns: Origins and Outcomes'. In *The Fate of the Bolshevik Revolution: Illiberal Liberation, 1917–41*, edited by Lara Douds, James Harris and Peter Whitewood, 77–92. London: Bloomsbury Academic, 2020.

'"Merciless War" against Trifles: The Leningrad Party Organisation after the Fall of the Zinoviev Opposition'. *Revolutionary Russia* 28, no. 1 (2015): 48–68. https://doi.org/10.1080/09546545.2015.1053697.

Kollontai, Aleksandra. 'Rabochaia Oppozitsiia'. in *Levye Kommunisty v Rossii*. Moscow: Praksis, 2008.

*Kommunisticheskaia Partiia Sovetskogo Soiuza v rezoliutsiakh i resheniakh s"ezdov, konferentsii i plenumov TsK, 1898–1988*. 16 vols. Moscow: Izdatel'stvo Politicheskoi Literaturi, 1983.

Konecny, Peter. *Builders and Deserters: Students, State, and Community in Leningrad, 1917–1941*. Montreal: McGill–Queens University Press, 1999.

Kostiuchenko, Stanislav. *Istoriia Kirovskogo Zavoda, 1917–1945*. Moscow: Mysl', 1965.

Kotkin, Stephen. *Magnetic Mountain: Stalinism As a Civilization*. Berkeley: University of California Press, 1997.

Kozlov, Denis. 'The Leningrad Martyrology: A Statistical Note on the 1937 Executions in Leningrad City and Region'. *Canadian Slavonic Papers* 44, no. 3–4 (1 September 2002): 175–208. https://doi.org/10.1080/00085006.2002.11092307.

Kozlov, Konstantin. 'Uchastie ural'skikh profsoiuzov v predotvrashchenii i uregulirovanii zabastovochnogo dvizheniia v gody nepa'. *Vestnik Cheliabinskogo Gosudarstvennogo Universiteta*, no. 12 (2013): 36–41.

Kropotkin, Peter. *The Conquest of Bread*. London: Penguin Classics, 2015.

Kukushkin, Iu. S. and O. I. Chistiakov. *Ocherk Istorii Sovetskoi Konstitutsii*. Moscow: Politizdat, 1987.

Kuromiya, Hiroaki. 'Edinonachalie and the Soviet Industrial Manager, 1928–1937'. *Soviet Studies* 36, no. 2 (1 April 1984): 185–204. https://doi.org/10.1080/09668138408411523.

*Stalin's Industrial Revolution: Politics and Workers, 1928–1931*, Reprint ed. Cambridge: Cambridge University Press, 1990.

Larionov, Viktor. *Boevaia vylazka v SSSR*. Paris: Bor'ba za Rossiiu, 1931.

Lenin, Vladimir Il'ic. *Polnoe Sobranie Sochinenii*, 5th ed. 55 vols. Moscow: Izdatel'stvo Politicheskoi Literatury, 1975.

*Leningradskaia Organizatsiia KPSS v Tsifrakh, 1917–1973*. Leningrad: Lenizdat, 1974.

Lenoe, Matthew E. 'Fear, Loathing, Conspiracy: The Kirov Murder as Impetus for Terror'. In *The Anatomy of Terror: Political Violence Under Stalin*, edited by James Harris, 195–215. Oxford: Oxford University Press, 2013.

*The Kirov Murder and Soviet History*. New Haven: Yale University Press, 2010.

Lewin, Moshe. *The Making of the Soviet System: Essays in the Social History of Interwar Russia*. New York: The New Press, 1994.

'Society and the Stalinist State in the Period of the Five Year Plans'. *Social History* 1, no. 2 (1 May 1976): 139–75. https://doi.org/10.1080/03071027608567373.

Lih, Lars T. *Bread and Authority in Russia, 1914–1921*, 1st ed. Berkeley: University of California Press, 1990.

'Zinoviev: Populist Leninist'. *The NEP Era: Soviet Russia, 1921–1928* 2 (1928): 1–24.

Lobodok, D. 'Profsoiuzy sovetskoi Rossii v usloviiakh novoi ekonomicheskoi politiki (1921–1928 gg.)'. *Vestnik Sankt-Peterburgskogo Universiteta*, no. 4 (2006).

Lomb, Samantha. 'Personal and Political: A Micro-History of the "Red Column" Collective Farm'. *The Carl Beck Papers in Russian and East European Studies* 2404 (2016).

*Stalin's Constitution: Soviet Participatory Politics and the Discussion of the 1936 Draft Constitution*. London: Routledge, 2017.

Luebbert, Gregory M. *Liberalism, Fascism, or Social Democracy: Social Classes and the Political Origins of Regimes in Interwar Europe*. Oxford: Oxford University Press, 1991.

Mally, Lynn. 'Shock Workers on the Cultural Front: Agitprop Brigades in the First Five-Year Plan'. *Russian History* 23, no. 1–4 (1996): 263–75.

Manning, Roberta. 'The Soviet Economic Crisis of 1936–1940 and the Great Purges'. In *Stalinist Terror: New Perspectives*, edited by J. Arch Getty and Roberta Manning, 116–41. Cambridge: Cambridge University Press, 1993.

Markevich, Andrei. 'Planning the Supply of Weapons'. In *Guns and Roubles: The Defense Industry in the Stalinist State*, edited by Mark Harrison, pp. 107–10. New Haven: Yale University Press, 2008.

Marot, John Eric. 'Trotsky, the Left Opposition and the Rise of Stalinism: Theory and Practice'. *Historical Materialism* 14, no. 3 (1 January 2006): 175–206. https://doi.org/10.1163/156920606778531743.

Marshall, Alex. 'The Terek People's Republic, 1918: Coalition Government in the Russian Revolution'. *Revolutionary Russia* 22, no. 2 (2009): 203–21.

Marshall, T. H. and Tom Bottomore. *Citizenship and Social Class*. London: Pluto Press, 1992.

Martin, Terry. *The Affirmative Action Empire: Nations and Nationalism in the Soviet Union, 1923–1939*. The Wilder House Series in Politics, History and Culture. Ithaca: Cornell University Press, 2001.

McAdams, A. *Vanguard of the Revolution: The Global Idea of the Communist Party*. Princeton, NJ: Princeton University Press, 2017.

McAuley, Mary. *Bread and Justice: State and Society in Petrograd 1917–1922*. Oxford: Clarendon Press, 1991.

Merridale, Catherine. *Moscow Politics and the Rise of Stalin: The Communist Party in the Capital, 1925–32*. London: Palgrave Macmillan, 1991.

Miasnikov, A. 'Partiinaia chistka 1921-go goda v provintsii (po materialam Kaluzhskoi i Tul'skoi gubernii)'. *Omskii Nauchnyi Vestnik* 12, no. 6 (2009): 37–41.

Murphy, Kevin. *Revolution and Counterrevolution: Class Struggle in a Moscow Metal Factory*. Chicago: Haymarket Books, 2007.

'Strikes during the Early Soviet Period, 1922 to 1932: From Working-Class Militancy to Working-Class Passivity?' In *A Dream Deferred: New Studies in Russian and Soviet Labour History*, edited by Donald Filtzer, Wendy Z. Goldman, Simon Pirani and Gijs Kessler, 171–92. Bern: Peter Lang, 2008.

Nedelmann, Birgitta. 'Individuals and Parties – Changes in Processes of Political Mobilization'. *European Sociological Review* 3, no. 3 (12 January 1987): 181–202.

Nikonova, Olga. 'OSOAVIAKhIM kak instrument stalinskoi sotsial'noi mobilizatsii (1927–1941 gg.)'. *Rossiiskaia Istoriia* no. 1 (2012): 90a–104.

*Vospitanie patriotov. Osoaviakhim i voennaia podgotovka naseleniia v ural'skoi provintsii (1927–1941 gg.)*. Moscow: Novii Khronograf, 2010.

Nove, Alec. *An Economic History of the USSR*. Middlesex: Penguin Books, 1982.

*Was Stalin Really Necessary?: Some Problems of Soviet Economic Policy*, Reprint ed. London: Routledge, 2012.

Nureev, Rustem. 'Kratkii kurs istorii VKP(b) v krivom zerkale partiinoi propagandy (materialy zasedania politbiuro 11 i 12 Oktiabria 1938 g. kak istoricheskii istochnik)'. *Zhurnal institutsional'nykh issledovanii* 3, no. 1 (2011): 83–92.

*O postanovke partiinoi propagandy v sviazi s vypuskom 'Kratkogo kursa istorii VKP (b)'*. Moscow: Gospolitizdat, 1938.

Ofitserova, Nataliia. 'Informatsionnye dokumenty o vzaimootnosheniiakh zavodskogo soobshchestva i vlasti v 1920-kh godakh: problemy i ikh resheniia'. *Nauchno-tekhnicheskie vedomosti SPbGPU* 2, no. 111 (2010): 155–60.

'Rol' Profsoiuzov v Bor'be s Rabochim Aktivizmom v Zavodskom Soobshchestve v 1920-e Gody'. *Nauchno-Tekhnicheskie Vedomosty SPbGPU. Gumanitarnye i Obshschestvennye Nauki* 3, no. 131 (2011): 165–69.

Osokina, Elena. *Za fasadom "stalinskogo izobiliia": Raspredelenie i rynok v snabzhenii naseleniia v gody industrializatsii, 1927–1941*. Moscow: ROSSPEN, 2008.

Palkhaeva, Elizaveta and Natal'ia Zhukova, 'Deiatel'nost' obshchestvennykh organizatsii Buriatii (vtoraia polovina 1920-kh gg.)'. *Vestnik Buriatskogo Gosudarstvennogo Universiteta*, no. 7 (2005): 96–100.

Pavlova, I. V. *Stalinizm: stanovlenie mekhanizma vlasti*, Novosibirsk: Sibirskii Khronograf, 1993.

Pethybridge, Roger. 'Concern for Bolshevik Ideological Predominance at the Start of NEP'. *Russian Review* 41, no. 4 (1982): 445–53.

*Piatiletnyi plan narodno-khoziaistvennogo stroitel'stva SSSR*. 3 vols. Moscow: Izdatel'stvo 'Planovoe Khoziaistvo', 1930.

Pirani, Simon. *The Russian Revolution in Retreat, 1920–24: Soviet Workers and the New Communist Elite*. London: Routledge, 2008.

Pospielovsky, Andrew. 'Strikes during the NEP'. *Revolutionary Russia* 10, no. 1 (1 June 1997): 1–34. https://doi.org/10.1080/09546549708575661.

Priestland, David. 'Bolshevik Ideology and the Debate over Party-State Relations, 1918–21'. *Revolutionary Russia* 10, no. 2 (1997): 37–61. https://doi.org/10.1080/09546549708575672.

*Stalinism and the Politics of Mobilization*. Oxford: Oxford University Press, 2007.

*Protokoly Odinnadtsatogo S"ezda RKP(b)*. Moscow: Partizdat TsK VKP(b), 1936.

*Protokoly X S"ezda RKP (b)*. Moscow: Partiinoe Izdatel'stvo, 1933.

Raleigh, Donald J. *Experiencing Russia's Civil War: Politics, Society, and Revolutionary Culture in Saratov, 1917–1922*. New Haven: Princeton University Press, 2002.

Randall, A. *The Soviet Dream World of Retail Trade and Consumption in the 1930s*. London: Palgrave Macmillan, 2008.

Rees, E. A. 'On Stalin's Team: The Years of Living Dangerously in Soviet Politics'. *Revolutionary Russia* 29, no. 1 (2 January 2016): 110–12. https://doi.org/10.1080/09546545.2016.1168998.

*Resheniia partii i pravitel'stva po khoziaistvennym voprosam. 1917–1967 gg. Sbornik dokumentov za 50 let*. 3 vols. Moscow: Politizdat, 1967.

Retish, Aaron B. *Russia's Peasants in Revolution and Civil War: Citizenship, Identity, and the Creation of the Soviet State, 1914–1922*. Cambridge: Cambridge University Press, 2008.

Reznik, Aleksandr. *Trotskii i tovarishchi: Levaia Oppozitsiia i politicheskaia kul'tura RKP(b), 1923–1924*. Saint-Petersburg: Evropeiskii Universitet v Sankt-Peterburge, 2017.

Rigby, T. H. *Communist Party Membership in the USSR*. Princeton: Princeton University Press, 1968.

Rimmel, Lesley A. 'Another Kind of Fear: The Kirov Murder and the End of Bread Rationing in Leningrad'. *Slavic Review* 56, no. 3 (1 October 1997): 481–99. https://doi.org/10.2307/2500926.

Rittersporn, Gábor T. 'New Horizons: Conceptualizing the Soviet 1930s'. *Kritika: Explorations in Russian and Eurasian History* 2, no. 2 (2001): 307–18.

'The Omnipresent Conspiracy: On Soviet Imagery of Politics and Social Relations in the 1930s'. In *Stalinist Terror: New Perspectives*, edited by John Arch Getty and Roberta Thompson Manning, 99–115. Cambridge: Cambridge University Press, 1993. https://doi.org/10.1017/CBO9780511626012.005.

Rogachevskaia, L. S. *Likvidatsiia bezrabotitsy v SSSR 1917–1930 gg*. Moscow: Nauka, 1973.

Rosenberg, William G. 'The Social Background to Tsektran'. In *Party, State and Society in the Russian Civil War*, edited by Diane P. Koenker, William G. Rosenberg and Ronald Grigor Suny, 349–73. Bloomington: Indiana University Press, 1989.

Rossman, Jeffrey J. 'The Teikovo Cotton Workers' Strike of April 1932: Class, Gender and Identity Politics in Stalin's Russia'. *Russian Review* 56, no. 1 (January 1997): 44. https://doi.org/10.2307/131485.

*Worker Resistance under Stalin: Class and Revolution on the Shop Floor*. Cambridge, MA: Harvard University Press, 2009.

Safonova, E. I. 'Moskovskie tekstil'shchiki v gody nepa: kvalifikatsiia i differentsiatsiia v oplate truda'. *Ekonomicheskaiia Istoriia. Ezhegodnik* (2001): 389–419.

Sanchez-Sibony, Oscar. 'Depression Stalinism: The Great Break Reconsidered'. *Kritika: Explorations in Russian and Eurasian History* 15, no. 1 (2014): 23–49. https://doi.org/10.1353/kri.2014.0007.

Sandu, Tat'iana A. '"Rabochaia Oppozitsiia" v RKP (b)'. Unpublished doctoral thesis. Tiumen', 2006, pp. 192–94.

Schapiro, Leonard. *The Communist Party of the Soviet Union*, 2nd Revised ed. New York: Routledge, 1970.

Schwarz, Solomon M. *Labor in the Soviet Union*. New York: Praeger, 1951.

Semanov, S. *Likvidatsiia antisovetskogo Kronshtadtskogo miatezha 1921 goda*. Moscow: Nauka, 1973.

Siegelbaum, Lewis H. 'The Late Romance of the Soviet Worker in Western Historiography'. *International Review of Social History* 51, no. 3 (2006): 463–81. https://doi.org/10.1017/S0020859006002562.

'Production Collectives and Communes and the "Imperatives" of Soviet Industrialization, 1929–1931'. *Slavic Review* 45, no. 1 (1 April 1986): 65–84. https://doi.org/10.2307/2497922.

'Socialist Competition and Socialist Construction in the USSR: The Experience of the First Five-Year Plan (1928–1932)'. *Thesis Eleven* 4, no. 1 (1 February 1982): 48–67. https://doi.org/10.1177/072551368200400106.

'Soviet Norm Determination in Theory and Practice, 1917–1941'. *Soviet Studies* 36, no. 1 (1 January 1984): 45–68. https://doi.org/10.1080/09668138408411513.

*Stakhanovism and the Politics of Productivity in the USSR, 1935–1941*. Cambridge: Cambridge University Press, 1988.

Skocpol, Theda. *States and Social Revolutions: A Comparative Analysis of France, Russia and China*. Cambridge: Cambridge University Press, 1979.

Slezkine, Yuri. *Arctic Mirrors: Russia and the Small Peoples of the North*. Ithaca: Cornell University Press, 1996.

'The USSR as a Communal Apartment, or How a Socialist State Promoted Ethnic Particularism'. *Slavic Review* 53, no. 2 (1994): 414–52. https://doi.org/10.2307/2501300.

Smele, Jonathan. *The 'Russian' Civil Wars, 1916–1926: Ten Years That Shook the World*. 1st ed. Oxford: Oxford University Press, 2016.

Smith, Stephen A. 'Introduction: Towards a Global History of Communism'. In *The Oxford Handbook of the History of Communism*, edited by Stephen A. Smith, 1–34. Oxford: Oxford University Press, 2014.

Solomon, Peter H. *Soviet Criminal Justice under Stalin*. Cambridge: Cambridge University Press, 1996.

Sroka, Marek. '"Soldiers of the Cultural Revolution": The Stalinization of Libraries and Librarians Hip in Poland, 1945–1953'. *Library History* 16, no. 2 (1 November 2000): 105–25. https://doi.org/10.1179/lib.2000.16.2.105.

Stalin, Iosif. 'Ob osnovakh Leninizma'. In Iosif Stalin, *Sochineniia*, vol 6, 69–188. Moscow: Gospolitizdat, 1947.

*Sochineniia*, 13 vols. Moscow: Gospolitizdat, 1946–52.

Statisticheskii Otdel TsK RKP. *Vserossiiskaiia perepis' chlenov RKP 1922 goda*, 5 vols. Moscow: Izd. Otd. TsK RKP, 1922.

Stites, Richard. *Revolutionary Dreams: Utopian Vision and Experimental Life in the Russian Revolution*, Illustrated ed. New York: Oxford University Press, 1989.

Stone, David R. 'Shefstvo: Lev Trotsky and the Military Origins of Revolutionary Patronage'. *Revolutionary Russia* 19, no. 1 (2006): 21–36. https://doi.org/10.1080/09546540600670100.

Stotland, Daniel. *Purity and Compromise in the Soviet Party-State: The Struggle for the Soul of the Party, 1941–1952*. Lanham: Lexington Books, 2017.

'The War Within: Factional Strife and Politics of Control in the Soviet Party State (1944–1948)'. *Russian History* 42, no. 3 (3 September 2015): 343–69. https://doi.org/10.1163/18763316-04203004.

Straughn, J. B. '"Taking the State at Its Word": The Arts of Consentful Contention in the German Democratic Republic'. *American Journal of Sociology* 110, no. 6 (May 2005): 1598–1650. https://doi.org/10.1086/428818.

Straus, Kenneth M. *Factory and Community in Stalin's Russia: The Making of an Industrial Working Class*. Pittsburgh: University of Pittsburgh Press, 1998.

Strauss, Julia C. *State Formation in China and Taiwan: Bureaucracy, Campaign, and Performance*. Cambridge: Cambridge University Press, 2019. https://doi.org/10.1017/9781108569163.

Suvorova, Lyubov'. *Nepovskaia mnogoukladnaia ekonomika: mezhdu gosudarstvom i rynkom*. Moscow: AIRO, 2013.

Thatcher, Ian. 'Trotsky and the Questions of Agency, Democracy and Dictatorship in the USSR, 1917–1940', in *The Fate of the Bolshevik Revolution: Illiberal Liberation 1917–1941*, edited by Lara Douds, James Harris and Peter Whitewood, pp. 96–98. London: Bloomsbury Academic, 2020.

Thurston, Robert. *Life and Terror in Stalin's Russia, 1934–1941*, New ed. New Haven: Yale University Press, 1998.

'The Stakhanovite Movement: The Background to the Great Terror in the Factories, 1935–1938'. In *Stalinist Terror: New Perspectives*, edited by J. Arch Getty and Roberta Manning, 142–60. Cambridge: Cambridge University Press, 1993.

Timasheff, Nicholas Sergeyevitch. *The Great Retreat: The Growth and Decline of Communism in Russia*. New York: E. P. Dutton & Company, Inc., 1946.

Tirado, Isabel. 'The Komsomol's Village Vanguard: Youth and Politics in the NEP Countryside'. *The Russian Review* 72, no. 3 (2013): 427–46. https://doi.org/10.1111/russ.10699.

*Trinadtsatyi S"ezd RKP(b). Stenograficheskii otchet*. Moscow: Gospolitizdat, 1963.

Trotsky, Leon. *The Revolution Betrayed*. Mineola: Dover, 2004.

*Trud* v *SSSR: Diagrammy, 1924–1926*. Moscow: Izdatel'stvo VTsSPS, 1926.

Tymiński, Maciej. 'Apparatchiks and Enterprises: The Case of the Warsaw Region in 1950–1970'. *Europe-Asia Studies* 72, no. 8 (13 September 2020): 1277–1304. https://doi.org/10.1080/09668136.2020.1767760.

Ulam, Adam B. *Stalin the Man and His Era*. London: I. B. Tauris, 2007 [1973].

Ul'ianova, Svetlana Borisovna. 'Formirovanie "Treugol'nika" na sovetskikh predpriiatiiakh v pervoi polovine 1920-kh gg.' *Noveishaia Istoria Rossii* no. 2 (2013): 169–84.

'"Leningradskii pochin": proizvodstvennye soveshchaniia v sisteme motivatsii i stimulirovaniia truda v 1920-e gg.' In *Rynok truda v Sankt-Peterburge: problemy i perspektivy*, edited by B. V. Korneychuk, 72–83. Saint-Petersburg: Nestor, 2003.

'Rabochie v massovykh khoziaistvenno-politicheskikh kampaniiakh 1920-kh gg.' In *Predprinimateli i rabochie Rossii v usloviiakh transformatsii obshchestva i gosudarstva v XX stoletii. Materialy mezhdunarodnoi nauchnoi konferentsii, posviashchennoi pamiati Professora Iu. I. Kir'ianova*, edited by A. M. Belov, 83–93, Kostroma: Kostromskoi Gosudarvstennii Universitet im. N. A. Nekrasova, 2003.

Urazova, Svetlana. 'Izmeneniie funktsii profsoiuzov v nachal'nyi period nepa'. *Izvestiia Vyshikh Uchebnykh Zavedenii. Povolzhskii Region*, no. 1 (2011): 36–42.

Varga, Evgenii. 'Kapitalizm nakanune pervoi i vtoroi imperialisticheskikh voin'. *Bol'shevik* 13 (1939): 11–20.

Velikanova, Olga. 'Stalinist Moderation and the Turn to Repression: Utopianism and Realpolitik in the Mid-1930s'. In *The Fate of the Bolshevik Revolution: Illiberal Liberation, 1917–1941*, edited by Lara Douds, James Harris and Peter Whitewood, 141–54. London: Bloomsbury Academic, 2020.

Vihavainen, Timo. 'Meshchanstvo, or the Spirit of Consumerism in the Russian Mind'. In *Communism and Consumerism: The Soviet Alternative to the Affluent Society*, edited by Timo Vihavainen and Elena Bogdanova, 139–60. Leiden: Brill, 2016.

Viola, Lynne. *The Best Sons of the Fatherland: Workers in the Vanguard of Soviet Collectivization*. New York: Oxford University Press, 1989.

*Stalinist Perpetrators on Trial: Scenes from the Great Terror in Soviet Ukraine*. Oxford: Oxford University Press, 2018.

Viola, Lynne, V. P. Danilov, N. A. Ivnitskii and Denis Kozlov. *The Tragedy of the Soviet Countryside: V. 1: The War Against the Peasantry, 1927–1930*. New Haven: Yale University Press, 2005.

Vorob'ev, Sergei. 'Sotsial'nyi portret kommunistov Urala nachala 1920-kh gg. Istochnikovedcheskoe issledovanie materialov vserossiiskoi perepisi chlenov RKP (b)', Unpublished doctoral thesis (avtoreferat). Institut Istorii Ural'skogo Otdeleniia RAN, 2003.

Weiner, Amir. *Landscaping the Human Garden: Twentieth-Century Population Management in a Comparative Framework*, 1st ed. Palo Alto: Stanford University Press, 2003.

'Robust Revolution to Retiring Revolution: The Life Cycle of the Soviet Revolution, 1945–1968'. *The Slavonic and East European Review* 86, no. 2 (2008): 208–31.

Whitney, Susan. *Mobilizing Youth: Communists and Catholics in Interwar France*. Chapel Hill: Duke University Press, 2009.

Wierling, Dorothee. 'Work, Workers, and Politics in the German Democratic Republic'. *International Labor and Working-Class History* 50 (1996): 44–63. https://doi.org/10.1017/S014754790001320X.

Willimott, Andy. *Living the Revolution: Urban Communes & Soviet Socialism, 1917–1932*. Oxford Studies in Modern European History. Oxford: Oxford University Press, 2016.

Wimberg, Ellen. 'Socialism, Democratism and Criticism: The Soviet Press and the National Discussion of the 1936 Draft Constitution'. *Soviet Studies* 44, no. 2 (1992): 313–32.

Wood, Elizabeth A. *The Baba and the Comrade: Gender and Politics in Revolutionary Russia*. Bloomington: Indiana University Press, 2000.

*XIV S"ezd Vsesoiuznoi Kommunisticheskoi Partii (b). Stenograficheskii Otchet*. Moscow: Gosudarstvennoe Izdatel'stvo, 1926.

*XV S"ezd Vsesoiuznoi Kommunisticheskoi Partii (b). Dekabr' 1928 Goda. Stenograficheskii Otchet*. Moscow: Gosudarstvennoe Izdatel'stvo, 1928.

*XVI Konferentsiia Vsesoiuznoi Kommunisticheskoi Partii (b). Stenograficheskii otchet.* Moscow: Gosudarstvennoe Izdatel'stvo, 1929.

*XVIII S"ezd Vsesoiuznoi Kommunisticheskoi Partii (b). Stenograficheskii otchet.* Moscow: Gosudarstvennoe Izdatel'stvo Politicheskoi Literaturi, 1939.

Yekelchyk, Serhy. *Stalin's Citizens: Everyday Politics in the Wake of Total War.* New York: Oxford University Press, 2014. https://doi.org/10.1093/acprof:oso/9780199378449.001.0001.

Zaitseva, Oksana. 'Metody predotvrashcheniia trudovykh konfliktov na predpriiatiiakh Petrograda, Leningrada v nachale 1920-kh gg.: sistema opoveshcheniia o besporiadkakh, kontrol' za povedeniem mass.' *Vestnik Leningradskogo Gosudarstvennogo Universiteta Im. A. C. Pushkina* 4, no. 1 (2012): 114–23.

Zaleski, Eugene. *Stalinist Planning for Economic Growth.* Durham: University of North Carolina Press, 1980.

Zarrow, Peter. *China in War and Revolution, 1895–1949.* London: Routledge, 2005.

Zinoviev, Grigorii. *Filosofiia epokhi.* Leningrad: Priboi, 1925.

*Leninizm: vvedenie v izuchenie Leninizma.* Leningrad: Gosudarstvennoe Izdatel'stvo, 1925.

# Index

For EU product safety concerns, contact us at Calle de José Abascal, 56–1°, 28003 Madrid, Spain or eugpsr@cambridge.org.

www.ingramcontent.com/pod-product-compliance
Lightning Source LLC
LaVergne TN
LVHW022155200926
848481LV00006B/1748
*9781009218849*